FROM ONE END OF THE RAINBOW

A Story about the Life Inside the Irish Defence Forces and Beyond

GW00771082

FRANK SUMNER

Strategic Book Publishing and Rights Co.

Strategic Book Publishing and Rights Co.
12620 FM 1960, Suite A4-507
Houston, TX 77065
www.sbpra.com

ISBN:978-1-62212-976-8

Typography and page composition by J. K. Eckert & Company

This book is dedicated to the memory of Private Hugh Doherty, from Ballmacool, Letterkenny, and Private Seoige Joyce, who hailed from the Aran Islands, and to all the Irish soldiers who lost their lives while serving the United Nations in southern Lebanon.

It invites you, the reader, to compare the author's recollection of events and to look at the Department of Defence files and then judge which is most likely to be the truth.

Notwithstanding the lies and untruths that have been told by our governments of the previous thirty years, whatever the makeup was to me and indeed to most people in the present economic climate, it can be seen that all our politicians are just a self-serving people.

But that said, this book is also dedicated to people like Private Micky Walker from Dungloe, who has single-handedly fought and highlighted the case of Hugh Doherty with various ministers of defence in order to have a proper enquiry held, down through the years.

Contents

Preface

This is a story about one's chosen profession, the journey through a career, that can be viewed through the eyes of any soldier in the world, no matter what army. The universal soldier is a breed apart—the balls, the dedication, the sacrifice, the loyalty, and the commitment that only this kind of breed can give. It's a life of sacrifice to the job, your unit, and your country; it's a profession that brings all sorts together and moulds them into one cohesive unit, capable of anything.

The Irish soldier, being in a defence force, has history going back to his first chief of staff, General Michael Collins, a legend who set the standards with guerrilla warfare in the 1920s. So even before the British realised there were more ways to fight than the conventional military way, the Paddy was years ahead; he has stood out since the formation of the United Nations and Ireland's first involvement with troops in the Congo as the world's best diplomat in the military theatre of United Nations missions. Our forefathers were the *Fianógliogh* in Irish, or young warriors; today Finn Mac Cool, the ancient chieftain, would have been very proud of his prodigy.

L.A. 89

ÓGLAIGH NA hÉIREANN

THE DEFENCE FORCES

Certificate of Service

WARNING

If this Certificate is lost or mislaid no duplicate can be issued.

Any alteration in the particulars given in this Certificate may render the holder liable to prosecution.

Any person finding this Certificate is requested to hand it in at any Barracks, Post Office or Garda Station for transmission (post free) to the OFFICER i/c. ENLISTED PERSONNEL SECTION, Department of Defence, Parkgate, Dublin 8.

ÓGLAIGH NA hÉIREANN

Certificate of Service

SERVICE No. 826929

SURNAME   SUMNER

CHRISTIAN NAMES   FRANCIS

ENLISTED ON 20ᵗʰ MARCH 1973.

NOTE :—

 Attention is specially directed to pages 3, 7 and 8.

TESTIMONIAL ON   *DISCHARGE   ~~PH~~ *Capt*   3.

~~*TRANSFER TO RESERVE~~

Testimonial: Cpl Frank Sumner gave 23 years excellent service to the Army. He is totally reliable and has shown himself to be very proficient in why many training and administrative activities. A very popular and industrious junior leader whose prowess as a sportsman was reflected in the magnificent grounds in hired military post

Bo Rwandoy LT Col (Signature and Rank)

Officer Commanding .... 28 WK Bn

Place .... Jinnen Camp

Date 28/9/96

*Delete words which are inapplicable. Otherwise this Page should be entirely free ~~from Erasures.~~

5.

FINAL ASSESSMENTS OF MILITARY CONDUCT ON ~~TRANSFER TO THE RESERVE DEFENCE FORCE~~

*

DISCHARGE

1. Military Conduct .... *EXEMPLARY.* ....

16·9·96.   P. Harris   Captain

(date)   (Officer i/c. Records)

TRANSFERS OR OTHER ALTERED CIRCUMSTANCES IN RELATION TO THE HOLDER'S SERVICE.

Each entry to be dated and signed by the Officer i/c. Records. Any transfer, etc., not covered herein will be covered by official notification in the reservist's possession.

Particulars		Signature of O. i/c. Record
66/	17·9·75	
216/	1·10·74	
4/6/ (LEBANON)	6·4·81	
3/6/	21·10·81	
5/6/ (LEBANON)	20·10·82	
4/6/	20·4·85	
5/6/ (LEBANON)	14·7·86	
224/	3·10·ε8	
5/6/ (LEBANON)	9·10·ε	
4/6/	4·5·90	
7·6/ (AL)	4·11·91	

* Delete words which are inapplicable.

7.

CERTIFICATE OF DISCHARGE

Serial No. .....W15140........................

Date of Discharge .2ND OCTOBER 1996........

Rank ..CORPORAL........ Grade/Class ...LINE........

Classification .....INSTRUCTOR......................

Reason for Discharge .DETERMINATION OF....

.......SERVICE BY THE MINISTER.......

.............FOR DEFENCE (VER)

(See below*)

Unit from which Discharged ....28 INF BN,......

Service on date of Discharge :—

Permanent
Defence Force : ....23....years ....197....days

Reserve
Defence Force : ....Nil.....years ...Nil...days

Military Conduct ..EXEMPLARY......................

*N.B. ....

....

....

......P. Harris........ Captain
Officer i/c. Records.

..............Western..............Area.

EDUCATIONAL ATTAINMENTS, TRADE QUALIFICATIONS, Etc.

8.

		Signature of Officer making entry.
1. Trade on Enlistment.	APPRENTICE BARMAN.	
2. Vocational training undergone and standard attained.	NIL	
3. Trade tests passed during service.	NIL	
4. Courses of Instruction passed and Certificates awarded.	POTENTIAL NCO's - PASS. M.T. DRIVERS - PASS. RANGERS COURSE - PASS. MESS ADMINISTRATION AND ACCOUNTANCY. - PASS. REGIMENTAL SIGNALS - PASS.	
5. Nature of employment during service.	INSTRUCTOR.	
6. Army Education— Certificates awarded.	2ND CLASS CERTIFICATE - 1978.	
7. Acts of gallantry or distinguished conduct brought to notice by order of higher authority.	NIL	

9.

10.

SERVICE IN THE PERMANENT DEFENCE FORCE RENDERED SUBSEQUENT TO DATE OF TRANSFER TO RESERVE DEFENCE FORCE

Date of re-entering Permanent Defence Force	Date re-transferred to Reserve Defence Force	Nature of Service	Signature of Officer i/c. Records

PREVIOUS SERVICE IN THE DEFENCE FORCES

Service No.	Rank	Enlisted	Discharged	Service in Permanent Defence Force	Service in Reserve Defence Force	Remarks
23244	PRIVATE	10.12.71	7.2.72.	0-60 Days.	NIL	E.C.T. DEPOT.

11.

12.

DESCRIPTION OF MAN ON ~~TRANSFER TO~~ ~~THE RESERVE DEFENCE FORCE~~

* _____

DISCHARGE

Born 10·3·1956.   Height ....

Complexion.............. Eyes............ Hair............

Scars or marks ....

....

(Signature and Rank)

Officer Commanding ....

Place ....

Date 3/10/96.

* _Delete words which are inapplicable._

131274. 20M BKS. 3/80. JFN

Acknowledgments

The writer, to whom I refer as Paddy, with whom I worked for almost twenty years, helped me formulate and type and aided me with this book. Without his help, this writing would not have happened.

Micky Walker, who through his personal friendship with Private Hugh Doherty, never gave up the chase to get justice for Hugh. Micky was instrumental in pursuing justice for Corporal Fintan Henehan, Private Mannix Armstong, and Private Tomas Walsh. Even though I decked him one when on Post 617c during our service with the Forty-Ninth Battalion, we have been friends ever since. His resilience can be seen through the article in the *Donegal News,* dated May 12, 2012, where he again took the case to the minister asking for an enquiry.

To all the lads of the Number Six Platoon, who have always been supportive all through the years and bear the pain of what happened on April 27, 1981, in equal parts and are always a comforting influence with regard to the truth being exposed at some time in the near future. Just to name a few: ex-Lieutenant Hugh Carthy; ex-Corporals Joe O'Brien, Jackie Quinn, Tom Frize, and Hands Lafferty; ex-Privates Joe Martin, Billy McKinley, Danny Calhoun, Joe McGirr, Brian Porter, Jock Kelly, the late Seamus McKinley (RIP), and Nicky Crabb; and Paddy McLaughlin (03), active, who gets a mention in the book from the report by Col. Savino.

1

The Early Years Living in the Midlands of Ireland

From my earliest recollection, I was destined to be a soldier. At the age of four, my earliest pulse of life, I remember being fed, dressed, and washed, my ginger locks carefully groomed, by my mother, herself barely twenty-two years of age at the time. My demanding young sister, Olive, just three years of age, was baying for attention from my mother, heavily pregnant, while my youngest sister, Eithne, had her midday sleep in the pram. We lived in a small rural town called Strokestown in the county of Roscommom. My father was an NCO in the army, attached to the FCA (part-time reservists, now called the RDF) as a training instructor. In the 1960s, for my mother with three children to feed on meagre military wages was like the five loaves and two fishes. My father got a house in his hometown of Elphin, just six miles down the road, so we relocated there. It might as well have been six hundred miles in those days. I recall my mother being very scared in the house when my father was away on duty with the army, and this fear permeated right down through her siblings. Apart from that, my memories were good, going uptown with my mother to my granny's or just down three doors to my cousins and aunt; her husband, Sean, was a lorry driver, so to be taken on a run in the lorry was a great treat. My father was a great handyman, from building blocks to plastering, something he learned after being conscripted in the fifties in England to the royal engineers. He built sheds and stables, and to aid, abate, and supplement the family he bought a blue-grey cow, which we called Muchie, calves and all.

Things in military life were never straightforward in those days, and my mother wasn't comfortable with the house, so we sold Muchie, and it was off to Athlone in the front of a flat-nose Bedford army truck, our only worldly goods, furniture, clothing, and bedding piled high in the back of the truck. We arrived in St. Ruth's Park, but how long we stayed I can't remember, and then it was another transfer to Assumption Road, still in the town. I was too young to let it have any effect on me, but it must have felt like musical chairs to my mother and father. I vaguely remember my father bringing home his Lee Enfield 303 rifle, with full magazines; seemingly, this was the norm for everyone in the army—no point in hiding it. My mother and father often had, what seemed to me as a child, horrendous arguments and pillow fights; whether it was hormones or what, I often wonder how one of them didn't go for the rifle and finish it, but now, looking back after nearly sixty years together, through it all they must have loved one another.

Back home, the family was getting larger, with the arrival of Loreto, which coincided with my father's return from the Congo. Loreto had a dark hue to her skin, and on making enquiries about where she came from, we were told she was the Congo baby, and we were found under a head of cabbage. To relieve territory around the house during the summer holidays, I was shipped off to Elphin to my grandmother's, and those memories are still very fond— having my own bedroom, my own bed, undivided attention, and new friends, including Benedict Morris and John Clancy, whose parents owned the two local grocery shops in the town, so tuck was always on hand, and of course the lads had to nick it. Then there was Ned McCormick's forge, where the local farmers had the horses shod (we were not quite into automation yet in agriculture). Those were great summers. Josie Kelly, a schoolteacher who gave up his career to take over the family farm, was a bachelor for whom my grandmother cooked and cleaned. He was a real taskmaster; I often observed that being at his school would have been a nightmare. My experience in primary school with the Sisters of Mercy was not a good one; whatever grey matter there was in my head could have been nurtured in a more humane way. Looking back, it was an army in itself.

So after the long summer, it was back on the bus to Athlone and another year at school—only this time, it was to be the start of secondary school, and that's where my problems started. In Athlone in the sixties, there were two schools of thought in learning. There was the technical college that prepared you geodetically and taught you trades, thereby grooming you for an apprenticeship and preparing you for a working-class life. Assumption Road had 118 houses, and at least 90 of them were soldiers' families. I wanted to go to school with my mates, Jessie Purtill, Kipper Lynch, and Sam McManus, but Mother was having none of it. Her eldest was going to the Marist College—a bad decision I thought, but my mother was having her way, her eldest was having the best, should it mean sacrifices for the rest of the family. Off she went to the principal's office to demand that her son get the best, a state-funded college with boarders and day students, mainly made up of sons of big farmers, business and legal people, and army officers. The Carmelite College in Moate ten miles away competed for the same brains of Ireland, so what chance did I have? So here I was making new friends, make-believe or other-wise. Two who stand out from primary school are Dino Maloco and Liam Clancy, not the brightest, but sound lads. The Malocos ran a big restaurant in the town, and Liam's father was a full colonel in the army. The vice principal, Brother Gerard, was known as the enforcer and did he do some enforcing. I am sure he taught some language or other subject, but the focus for us was to keep out of his way, so much so that I can't pretty well remember the reasons. Then there was this guy, a lay teacher, who broke the mould, coming from a similar background to my own. Lucey Walsh was his name and he taught Spanish, but his facial expressions when he was talking to you gave away the game—"Sumner, you have no chance." I tried my best; I was reasonable in most subjects—at least that was the opinion of Dino and Liam, as they copied my homework—but it was never going to last.

When my mother fully realised this, preparations were made to ship me out to the countryside under the stewardship of my grandfather and grandmother on my mother's side, in part to protect my character and keep me out of the young offenders' home—not that I was ever in court, but another year or two would surely have seen me going that way. Welcome to the real world of farming and a fourteen-hour day, between going to technical school and doing my jobs around the farm. My mother had eight children by then, with three of us on the farm, myself, Donal, and Des. I took well to school in Moate and had the honour of having Mary O'Rourke's mother, Mrs Lenihan, teaching me. She was well past retirement but must have loved her profession so much that she stayed on for years later. My grandfather was the best taskmaster I have ever met and translated his work ability to me like a sporting challenge, and in time it became enjoyable. I often thought had he been a teacher, he would have created geniuses. I didn't know what to do. I enjoyed joining up with the FCA, training nights in Boher Hall, and if you put the right hours in, you were guaranteed a two-week training camp in Athlone with a big payday at the end of it.

I was now sixteen, Dana had just won the Eurovision Song contest with "All Kinds of Everything," and it was now time to make a break for it, so I hatched my plan: three of us were going to get on the boat and head to the streets and the bright lights of London. Looking back now, as a parent, I would have had a nightmare, but I was young and had been toning my body on a farm for three to four years; I was sure up for it and probably looked more mature than the average sixteen-year-old of today. So off we went without consulting anybody, which, in hindsight, wasn't a very smart move. I think my uncle Liam, who was ten years older than I, made contact with my parents. My mother arrived, and when she saw we were settled in, she had the presence and wisdom of mind to allow us to get on with it and make our own way in the world, as there were not many opportunities back in Ireland. The first few weeks were hard, as all the money was spent attending places such as the Galtymore Ballroom in Cricklewood, the National Ballroom in Kilburn, and the Odean Cinema. Sure, we were having a great time, but soon the hunger pangs set in, and when we were to the point of trying to get the tenth cup of tea out of the same teabag, we knew we were in trouble. Eventually, work and that first wage, the equivalent of the money for our two weeks with the FCA, arrived, and it was a lot. We were going to be frugal with our money. Six months in London as a sixteen-year-old—maybe I was really only fifteen, I can't be sure—was enough for me, and it was back to the emerald isle again, but now my priority was to enlist in the army. The pay might not be that good, but three square meals a day and an opportunity to get a head start was an option. England had been a good eye-opener to see where you could end up, like the rest, if you didn't watch out for yourself, confined to the streets and a life revolving around alcohol. In those days, if you looked seventeen years old, then you were indeed seventeen, and on the advice of my father, the Eastern Command of the Army might be the place to go and enlist. This was the Dublin command. I enlisted and was assigned to the Second Motor Squadron, and what a shower of recruits. I married up within Cathal Brugha barracks in Rathmines; this place was like the H Blocks prison in Northern Ireland. There were two kinds of people here, the "Dubs" and the "Culshies," and the Dubs were hardened bullies. It's incredible now when I recall that even the NCOs tasked as our instructors, and Dubs themselves, showed all the favour to their own people, and after about ten weeks, it was as much as I could take, with getting mugged in Cable Street in the city centre to being mugged every day in training. I was a broken kid; it was if the older guys sort of knew that I was underage, and they took every advantage going. I knew if I returned home a failure, my father would go ballistic, so I did a runner and went home, telling a cock and hoop story that we were on a midtraining break. It was nice being home again among my brothers and sisters; it was as if I flew the nest and returned to perch. The two weeks had run out very fast, so with my thinking cap firmly on, I decided to enlist for a second time, but this time in Coloumb barracks in the town of Mullingar.

So off I went thumbing for a lift up the road. I got a lift in a car driven by then Lt. Col. Johnny Kane, commanding officer of the Fourth Field Artillery Regiment based in the barracks in Mullingar. He enquired as to who I was and where was I going. I replied I was going to "enlist, sir," and with that, he was delighted, as he was heading into the barracks himself. He took me straight to the recruiting sergeant, and when he asked me my name, I was quick off the mark and used my uncle's name. "Tommy Egan," I stated, so I was sworn in under that name and advised to report the following morning for a medical exam. Col. Kane gave me one of his see-through rain macks to aid me on my way home to my grandfather's, as it was raining cats and dogs that day. So I was Private Tommy Egan; sure it would be grand. I would soon get used to it.

Back I went to Mullingar the next morning and got kitted out with my new clothing and back into the drill of it. With the troubles breaking out in Northern Ireland on a large scale, the army was very wary of IRA "sleepers" coming south and joining up for training, so the platoon officer, Captain Paddy Keogh, briefed everybody to be on the lookout for anyone acting in a suspicious manner or being overly familiar. Now a guy called Christy Molloy, who had been a corporal in the FCA and came from a large family with most of them in the army, became wary of me after about five or six weeks of playing Tommy Egan. We were in the fields playing a game of football when a military policeman walked on to the pitch and hailed Private Sumner. The game was now up, and I was dragged off and put in the guardroom until the Second Motor Squadron came along in its black Zephyr car to escort me back to Cathal Brugha barracks. Chalkie White and others with their nice two stars sewn on their uniforms escorted me—Tommy or Frank, they didn't know. I was fired into the guardroom in the Brugha and was going to have a long five days in the cell before being called in front of the battalion commander of the Fifth Infantry Battalion, Lt. Col. "The Bull" Callaghan. I was run out the gate so quickly because I was still underage. Well, I tried; I guess military life was not going to be for me, and back home I got a meaningless job as a waiter in the Hudson Bay Hotel, but at least it kept me out of trouble. I was going nowhere fast, though, and the manager of the hotel, who was friendly with my parents, knew about a job in London, doing bar work. At least I would get to have another go in the big smoke of London.

The position was as a live-in barman in the Castle in Kentish Town; the governor's name was Denis O'Brien, a jovial, heavy man from Kerry, and his wife, May, was from Mayo. They had a daughter, Margaret, aged seventeen and drop-dead gorgeous, and a son called Tony, aged eleven, who was a real brat. So here I was in a new home with a new job and new family. As I was introduced to the part-time staff, I took stock of them all, as I was forewarned by the manager of the Hudson Bay that they were all on the take and fiddle, and here was this jumped-up teenager from Ireland who could wreck their lucrative trade and extra earnings. The simple fact of the matter as I learned later was that both Denis and May were alcoholics. I was faced with some responsibility, and Denis trusted me implicitly. I could see the pub was doing a roaring trade, and one by one I ousted the crooks until we had an honest staff, who were rewarded in turn.

Sometimes I might go three weeks without pay, and Denis would meet me on the stairs on one of his better mornings and ask when I was paid last. Reaching into his inside coat pocket, he would pull out a wad of notes and say, "There you are." When the opportunity arrived, I would count it, only to remind Denis that he overpaid me, but he would retort, "Keep it—you earned it."

I suppose, looking back now, I put my heart and soul into working in the Castle, hoping somehow my effort would catch the eye of Margaret, but she was going out with someone, ironically, the son of an Athlone woman who played piano accordion in the pub, and as it turned out, she was having an affair with Denis. I can only think now that it was my acne that put her off, but then he also had it, just not as bad as mine.

I had only one day off in the week and spent it in Leicester Square or in Shaftsbury Avenue. Believe it or not, through the help of a big Cork bouncer who made it clear he would break my legs if I disinherited his trust in me, I was in Tiffany's every Monday night—that was one of three places to be seen in while in London—and, man, did I love those Monday nights. Working my bollocks off all week was worth it for this one night; however, things at the Castle were starting to go from bad to worse, with the constant rows—more serious ones than when I was growing up. If there was a Lee Enfield 303 on the premises, it sure would have been used by either Denis or May. So once again, I had enough of London, and after nearly a year and a half in the Castle, it was time to go home. The family on a good day expected this, and we parted on good terms; at seventeen, I had become a diplomat at integrating with other households. I said my goodbyes and returned to Ireland.

Money to hand and being the alpha male, it was time to get stuck into the local social scene. My mother and father had become more placid toward me; nonetheless, out of respect I never went home with drink in me. Maybe I remembered how hard they had worked.

My father was planning the next stage of his life, thinking about going on his ticket, which was the military slang for leaving the army. The army being the institution that had provided for his family up until this time, it was a brave decision but one that he had confidence in. He enquired as to where I was heading in life, and when he suggested the army again, my mouth dropped.

"Are you mad?" I asked. They would never have me back. F̣ₓ
that he had his contacts and there would never be a record of me ͻ
army before, as I was then a minor.

Having discussed it with my mates, Pauric Sheriff, "Cock" Roach, ͻ
Kelly, and a few more, we all decided to go in on the following Monday
morning and enlist. I held on at the rear of the group, shading myself, as I full
well was expecting to be run straight out the gate again. This was March
1973, and two full platoons in blues taking lumps out of the square with the
square bashing were very impressive. To my astonishment, I was sworn in and
kitted out, head shaved, and sent to the cookhouse to wash pots and pans. We
had to wait our time until the right numbers signed up to form a full platoon.
The company sergeant of Headquarter Company was a Clare man with a tor-
rid reputation. I was to witness his death later in St. Bricins Hospital in Dublin, and he was a fighter to the end. One day on the 1400 hours parade, he
informed ten of us that we were going to Mullingar to make up the numbers
for a new platoon going into training there. Surely after two years they
wouldn't have forgotten me, but my luck was holding, and after nearly a
month cleaning the pots on eight pounds a week, there was a slight outside
chance it would still hold up. We arrived in the back of a truck at Coloumb
Barracks in Mullingar, and unless you ever travelled in the back of one of
these trucks, you haven't a clue as to what it is like. So here we were, and,
Jesus, there was Captain Paddy Keogh as gildy as ever; it was as if we were
always together and who else did I spot? The one and only Corporal Molloy,
yes, the same Christy Molloy who was in Number Nine platoon with "Private
Tommy Egan," so my heart sank. Fucked I was now, as they both recognised
me, and after the normal barking introductions, they both took me to the one
side and gave me an ultimatum—walk now and have a quiet life or be pushed.
The only thing going for me was this time everything was legitimate. I was
now 828929 Private Frank Sumner. It was testimony to them and me, as we
were each more determined than the other. It reminds me now of the film from
the early eighties called *An Officer and a Gentleman,* but I was in no film. It
was shitting real, and it was my last chance. The crap that I went through, the
CB (confined to barracks), and so on—yes, this time they couldn't hurt me; I
was insulated from all my experiences, and this time I would win.

After three months of the most unbelievable shit that could be dealt out to a
human being, I passed out proudly on July 13, 1973, in a final class of thirteen
out of the thirty starters in the platoon. Some achievement, though that number has never been lucky for me since, so maybe we just get the one lucky
shot. Marching down home that weekend from the top of Assumption Road in
Athlone with my mate "Cock" Roach, with our white lanyards and collar
badges, we were almost marching in step. This was the proudest day of my

.fe so far; I had made it, God help the army. We were all posted back to Athlone to take part in the next stage of training, the 3star course, back to the legendary B Company, Sixth Battalion. It was a ranger-style company set up as the only standby company for the Western Command of the army. Dressed in combat uniform all the time, it was a great soldiering approach to a military life for a young lad, as one must realise within a big barracks such as Custume Barracks, Athlone. There were more than a thousand troops based there during this time, and there was a lot of cronyism and cushy numbers to be had; after all, it's only human nature to make life as comfortable as possible, but this was not the case in B Company under the command of Comdt. Vincent Savino and Company (Coy) Sergeant McCarthy, a very respected senior NCO. The hardiest NCOs in the command were part of this company, as they were all handpicked. This is a memory that will always last with me, to see Coy Sergeant McCarthy marching more than one hundred men out onto the square for the daily parades all dressed in their combat uniforms. Every other unit went on the parades in their number two dress uniforms, so one knew that this was a special unit.

My father was leaving the army at this time after twenty-four years' service. Along the way, he had built up a close circle of friends and, I am sure, the odd enemy. Passing out with the third star was "mission complete," and I was a fully fledged soldier. Lt. Col. Pat Stapleton (RIP) was the battalion commander, and we all fell in on the square, ready to be presented with our extra star. The army had now just introduced name tags for the uniforms, and as he walked down the ranks presenting in turn each man with his three stars, he came to me. On examining my name tag, he asked, "Are you the son of Frank Sumner?"

Proudly I replied, "Yes, sir," and he retorted, "Well, there is not room in the army for both of you," referring to my father's imminent discharge.

Even then, as a young man, the bitterness of his attitude hurt. The ironic thing about Col. Pat Stapleton was that he was the barrack officer commanding a long time and pronounced severe penalties on men from around the town of Athlone if they were up on charges before him. He cycled in and out of the barracks, and when he eventually retired, he took up voluntary work with St. Vincent de Paul and often went around to the same men's houses looking for charity donations. You can imagine the reception that he got; the stories are not printable.

After we passed out with our 3 star course complete and before we could settle down to barrack routine, Private Ollie Kelly and I were sent to the Curragh Camp in County Kildare in the back of an open-back land rover. We were assured that it would be a short sojourn; however, it turned into a nine-month stint in the military college, the cadet school; this was the location where they trained the commissioned officers. Every day showed an example of these robots marching all over the place; it really looked as if they took their brains out upon arrival and put them into cold storage until needed again. Life in the Curragh Camp was indeed an experience in itself.

Back in Athlone and B Company, after too many military engagements to mention and a change of personnel, a certain Captain Paddy Keogh, a hammer of a man, was now second in charge of the company. We were on one of the biggest operations in the history of the army; the prime minister of Great Britain, Mr. Ted Heath, was to be the first prime minister to put foot on Irish Republic Soil postpartition. With every IRA man and woman in Ireland baying for his blood, we were billeted out in two-man tents as part of two brigades based in the Glen of Imal in County Wicklow. One night there was a confrontation between two guys from different units that had the potential of turning into an internal riot. A company sergeant from the southern brigade was throwing his weight around, when out stepped Captain Keogh in string vest from his billet and planted the best right hook that I ever seen onto the jaw of the bullying company sergeant. He then shouted to everyone, "Get to bed," and that was the end of the matter.

After this, it was back to Athlone, and I was sent to work in the officers' mess as a barman, due to my previous experience in civilian life in London. This was to be some job; the commanding officer of the Western Command was the infamous "Murt" Buckley, a full colonel—the place quaked in his presence. One of the many tales that carried through the years about Buckley I observed for myself. It was a passing-out parade of a recruit platoon that was held in the gymnasium due to inclement weather. The platoon fell in, as did the rest of us for the occasion, and the band in the gallery was tuning up. Everybody was waiting for Murt to arrive (dignitaries are always late); however, after a few minutes, in came Murt with the band playing the general salute, and the platoon officer handed over the parade, when low and behold this young lad in the front rank hit the deck like a brush, having fainted. Three or four of the platoon NCOs ran to his rescue, and Murt bellowed out, "Leave him alone. He'll be all right."

My experience there made me feel that the young fellows in the canteen were more grown-up. One inevitably got caught up in the politics of the officers' mess and had to be a real diplomat to remain above their evening wars about promotion and so on. It was on one of these occasions that a Captain Joe Leech was promoted to commandant; his promotion was to be as company commander of Lifford Barracks. *Where the fuck is that?* I thought. With the celebrity drinks in the mess flowing, the newly promoted Joe turned to me and said that he wanted as many Athlone men as possible to go to Lifford with him and, making some complimentary remark about my father, asked me if I would serve under him. My answer was yes, anything to get out of this bitch trap of a place, for my conscience was carrying the pure bitchiness that they had for each other. When they left the cadet school and had their brains put back in, some of them had the misfortune of having them put in back to front.

Before I had time to think it through, I was getting ready to depart for Lifford in County Donegal. I was in the back of one of the two trucks as part of a full platoon heading to Lifford, and, thanks to Joe, I would now be on an extra eleven pounds a week on top of my weekly wage of sixteen pounds. Back in those times, the cost of a pint was eighteen pence and a packet of cigarettes seventeen pence. So four to five hours later, we arrive in Lifford military post, which was an old school from the beginning of the century with high walls. It was now turned into a military establishment, albeit pretty basic one, but this was a new challenge. On getting our brief, it soon became clear that we were in a hostile environment, and when we got to go out of the camp, we had to go in packs and, mad as it must now seem, were barred from every pub in the town except one.

The first year or so in Lifford was full of incidents, but we were settling into it. The post was of company strength made up from elements of units from the Southern and Western Commands. It was meant to be only tempo-rary, as the Twenty-Eighth Infantry Battalion was formed in 1975. Joe Leech (RIP) finished his stint in Lifford and was heading back to Athlone; he would be missed as a great man in charge of that military post. The post also had the pleasure of a Lt. John Pickard in the early years; now when they were putting his brain back in at the Curragh cadet school, they sure did miss a nut. He was generally a sound man but very unpredictable and could do anything on impulse. One Sunday morning when he was on duty as orderly officer, there was a man missing from the guard mounting parade. A guy called "The Rat" Sweeney, who was the company store man, was in bed. Lt. Pickard told the barrack orderly sergeant (BOS) to detail him as the replacement for guard duty. The BOS returned to Pickard and informed him that The Rat had refused to get out of bed. Now, The Rat was known to be a bit lippy. Pickard went over to the prefabricated billet where The Rat was in bed and detailed him to get out of it, as he was needed for guard duty. After a litany of verbalism from The Rat, Pickard took out his Browning pistol and fired a shot about twelve inches over The Rat's head. We never saw a man get out of bed so quickly.

I was promoted to the rank of acting corporal in charge of the transport sec-tion. I was fairly good with figures and with about nine drivers and a mechanic under me, I wasn't exactly Rommel, but it had its perks. This was until one day when Private "Pastry" McDonald and I were on a driving detail to Athlone. We had stayed overnight in the barracks in Athlone and were on the road back to Lifford, travelling through the town of Boyle. Just as we left the town, I observed these two beauties standing on the side of the road, thumbing a lift. Before Pastry knew it, I had pulled over to the side of the road. Pastry shouted at me, "What are you up to, Reggie?" as we were not allowed to carry any civilians in military transport. In jumped the two girls, one from Australia and the other from New Zealand. I carried them the whole way to Donegal, even past Finner Camp in Ballyshannon. Two young second lieutenants were heading back down the country for the weekend and spotted us with the ladies on board, and then stopped to phone the military police. The long and short of it was that for looking after the two lovely ladies I was brought up on charges and stripped of my acting corporal rank. Somebody else got the stripes, but I still had to do the books for transport.

Because the subunit was part of the newly formed battalion, there was plenty of opportunity to go on NCO courses. One day, the company sergeant called me in and informed me that I was going on the next NCO course. With me were Privates Gerry Driver, Pastry McDonald, Micky Devlin, Micky Coyle, and Terry Doherty. So off we went to Finner Camp in Ballyshannon for a month-long preliminary course under the supervision of Corporal Jim Brennan. This was to bring us up to speed in all things military to give us a foot in the door for when the course would start properly in Custume Barracks, in the Athlone training depot.

An NCO course is considered the alpha-omega of all military tactics planning—that is, ground, situation, mission, execution, service support, command, and signals. Its duration is six months and, with exceptions, maybe longer. The first part of the course is instruction learning, and students are taught how to instruct. Upon qualification, these guys will be the personnel doing the training, and, as the saying goes, the cream always rises to the top and the top guns will go on to be top instructors in whatever field. As everybody isn't cut out for teaching, so others will go on to hold logistics or administration appointments, working in stores and offices as part of any well-oiled unit. Every infantry weapon in the field—from a ground 90-mm antitank gun, 84-mm antitank gun, and 60-mm and 80-mm mortars to .5-m heavy machine guns along with the smaller personal weapons like the 9-mm pistol, FN rifle, and general purpose machine gun—is taught in this course. With that instruction, lectures are given on defence force regulations, military law, and so on, which all have to be completed within the course's allocated time frame, followed by individual tests for the students. On successful completion of the course, corporals have to have the ability of a general, and within the system of the army, they are the most important rank because it will be their tactical input and awareness that decide the day in any battlefield. As with all courses, there is failure as well as success and ongoing tests during the course.

Starting the course, each student receives up to twenty hardback instruction manuals covering every subject to digest; for the period, each student puts in about eighteen hours every day, including the weekend. It also gives the student great personnel management skills, and it is well known in civilian life that applicants with these military skills are highly sought after by employers purely because of their training. The natural line of progression after completion of this course is the rank of sergeant, company sergeant, and the highest non-commissioned rank of sergeant major. Some guys get the opportunity of going from the rank of corporal on to a commissioned officers course and, thereafter, the rank of lieutenant. These courses were periodically run in the military college separate from the cadet intake for these guys. The only difference is, in most cases, they left in the well-schooled military brain, but not always, as some came back as different people with a completely new identity and approach to personnel.

All told, the NCO course was a very satisfactory one for me, and on completion, there was a passing-out parade and ceremony when the instructors pinned on our corporals' stripes. Our course was the first in the Western Command to give a ranking from first place to last. I remember the late Harry Cassidy came first, Benny Barber and Gerry Driver were either second or third, and I came in at sixth place from a class of forty; however, I will never forget what Jeff Cuff, the old company sergeant from that time, always said, "Whatever about coming first; never be the last."

This brings me on to another course that I underwent shortly after being promoted to corporal; it was a command ranger course that had a completely different emphasis. The chief instructor for the course was Sergeant Willie Sweeney from Assumption Road, Athlone. On entering the classroom, Willie had a blanket hanging over the blackboard. All students were referred to as "ranger," as rank didn't carry in this course, and indeed the students were not allowed to wear any. When Willie partly removed the blanket from the blackboard, it read, "Rule One: The instructor is always right," and when he removed the blanket further, it revealed, "Rule Two: Even if the instructor is wrong, he is still right." The ranger course is a survival course with skills such as mountain climbing, cliff rappelling, endurance training, field engineering, and explosives. It's crippling and intensive, and the attrition rate was high. The course lasted almost three months, and we were on the go 24/7.

After returning to my unit, I was sent back a few months later to instruct on a command ranger course for officers and men. We carried out a prelim in Rockhill House outside Letterkenny. There were ten applicants for the course—my job was to make life as uncomfortable as possible, and, believe me, I did that. We had four officers and six NCOs from the unit. I can't remember all their names, but from my own unit there was Lt. John Durnan,

Sergeant Eddie Crawford, and Corporal Micky Devlin. Once, on a strip-search for a survival day, when nobody was to have any food, I was searching John, and he had tucked up inside the bottom of his combat trousers a full packet of cheese squares. I had a drink with John two years ago while attending the funeral of an uncle; he was then the commanding officer of the Sixth Infantry Battalion with the rank of lieutenant colonel. John was a good guy. There was also a lieutenant from Finner Camp whose name I now forget, but he was up for anything. The officer in charge of the course was a Comdt. Sean Kilbride, and he wasn't happy with the application that we were giving the students, so those poor bastards really did get it up the ass; some fell by the wayside and on completion of the course a soldier from Derry who was stationed in Rockhill House as a corporal wanted to have it out with me now that the course was over. Such was the nature of the job as a ranger instructor.

Around that time the army was to form a new unit called the army ranger wing, an independent unit answering only to the chief of staff. I was back in Athlone on a command signal course, when one day two new jeeps from the newly formed rangers swept into the barracks and straight to the training depot. One of the passengers was an officer whom I had earlier trained, and he asked me to join the unit, with the promise of quick promotion through the ranks. While this was appealing, it was not practical with a wife and two children in Strabane. She would never have moved to the Curragh Camp in County Kildare, so I was held back from the one thing that I wanted to really do in my army career not for any military reasons but for domestic ones.

Back in Lifford, we were kept busy with our own operational duties. The lads were always having a kick about with a ball on the barrack square. One of the local NCOs, Corporal Hugo Rooney (RIP), formed a now-infamous soccer club, Prior United, which went on to play in the Donegal League. The club gave most of the lads in the camp an outside focus. Hugo was a great organiser; even at Christmas, Hugo was in the thick of it, organising pantomime for the kids of the soldiers. He was always a busy bee who died suddenly at a young age in 1984. Soon after that, the barracks got some money from the military budget, and the NCOs got a new mess built. This was my life until my first overseas posting in 1981, which I now go on to deal with, taking you from one end of the rainbow to the other.

2

1981, The Start of My Adventures in Lebanon

As we cast our memories back thirty-one years, it can somewhat cloud the past, but when it is set in the granite of your brain, it pops out like the umpteenth slice of toast, fresh, well-done, and tasting the same. That's reality, yet perceptions of others who are immune to the facts keep changing the script. Even worse are those who were never there but become an authority on all issues, and so the waters get murky.

What has all this to do with, you might ask. Well, it goes back all the way to a village in Southern Lebanon in 1981. On April 27 of that year, the village of Dynater became famous after the murder of Private Hugh Doherty from Letterkenny, County Donegal, an Irish soldier serving with the Forty-Ninth Infantry Battalion, and the disappearance of Private Kevin (Seoige) Joyce, who hailed from the Arran Islands off the coast of Galway. Private Joyce has never been found dead or alive, and the file on this incident is still open, thrashing out the same rhetoric for the past twenty-six years. There has never been an inquiry set up to get to the truth of the matter—just the government line on how things were then as they are now.

In the twenty-first century of modern Ireland, we have enquiries into everything and anything, from a shady few bob right up to Garda corruption, yet when it comes to something such as a young man from the Arran Islands serving his country as part of the United Nations, his family has to accept that now he is officially declared dead—so that is the end of the matter. The govern-

14

ment's defence will be that they had a military police officer assigned to the case exclusively for a period of eighteen to twenty-four months in 1986 that drew a blank in the investigation, and right up to the time when the Irish Defence Forces withdrew from southern Lebanon, the matter was always under review. The obvious—a thorough examination of the facts and interviews of everyone in the village of Dynater, including myself, on that fateful day in 1981—has never happened. I can only now conclude with the passing of time that any investigation included only those people who could construct an official timetable of events to form the basis of the department's findings into the death of Private Doherty and the abduction of Private Joyce.

The Irish Defence Force's involvement with UNIFIL (United Nations Interim Force in Lebanon) commenced in May 1978 with the deployment of the Forty-Third Infantry Battalion. The Department of Defence had bolstered its numbers with a huge recruitment drive during 1976 and 1977; a lot of things were changing, with the escalating troubles here in Ireland and Northern Ireland, including the formation of new border battalions, new equipment, and new units and promotions. When I look back at that era, it was courses, courses, and more courses, as everyone wanted to get on ranger courses, NCO courses, and signal and mountaineering courses, and thereafter to instruct on these courses.

It was 1981 before it was my turn for overseas service. The names were published for the Forty-Ninth Infantry Battalion and I was on it. Brilliant. We formed up as a platoon in Finner Camp, Ballyshannon, County Donegal, a total of thirty other ranks, under the command of Lieutenant Hugh Carthy. He was a very easygoing fellow who hailed from Longford, and as I was from Westmeath, we seemed to get along well. I had just finished instructing on a command ranger course for officers and NCOs in the command training depot, so to then get my first overseas posting was just the icing on the cake.

The first three weeks in Finner Camp were for bonding training, finding out the strengths and weakness in every individual. The Irish were only three years into the Lebanon mission, so information filtering back down the line was minimal. We learned about the civil war, the different political factions operating in our area of operations, and, yes, basically southern Lebanon then was a time bomb. The Irish already had taken casualties as early as 1980 when three men serving with the Forty-Sixth Infantry Battalion were killed in April, so Lebanon was proving to be no cushy trip like Cyprus (UNFICYP) was before it. This was the real thing. I was young, an NCO at twenty-five years, and all up for it. I considered myself professional and gung ho and was nicknamed the Reg. Little was I to know that I was to travel on five further tours of duty to southern Lebanon, six in total (with the Forty-Ninth, Fifty-Second, Fifty-Ninth, Sixty-Sixth, Seventieth, and Seventy-Sixth Battalions). After the initial three-week training, we went to Custume Barracks to form up as a company, so down the road we travelled in the back of 4x4 trucks. The platoon sergeant was a guy called Jim Brennan, who had instructed me on my NCO course, so at that time I had rated him highly, and he had good man management skills, which were important to keep everybody happy. There were other corporals with me: Corporal Jackie Quinn (considered an old sweat due to his longer service); Corporal "Hands" Lafferty, such a worker that when the French engineering company came to us looking for a work detail, they would ask for a section of men or Hands Lafferty; Corporal Tom Frize, who had just completed his NCO course; and Corporal Joe "Twinkle Toes" O'Brien, whose nickname came from his love of Irish dancing.

All personnel from the Donegal platoon had border security duty experience behind them so they were not wet behind the ears. One of the youngest in the platoon was Private Hugh Doherty from Letterkenny, and he had just finished an army tailoring course; as such, he was handy with the Singer sewing machine, so he was definitely travelling overseas. On these training weeks, there were always a number of subs selected as part of the training, so if anything untoward happened, they would always make up the numbers very quickly. This always helped to keep people on their toes, so to speak, and over a three-month period of training, anything could and did happen, from a guy not being up to standard to a domestic situation; if you were a sub, you had a good chance. I remember one time with the Sixty-Fifth Battalion when Corporal Martin McKnight and I were the NCO subs. We had a great time, but we did not get to travel; however, we had to travel up to the airport for each flight to Lebanon just in case of a mishap. I remember one NCO from the Southern Command who was also a sub cracking up; he was definitely ready to go, as he was pointing out different individuals to me, saying things like, "His wife won ten grand on the lotto, and I should be in front of him," and then pointing out someone and said he buried his father only last week and should not be travelling. I remember going back to my barracks, thinking how glad I was not to be travelling with him.

When we formed up as a company in Athlone, there were another two platoons and the company headquarters. Now was the time to form into one cohesive unit, which always happens, with every battalion and every platoon retaining its own identity. Our company commander was an artillery officer by the name of Comdt. Jim Gavin, a very jilty officer. The second in command was Captain Brian O'Keeffe; the company sergeant who was promoted acting up followed these from the rank of quartermaster sergeant.

These two NCOs were drawn from the training staff of the FCA (reserve defence forces), and such were regarded as part-time soldiers. The company sergeant was to keep a low profile during the training period but became a much-hated figure throughout the tour of duty. I can never recall over my twenty-three-plus years in the army someone abusing power and trust like he did. In those days, the officer cadre didn't mix with the other ranks as much as they do today; there is no way that this individual would get away with it, but I will talk a bit more on this later on.

We had a great platoon: characters like Private Billy McKinley, who retired only a few years ago, and his cousin Thomas, who died at the age of thirty-seven. I will always remember Thomas for three things. First, the night we were due to fly, his wife phoned him. I was the duty NCO and had to take him to the signal centre for the phone call. The call was not private, and it was touch-and-go if he would travel or not, but he did. Second, after about five weeks into the tour, it became evident that he made the wrong decision, but he worked his way through the six months, and finally, during a very hot summer in Southern Lebanon, he got an ingrown toenail that had to be removed, and when sunbathing on the roof of our observation post the flies would torture him. That's one thing Lebanon had plenty of—flies. I remember climbing the stairs onto the roof, and I could hear this solitary voice talking to himself. It was Thomas. He caught the flies with both hands clasped, shook his hands violently, dropped the disorientated flies, and then plucked off one of their wings to watch them struggle to take off again. He shouted, "Suffer, you bastard. Suffer, suffer!" He then took mercy on them and killed them with his flip-flop sandal. Then there was Danny Calhoun from Lifford, a walking bag of nerves—something Lebanon did not improve—and boy, could he chat. You could never shut him up. I was to calm him down months later in Lebanon.

Now the time of departure was drawing near, and the romance of the situation was coming to an end, with final injections, the making of the last will and testament, and the final weekend with the family at home. This was the one thing that nobody was looking forward to; we were to travel in three flights (chalks), one a week. I was on the first out along with the platoon commander, Lt. Hugh Carthy; the platoon sergeant, Jim Brennan; and my entire section.

It was one hell of a long weekend, as I was married with a son just two years of age and my wife, Sheila, was three months pregnant. We had just moved into our new house in Lisnafin Park in Strabane, County Tyrone; she was happy for me and always supported me during my army career, but it was tough for her, as well. Luckily, she had her family beside her supporting her.

It's funny now looking back, me as an Irish soldier living in what was one of the most republican, blown-up towns in Northern Ireland. My brother-in-law was serving in the now-disbanded RUC, him a Catholic, which put undue pressure on my in-laws for their whole lives. The now-infamous republican hunger strike was in full swing. There were two areas of the world gaining prime time news every day, Lebanon and Northern Ireland. It felt like I was going from the frying pan into the fire. Time to pluck the courage up. That Tuesday morning, Sheila and I sat up the night before crying our eyes out; there were no tears left come morning. I was sitting there wishing the time away, waiting for the minibus. Such a morning to be late, as if things weren't hard enough. I had resolved not to look back after I left the front door, just one kiss and keep going. The bus arrived, and I executed the plan accordingly. We arrived at Gormanstown Camp in County Meath at about 2:00 p.m., after which we passed the day doing final checks, eating, and playing cards. The big buses arrived at 9:00 p.m. to take us to Dublin Airport after final mass and general absolution, something I always found amazing—that before the soldier goes to the battlefield, his soul is totally absolved from all sin. We flew out with Aer Lingus on two 707 aircrafts, a bit cramped, but the food was great and the cabin crew friendly; after approximately five hours, we landed in Ben Gurion Airport, Tel Aviv, Israel.

We had to take off our berets, as you are not allowed to wear the cap badge of a foreign army on Israeli soil. The heat was serious; it was eight o'clock in the morning, and it was already around 30 degrees Celsius. From the airport in Israel, it was a long journey to the Lebanon border, sitting in the back of French army trucks. One of the lads from Athlone who had been out with the Forty-Sixth Infantry Battalion sat beside me. I kept saying what a beautiful country, and Liam said to me, "Frank, tell me that in a month's time."

When we arrived at the border and treaded down the road to Naqoura, Southern Lebanon, which was UNIFIL headquarters, it was dark—and I mean dark. We were informed that due to trouble in the area of operations, we were being held overnight in Naqoura. The priority was to get fed, washed, and rested, as we had had a long journey. The logistics of running a convoy of UN vehicles from the airport was longer than the flying time from Ireland, but we were here at last. The first impression of Naqoura was brilliant. We were advised before we settled down to sleep that we could avail of the canteen facilities of the Swedish contingent, something most of did, and boy, did we get some surprise. The Swedish were light years ahead of us with everything, from the sounds of ABBA to cans of Heineken to beautiful tanned female soldiers in uniform walking around the place. It was too good to be true. Private Brian Porter (a veteran with eighteen years of service) and I were sitting on two reed chairs looking out on the Mediterranean Sea, just full of ourselves, saying this isn't the Lebanon from the stories that we had heard prior to our departure from Ireland. Brian remarked that maybe the stories were put out to prevent us from volunteering; it was something to think about.

The next day we travelled north to the area of operations, and climbing mountain roads barely wide enough for a truck was daunting. I was an army driver in my earlier career, and I wasn't impressed with the French detachment of drivers taking us there, but, then again, I was always a nervous wreck as a passenger at the best of times.

Lebanon, as we drove into her very soul, was becoming more like the Lebanon we were told about at home. Houses with their gables exposed to the skyline from tank shells and walls peppered from heavy machine gun fire were a final reminder that our illusion from the night before through a can of Heineken was nothing other than that. We finally arrived at Sultaniayh, which was our company headquarters, to be met by old faces heavily suntanned and glad to see us, as their time was coming to an end, and all were looking forward to travelling home to their families. Over the next two weeks, things were going to be hectic, taking over from the Forty-Eighth Infantry Battalion, getting briefings and ground orientation, learning the identity of armed elements, and learning the duty rotation system and the local customs.

To continue at this stage without examining the military and political situation on the ground prior to our deployment would be criminal, so let's look at events during early 1981. The Israelis had created a buffer zone some twelve miles deep from the international demarcation line right into southern Lebanon. They brought together approximately six to seven thousand men mostly recruited from that area. Add in the odd mercenary soldier and give it a command structure under renegade Lebanese officer Major Said Haddat. The Israelis equipped them with half-tracks, which were World War II vehicles, and Sherman tanks; their mission was to control that area and to repulse any attack in Southern Lebanon from Palestinian soldiers of the PLO. In the south of the country, the Lebanese government had lost control mainly because it was in a continuous state of fracture and the Lebanese army was very weak after the civil war during the mid-seventies. The landscape of southern Lebanon is very mountainous, but along the sea belt is a very fertile area given over to miles of banana and citrus groves. This was natural ground cover for the many different PLO factions that were operating openly in the area. We have to remember that there were up to fifteen thousand PLO operating from the port city of Sidon right down to the enclave, and these guys were an army on their own, heavily armed with antiaircraft capability, both mobile and stationary. A lot of the time there was infighting among the different factions and then constant attacks against the Israeli-backed South Lebanese Army (SLA). Caught in between was the local Lebanese population, who felt very vulnerable despite the presence of UNIFIL. Remember, in guerrilla warfare, all kinds of tactics are used, creating informers, kidnapping, and even targeting the local population. The south was mainly inhabited by Shia Muslims who, in the main, were farmers. Their spiritual leader was the Imaam Musa Sadr, who was affiliated with the political-military party Amal, which armed itself in every village and town of Southern Lebanon. They had a very loose command structure as can be imagined, and so it was their policies that were different from village to village. Their main foe in the beginning was the Palestinians, and figuring out how to contain them in the refugee camps, which was near impossible, and how to protect themselves in the Palestinian villages. This had a two-pronged effect: a strong Amal presence inhibited the Palestinians and kept the SLA in check. They were the only armed group in the area that supported UNIFIL as policy, but on the ground this did not always work. There were renegades in their ranks, and one such guy was the local Amal captain in the village of Brachit, named Hassan Hanowee. I was to have an altercation with him during the TOD that kept me on my toes for the remainder of the tour. In early 1981, the PLO stepped up their attacks on Israeli targets and the SLA. Their favourite method of travel inland was through the wadis (dry river beds). The Forty-Eighth Battalion was stretched on the ground, and it was impossible to cover every track, but something had to be done. C Company, under the command of Comdt. Sinad Downes, moved into the village of Dynater and set up a platoon strength command post about a half kilometre outside the village. On the far side of the village was a natural plateau overlooking the ground west and right down to the city of Tyre on the west coast. This area became known as the iron triangle. There was natural woodland that housed batteries of PLO antiaircraft, and this was the natural route east to gain access to attack the IDF-SLA positions north of the Israeli border.

From several vantage points, from the village of Harris under the control of the Dutch UN contingent to Tibnin, Sultaniayh, and Dynater under the control of the Irish, listening posts were set up to restrict the PLO activity. This operational tactic stretched our resources to the limit—indeed, beyond the limit— so a decision was taken, at what level I don't know, to send two armed private soldiers with a radio to man these observation and listening posts (OP-LP).

Military tactics dictate that the minimum deployment requires an NCO with a half section on the ground, about five or six men in total, and this depends on the situation, with the reinforcement level having been judged on reaction times and speed to the location.

So at this point in time, the Forty-Eighth Battalion was conducting operations that were not to a good military standard. The walk from the command post in Dynater to the OP-LP 612D on the plateau was a twenty-minute trek through the village. The only military vehicle allotted to Dynater was a platoon soft-skin vehicle that was not guaranteed to be there at all times, as it had to travel to company headquarters in Sultaniayh, fifteen minutes in the other direction, so there was no real backup if anything was to happen on the two-man OP-LP.

Let us look at Dynater and the villagers. Shia Muslims are broken into two groups: (1) liberal and pro-Western and (2) orthodox religious pro-Iranian, where the men and women dress in black. Dynater was of the latter, very conservative. During March 1981 in the village of Brachit behind the mosque, three men were executed by what is believed to have been IDF-SLA forces that came into the area from the enclave. What's interesting is that one or two of the causalities were from Dynater. In Southern Lebanon, "blood money" is often sought, if you're lucky; if not, revenge is guaranteed. During the tenure of the Forty-Sixth Battalion, a young boy of fourteen years came out from a crowd protesting at Attiri Village, brandishing what was considered a gun. He was shot dead by the Irish. His uncle Mohammad Bassi, who was in the SLA, promised revenge, which he exacted on two Irish soldiers, Privates Barrett and Smallhorn. The lead-up to their deaths was what we soldiers called a CMFU, a complete military fuck-up, but this can be dealt with by someone else. In the earlier years of UNIFIL, blood money was sought and paid. Though no one can prove or disprove it, it was local knowledge that the family of the Dynater victims sought blood money from UNIFIL, as the victims were executed on the Irish watch within the area of our operations. On this occasion, because UNIFIL was not directly involved, no money was paid over.

As we billeted down in Sultaniayh, our conditions were very different from Naqoura, a complete reality check. We were moved into a barn under the house, and it must have housed half the small birds nesting in Southern Lebanon. You made sure that you had your mosquito net down at night, or you would have a very messy face come morning; however, you were sure to get done by the mosquito, as they would get in ahead of a draft. They were worse than the gunmen in Lebanon at the time. I was to observe later the birds' talent for staying alive and safe, as in Lebanon, small birds are considered a delicacy. It was often you would see a young boy with a single-bore shotgun and a string of birds dangling from his side. The birds were quick on the pickup, as they knew they were safe in a UN post. We were soon moved into a routine that was to last for six months, with six hours on duty and twelve hours off; during times of need, which weren't far away, it was six on and six off. The first few days were spent getting kitted out in UN clothing and getting rank markings sewn on, which you would not think would be a problem with a tailor in the platoon, but poor Hugh Doherty was snowed under with work carried on from our time in Gormanstown. Like everything in the army, it works from the top down. C Company had responsibility for a major checkpoint on Tibnin Bridge, added to Camp Guard, patrols checkpoint at Barasanasil, and the platoon detached to Dynater, rotating personnel every four weeks from post to post. The companies then rotated every two months with 120 person-

nel moving from one company location to the next. This was a heavy work-
load on any level of organisation, and thankfully in later years this was to
change.

After two days in Sultaniayh, the Donegal Platoon was moved out to
Dynater to allow the personnel returning home with the Forty-Eighth Battalion to move back to company headquarters in preparation for their repatriation. The remaining battalion personnel stayed behind in Dynater to conduct a
handover and to allow us to familiarise ourselves with the terrain and the mission. The strength of the post at that time was two officers, sixteen NCOs and
privates, a cook, and a driver. It was pretty straightforward: we provided one
NCO and three privates for checkpoint duty on Tibnin Bridge on an eight-
hour rotation, one NCO and two privates for post guard, and two privates for
the OP 612D.

Into the second day, I learned that there was a five-a-side football match
being played in the village. The land rover was down in the village, so I asked
Lt. Carthy if I could go down and watch the match. In reality, I just wanted to
get out of the house for an hour. Private Danny Calhoun and I slung our rifles
over our shoulders and headed down. The village was quite small and horse-
shoe-shaped with the watering hole in the centre, a few grocery shops, a
butcher shop, and a few clothes shops. We did expect a friendly welcome like
we had received in Sultaniayh, but, no, there was an air of hostility; as we
went into one shop, the guy behind the counter even produced a 9-mm Beretta
pistol. Call it what you like, but I felt very uneasy about the atmosphere, and
we left the shop to return to the house. In truth, you didn't get much time to
think because of the shift system; it was duty, food, and bed, although some of
the middle shift got time to touch up on their suntans in the afternoon on the
roof of the house. I can remember being struck with the architecture of the
buildings—completely different from our housing in Ireland, all big buildings
with flat roofs. The smaller ones were of a single story, with the necessary
steel works jutting up from the four corners in preparation for the next phase
of construction when it became necessary to expand for another member of
the extended family.

Now here was I, still no rank marking sewn on my uniform and the asshole
of an acting company sergeant on my back 24/7. I just gave up on Hughie
Doherty, our tailor, and took my gear into Mama Tabs, adjacent to company
headquarters. Mama Tabs cooked Double Double (egg and chips) for a dollar
a time. These women were so ingenious they could do anything, and this
included the sewing, so, price agreed, I handed my gear to Mama Tabs. The
reason she was called Mama Tabs was that she was a tall woman with massive
feet in comparison to her husband, a local farmer who was quite small. The

homey feeling brought back memories of my grandfathers, who were farmers, a nice warm home, and the kettle always on.

Day four, I had a shift on Tibnin Bridge that night, just one NCO and three privates complemented by three Lebanese soldiers who might or might not turn up. Presidential election was the fever of the day, and the front runner was a Christian called Amin Gemeyal. Even the Shia in the south were shouting "Amin"; he was seen as a unity candidate, and for the first time since the start of the civil war, there seemed to be a determination by the Lebanese people to rise from the ashes. With a curfew from 10:00 p.m. until 4:00 a.m., Tibnin Bridge was quiet, and we passed the time telling yarns. Anyway, 7:30 a.m. came, and the changeover took place. I told the driver to call into Mama Tabs to check if my rank markings had been sewn on, only to be told that she would have them for me that evening. The CS called, and I thought, *Fuck, here we go again,* but no, he just wanted to show me the new company lanyard, which he made himself. He and the company second in command were going to make sure everyone had one for eight dollars each. "Make sure you tell the lads, Reg." Not likely, as we had all already paid six dollars for one back in Gormanstown before we left for Lebanon. The feeling of being on the make was creeping in far too early on the trip.

We arrived back at the gate in Dynater, and I noticed Doherty and Private Seoige Joyce outside, one helping the other put on the 77 radio back set. "Have you got the *mungeriia* (Arabic for food)?" asked Joyce.

Doherty nodded, turned his gaze toward me, and said, "Reg, I'll sew those rank marking on for you tonight."

Sadly, my response was, "Hughie, fuck off," the last words I ever spoke to him. Even today, that rankles me. It could have been said a nicer way. Hughie rolled his eyes, and the two of them headed off down the road.

Private Joe Martin, the cook, met me inside. "Reggie, the kettle is on and there is a bit of breakfast on."

"Right, Joe," I said as I went to put my weapon and gear away. A mug was a precious implement out here, and everyone had their own, be it Celtic or Man United type. I gathered mine and headed for the breakfast as promised by Joe. Corporal Joe O'Brien was guard commander with 03 Private McLaughlin and Doherty. Prior to our return from Tibnin Bridge, Joe had tossed a coin to ascertain which of the two lads would go to the OP with Seoige Joyce, and 03 Private McLaughlin had won the toss. "Any news from home?" I asked Joe. "Or anything on the BBC World Service?"

"The hunger strike is getting bad, and there is a lot of trouble in Northern Ireland."

While I waited on my toast, I asked him if there was any mention of Strabane.

"Naw," he said. "Sure, who would mention that place?" Then he laughed.

At 8:30 a.m., I gathered myself to get to bed after the breakfast. I had slipped into a routine after five days: I grabbed my Walkman radio, because with people to-ing and fro-ing, the sound of Anne Murray singing "I'll Always Remember" was guaranteed to get you off to sleep. At about 2:00 p.m., all hell broke loose. The walls of the building were wobbling from the noise of explosions, and at first, I thought it was a nightmare, but within milliseconds, I was in my bush green uniform, grabbed my rifle, and ran to the roof. By now, everyone was on the roof, and what a spectacular sight we beheld to the north of our position. The village of Maruna was being bombed by Israeli war jets, and other villages in the Tyre pocket were getting it also. There was no immediate threat unless they started heading our way; however, it felt like you could just reach out and feel them, and for us first-timers it was as if John Ford, the film director, was on set. Then you thought of the poor bastards who were being bombed. I am sure it must have lasted a couple of hours with one wave after another.

At about 4:00 p.m., the radio operator at company headquarters became alarmed when he could not make contact with Dynater House or the two-man OP. Private McLaughlin was on duty on the roof, and just like us he was more fascinated by what we were all observing and probably didn't hear the radio. The operator called the second in command of C Company, Forty-Eighth Battalion, Captain Christy O'Sullivan, to inform him of his concern. It was normal to give a radio check every fifteen to thirty minutes so contact with the forces on the ground was maintained. Human nature derives all the human excuses it can muster—bad battery, signal block, whatever—then the guys turned up. Anyway, things were busy at company HQ as there was a big barbecue in UN whites, the last big session for the Forty-Eighth Battalion before departure. This is normal in military life, for the *esprit de corps* of any unit. It's rewarding, saying thanks for a job well done.

The day moved on, and at about 5:00 p.m. Lt. Carthy told me to pick one man from last night's duty, and the two boys came back at 6:00 p.m. to get ready to do an all-night two-man OP. I just said, "Yes, sir." Jesus, it's one thing doing something crazy during daylight, but in the dark of night it was madness. I picked Private Joe McGirr, a bit rock solid. I made sure I was well armed, with hand grenades and the lot. If something was going to happen to two men, I was going to bring company with me. We moved outside at about 6:30 p.m., and concern was raised by Joe Martin, the cook, as he was keeping two dinners warm.

"Where is the lads?" he asked. You did not fall out with Joe Martin, because he baked better bread than my granny. Somebody remarked that they were probably drinking *shi* (tea) in some house on the way back. Well, the platoon sergeant, Mossy Scanlon, and his driver, Private Rabbit, jumped into the Jeep and headed down the village.

I remarked to Joe McGirr, "It's near 7:00 p.m. Our shift will be shorter." Then I heard the revs of the Jeep speeding back from the village, and somebody was shouting to open the gate, which I did. The sergeant and the driver dismounted at speed, running toward the house. Private Rabbit shouted, "One of your lads has been shot."

My first reaction is, *Silly bastard, messing with his rifle, probably shot himself in the foot.* "Is it bad?" I enquired.

He shouted back to me, "He is dead!"

Where was John Ford now? Panicked, I instinctively mustered red alert, and everybody grabbed flak jackets, helmets, and rifles and ran to firing positions. I hadn't time to think; this is where your professionalism kicks in. We had an ammunition store in a back room, and I ran to get the heavy machine gun and a belt of 7.62-mm ammunition, twenty-five-feet long and packed with one in five tracer rounds. I put my best man, Private Billy McKinley, on the weapon and sighted him and got the 84-mm antitank weapon. While one man shouted out the orders, the first to take the initiative, the other NCOs, irrespective of seniority, chipped in. The two officers were frantically relaying the situation back to company headquarters and requesting backup. Nobody knew what was going on, whether the post was going to come under attack, whatever, so we were primed for anything. I went from position to position checking on everybody; there was a sense of disbelief and tears, but most were holding themselves together. One guy, Private Danny Calhoun, was very disturbed, banging his head against sandbags, saying, "Why didn't I listen to Roy and Maureen? Come on, Danny, pull yourself together and don't let the side down." He did his best, but it was obvious that he needed to be watched.

The company mobile reserve arrived in two armoured personnel carriers (APCs) to back up our position. A sense of calm and relief spread throughout the house. You could hear a pin drop, and nobody was going into the village until the force mobile reserve arrived. They did at some time around 8:00 p.m., and then the village was secured. Negotiations with the village mucktar (local headman) and Amal took place, and it was agreed that UNIFIL could search the village but that no buildings could be entered. The Norwegian dog unit arrived and were taken to the scene of the shooting at about 9:30 p.m., but they could not be used until the morning because of the darkness. Word filtered back to the house that one body was found and that Private Joyce was missing, along with the radio and both rifles. Being quite honest, the army, to improve its capability to carry out drills, most parts of me were thinking this was a dress rehearsal operation and everybody had to play their part. I remember that thought keeping me focused. It seems crazy now, but fiction and fact kept my mind calm—it was as if my brain was in denial. At about 9:30 p.m., the ambulance came back from the village with the remains of Private Doherty. Lt. Carthy had to go into Tibnin village hospital to identify the remains. He decided to take Calhoun with him; that was a relief. Now was the time to stand down, get people to bed, as duties were needed the following morning. More than likely, there would be extra duties now because of the situation. Everyone mulled about in the kitchen with a cup of tea or coffee. A checkpoint was set up outside the post to check all vehicles coming and going out of the village; with a man down and another missing, it was imperative that we keep everything watertight. Carthy briefed us on what was happening the next morning. I was on the checkpoint at 6:00 a.m., so it was time to put the head down for the remainder of the night; however, I don't think one person slept that night. This was sure a baptism of fire after only six days in the mission. Welcome to Lebanon.

Lebanon comes alive quite early after the 4:00 a.m. curfew is lifted; the vehicles start to pile up, ordinary people go to work and about their business, but still everyone has to be checked. I think I took over the checkpoint from Corporal Jackie Quinn; he was relieved to get to his bed, though it was to be a short sojourn. At about 6:30 a.m., a young fellow from the village approached the checkpoint, talking in Arabic to me. He seemed quite concerned, trying to explain something to me. "No English, am parleo Francie."

"Hold it there," I said, and I went to get Carthy, who spoke fairly fluent French.

Carthy came out to the lad and started to converse with him in French. I observed with a sense of envy, realising how important it is to be able to speak a second language. There was a lot of pointing and verbal exchanges, and it was obvious that this lad knew something. Then all of a sudden, Carthy dismisses him. The lad seemed confused, as if he was taking a big chance approaching us in the first place; anyhow, he headed back to the village, looking annoyed. I asked Carthy what the lad said, and he replied, "Typical Arab. He claims he knows where Private Joyce is being held in the village, and he will show us if we give him dollars." With this, Carthy headed back into the house.

From 7:00 a.m. onward, there was a lot of activity at the checkpoint, so working with one NCO and three privates was akin to one and thirty. A search party was mustered from within the battalion from all the companies, between 130 to 150 personnel. They came in all sorts of military vehicles, some familiar faces shouting words of encouragement to try to keep morale up. One of them, Sergeant John Touhy, was a brother-in-law of Hugh Doherty. It was my brief to allow no one into the village unless they were indigenous, and everybody's ID had to be checked. Every armed group in Lebanon had a liaison officer who carried a UN ID card signed by the force commander. At this stage, during 8:00 to 9:00 a.m., there were many theories going about, and one of the stories was that the PLO shot Doherty and took Joyce as hostage.

A car approached the checkpoint and stopped. I asked the occupant to get out, spread-eagled him, and, while being covered by one of my sentries, proceeded to search him. I recovered a 9-mm star pistol on his mid-back; he was speaking fluent English, and on his right arm was a small box-like item. I insisted that he take it off his arm, only to discover it was a religious item. At this stage, everyone, bar the essentials, was out on the search including officers. This guy showed me his ID, wanting to speak with someone in charge. I passed this information on via radio and told him he would have to wait at the checkpoint until someone came along. I took the magazine out of his weapon and returned it to him, as nobody other than us was going to have a loaded gun on my checkpoint. Now when I look back, whoever came through the checkpoint got a grilling, as the adrenaline was high. This PLO guy was all right; as he waited, he went to some pains to reassure me that no PLO personnel were involved in the murder scene. He went through various scenarios and seemed genuinely remorseful.

There was too much going on to get my head around everything. In the village to the west, the OP was about a half mile behind the village. The search dogs were deployed in the direction of Tyre, and a full skirmish line of men searched for any clues. The OP was cordoned off as a crime scene, and so the search started looking for anything in the very rough terrain. As day one ended, I watched the search parties coming back in small groups totally exhausted; just one look at the faces told the story. They had given it everything, and there was a sense of disappointment that they had found nothing. Eventually during the day, somebody did see the PLO liaison officer, and I gave him his magazine back, and he headed off. I did see him back at the checkpoint the next day, but that day I was going out on the search.

There was a sense of desperation setting in, but nobody was giving up. Things for the first week were so hectic; we were still in Irish combat uniform, and with temperatures thirty to thirty-five degrees, our own Irish kit was not fit for the purpose of conducting searches. We trekked through the terrain ever mindful of our own vulnerability, and after a while we took a break. I remember Commandants Gavin and Downes sitting down. Gavin beckoned me over and asked about the welfare of the men. I said that they were, in the main, okay, given what had occurred and that they were concerned about being exposed to the two-man OP with no NCO in charge. He told me to reassure them that this was the end of such operations. Later it was confirmed that the search dogs found no scent in the area forward of the ill-fated OP, and the reason given was that seven hours after the incident the scent would be lost, but it was later known that the dogs were not used in the direction back to the village.

On the third day of searching, the search was extended up to the wooded area known to house the PLO antiaircraft guns. At this point, the PLO opened fire over the heads of the search party to indicate that they thought we had gone far enough. This was nearly four kilometres from the OP. At the same time, the SLA had a private propaganda radio station on the airwaves, and at times they used to encourage UNIFIL personnel to defect or desert over to their side, where they would be well paid and looked after. The rumour mill got going again, and it came out the Joyce had shot Doherty, taken the missing pieces of ordnance, and headed off to join up with the SLA. Trying to fathom what happened was a full-time topic of conversation; it was also suggested that Joyce had defected to the PLO, and so on. A couple of years later with the Fifty-Fourth Battalion, it was rumoured he turned up at a checkpoint in Brachit and had a conversation with the lads; the rumours really did the rounds in Lebanon and at home in Ireland. Remember, during and after the searching, the mission had to continue, and there was no doubt in anyone's mind that we were in a very hostile and dangerous situation. Hugh Doherty's body was removed to Ram Bann Hospital in the port city of Haifa, Israel, in preparation for going home. The final chalk of the Forty-Eighth Battalion departed for home, and now the Forty-Ninth Battalion was in charge under the command of Battalion Commander Lt. Col. Fergi Nichol, who had taken over from Lt. Col. Steve Murphy. The battalion commander was now engaged in touring his company locations, especially C Company.

For a man to be defecting to any armed group operating in Southern Lebanon, it must have been a last-minute decision, I thought as I gazed down at Private Joyce's neatly packed bag and case, meticulously packed in anticipation of returning home.

It soon became clear that we had a month to serve in Dynater, and then we would be moved to Tyre Barracks to do barrack duties. This would be a rest period after what we had been through. Tension in the area was still high, and I was on Tibnin Bridge at 7:30 a.m. with three privates and, of course, my Lebanese army commitment. Joe Martin, our cook, had the sandwiches ready and had saved a bit of scone bread for me. Joe was a good one; he was under as much pressure as anybody else, for he always managed the five loaves and two fishes job with the rations supplied.

I called into Mama Tabs to collect my now-tailored UN bush greens, and when I looked at them with rank markings all sewn on, I got a lump in my throat. No time to dwell. Mounting back into our vehicle, I heard the call. "Reg, did you tell the lads about the lanyard?" He pointed to the ceremonial one he had on his right shoulder.

"Yeah," I shouted as I beckoned our driver to move on. *Fuck you and your lanyard,* I thought.

"*Quise,*" he shouted back, knowing full well by my mannerisms that the lanyard had to wait for another day. *Jesus,* I thought, *does he know no other word than* quise*?* He always said it, and even though it translates to means "good," I might add that that was all the good there was in that man.

Down at Tibnin Bridge, there was a quick handover as the lads coming off were knackered and headed home to their beds. After two weeks into the mission, we soon came to realise how important sleep was. Tibnin Bridge is one of the most important hubs for traffic in Southern Lebanon as three roads lead to the one bridge. A sentry was posted at each juncture with one at a time being allowed through to be checked. The tailback on the three roads was terrible, so we used as much common sense as possible. Holy men such as sheiks or imams were ushered through with due respect, which they appreciated, and funerals, likewise. My first was coming down the road from Sultaniayh: what looked like an ambulance with flashing lights and sirens with music ringing out, and a fleet of cars with black flags swirling from them. It was some sight. Lt. Tony Bracken (DSM) was operations officer and also in charge of the recce section, the armour car element of the company. He rang me on the landline to inform me that Hassan Hanouee was touring our area of operations in a green Mercedes and that his vehicle was to be stopped and thoroughly checked. Low and behold, within the half hour, he was approaching our checkpoint. There were six people in the vehicle, four men and two women, and Hanouee was driving. He offered me a cut rose, which, at the time, I didn't know was Lebanese custom. It was important to separate the women from the men with respect and then search the men. I positioned Hanouee spread-legged across the car and found a pistol on him; he resisted, so I shoved him up against the sidewall of the bunker and gave him one. On completion of the car search, we found three more weapons, including a Kalashnikov. Hanouee was very irate and embarrassed in front of the heavy traffic that was gathered. Reading off my name badge, he threatened that he would later kill me, and then turned to one sentry, Private Micky Walker, and told him that he would kill him, too. Micky became very nervous; he was about twenty-one years old and best friends with Hugh Doherty. I needed him to snap out of it, which he did. The military police—the "appeaser brigade"—were called, and to be fair, they can only do what's laid down. They took the offenders off to Tyre, took statements, and confiscated the weapons, only to hand them back to their liaison officer.

About four to five days later again on Tibnin Bridge, about 2:30 in the afternoon, a small convoy of cars came down the hill from Tibnin. They pulled in at the waterhole just short of the checkpoint, and the men got out

armed. It was Hanouee, back to exact his revenge. I looked around, and the
Lebanese soldiers were skipping off (the nickname we had for them when
trouble appeared was "Dash Batt"). With just my three men, Privates Nicky
Crabbe, Joe McGirr, and Micky Walker, I ordered the men to cock weapons.
Private Crabbe radioed back to headquarters for reinforcements from his
machine gun position, and the gunmen proceeded toward our ranks. On my
instruction, we fired three warning shots above their heads. The cadets at John
F. Kennedy's funeral would have been proud of us. There was a rank on the
middle of the bridge, and Hanouee was in front of me, armed. I had my rifle
lowered toward his midriff, and he was shouting abuse about killing me again.
I was probably shitting myself, but I didn't have the time to dwell on it. I
could only tell him he was coming with me, whatever happens. The cavalry
came down the hill with Comdt. Gavin, and the liaison officer from Amal had
arrived on the bridge to speak with Hanouee. The reinforcements, armoured
personnel carriers, and about twenty personnel arrived at the checkpoint.
Gavin arrived on the bridge, and I asked him if he wanted to take over. "Carry
on, Corporal," came the reply. The liaison officer suggested that I assaulted
Hanouee at the time of his arrest. I didn't want to get into a debate about what
happened that morning, so I flatly denied it. He ordered the Amal personnel
off the bridge, so they dispersed, and Hanouee repeated his threat to kill me
before he finally left. Corporal Joe O'Brien took over the checkpoint duty
from me at 4:00 p.m., jovially fucking me out of it for causing hassle. I had
had enough for that day. I called into company headquarters for a debriefing
with Lt. Tony Bracken, and he commended me for a job well done. Bracken
was stationed back home with the Fourth Cavalry in Longford; he was a great
skin, a brilliant musician on the guitar, and always up for the craic. We as a
unit were well into the swing of things by now. The scene of crime report was
now out from the Swedish forensics; Hugh Doherty was shot once in the back
and struggled eleven paces to his right and collapsed, and then received two
gunshots to the back of his neck, which left scorch marks. This indicated he
was finished off from close range by a 5.56-mm round of ammunition, not
7.62-mm, which was the standard ammunition on issue to the Irish Defence
forces at that time, so that put to bed some of the theories going about.

Back to the OP, a place I have been many times since, as recent as 2005,
when I was with the TG4 (an Irish TV channel) reporting team. They were
doing a documentary programme about Kevin Joyce's disappearance. I am
now convinced more than ever about my theory on what happened. First, let's
look at the PLO: to break cover from the hidden-from-view location that was
three to four kilometres away from the tragic OP during a very heavy bombardment by Israeli war planes and then travel back to their cover position
would have been nothing short of suicide on their behalf as F-16 fighter jets

pick up infrared, which is transmitted through body heat. Over the rough ground, they would have been sitting duck targets for the Israeli fighters. It certainly would not be farmers out in the fields during this time of heavy aerial bombing. To come too close to Amal on that day would not have been wise either. We know that Hugh Doherty was shot in the back with his back facing the village. Children used to come down that way every day all day selling Coke and Mars Bars to our soldiers on duty. They were more torture than anything; however, it is believed the children on that day were trying to warn them about gunmen behind them—so where did these gunmen come from and why? Now let's go back to the young lad who came to me the morning after the shooting and who spoke in French with Lt. Carthy, and also take into account the *mucktar* not allowing any buildings to be searched. What if, during the Israeli aerial bombardment, Amal knew that the Irish would not be moving from their positions and decided locally to take the two Irish lads hostage only for something to go wrong? Then their situation changed. With one person dead and one person alive, it would be easier to kill the second and abort, rather than be laden with a prisoner, unless they were not bloodthirsty killers and took Joyce back to the village to buy time. Now the situation has become international with all parties involved; if this was an indiscriminate act carried out by the local Amal of Dynater, not authorised by the regional command, then it's a different scenario, so back to the PLO position. It was the case that they suspected the Irish OP position as an early warning system for the Israelis to monitor. So, to make their escape, taking a prisoner would not aid their speed of getaway.

So what can we conclude? Well, we know that Amal nationally and regionally supports the UNIFIL position; if it became public knowledge that they were responsible, it would have put severe pressure on the Irish to withdraw from UNIFIL. I don't think the UN wanted to go down that road, so what can we say happened to Kevin Joyce? I believe he was kept alive for two to three days in Dynater, and then a decision by his captors was taken to get rid of him, and I always believed he was disposed of in and around Dynater, a lime pit more than likely, as Dynater is a dead-end village. This way, those responsible got away, but why would local Amal do this? I believe they would have been held hostage for blood money, which would have been paid and released safely, but the whole thing went wrong for them.

Reaching a conclusion regarding Joyce's disappearance too quickly handed the initiative to the killers. The PLO had earlier voiced their concerns about Post 622D to Irish Battalion Operations, so they were deemed the most likely threat. Dynater was never really considered a factor, so it was dismissed far too quickly. The force mobile reserve was a unit of company strength with their mission, as the name implies—a force in reserve. Should they have been deployed all around the village like a ring of steel for a protracted period? Of course, hindsight is an exact science, but had that been the case, if Joyce was in the village, time would have flushed out his abductors and disposal of his body, dead or alive, would have been highly unlikely or not feasible. The presence of search teams in and around the village lasted for three days. The young fellow coming to the checkpoint the following morning has always bugged me. Not passing judgement on then Lt. Hugh Carthy, who, like all of us, was young—he was a fine platoon commander and looked after his men. Everything in the Middle East costs money, even information, so let's look at other motives the young fellow had. The Irish employed a lot of local youth in dining halls, etc., so maybe he might have gotten a job, and what about the risks he was taking? These cannot be taken too lightly. If he had seen Joyce and his abductors moving into a house, for him to pass information or be known to could have been fatal, something a fourteen-year-old doesn't envisage. If he were living, he had nothing to gain, as I am sure that, even at fourteen, he would have known no money would have been paid until the information checked out.

Another aspect that came to mind a few later years was, prior to going to Lebanon, Hugh Carthy was stationed in Lifford for two years. In my twenty-two years in Lifford, he was one of the most approachable young officers ever stationed there, and the same in Lebanon; however, his attitude changed when he returned. He became more distant, very strict, and hard to work with. He then got promoted to captain and shortly afterwards was posted out to Rockhill House in Letterkenny. While there, he remained aloof; his reputation among the men there was not a good one, and very soon afterward he retired from the army. I got the sneaking impression he was carrying a lot of responsibility on his shoulders, not for discarding the young lad's advice, but that he was trapped by his conscience regarding the way the whole thing was handled. Dynater today is no longer a village but a sprawling town brought into the twenty-first century by exiled American dollars. A lot of Lebanese emigrated during the civil war and became very wealthy in the United States, and then came home and built very remarkable buildings. Over the years, the remains of Kevin Joyce may have been disturbed by excavation and lost or buried under one of the many buildings now a part of a very different Dynater from 1981.

It may be getting too late, but what if that fourteen-year-old could be located? He would be in his early forties by now, and he could be the key that unlocks this mystery. Having been to Lebanon in 2004 and 2005 and seen the vast improvements in the infrastructure of the country, the self-belief of the people, I can't help but wonder if all that was lost after the short summer war of 2006 between Hezbollah and the Israeli Defence Forces. Could anybody be so bothered? For the life of me, I can't understand why the crime scene and immediate area weren't then or in the years since given more priority. It just seems as if a theory was developed after the abduction and, like lemmings to the cliff, succeeding administrations followed the official department line.

The Number Six Platoon (Donegal Platoon) was nearing the end of their stint in Dynater. We were now getting mail from home more and more, so national papers carrying reports of the incident were well dressed up, but we just got on with it. Something else was occupying our minds: we had a thief among us, and a lot of stuff was going missing. The one thing a monastery of men such as soldiers can't have is a thief. It can cause pandemonium.

Now the thieving was getting worse. A lot of money and kit were going missing. Dealing with Hugh Doherty's death and the ongoing situation was enough, but among twenty men or so, looking into one another's eyes and wondering was putting a strain on relationships. It was imperative that this thief was caught. Two sections of the platoon from Donegal and one section from Athlone were to be relieved after four weeks and sent to Tyre Barracks. We were being sent there for a month to accommodate a platoon of Lebanese for barrack security duties. I considered it a bit of a swan trip, a bit of R&R, but it was good thinking by the company commander, as we had come through a rough initiation. It would help us to recharge the batteries, but the *cliffiter* (Arabic for "thief") still had to be caught. We had him narrowed down drastically, but it was hard to accuse someone directly without proof. One day on duty with him, I concocted a ploy where I told him that Lt. Carthy knew who it was and was going to give the individual twenty-four hours to own up or he would face a very public exposure. He became concerned and owned up. I can't put on paper what I felt, but in military terms he deserved next to a firing squad. He made a full confession but was treated very leniently. The irony of that was he went on to become a military policeman, and then a number of years later again in Lebanon, in a place of trust, was checking parcels being sent home, and he robbed thousands. This time, the hatchet fell heavy. The weapons platoon commander from Athlone was the Tyre Barracks commander, ably supported by Lt. Carthy. We were situated inside one of the largest concentration of PLO in the south of the country, so it was important that we monitored their movements. Nonetheless, they were the authority in the area.

One source of recreation was to head to the beach, about one hundred metres to the rear of the barracks. We could swim in the Mediterranean Sea and play beach football. The weapons platoon captain was a real sun god. One day he was lying down taking in the rays when a PLO patrol of about twelve men and boys approached us from the city side, throwing the odd hand grenade into the sea. This was considered fishing, war style, which always yielded the participant a healthy supper. It was hard to gauge whether they would be hostile. Our choices were few and far between—(1) reaching for our gear and hightailing back to the barracks would be akin to running away from the owner of the orchard or (2) just act naturally and keep playing football—as they got very near they started shouting, "Bobby Sands *quice,* Maggie Thatcher *la quice* (Bobby Sands was very good and Maggie Thatcher was no good)." We had suddenly adopted Bobby Sands as our Che Guevara; it seemed to fit in well. They wanted to play football; it reminded me of the stories of the trench warfare during the First World War when, at Christmas time, opposing sides stopped firing to play football. Though not our enemy, we had to be seen once removed. What the heck. There were no internationals on our side, and these guys were useless but enjoying themselves. I subbed myself out for a fag, and as I approached my towel beside the captain's, I noticed him taking a keen interest. It was as if we had just passed our first test in diplomacy in this area. "Reg," he quipped, "what's the score?"

I retorted, "It's about eighteen to zero to the Irish."

His face contorted as he gasped, "Reg, let them fucking win, for fuck's sake. This was to be our benchmark. Don't annoy or fall out with anyone."

Our time in Tyre Barracks was punctuated with the odd barbecue, though on the whole, the food was not great, having to adapt to a new diet. Believe me, goat's milk is not nice in tea, a far cry from ten years later when the food was like that at the Shelbourne Hotel. By the time our stint ended in Tyre, the company was getting ready to move to our new location in Brachit. Moving up on 120 personnel was a logistics nightmare. Every two months was akin to starting the tour of duty all over again. It was a crazy situation, and I think it was nearly another year or so before somebody had the good sense to sit down and decide that the company location should remain the same for the entire tour. Whoever made this decision will now know that every Irish soldier who served in Lebanon since owes him eternal gratitude. The one thing that was to be foremost on my mind was the fact I was moving into the backyard of Hassan Hanouee, the guy who threatened to kill me. I was going to have to be on my toes, but first our company second in charge was advising us to start planning a leave rota, which meant I could apply for a week off to visit the Holy Land. This, to me, was worth more than anything else. Remember that Southern Lebanon was also the workplace of Christ, so the notion wasn't lost on me for the first two months. The opportunity to walk in the footsteps of our Lord was going to be an experience I was going to cherish for the rest of my life. Personnel did not have a choice about whom they were paired off with, and the guy I teamed up with was the person indicted on the thieving. Added to that, he was an atheist, with no interest in religion whatsoever. Now, I wouldn't like to create the impression that I was a saint, but I always felt the mystery of theology to be fascinating. I also had a responsibility to this other chap. I had to be forgiven and had to facilitate his desires while in Israel. It was a memorable week.

The night before I left Lebanon, I was on duty with a guy from the Sixth Infantry Battalion in Athlone. He was a neighbour of mine from Assumption Road before I moved to Lifford, so we knew each other quite well. He was about twenty-two years old and married, and I remember the conversation, roughly planning what to do with our money—about £2,200 or whatever was left—when we got home. As I crossed the border back to Lebanon from Israel, I met a few guys from Athlone who were down on patrol. Reaching out his hand to give me a lift up onto the back of the truck, I asked, "Any crack, lads?" The reply was, "Did you not hear about Noel Burns? He was killed during the week." I nearly fell out of the truck, thinking *not again,* only to discover he was killed in a traffic accident. It was still such a shock and hard to deal with, but Lebanon didn't allow the mind to dwell. It was up the Burma Road again in convoy back to company headquarters in Brachit. The eerie thing about his death was he was in bed in Dynater, when Chalkie White, a driver, was going into headquarters. It was standard operational procedure to carry a shotgun passenger, so when Chalkie requested, Noel volunteered and insisted he travel. A number of years later, an NCO from my own battalion stationed in Finner Camp, Corporal Dermott McLaughlin, who was home on leave for the Christmas period, had a bad premonition about his death; therefore, he went to see his company sergeant in Finner Camp before travelling back and gave him two letters, not to be opened until after his death, one regarding funeral arrangements, the other for his wife. He went back to Lebanon and his post, which housed about sixteen personnel. It was dinnertime, and everyone was downstairs. Dermott went upstairs to pack his gear into his locker, when a Mecava tank on a position overlooking our post fired a single tank round into the building on the floor Dermott was standing on. He was killed outright. Things like that stick with you for life.

The task of C Company in Brachit was to secure the village and also the smaller village of Byjhoun and carry out foot patrols of the area to prevent any IDF/DFF incursions. Our presence also meant the limited movement of Amal and the PLO. During daylight hours, the locals would invite us into their home for *shi.* They were very friendly, especially the children. One wonders years after why we kept going back for further tours of duty. The money was good for the six months, but by now Ireland was getting into the throws of an economic boom. It was the kids and the many friends we made there that kept us going back; arriving and leaving was much like leaving family at home. When the last goodbyes were said at home, the pain was dulled by the

familiar welcome, and vice versa. This was the pivotal thing about not rotating the company locations—lifelong relationships were born.

Brachit was considered the hot spot in the battalion area, and so it turned
out to be. The time there was peppered with IDF/DFF incursions. These for-
ages were for different reasons; sometimes it was kidnap, and others were for
house demolitions. This was a favourite tactic of the Israelis. For anyone suspected of involvement with militia or attacking their positions, if it was not
possible to get them there and then, they would go in and blow up the family
home. The one thing that was different from Northern Ireland was here there
was no early warning system. One night in Brachit, we had two listening
patrols approximately a mile apart watching over the wadis (dry river beds)
and we had the guard on the roof on our post 617, when all hell broke loose—
the IDF attacked the post and the dispensary ops, while down the graveyard
road between the two listening positions our own armoured personnel carrier,
with Lt. Carthy as patrol commander, was also under fire. You didn't have
time to think. "Return fire" was the order. Private Billy McKinley grabbed the
heavy machine gun in the sandbagged position and started firing, followed by
at least twelve FN rifles on full automatic. The radio crackled; it was Carthy
requesting Ilium. I reached for 00 Private Kelly and headed downstairs for the
84-mm antitank gun and an Ilium bomb, set the dial for 800 metres, and
returned to the roof, only to discover such heavy incoming fire that it would
have been suicide to stand outside to fire. I made a snap decision. The 84-mm
antitank gun has a venture that gives equilibrium of force forward and to the
rear. It's definitely not recommended to fire indoors. I was four steps from the
top of the stairs with the gun barrel pointing toward the skyline. I shouted to
Private Kelly to load, and then, as an afterthought, shouted, "Get off the
stairs!"

Joe, the cook, was running toward the ground floor when I squeezed the
trigger. The bang was like the end of the world, perfect shot. The walls wob-
bled and the backblast ran like sheet lightning, almost catching Joe to the
point it singed his moustache. This was followed by a further explosion on the
outskirts of the village; a family home had been reduced to a lump of twisted
metal and concrete. The Israelis came in, attacked our positions as cover to
their engineers who wired the house, and then they slipped back through the
cover of darkness to their own positions.

Periods came and went where little or nothing happened, and the economy
of the area returned to normal. Leave period was in full swing with anything
up to 15 per cent of company strength on holidays, places such as Jordan,
Israel, and Cyprus; as a result, the duty roster never got any easier. The canteen was the only social outlet, where every third or fourth night one ambled
in for a few beers, and sometimes this was accompanied by a singsong. Tony

Bracken was brilliant on the guitar. Then there was the post and the newspapers from home; the simple things kept us occupied, and added to that was the dreaded letter writing in reply. It was the only time in your life when you felt like a bishop, some truth, some lies, but mostly lies, and you couldn't worry your immediate family. When you were feeling down and out, it was time to write the love letters.

For as far back as I remember, I was never a romantic soul, but years later I was to find out what those letters meant to my wife. We are opposites in character; she is a magpie and hoards everything, whereas if I take a notion and put my head to it, everything goes, no matter what. One evening, after enlisting the children's help, I started to clear room by room, bin bags at the ready, when we came to Sheila's and my room. At the bottom of a drawer, I came across hundreds of letters. I sat on the bed, flicked through them, and thought, *Did I really write that?* Then into the bin liner. That evening was followed by a big bonfire, and of course the kids told Sheila everything. I never realised how much these letters meant to her. If I am ever asked about regret, then it definitely is burning those letters.

We are now well into the trip; one more move to Haddata, and then it was all downhill. The big thing on a Sunday, if you were not on duty, was mingi shopping up on the back of a truck and off to the town of Harrish, about five miles from Brachit, which was occupied by the Dutch UN force. They were friendly toward the Irish and were very generous; of course, they were paid far more than us. An hour to an hour and a half was the time allowed, and gold, hi-fis, and clothes were the normal purchases. It was possible, if one was inclined, to buy the most up-to-date handgun, ammunition and all. I remember going to a shop I was told about, just to see, and the guy behind the counter was selling me a .45, the round about twice the size of the 9-mm round. I thought about getting hit with that thing. The price was about $350, and of course I asked to see the silencer, which was massive and nearly as heavy as the gun itself and nearly the same price. I examined the pieces, seemed interested, and told him I would give his price consideration, shook hands, and left. Some lads bought .22 revolvers; most of them didn't try to bring them home and sold them on. The one thing on the ground that seemed to be scarce was food. Experience has since taught me that not only does an army march on its stomach but also a good unit ensures there is a good backup supply, and with my years later with UNIFIL, this would always be the case. With C Company Forty-Ninth Infantry Battalion, it was different—there was always a shortage, and we were forever having to buy from the local shops. Nobody complained. It was the same for everybody until one night I was on patrol after curfew, no traffic allowed, when suddenly I noticed the lights on a vehicle coming toward me. I put my patrol into cover, weapons at the ready, and as the vehicle got closer, I knew it was a UNIFIL land rover. What was it doing on an unofficial route? I stopped it to find the company sergeant, quartermaster, and the cook corporal in the front and the back of the land rover laden with rations, somewhat relived that this was all I had to deal with at this time of night. I asked the company sergeant where he was going.

"Around the Ops, Reg, with rations," he retorted.

"Be on your way," I said, never thinking that my patrol was due its first break. The thought of fresh bread and jam and a mug of coffee was excruciating. We got back to the post, and I shouted to Joe the cook, "Where's the rations?"

"What rations?" he replied.

It then dawned on me what was really happening. I really could have shot the bastard, and he was flogging the rations to local shops. I never believed the quartermaster was in on the act, as he was such a nice guy but was taken for a ride. It was well within the cook corporal sphere, and to think I could have had them caught cold nearly killed me, as you can't point fingers without any proof. That was basically what we had to deal with for the remainder of the tour of duty. The officers were fed well, and that was the cook corporal's cover. Next to your weapons and kit, food is the most important item to a soldier.

The time was drawing near for the move to Haddata; I was to be in the forward section, moving in on advance ten days before the rest of the company. I familiarised myself with the checkpoints and area; things were so primitive, in some senses of the word, that for home comforts you just had to improvise. The sergeant from the south called me. "Reg, here is a nice bed for you."

Wow, it was a civi bed with a deep mattress. I hadn't a good night's sleep in months. I carried a pair of sheets I had made out of a parachute that I had cut up in Tyre Barracks. I felt like a king. The one unwritten rule in the army is don't invade a man's bed space unless invited in. We were now well settled in, and the companies were changing. I was on checkpoint duty from 8:00 a.m. to 4:00 p.m.; it was mid-August and very hot, about thirty-five degrees. Corporal Jackie Quinn was taking over from me and said, "You have lost your fancy bed."

"What do you mean?" I asked.

"The platoon sergeant, Jim Brennan, has fucked you out of the room."

"By fuck, he has not," I said and started marching up the dirt track to my sleeping quarters. Jimmy O'Connell was in the room, somewhat embarrassed. "Nothing to do with me, Reg," he said.

"Where is my stuff?" I asked, and I was told it was in the guardroom. I footed it over to the guardroom to find my gear fired into the corner. This was abuse of power, and I could have made a big thing of it, but I didn't. I never spoke to Jim Brennan again, even to this day. As the tour went on, he lost the trust of the men and became an isolated character. His army career didn't last much longer.

The remainder of the trip was pretty routine, eight hours on and twelve hours off, and leave and sixty-hour breaks to fill the duty roster. The last month was spent getting ready to go home, checking presents for everybody. The Damascus tablecloth was a nice present and not too heavy, which allowed you to complement your forty-five-kilo allowance with cigarettes and booze. It was the same procedure for going home, with first, second, and third chalks organised and the goodbyes to the locals, who generally hated to see you leave, as they really felt protected by our presence. We headed for Beirut by convoy. This time the airport was open, and, for logistical reasons, avoiding the hassle of entering Israel seemed the best option and not as long a journey. When the convoy roared in with more than two hundred personnel, screaming and whistling like a scene out of *Braveheart,* you really felt great. This was not quite the end, but you really felt good. The only downside was that the French transport company were your chauffeurs, and this felt more like Formula One racing. As we arrived at the airport, the sight of a KLM 747 standing like a majestic peacock on the runway reassured us that our relief, first chalk of the Fiftieth Infantry Battalion, had arrived. They were also on the runway—we referred them as "milk bottles" for having come from cold Ireland. We got to mix with them for twenty minutes or so while the aircraft was loaded, saying our welcomes and goodbyes, wishing them all the luck. Those gestures were said with true meaning as we knew their task was even greater now going into winter.

3

Happy to Be on Home Shores Again

Up the aircraft went, and it was more than five hours' flying time to Ireland. The atmosphere on the plane was electric as we arrived into Dublin airport. The top brasses from the army met us; the first man on the plane was Major General Joe Leech, who was a near neighbour from home in Athlone. I went to school with his two sons, and as I was disembarking, he said, "Well done, young Sumner," which I will always remember, and then the special moment for every man returning: meeting the wives and girlfriends for the first time in six months.

It was Beatlemania, and you can guess the rest yourself. My daughter, Sarah, had been born only the week before, so I was not really expecting Sheila, but she was driven up by a good friend and neighbour Frank O'Rourke, who himself had served with the Forty-Sixth Battalion, ironically one of the harder trips when four men lost their lives. Mathematically, very few of those who served with the Forty-Sixth ever returned to service in Lebanon; that was Frank's one and only venture overseas. We headed up the road to Donegal, Sheila and I, like two lovelorn teenagers again; after all, I was only twenty-six years old. I don't know how O'Rourke kept the car between the two white lines. The funniest thing about the whole trip was that, as we approached Newtownstewart, ten miles from Strabane, and came to the T-junction entering the town, Frank turned right, straight into an orange parade, band and all. Panic gripped his voice as he barked out to me, "Get that fucking jumper off you," which was my army jumper, with rank markings. I replied, "Drive on to fuck." Frank's heart must have stopped, but nobody even noticed us as police directed traffic.

Back home, the next few days were spent seeing friends and relatives and generally relaxing. You have to remember that, with the training period and tour of duty, we had been on the go for ten months. The next month of UN leave was used up doing the jobs that were missed out on, socialising and telling war stories. That was long before the Internet and mobile phones, so everything was manual, for the want of a better word.

The next thing was reporting back to the unit for duty. Nobody liked that. We were now back to the routine of barrack life, which was not too bad, as the duty commitment was high on the border. Weeks passed into months, and the itch to go again was high on the brain; however, by means of elimination, you knew it would be three to four years before your turn came around again. I filled in the time doing courses or instructing, and then in August 1982, while instructing on a regimental signal course in Finner Camp, I was approached by Lt. Sean Curran, who had been selected as the platoon commander to travel with the Fifty-Second Battalion on a winter trip, a little more than twelve months since I had returned. He asked me if I wanted to travel, and being the type of person he was, it had to be an immediate answer. Given that I had now two young children at one and three years old, I had to phone my wife. I was surprised she did not stand in my way, so here I was preparing for my second tour to Lebanon.

Most of the guys selected to travel were on their first tour. Apart from myself, maybe another two NCOs had served previously, the platoon sergeant, Sergeant Martin Doherty, and Corporal John O'Brien, both stationed in Rockhill House, Letterkenny. This was the makeup of the platoon, with one section from the three posts in Donegal, all young lads ruled by Lt. Curran. Curran was commissioned from within the ranks. At the military college where he trained officer cadets as a corporal, it was his way or the highway. People were in genuine fear of him; he never mixed and found it hard to integrate with barrack life. The main thing in overseas service was the extra money, so you generally put up with any unpleasantness.

4

My Return to Lebanon after One Year

As with the Forty-Ninth Battalion, we formed up as a company in Athlone under Comdt. Gerry McNamara. The company sergeant was John McManus (an army legend), and one could not feel in safer hands around these guys. The situation in Lebanon had changed all over again; such was the turmoil of the civil war. The Israeli Defence Forces had reinvaded the country. Over the previous eighteen months, the PLO mounted greater attacks on Northern Israel. Beaufort Castle, lying approximately nine kilometres northeast of the Irish area of operations, was a PLO stronghold. The outer wall of this castle was about fifteen feet thick and withstood every known assault since 1978. It was from there and Tyre that the PLO fired their long-range rockets into northern Israel. The Israelis invaded, using the most-feared brigade within their forces to attack. Beaufort Castle had never been impregnated in history by any army—the crusaders built it, and these castles dot Southern Lebanon. This time, the Israelis pushed beyond the Litanai River, sweeping pockets of PLO who were retreating north toward Beirut, bypassing the refugee camps in Tyre and Sidon. They surrounded Beirut for in excess of three months, with Mecava tanks and heavy artillery causing a total blockade. The European Union interceded and tried to negotiate a settlement, and a multinational force was deployed, mainly composed of the American Sixth Fleet and Italian and French forces. There was also company strength of British forces. This force's mission was to oversee the safe evacuation of fifteen thousand-odd PLO fighters by sea to Tunis.

While this was all going on, there was a major battle taking place between different factions of Christians in east Beirut and the Druze forces in the Cheauf Mountains. During the siege of Beirut, one of the worst modern atrocities happened. Allied with local Christian militia, the Israelis, under the control of the then IDF Major General Ariel Sharon, entered the refugee camps of Sabra and Chalitta and slaughtered three thousand men, women, and children. This was the prelude to a complete withdrawal that took some months to complete.

Again I was out on first chalk of the Fifty-Second Battalion landing in Beirut. I could not believe the difference in one year. It was like something out of a war movie to see the sheer might of the American Sixth Fleet—ships, destroyers, cruisers, and aircraft carriers as far out to the horizon as one could see, both to the left and right, and what can only be described as a swarm of Chinook helicopters travelling between ships and the shore. The sight was awesome. The security involved in moving our convoy on the coast road through American lines was something else. The looks on their faces were as if we were from Mars; they had not a clue. Six months later on my return to Beirut at the end of this tour of duty, I was behind a truck changing out of my bush green operational dress into my UN whites for the homeward flight when this black US Marine, about six feet, five inches, with full combat dress and flak jacket with beads of sweat dripping from his locks, stood rigidly close by. I struck up a conversation with him. He saw me as some war hero after doing six months in Southern Lebanon with the minimum break; he was doing three weeks on with ten days' break in Cyprus.

Unfortunately, the Multinational Force (MNF) involvement in Lebanon ended very quickly. The next phase of conflict was about to take on a new political concept with the emergence of a new kid on the block called Hezbollah. They first came to light with the kidnapping of Irishman Brian Keenan, along with Englishmen Terry Waite and John McCarthy, who were held captive for up to five years. Ironically, years later in 1997, I was in one of the buildings, six stories underground, where Brian Keenan was held. Hezbollah loaded a pickup truck with a half ton of high explosives with a suicide driver, drove directly at the main residential area housing the US and French forces, and caused the deaths of more than 168 US and 53 French forces. The American Sixth Fleet and the MNF were literally gone overnight, but not before they had caused some major changes to the political structure of Lebanon. Maybe sixty miles away, when the BBC World Service was issuing news bulletins, the US destroyer USS New Jersey was firing one-ton high-explosive shells into the Cheauf Mountains at the Druze militia led by Wally Jumblatt.

Families or warlords who inherited their positions by family lineage led most dynasties or militia. More ingredients were to be added to the cocktail, as the Syrians were to be invited in as a peace force, where they remained until 2006.

It is at this point that I must add that the second in command of the Twenty-Eighth Battalion, Comdt. P. J. Kane, who had been the company commander of C Company the previous year with the Fiftieth Battalion, was by now the most-feared officer in the battalion. It was his routine to address all the troops prior to their departure to form up as in company in Custume Barracks, Athlone. So at 1400 hours, in an assembly room, he walked in, and everyone stood up to attention. "Sit down," he barked and proceeded to lecture us on our conduct while outside the battalion, that we were ambassadors, both at home and abroad. Then he told us that our wives and partners would worry about us while serving abroad and for us to write home frequently, and we had one thing in common—we all had mothers, and they would always worry about us, so we were never to forget about writing to them, as if we would. P. J. must have been a long-time second in command of the battalion, because three and a half years later, while I was formed up with the Fifty-Ninth Battalion, he was to lecture us again, this time before heading off to Mullingar. I remember somebody at dinner saying that P. J. gave the same lecture, word for word, to every unit going overseas. I thought, *How odd,* so at 1400 hours, P. J. entered and then proceeded with his usual mantra. I didn't know what I was thinking, but this idiot inside my head was brewing up trouble, and as soon as he came to the "mammy letters," I just burst out with an uncontrollable laugh. I couldn't stop; proceedings disengaged; and I apologised, explaining that something came into my head. P. J. took one disdainful look at me. "Seanie" was furious, but he must have rated me, because a man could be returned to his unit (RTU) for less.

Little was I to know that some years later P. J. would have his revenge. His revenge was not isolated, as I recall the best officer I ever served with, Comdt. Tony Kiely, had an altercation with P. J. many years earlier, and, as a result, P. J. held Kiely's promotion up for years, causing the man a lot of undue hardship. His bad ways knew no boundaries. That was borne out many years after I retired. I was invited to Finner Camp for the thirtieth anniversary of the formation of the battalion. What a spread, what a crowd—after the mass and all the pomp, it was to the dining hall and the respective messes. In the dining hall, P. J. cut a lone figure, sitting and eating by himself. Not one to rush to the front of the queue, I stood in the entrance hallway, having a smoke (before the smoking ban). Lt. Col. Vinnie Blyth and former battalion commanders Lt. Col. Maloney and Captain Jim Dwyer (retired) were all standing in the hallway, clearly hanging around until P. J. departed. I thought to myself, *What a legacy of a career he was to have left.*

Back to the Fifty-Second Battalion…we arrived at the area of operation and company headquarters for C Company. Nothing much had changed here in my one-year absence, just new faces. Now we had a good meal to help rescue us from our travels and then some decent sleep. As we were awakening from our slumber, a new mission was about to be undertaken; orders shouted out, and we gathered our gear for transfer to our new homes. The overall mission had changed in its concept; due to the Israeli invasion, half my platoon was to be deployed behind the lines in the enclave, in Israeli-held territory. It was a daunting task, as some three years earlier the Israeli-backed DFF militia in this area executed two Irish soldiers. The Irish who lost their lives were Privates Smallhorn and Barrett. It was a scenario that was going to up everyone's game. During a wet and windy morning, we mounted our vehicles up and headed off to an outpost called Mahibebe, heading through the familiar village of Shaqoura, and then on to Houle. Now we were behind the lines, passing IDF and militia patrols. It all felt surreal. About an hour later we arrived at our post, which had earlier been vacated by UN soldiers from Ghana. Now, I'm casting no observations on any nationality, but the Ghanaians had a totally different lifestyle than that of the Irish. We established security for the camp and set about checking the accommodations and cleaning the place top to bottom to bring it to our own minimum standards. For the first few days, we were all bitten by flies that paid particular attention to our ankles. At this point, Swedish Medical Company was called in to fumigate the whole outpost. The Ghanaians had a particular love of dog meat and used to round up all the local strays and cage them.

Certain characters came to mind during this time: Private Mannix Armstrong from Sligo, who was later to lose his life while serving with the Sixty-Fourth Battalion along with Corporal Fintan Henehan and Private Tomas Walsh from Sligo. The three were killed when their truck drove over a tank mine.

Mannix was always up to the thick in it; a rascal with a halo would be the best way to describe him. Now, as I was the senior NCO in the post, Lt. Curran would always hold me responsible for checking the ammunition, bottled water supply, and ration packs along with the diesel log for the generator supplying power for the post. At least twice a week everything had to be checked. We had this bunker where sixty boxes of ten-man ration packs were stored along with a month's supply of bottled water, and this was Curran's pet. He used to check every box separately. There's a point of reason with everything, but Curran took it beyond rational, and if anything was missing, it would be my fault. This day on duty I noticed Mannix smoking the Gitang French cigarette, which had an obnoxious smell. I asked him where he got them, and he either noticed the rogue in me or I in him and told me he stole them from the ration packs, knowing that I would not hang him. However, the thought of Curran finding out sent a sense of panic through my body. Mannix reassured me by showing me that by cutting the Cello tape at the bottom right-hand side of the ration pack and gently sliding your hand in, two hundred cigarettes could be extracted, along with a quart bottle of Martell brandy. Simply reattaching the tape to the box rendered the box "never tampered with." Now in a dry post for more than a month, two guys always had wee toddy every night, and throughout the checks by Lt. Curran, he was never the wiser to our scheme. I did have the presence of mind to inform him at the end of the tour to arrest his ego, but there was nothing he could do about it at this late stage.

Then there was a medic called Private Ray McEvoy, and we went to school together. He was also a character but somebody who was very important to the welfare of the squad. He was the nearest thing to a doctor you were going to get in these parts, but his other job was liming the latrines (long drops), holes dug by mechanical diggers to a depth of twelve feet, with the caricature of a toilet made of timber built over it. Ray was very proactive within the unit and had proved here before with the Forty-Sixth Battalion. Every day the local population of the nearby village would arrive at the post entrance looking for the doctor. Ray would see to them and administer medication, but after a few weeks and no resupply of medical stores, they were running low, so we had to retain the minimum supply for ourselves. I was on duty this particular morning when the usual stream of local villagers arrived for treatment, and with the language problem, it was impossible to relay our situation. I called Ray and told him to deal with the issue. From old men to heavy-laden pregnant women, Ray issued them with salt tablets and told them to take one in the morning and one in the evening. I never witnessed a placebo working before, but that evening several baked cakes arrived at the gate as a thanksgiving for the doctor.

On a more serious note, one week after taking over in Mahibeb at approximately 6:30 p.m., radio traffic on the 46 radio set all of a sudden was spoken in Irish. With a sense of panic, I knew straight away something serious was happening. All units, including ours, were mobilized into a state of stand-to, ensuring all round firing positions were taken up. We deduced from the radio transmissions that three Irish soldiers were shot dead. With the fear factor of not knowing the details, being behind the lines, and the country still under Israeli control, it was pandemonium. The radio transmissions in Irish were to keep the Israelis in the dark, but also aided in keeping most of us in the dark, as we were not fluent in the language either. Basically we were twenty-four hours in the state of unknown until a patrol arrived the next day with the rations and the much-loved post, a topic that will be mentioned many times again. The three personnel killed were Corporal Gregory Morrow and Private Burke from the Fifty-Second Battalion and Private White from the Fifty-First Battalion, who had just one week left from the end of his tour of duty. It transpired that a fourth member of the checkpoint duty, a Private McElevey, was the triggerman, something that was never communicated to us for the whole month that we spent in Mahibebe.

Our stint behind the lines over, we were relieved by the platoon from the First Battalion soldiers back home who hailed from Galway, and so we returned to company headquarters to perform routine camp duties. Things were a little better than with the Forty-Ninth Battalion. As there was no company rotation, we were to serve the six months in the town of Brachit and surrounding area. This seemed the sensible approach, but it took the army top brass more than four years to figure it out. The food had improved a lot, and in between meals we had two mingi shops, Marie and Moussa's outside the camp gate and Rosie's inside along the camp perimeter. Two different families competed for our dollars, and services included laundry, double double (eggs and chips), soft drinks, sweets, and the legendary *shi*. Many an hour was spent in either shop being entertained by the locals, and down over the years they became like family. Rosie, years later, came over to Ireland to visit all her friends in Galway, Athlone, and Bundoran. Letter writing was still the only way of communicating, so it was important to write more than five letters a week. The post was free both ways, so if you did not get a letter from the wife or girlfriend, the head would go down for the next few days, and I witnessed over the years the effect of that form of communication both in the positive and the negative.

The odd opportunity presented itself when you would be picked for the convoy down to UNIFIL headquarters in Naqoura. This convoy travelled three days a week to get supplies for the battalion. In Naqoura, you could use the international phone. On one occasion near to Christmas, I phoned my wife, Sheila, something which I regretted afterwards. Maybe it was the depressive time of the season, but one such guy from Belfast, who was stationed in Finner Camp back home, an APC driver, got worse news: his wife informed him that she had left him. His nickname was Motor Mouse, as he was small and ideally sized for driving the APCs. He had to be disarmed, and on return to company HQ arrangements were made to repatriate him the next day. I was ordered to supervise him all night in case he self-harmed. What I had to listen to that night I will never forget; he was packing his gear and what I can only describe as about $1,000 worth of gold for the wife and toys for the kids. It later transpired she left him to live with a guy who had done his NCO course with me.

The frequency of duties was such that if you were caught sleeping on duty it was automatic jail. One such evening, I was asked by CS John McManus to escort a Galway lad to Gallows Green prison in Battalion HQ in Tibnin. He had received seven days for sleeping on rooftop duty. Because of the security regarding Private McElevey, who at this stage had not been convicted, the place was like Fort Knox. I had to sign this prisoner in, and there was Ollie McNamee, a military police NCO who was stationed in Mullingar Barracks back home, and he invited us in for a cup of tea. I was sitting next to this guy talking about football, when my driver, who was agitated, asked me to leave. While travelling back to Brachit, I asked what his problem was. He said, "That was McElevey you were talking to back there," and the hair stood on the back of my neck.

On another occasion, we had an incident with a guy from Derry, Private Jim O'Hagan with the Athlone platoon, whose platoon commander was Captain Harvey, a nice guy who should have been a priest. He was a Jehovah's Witness and had two or three like himself in the platoon. He was duty officer one night and was going around the posts on an APC, which you could hear for miles. He arrived at Private O'Hagan's post, and the driver had copped that Jim was not out, so he revved up the engine of the APC to ear-splitting level, but still no sign of Jim. Captain Harvey, on entering the post, observed Jim cuddled up in a blanket. He informed Jim that he would have to charge him and asked for his forgiveness. Jim got seven days for his troubles in staying awake and had a song written about him and the incident. As a footnote to this, you lost two weeks' pay, one from the UN payroll and one for the same period from the home payroll.

About two months into the trip, there was a darts match at company headquarters, transport company versus Charlie company, and an uncle to me (now deceased), Sergeant Noel Graham, who was in charge of UN vehicles for the battalion, was there for the darts match. So after buying him a drink, I asked him to provide me with a minibus for two weeks in Israel. The look on his face spoke volumes as he said he couldn't even provide one for the battalion commander. Tongue in cheek, I told him I would destroy him back home in Mullingar if he didn't come up trumps, and the darts continued.

Less than a week later, one of the lads on Post 617 in Brachit village called me to say I was wanted on the landline, only to find Sergeant Noel telling me that there was a transit available from March 9 until March 22. Over the moon with this news, I started to plan a budget holiday, taking along six lads from my platoon, sleeping bags and ration bags packed, everything we could get for nothing. After all, I was building a new house when I returned to Ireland. At this stage, I would like to interject the not-too-often jealous traits that can raise their heads periodically when one has bitten off more than he can chew. I sat around offering the positions on the minibus to my own crew first and then the rest of the platoon. Before long I had a full load, but as the days passed they fell off one by one. The rumour machine was in full swing, regrettably by fellow NCOs, who were advising that no way could I have gotten my hands on a vehicle for the two weeks for free and that each and every one of those travelling would have to exact a high charge for the tour to Israel. Of course, I did not know the reason until much later. However, I had a full complement come time for departure, and, sure enough, Noel had everything ready. As I was a transport man myself with a full army driving licence, he passed me a full book of petrol vouchers and off we went.

The first day's programme was to travel down to Eilat, the most southern point of Israel, near the Red Sea. The journey was first to Jerusalem, and then a short break, and then onto Jericho, the last stop before setting off on a six-hour drive through the Negev Desert. We held back in Jericho until the sun began to fade in the early evening, and then with a full cargo of beer, we set off on our journey. The desert is somewhat different to what you might expect. The stream of mountains and ravines drew your attention to the whole landscape. Six hours later with a full choir in full song, we rolled into Eilat. After briefing the guys about their behaviour, as these guys were by now pissed drunk and as the driver I was only half-pissed, we pulled up outside this hotel with an Israeli wedding in full swing. We were invited in and joined the celebrations, dancing to the Hebrew music and already feeling half-Jewish. When the night came to an end, we proceeded back to the minibus to get into our sleeping bags; seven guys in a fifteen-seat bus, laying out full stretch, took some organising, because floor and seat space was fully booked down to the last inch. After thirty minutes or so, the guys were asking if I could find a quieter place, as there was a lot of activity in Eilat, even at 2:30 a.m. I unzipped my sleeping bag, jumped behind the wheel, and headed a few kilometres out of town. Observing a gap in a fence, I drove in off the road. We had peace at last, feeling a sense of a job well done. Perfect day one. I was into the sleeping bag again when some twenty minutes later I was awakened by the butt of a rifle thumping against the driver's door and an irate Israeli soldier shouting in Hebrew at me. I got up, could not understand him, and got out only for him to point out I was parked on the middle of the runway of the Eilat international airport. Making my apologies, I jumped into the driver's seat and made a hasty escape to the jeers of the lads accusing me of trying to get them killed. I retorted that the pilot would have seen the big black letters of UN on the top of the vehicle; this provided the scale of banter for the next few days. Everybody in Eilat was informed of my bravado. The one thing I learned very quickly was the ability of the Jews to barter. After filling up at the designated petrol station, I was soon to learn that petrol coupons could be exchanged for cash, eighty cents for every dollar's worth. Needless to say, my petrol holiday was very successful. On our return journey through Jerusalem, we all chipped in for a present for Noel. After this, his job in allocating fuel to every UN vehicle took up the time for the rest of his tour.

Back to the shooting incident on Tibnin Bridge—after the Swedish forensics came up with their findings, the Irish gardai were flown out to Lebanon to assist the military police with their questioning of Private McElevey, now some eight weeks after the incident. He pleaded guilty to the crime and was returned home, charged with the offence, and sentenced to life in prison. (He was released from prison in Northern Ireland in 2010.)

The main trouble in Lebanon at this time was centred on the Beirut area. The main Christian militia, being pro- and anti-Syrian, were at it head-to-head. One faction was led by Lebanese General Michael Ayoun, an ex-army chief of staff, who was central to the conflict. After the evacuation of the PLO to Tunisia, the Arab League sanctioned the Syrian Army as a peacekeeping force. They became much more than that and stoked up further unrest between them and the Israelis, when they set up Sam Six missile batteries in the Bekaa Valley region. The presence of these batteries allowed the Syrian Air Force to fly their MIG 29s, the most up-to-date Russian aircraft, up there with the American F-16 aircraft. They flew deep into Southern Lebanon, at a time when Syria and Israel were still technically at war over the Golan Heights region. Every time there was a violation, we observed the IDF Air Force flying at low altitude over our positions on route to engage the Syrians. Once these aircraft broke the speed of sound, an aerial explosion would cause you to fall out of the bed, and this constantly caused much fear among our troops. Amal was still the dominant force in the south, led by Speaker of the House Nabbi Berry, a position allocated to the Shia under the constitution. He was also local, from Tibnin.

The only concern now in the south was the PLO breaking out from the refugee camps, and when the occasions arose, there were massive gun battles between Amal and the PLO. This tended to take up most of the time, and these battles were mostly launched near UN positions. One that comes to mind was a battle near a Fijian post on the Lebanese coastal road; the Fiji unit had taken casualties, and the Irish were sent to reinforce where they had the dig in for five days. The Israelis, now completing their withdrawal, set up a third force within the Irish area of operations. With themselves and the DFF force in the enclave, they recruited a maverick group led by an infamous local gangster named Hussain Abdel Nabbi. The IDF armed and paid them, and their mission was to cause as many problems as possible for UNIFIL and the local villagers and gather information on the Amal group. They had freedom of movement throughout and did cause serious concern within our area of operations. They used their sense of power to abuse the locals. On one such occasion, Nabbi went to this household to take a young sixteen-year-old girl as his wife. The family could not resist or he would have murdered every one of them, and, rather than give herself to him, she doused herself with a gallon of petrol and burned to death. To exact this on one of your own villagers, out of a population of about eight hundred, shows the level of his compassion. He was a hated figure, and Amal made several attempts on his life. The story goes that he was born with an outer womb and had a sealed skin over him; when this happens, the Shia believes such a birth to be a very lucky person. He was eventually killed around 1992 or 1993 after causing ten years of hell for his people. The Amal or Hezbollah were believed to be responsible, and his lieutenants were hanged in the garages outside Brachit village.

The one thing I can remember about the Fifty-Second Battalion was the weather. It was atrocious, a very bad winter for Lebanon, which usually has very mild winters. Because of the weather, the only form of heat was the Damascus heater, which was a fire fuelled by a drip of diesel, and its main job was keeping you warm and drying clothes.

The remainder of this tour was uneventful apart from the routine, and April could not come quickly enough, as I had gained planning permission for my new house. The electric connection was gained by correspondence during my six-month tour. I had the mortgage all sorted without my wife's knowledge.

Back in Dublin at the airport, there had been some bad press about the Irish troops coming home from Lebanon with contraband, so to say we were raped by customs on arrival was an understatement. This all stemmed from one of our navy frigates doing a resupply to Lebanon. Some of our armoured personnel carriers (APCs) were sent home, and on docking customs boarded the ship and noticed the main doors of the APCs welded shut. Of course, they had to be opened, and they discovered an Aladdin's Cave on the inside. So future tours would have to be more innovative about getting their stuff home, as it was seen as a perk from the six months away from home.

One thing that I must mention at this stage is that survival is based on common sense and the application of our standard operational procedures (SOPs), which is the text that applies to everything that happens in the area of operations. Corporal Ritchie Calhoun, "Big Ritchie" he was called, was stationed in Rockhill House outside Letterkenny. Big he was, about six feet, three inches, and about eighteen stone, a pure bull of a man. As checkpoint commander with three private soldiers, Ritchie was on duty at the Black Hole OP and checkpoint when a large convoy of IDF was coming down the road from Saff El Howa (a village in the occupied enclave). The SOPs stated that a stopgap would be put in place and the senior IDF officer would give his name and ID number, which in turn would be radioed into company headquarters, before the convoy would be allowed to proceed through the checkpoint. These arrangements must have been agreed to by the Israelis, but the reality on the ground was different. At all times, you couldn't stop them, as they did not want to stop, and when they passed through, we would call to company HQ with a fake ID. This was our SOP for survival. The convoy arrived at the Black Hole, with stopgap (large rolled steel joists cut and welded in the shape of a triple X that took two men to shift and set in place) in place. Ritchie had put four of them out as the convoy arrived. They stopped, and Ritchie, fully kitted out with flak jacket and Gustaf submachine gun, approached the lead vehicle and asked the IDF major for ID. The officer, with a brazen look, issued an order in Hebrew, and about twenty men jumped out of the vehicles and rolled the stopgap triple Xs down the steep wadi. The three privates with Ritchie must have shit themselves. Ritchie, now welded to the road, watched the convoy then proceed, after which he radioed the result to company HQ. The company commander, Comdt. McNamara, having taken in Ritchie's report, had a look and told Ritchie to get the stopgaps back up onto the checkpoint from down the wadi. It took the lads the rest of their shift to get them back up onto the roadway. Some years later, Big Ritchie died from a massive heart attack at only forty-seven years old. I sometimes think these stopgap fixtures maybe contributed to his demise.

An occasion that raised its head and further drove my interest into the events that took place in Dynater in April 1981 was the arrival of Lt. Dwan, a military police officer in Brachit village during my tour in 1986. After some five years of public outcry at home about the disappearance of Private Seoige Joyce, the rumour mill of where he was, which varied from sightings in and around the area of operations to stories that he had opted to join the PLO and was now living in Beirut, was just endless, so the Department of Defence sent out this officer for a two-year stint to investigate all avenues.

After finishing evening dinner, the CS, John McManus, beckoned me to his quarters, informing me that a full section and I would be assisting Lt. Dwan the following day at a dig, a known PLO stronghold within the iron triangle. *How appropriate,* I thought. John gave me ten trowels and told me that C Company was working this week with the officer, a different crew each day, and then the baton was being passed to A Company, followed by B Company. *Wow,* I thought, *a big operation.*

The next morning at 0630 hours, my crew ready, Lt. Dwan rode into camp, and off we went down through the village of Dynater, through the crime scene, and further through the iron triangle until we arrived at the remnants of what was once a PLO camp with dug-in tank and anti-aircraft positions. The lot was all but desolate, and there was a house about one hundred metres away. Dwan had two civilians with him who were obviously being paid by the

UN. He proceeded to brief us on the situation, totally unaware that any of the ten of us had any connection with the situation, as it had happened in 1981. His brief was completely alien to what I knew of the facts, but I decided to stay quiet. After all, what was I but a mere corporal, so why would I interfere with a major government investigation? The brief was that a local farmer who lived in the nearby house observed the PLO dragging a male Caucasian into the camp around the time Private Joyce disappeared and sometime later they shot and buried him within the compound. We had to dig and look for any clothing clues that could relate to Irish Defence Force issue clothing. This was a fair but not strong point, as the Irish were flogging their kit to everybody since they arrived in Lebanon in 1978 with the Forty-Third Battalion for watches and cigarette lighters and any such items for presents back home. Southern Lebanon was awash with Irish issue kit. Robbie Barlow and "Fly" Gethins, two corporals based in Finner, were involved in the dig. Fly, being a character, always kept everybody on their toes with his banter. This was an archaeological dig with our little trowels. I found a medallion of George Habash, the leader of the PFFLP (Popular Front for the Liberation of Palestine), which proved one thing—we were definitely in an old PLO camp. I am sorry that I did not keep the medallion for myself as a souvenir; however, come lunchtime, I decided to open up to Dwan about my involvement with Dynater. He was a little shocked and did not engage, which further fuelled my suspicions. After telling him what actually happened on the ground, he really did not want to know, which years later I realised was only a public relations exercise. We returned to Brachit Camp later that day with the trowels. I cannot recollect anybody else using them. What Dwan gleaned over those eighteen months was nothing more than a mirage that was carefully concocted for him to follow. I can only reflect and state that after engaging him on that day he himself realised he was set up as a patsy. There was a cover-up of immense proportions, but why? My only conclusion is the one I mentioned earlier, and it goes back to the UN resolution on the formation of UNIFIL. Amal was the only organisation that accepted the involvement of UNIFIL in Southern Lebanon, not the PLO, IDF, DFF—nobody but Amal. You just can't form up a UN force and deploy into any country you like. Why was the UN not invited into Afghanistan or Iraq? Simple...they were not invited in. The Iraqi people in power did not welcome even the weapons inspectors during and prior to the Iraq War. If the truth of the Hugh Doherty and Seoige Joyce episode came to light, the Irish government would have had no choice but to withdraw its contingent from Lebanon. How could we participate with an organisation that invited you there, only to kill your troops? Not now, before, or after was ever responsible for the death of an Irish soldier.

5

Home to Build My New Home

Back home I was now, after spending nearly eighteen months out of the previous three years away from two very young children and my wife. It was time to be domesticated, and one week after arriving home, the foundations for the new house in Donegal were dug. A local contractor, Paddy McCullagh, was doing the building for me, and whatever annual leave I had and my UN leave of thirty days was all directed at this project. The house was finished in November of that year, and we moved in January 1983. So back to barrack and border duty life—we kept in touch with the ongoing situation in Lebanon from guys who were home on leave and at the end of tours of duty. It's fair to say there was the odd cushy trip where the status quo stayed the same, but Lebanon was anything but predictable.

As an instructor, I found time passing by instructing on courses such as 2–3 star training, and then there was the odd course away from home for up to three months, getting home just at weekends. It was hard on any kind of relationship, but my wife had her immediate family, and they were always close anyway; sometimes I felt like I was butting in. We had our own situation here at home—never mind Lebanon. One day in barracks, without any warning we were deployed to Ballinamore in County Leitrim. Don Tidey, a businessman, had been kidnapped by the IRA. He had been missing for two months when the gardai and the army mounted a massive search in the Ballinamore area. As they closed in with their cordon, a young gardai and a soldier, Private 09 Kelly from the Sixth Battalion in Athlone, were both shot dead. I ended up in Ballinamore for ten days, informing my wife by phone from Finner Camp.

There was general pandemonium in Ballinamore; after a briefing, we were deployed into an outer cordon. I, along with three men from Lifford, was positioned on the side of a mountain road. It was to be twenty-two hours before we were relieved. The man who relieved me I had trained on a command ranger course, and that was the last time I had spoken to him. He was the same rank as me then, but now he was a lieutenant, having come up through the ranks to get his commission. His name was Jimmy Doohan, and he had told me years earlier that he would one day be a commissioned officer.

A soldier has a hard time trying to balance married and military life, so going overseas is a two-pronged solution; it provides much-needed extra cash and also gets you away from the one side of life that you have not trained for, and pay in the army in those days was not great. Every time I went back to Lebanon, the political scenario changed, and it was always good to be up to speed with events to have a slight advantage on the ground. The time had come again for me to travel. It was now the Fifty-Ninth Battalion, and it was the summer tour from April to October, one of only two summer tours I did. The list of names was out, and on it again was Lt. Sean Curran and Comdt. Gerry McNamara. Now, I would have gone to hell and back with McNamara, but Seanie left a question mark. The platoon sergeant was Brian Doherty, a blow-in from Finner Camp to Lifford, and I did not know much about him. The balance of the platoon was good; at least I knew what to expect with Seanie and was prepared. A number of years before, I was on a mountaineering course with him, and we were issued with a great wetsuit at the time, which I kept. Having the ranger course done, I stuck out a bit. In those days, you had to look after yourself.

Lebanon had a very weak Amal in the south, which created a vacuum for Hezbollah, an Iranian-backed group. The spiritual leader was Sheik Mohammad Husain Faddhala, and they were armed and financed through Syria and Iran into the Bekaa Valley in the north region of Lebanon, with the weapons then smuggled south. The southern people took to them, and of course they knew how to win the hearts of the people by pouring large sums of money into the area. When the Israelis bombed or fired a tank shell at a house, it was Hezbollah who rebuilt it, and if there were any casualties, they would help the family financially. Like any well-run organisation, they had a military wing and a political wing. This new kid on the block was made up mostly of ex-Amal; they soon built a support base and for the most part made the Amal redundant. A lot of strange faces cropped up in the area, mostly Iranians overseeing the construction of this new enigma whose main mission was the destruction of the Jewish state. This was a completely new scenario, though it was what the PLO wanted; this was seen as a more potent threat, one that was state-sponsored. We were to witness in coming years a more militarised campaign against the IDF and their support group, the DFF. This was no longer the local goat shepherd taking up arms; these were highly trained and skilled fighters who just melted into the local population. One such incident that occurred midway through the tour was a patrol led by Corporal Butch Brennan, a great character from Athlone who was stationed with the Twenty-Eighth Battalion in Finner Camp. He was leading a patrol in Brachit at an area known as the chicken farm; this location in the village was out of view and out of range from the IDF. It was here he noticed three or four men acting very suspiciously; he kept his patrol in cover, and when these people made their escape by car, he went to the building to investigate. What he was met with was unreal—an arms dump with enough high explosives to blow up half of Southern Lebanon. He radioed his findings into company HQ, and a recce section led by Lt. McNamara and Captain Tom Cox, the company second on command, came out to the scene and made a decision to call out the ordnance section. Katuska rockets by the mile were the main weapon being stored; these had the range to strike the main northern towns of Israel, such as Nahariyah. The order was made to remove the lot, four full truckloads, but what happened next was unreal. When Hezbollah learned about the situation, they, through their liaison officer, informed the authorities that if everything was not returned, they would mount an attack on our company HQ. We were surrounded by high ground on three fronts, and literally within the hour up to two hundred Hezbollah fighters surrounded the camp. Tensions were high; this was ground-breaking territory. Whose authority would win out? Was this going to be the mother of all shoot-outs or what? I think some guys penned their final letter, and the whole company was on stand-to, and it was amazing the calm leadership that was shown by some people and the sheer panic of others. This incident sorted the boys from the men, and even in the heat of the moment some humour emerged. Some of us thought that better than crying. The stand-off lasted two hours when two trucks were seen heading back to the village. The marker was thrown down, but we never learned the lesson properly.

Later we were to lose a much-loved young man through serious negligence; his name was Lt. Angus Murphy. I met him only briefly. A colossus of a man, he was escort commander to Naqoura, and when we were heading back up later that day, the recovery truck driver had got drunk. Angus wanted to keep the issue low-key, so he asked who had a military driving licence (AF 154). I was the only one there, so I took the truck back up to our area of operations. He thanked me, and we went on our way. The next morning I was on duty on Post 617C, and while on the roof observing the early morning activity in the area, I glanced towards the Haddata direction and observed this mushroom of dust ascending toward the sky, momentarily followed by a massive explosion. It was hard to figure out what happened, but we were later told that Lt. Murphy had been killed by a landmine. What I say next is the story that circulated in the AO. Angus was stationed in Custume Barracks, Athlone; part of his mission was to carry out a mine sweep at 0630 every morning, covering a route used by the IDF and DFF forces. The Hezbollah, at great risk to themselves, infiltrated the area on several occasions to put landmines intended for the IDF and DFF. On at least two occasions, the Irish discovered these mines and made them safe. Through its representatives, Hezbollah asked the Irish not to do mine sweeps before the Israelis did theirs. I think they were politely told where to go. The order went out the next day after the death of Lt. Murphy that all mine sweeps in the area be suspended until the IDF did theirs, so draw your own conclusions. Lt. Murphy's father was the general officer commanding (GOC) the Fourth Western Command, our own command back home.

It was a very hot summer, and with a big rise of attacks on Israeli positions, we were kept very busy. It was our platoon's turn to take over the village of Byjhoun; half of the platoon would go to the Black Hole with the platoon sergeant and the balance to Byjhoun. Just below the village on the Tibnin side by four hundred metres was a DFF position with maybe up to twenty men in strength. The craziness of the position was the DFF had to go through our checkpoint position, but, rather than be stopped by us, they made a pea track around our position. There were times they came through, and when Seanie Curran wasn't around, you did not stop them. They were all local Lebanese just fighting for a different side, but you could see by the looks on their faces they were afraid of the Hezbollah, very afraid. One fellow, Private Ganch Friel from Lifford, was some character; again, most of the younger guys in the platoon were trained as recruits under the eye of Curran, and the Ganch was fearful of him. One night a major attack was launched on the DFF position—heavy machine, mortar, RPGs—it was like full metal jacket, and all fire wasn't accurate. We had as much incoming from both Hezbollah and DFF. We were in ground hog in the bunker, with Seanie very pensive and nervous, and Ganch, in his usual stream of banter, was getting on his nerves, when Seanie said to me, "Take Private Friel and go and close the swinging gate."

Now, this was a mad order, which was reflected in Ganch's face; however, I said, "Let's be having you, Private Friel," as we made our exit from the bunker. I crawled to the safety of cover to observe a half track coming up the road with bodies hanging out of it and making its way through our lines back to their HQ. It was racking all-round fire on its travels, and I wasn't going to be Kevin Barry. I returned to the bunker, and Seanie asked if the gate was closed. I said yes. What he was saying was madness, giving him a sense of control. Seanie was promoted to captain during the tour, which relaxed him a bit.

The one thing about going with the Fifty-Ninth Battalion was that my wife, Sheila, was heavily pregnant, but with the training before departure lasting three months, we had agreed on everything. Two weeks after we left for Lebanon, our son, Patrick, was born. He had problems and was just a little over six pounds in weight. The company commander threw a party and had a cake baked, as well.

I made plans to go home in July; a Private McGlinchey from Strabane was also travelling, as his father was dying. Seanie was to arrange the travel documents. This was the one and only time I used the travel officer; every other time, I made my own arrangements. We landed at Mona travel agency on Bograshof Street in Tel Aviv, Israel, only to be told there were no tickets. This was day one into a ten-day leave pass, which is the maximum period that Seanie would give his platoon. Everyone else got twenty-one days. The travel agent had a direct line to the battalion adjutant, who told me to furnish him with all hotel receipts when I returned, and he would then reimburse us. Needless to say, I had a very good five weeks at home when we managed to get stand-by seats on a Dan-Air flight to London that very night. Armed with hotel receipts from two Irish lads going on holiday to Cyprus, I was going to make Seanie pay for his arrogance.

On arrival back to the AO, I was welcomed back to the fold by the CO, who knew all about the cock-up. Seanie was not as welcoming; he directed me to Post 617C and told me not to even look to go to the canteen for the rest of the tour. Unfortunately for Private McGlinchey, his father died about two weeks or so after we arrived back. He had to be repatriated and accompanied to Ben Gurion Airport by an NCO who knew the Mona travel agency, and guess who was selected? Seanie went berserk, and Reg was off for another long weekend. My luck was certainly in, as Israel was some place for the weekend. Corporal Myles McDonald, who was stationed in Lifford, also a character, took his holidays in Cyprus; he was always in trouble with Seanie, even during the training.

Platoon Sergeant Brian Doherty was one to be watched, as we learned as the tour went on. He was an officers' man, and where he gained, he did not care who suffered. Seanie was away for a weekend from Byjhoun, and I was on duty as checkpoint commander with Ganch Friel, Tommy Moran from Mayo, who served only a brief period in the army before he immigrated to the US, and another two lads whose names I can't remember. As the senior NCO, I was in charge of the post, and a junior NCO, Corporal Titch Gavin from Sixth Battalion in Athlone, was also there. Tommy asked me if he could leave his post to make a cup of tea, and I gave him permission, but after thirty minutes or so I went in after him, only to hear as I approached, him and Titch discussing my ability to run a checkpoint. One look at Gavin said it all. Later that night in an APC, I decked him, but not before I decked Moran outside. Needless to say, in sweltering heat for the next three hours, I made their life tough, and they knew they had put in a shift. The word in the grapevine had reached Brian Doherty, and later that evening Moran came into my room and apologised, and we put the matter behind us. That night we all went to the canteen and were in camp an hour before it opened. Brian Doherty spent an hour trying to extract a statement from Tommy Moran, a route Tommy did not take. When the canteen opened, Brian bought me my first drink, something that galled me when I learned from Tommy his real intentions. I never got on with him after that and made sure he was always on my port side.

On nearing the end of the tour, we were all rearing up for going home, so we decided to pair off relating to cigarettes. We bought ten thousand (five thousand each) and, because customs were really going to town on us returning home, the decision was made that if you were caught, you had the choice to either leave them there or pay the duty on them, but either way your buddy gave you half. Myles McDonald was not long in pairing off with me. "Okay, buddy," he would say. This was the only tour I ever encountered where people were not allowed to be paired off for cargo weight and your allowance of forty-five kilograms was final; if you were over, you were out, even if the next man had only twenty-five. This was obviously a rule to facilitate the officers, who had wooden crates made and stencilled as army records and confidential documents. The one factor they had not thought of was the baggage crew, who were responsible for transferring all cargo onto a forty-foot container, heading for Ben Guerin Airport. I was that man in charge. The rattle of bottles in these large boxes with rope handles was like an orchestra playing. Placing them at three to four feet high, counting one, two, and three bangs as the container headed down the highway, there was a trail of whiskey to the aircraft. I was not going to be going home for two weeks yet, but I would not have to sweep up the broken glass.

Two things I remember with fondness from the Fifty-Ninth Battalion is the baptism of my son, Patrick, named after his grandfather. When we got married, I did not want to name the children after family, and we agreed on Biblical names—hence John, Sarah, David, the P word, and Aaron. I phoned from Harris village with the patrol waiting outside. Sheila came on the phone. It was 7:00 p.m., and she was in a hurry, as it was the Friday night of the baptism, an occasion held generally for single mothers who wanted to remain in the background on a Sunday. I asked her the name, to which she replied Patrick Francis, and then a pause. "Is that okay?" she asked, and I said yes, as really, what could I do from some three thousand miles away? I came out from the phone, raised my arms to heaven, and roared out a loud shriek of frustration. The second thing was in Byjhoun, one morning when the traders from the enclave were heading to Tyre city with their pickups full of merchandise from sand trucks, loads of shoes, clothing, and food items. They would be backed up the road for a half mile waiting for the UN to open the checkpoint, ending the curfew that was in place from 10:00 p.m. to 4:00 a.m. every day. The irony of the situation was that these goods were going to Tyre, the fifth largest city in Lebanon after Beirut, Sidon, Tripoli, and Nabatiyia. These goods were to be sold to the Palestinians, coming from an area under the control of Israel, so this proved that the power of the dollar is greater than the gun. One such morning, the IDF and DFF were carrying out a mine sweep back to the opposite direction of the oncoming traffic. It was normal to hear shooting, as they would fire up the road at large rocks that could easily be disguised as roadside bombs. This time, a Hino van, laden with shoes, was hit, the front grill badly shot up and the driver in shock from being shot in the leg, because he would not pull his vehicle further in off the road. I took him into the dining area and made him a strong cup of black coffee. The wounds were clean and fresh, clearly open with no blood. We arranged a medical evacuation to Tibnin hospital for him, where he was treated. If you were walking wounded in those days, they did not keep you in hospital. He returned to thank me for my humanitarian aid, and it was good to know he would live to make another few dollars.

Chalk three of the Fifty-Ninth Battalion returned home after successfully handing over to the Sixtieth Battalion, as at this stage everyone was nearly an old hand with previous Lebanon-UNIFIL experience, with the proper balance of some young blood. One of the reasons guys kept going back was that we felt the job was not done, and with the ever-growing number of casualties been ratcheted up, we felt Lebanon a job not finished. Back home, things were getting no better with the shoot-to-kill policy operating in Northern Ireland, the Lough gall ambush, where a number of republicans were killed, touts turning up on the border executed, and the ongoing bombing of commercial targets. You never got away from conflict, and some form of normal life was hard to establish. None of us were getting any younger. We had a football club, Prior United, formed from military personnel and playing in the Donegal League with a reasonable degree of success. This was a public outlet, which bonded local players and soldiers together. Less than two weeks after we returned, we were to learn that a Private O'Brien from Athlone was shot dead at the checkpoint in Brachit. Having a drink in your local and hearing that news is very sobering.

It was now 1986 and yet more to follow. Back to work again with every day a challenge, family life, mortgage to pay, keeping a car on the road, and children to school, all nicely fitted into a regime at camp level that saw the Prior School army camp no more than a training ground for blooding new officers and company commanders doing their grooming here before getting saucier roles down south. They could always say they served in Lifford or with B Company in Rockhill House, Letterkenny. These two locations had great rivalry, and at times one would think they were different armies. The battalion headquarters in Finner Camp some fifty miles away was a world apart. Camp life was now stagnant because of the way the battalion was subdivided; any activity took place in Finner Camp, and promotions and courses, etc. were all handed out there. Prior School will always be in the folklore of army life and written into the history books. It was an institution that in an odd way contributed to the peace process years before any dialogue was ever entered into, by mass integration through married life and recruitment and how it made a success of the local economy. In 1989, the nominations selection was again taking place for the Sixty-Sixth Battalion to serve with UNIFIL; I—with a wife and four children and always some sort of a financial tsunami hanging around the corner—was once again in the mix for selection, as this seemed the best option of a bad lot.

Years earlier I became disillusioned with army life and had pursued my interests in horticulture and opened myself up to the local economy. Work was coming in hard and fast, with new developments in the camp with extensions and new buildings; my talents were harnessed, and with the inclusion of a garden pond, tree planting, and lawn areas, this allowed me to escape a lot of the bullshit that entailed general duties. I was very independent and struck up a great relationship with the incoming company commander, Comdt. Tony Kiely, who had served as second in command to several company commanders and went on to become the longest serving company commander in Lifford ever. A very astute man and nobody's fool, he could see through you like glass. Several individuals were to feel the wrath of his management style, even the officers. I cannot remember ever a man being charged or on orders in front of him. I may stand to be corrected; he had his own way of dealing with things without hitting you in the pocket. After fifteen years and with no prospects, I put in for predischarge leave, which is for ninety days to consider your position and future.

Lt. Col. Vinnie Blyth was the battalion commander, and he introduced a policy of interviewing all NCOs with long service before allowing their leave. So off down to Finner Camp, in best bibs for my interview, I was somewhat shocked at the introduction: sit down there, Corporal Sumner, would you like a cup of coffee, mad but nice, one or two sugars, now tell me what is a man like you with only six years left to serve for the pension, making a decision like this...he went on to advise me that he would create a position as environment NCO, and apart from doing my duties I was answerable only to him and Comdt. Kiely. Armed with that offer, not only did I stay for another six years but also I actually completed another nine. Lt. Col. Blythe was the battalion commander of the Sixty-Sixth and an old friend from ranger days; Comdt. Sean Kilbride was company commander; and Captain Joe Gaffney from Galway was second in command. Captain Dave Lannon, who had served in Lifford, was going as platoon commander with the weapons platoon. The list goes on, and most will be mentioned through the column of the best ever battalion to have served overseas. The most important element in any organisation is the *esprit de corps,* coupled with good discipline and having a professional crew to do a professional job. As part of the Sixty-Sixth, we had the greatest motley crew ever assembled. Training in Finner was fun. The platoon sergeant was Sergeant Martin Doherty from Rockhill, originally from Galway, a single man, who would remind you of Pauric O'Connor, who sits in Eyre Square in Galway, pipe and all. Martin was a good organiser, and he never courted controversy. His famous quote when something was wrong was "Another CMFU," which is short for complete military fuck-up. With the weapons platoon, there were five sergeants' vacancies, as we had a 60-mm mortar detachment, a .5-mm HMG, an 84-mm a/tank, and a heavy machine gun detachment. Rank was allocated according to qualification and seniority. Captain Dave Lannon was the John Cleese of C Company, very able. It was just the way he did things. As the full list was not complete, the platoon was not fully formed. We were down in the NCO mess playing snooker with Corporal Spud Murphy, a lifelong friend and neighbour. Spud was a cracker who has a speech stutter and was in line for the vacancy of 60-mm mortar sergeant, with myself in line for the vacancy with the 84-mm a/tank. We decided to set Spud up, still playing snooker. Spud fancied himself in every sport; after all, he was the goalkeeper with the Prior United football team. I met with the Athlone lads as they arrived in Finner Camp, including a lad by the name of John Regan, a real character, who had been overseas with me before and was just completing an NCO course; as they say, his stripes had hardly dried on his arms. I asked him to go into the mess and tell Spud that he was the 60-mm mortar sergeant and to get his men fell in on the parade ground. Now, John could play the part brilliantly. In he goes to the snooker room to inform Spud, who was about to take a shot. How he did not rip the cloth from the table, I will never know. The stutter was now in top gear. "When did they promote you?" asked Spud. "Long enough to make me detachment commander," was the reply; I think that between 1:30 and 2:00 p.m., every phone number from Albert Reynolds, the Taoiseach of the day, down was sought.

When we had everything done in Finner, it was off down to Mullingar Barracks, with the same bonding session as before and then preparing for chalk one. The one thing that was going to change was the concept of the canteen. Captain Joe Gaffney, the company second in command, went to Dublin to a famous nightclub and got the promotional billboard of the famous Bad Bob's, and when we got on the ground, there were billboards from Johnny Cash to Daniel O'Donnell all over the canteen walls with the name in neon lights over the canteen door. Lebanon had never seen the likes of this, and all nationalities serving with UNIFIL were to become regular patrons of Bad Bob's canteen; on Saturday night, it was the only place to be, but still our job was executed to the highest standard. The first few weeks were spent in Shaqoura, which had three posts, 6–8 in the village itself, and then on the outskirts was post 6–28, platoon HQ, and behind the lines was post 6–28a, which had beside it a DFF compound only one hundred metres apart. Nothing was allowed through the village and 6–28 to the direction of their compound without the DFF consent; otherwise, it would have been blown off the road.

One night, Captain Dave Lannon was returning from Bad Bob's the worse for wear; he just could not drink. As a young lieutenant in Lifford, he was the same, maybe because of his height—he is six feet, five inches—and the alcohol had so far to travel that it emancipated every atom of his body. We had a dog in Lifford when he was there. The dog was called Darkie, and she was a sex maniac constantly in pup, bedded up under an observation post inside the main gate. Dave came in one night and asked the gate policeman if Darkie had pupped, and the policeman said he did not know. Dave was orderly officer the following morning but could not be found. After checking the main gate to see if he was signed in, his accommodation was checked. A full manhunt now in operation, he was sighted in Darkie's den, cold out and with newborn pups climbing over him, afterbirth and all.

Dave asked me who was on duty at 6:00 a.m. I told him that I was, and he asked me to call him when I heard the CO was coming. The next morning, I was out on the road dealing with a Mingi man over the purchase of a jumper, when low and behold the CO's car appeared about one hundred metres away. Fuck, I should have had the checkpoint personnel fell in, so I was now in deep shit. Comdt. Kilbride asked who was on the radio and proceeded into the radio room. It was Private Clerkin, a lost soul and completely harmless. "Did you not hear me saying I was on route from 6–8 to 6–28?" the CO asked. He then started to give Private Clerkin a tongue lashing, when I tapped him on the shoulder, asked him outside, and explained to him that the buck stopped with me, and I was in further trouble as Captain Lannon was still in bed. He said because I was honest about the situation, he would allow this lapse to pass, but to tell Captain Lannon he went through on to checkpoint 6–28a and would call with Lannon on the way back. Lannon, busted from the bed, had a quick shave, dressed, had a cup of coffee, and went up to the guardroom where I had the guard turned out. I don't believe I ever handed over a duty as good in my military life as I did that day.

"Good morning, Dave," the CO said.

"A great morning, sir," says Dave.

"I was just saying to Sergeant Sumner at 7:00 a.m. how high the sun was in the sky." The CO looked at me, and the look said it all.

You teamed up with buddies only maybe once every week or so and got together for a few beers. I was planning to go home for Christmas and bring a load of drink and cigarettes home with me. The plan was to book a direct flight through Tel Aviv to Belfast; this was going to be tricky, flying into that part of the United Kingdom with a Tri colour on my jumper, rank marking, and all. The plan was hatched. Of course, I wanted Sergeant Spud Murphy in on the deal with me. Spud was a windy sort, and any initiated or organised activity outside of military protocol was viewed with high suspicion, so he was reluctant until he found out what plans and costs of the travel officer were first. I was up on Post 6–28a, and he promised that he would call me on the radio the next day. We had an arrangement where we would give a radio check at 1900 hours and then drop down five numbers on the radio frequency and then we could talk freely over the airwaves. The time arrived, but simultaneously Capt. Lannon was going to the main signal room, where he asked the operator to call the post commanders on Post 6–8 and 6–28a, Spud and me. Now, the operator knew we were off the air, but with 960 frequencies on the 46 radio set, he demanded to get us on line. All 46 radio sets have only one-way traffic. I asked Spud if he saw Captain Gaffney, the travel officer.

"That fucking money-grabbing bastard knows nothing," he said, and then I asked if he saw Captain Lannon. He replied, "That fucking alco, he has his head up his fucking Almaza arse."

All we heard next was Captain Lannon's voice instructing us to return to our proper frequency and that he would deal with both of us tomorrow. *Shit, what did I say,* I thought, and then realised that Spud did all the damage. The next morning we were on the mat. It was a pantomime, seeing Spud grovelling. Lannon was angry but decided, due to our relationship, not to take the matter any further. Spud did everything but lick his arse, as the saying goes. He was the only man in the history of the army who wore GI-style issue pyjamas, and that's a fact. Anyway, Spud relented to my plans, and I booked the tickets. Christmas was coming, and we were going home. The crack was so good in post, it was lousy leaving, as I knew I was going to miss out on one of the best Christmas times overseas, but I was still looking forward to Christmas at home. So off we went and arrived in London, standing out a bit in full UN regalia but enjoying the attention of the moment. We had a three-hour wait for our connecting flight, when this Irish guy who had been in the United States for thirty-five years and had served in Vietnam joined us in conversation about Lebanon and the Middle East region. After an hour or so, he broke out this bottle of Jameson Irish whiskey to toast our heroics. This was now getting a little out of hand, but Spud loved the limelight. With the flight time arriving, I had to literally prise Spud away, and as we walked down the terminal with thousands of people, about one hundred metres, this guy stands up and shouts to us. As I looked back, he was shouting at the top of his voice and making the shape with his hands. "You guys have balls this size?" We arrived in Belfast to the sight of heavy police security in and around the airport. I was later to learn they would have been aware of our flight itinerary and wanted to ensure there was no international incident due to the fact we were in UN dress. Later that evening, the Reverend Ian Paisley went on the BBC news to condemn the fact that Irish soldiers were landing in Belfast. After collecting our cargo off the conveyer belt, we went out to the reception and were met by our wives. My preoccupation after making the initial greeting with Sheila was to get as far away as possible. Spud was making a bit of a pantomime of his love, and as usual I had to prise him away. We arrived at the border crossing from Strabane to Lifford, when the customs man, Derek, stepped out. On looking into the car he said, "Hi, Frank, would you mind opening the boot?" to which I retorted with, "Have I to do this all over again after coming through Dublin?" Derek paused, and then said, "Go ahead."

Ten minutes later, the eagles had landed home in the town land of Cavan, where we lived. As I recall, this was four or five days before Christmas, so before we knew it, Christmas Day was on top of us. For almost thirty years, the routine on Christmas Day was an early start, light the fire, and pour a drink on the only day I took alcohol in the morning. After all the presents were opened, it was time to head in to the army post in Lifford for morning mass. The usual people came, and over the years it became more popular, as after mass the bar in the NCO's mess opened for two to three hours; war stories were told, the crack was always ninety, and by the time the bar closed, some of us were well snozzled. Back home, I tended to keep away from the panic of preparing the Christmas dinner; my usual routine was a round of the neighbours to wish them a happy festival, usually topped up with the annual glass of whiskey. Looking back over the years, I don't think I ever took much Christmas dinner. That was usually my day done.

After a good Christmas, it was time for us to head back to Lebanon. As usual, it was hard saying the goodbyes all over again, but we were getting used to it by now. Spud Murphy's brother-in-law collected us at 4:00 a.m. for our trip to the airport, as our flight from Belfast to London was at 8:00 a.m. I remember a difference of opinion between the both of us about which gate to go to, but there was nothing new in that as Spud and I always had a difference of opinion. We arrived back in Lebanon and Brachit to a hearty welcome, coming back from family at home to another. We were soon back in the swing of things. You could go on forever, day by day, but the emphasis has to be on how well that company performed its job. The area was relatively calm, and any issues were dealt with the highest level of diplomacy. One shock was on hearing of the suicide of the assistant operations officer in the battalion head-quarters camp called Camp Shamrock. He was a captain based at the Curragh Camp in County Kildare. I think he was a classmate and friend of Dave Lan-non. Nothing looked untoward, but it pointed out the fragility of the mind. Then with about two months to go, the shit hit the fan.

A Company was drawn largely from the Eastern Brigade and the barracks in Dublin, and most of them were okay, but their attitude was generally reflected by their chain of command, which on this trip was very gung-ho. Their company commander, Comdt. O'Donnell, used to have an 84-mm anti-tank detachment in the back of his land rover, and he carried a Steyr rifle in addition to his personal 9-mm pistol. I remember Comdt. Kilbride saying that he knew he would draw trouble on himself by his demeanour. One day in Haddata, the local resistance mounted an attack on the Haddata compound, which had a Russian .5 heavy machine gun mounted on the roof of the house. The assault group numbered five or six personnel armed with AK47 rifles and rocket-propelled grenades, and when the assault was mounted, the company reserve of A Company was called out. Comdt. O'Donnell in his land rover, accompanied by the SISSU APC, headed to the scene, which was a short jour-ney from the headquarters. The local militia were retreating from the scene of the attack when they were surrounded by the Irish. They tried to escape, and a member fired the RPG at the company commander's vehicle; all persons on board escaped before the land rover was hit, the grenade ripping through the driver's door before exploding. I saw the land rover a week later, and there was no doubt it would have killed anybody that was in it. Some of the combat-ants made good their escape but not before Comdt. O'Donnell shot the two Higzassi brothers, a seventeen-year-old and a nineteen-year-old. What hap-pened, from reports on the ground, is that when they were rendered neutral, Comdt. O'Donnell emptied his magazine into both of them. Mousa and Maria, who ran the shop at the Brachit checkpoint, both worked at the Tibnin hospital as nurses, and that evening when they returned from hospital, I asked Mousa about the condition of the two boys. Very depressed, he described the head of one of the boys as like a boiled egg with the egg scooped out. These two lads were the nephews of the district Hezbollah commander with whom I had a later encounter. An immediate threat of retaliation was made against the Irish.

The next few days saw some smart decisions being taken by Lt. Col. Blythe. First, Comdt. O'Donnell and all personnel involved in the incident were removed from the area of operations to Israel, and he was relieved of his command. The second decision was to remove *en bloc* the whole of A Company from Haddata and relocate them to the B Company area. Duties were doubled, which put a heavy strain on a six-on and twelve-off rotation, and anxiety levels were high, because we knew a threat from Hezbollah was severe. Some eighteen months earlier, Corporal Henehan and Privates Armstrong and Walsh were out collecting rocks to fill gabions when they were blown up by a landmine planted by Hezbollah. (It took twenty-five years for the Department of Defence to own up to negligence after their families pursued them through the courts.) So any threat now was being taken very seriously—no slacking.

About six weeks had passed since the incident, with no casualties, and with two weeks to go before the arrival of the new battalion, the Sixty-Seventh, we were getting the place spic and span. I was on duty at Post 616, company HQ, and my job was checkpoint duty. A radio transmission indicated that a known car belonging to Higzassi was operating in our area, and if it came to any checkpoint, stopgap was to be carried out, as the occupants were heavily armed. Some ten minutes later, a gold BMW 750 series was heading in my direction to Brachit, which was a dead end. As the car pulled alongside, I gave the orders for stopgap, totally closing the checkpoint. The driver was Higzassi, wearing dark camouflage combats with an AK47 on the dash. I never saw more evil in a man's eyes, and with the dark beard, he looked about forty-five years old. Everything seemed to be going in slow motion as I asked him to open the boot of the car. His passenger was a little younger and more nervous, as if he anticipated something was about to happen. Higzassi reached down with his right hand to lift something from the car, at the same time getting out of the car and pulling the pin out of a grenade. My life flashed before me, as I have no doubt he was prepared to sacrifice his own life to bring me with him. As if by instinct I ordered the stopgap to be opened in the direction he was travelling, because searching his vehicle was now a non-issue. He got back into the car and proceeded, still clutching the grenade; when he passed the checkpoint, he threw the grenade into the wadi. From the thump of the explosion, I had no doubt that I would not be writing this today. The whole saga lasted ten minutes, and afterwards this captain, who came up through the ranks, came down from the camp and proceeded to tear into me for allowing Higzassi through. When he had said his piece, he went back up the camp. Comdt. Kilbride, the company commander, was on his way back from battalion HQ and could hear everything on his radio. He pulled up at the checkpoint to hear my version of events and told me I had done the right thing. I informed him the captain did not think so and told him about the abuse I received. Fifteen minutes later, I was relieved from the checkpoint and told to go to Comdt. Kilbride's quarters. On entering, I noticed the captain standing to attention in front of the commandant's desk. He was made to apologise to me, but not before the commandant tore stripes out of him.

Another incident took place at 617c. Sergeant Gerry Monaghan was post commander, and the IDF and DFF broke out of their compound and entered our area to search houses. The company reserve was called out, about twenty-two personnel, to reinforce post 617c. When we got there, an Israeli Mecava tank and a half track were on a ridge about one hundred metres from the post with men deployed in firing positions. We had an 84-mm antitank gun on the roof, a .5 HMG, and two more .5 HMG on the SISSU APCs. With all our personnel covering their troops, the air was tense, and the stand-off had already lasted an hour or so. I asked Comdt. Kilbride if he would like a cup of tea, to which he replied, "That would be nice, Reg." I detailed somebody, I think it was Private Dullaghan, to put a big saucepan of water on the gas cooker and collect all spare mugs. I made the tea and broke cover giving everybody a brew. I went out to guys in the APCs with my Steyr rifle on my back; it was mad, as I was making a target of myself. It looked more like an advertisement for Tetley Tea bags. Corporal Eddie Derry, who was driving one of the APCs, said, "Reggie, you are a mad bastard." The IDF and DFF then jacked up and went back to their compound; maybe they also thought I was mad.

Appendix C (page 199) includes an interview with Timur Goskel in which he outlines the way matters were sorted out in Lebanon, in particular, the way Comdt. O'Donnell's lack of judgment and common sense was covered up with lure of the dollar and how it was all portrayed back home in Ireland at that time, making him out as a hero. However, the truth now tells a very different story. The copies of the paper cuttings are from the *Daily Star.*

§ § § § § §

Actually, some of these cases can get pretty serious. I remember an incident in Haddatha village, which was in the area patrolled by the Irish. The Irish were very outgoing, probably the most beloved soldiers in the south, but a couple of them got into a quarrel with some Amal guys and two brothers were killed. This was in the late 1980s, when the Amal movement was the dominant force in the south, and these brothers were from a large militant family that would wipe out the whole Irish contingent if something wasn't done. A nightmare situation. I immediately contacted Nabih Birri, the head of Amal. I said, "Ustadh, I need you. This is a very serious case. We cannot have bloodshed. I know you don't want that." He says, "Of course not." So he sends me his deputy, the highly respected Dr. Ayoub Humayed, to take me to visit the family. On his advice I took the UNIFIL force commander, a Swede at the time, along. When we got to the house, the other brothers and the relatives all grabbed their guns—if Humayed hadn't been with us, who knows what would have happened? But because of his intervention, we were able to pay our condolences. All we could do was say how terribly sorry we were, that something had gone very wrong, that the Irish fellows had nothing against them, that there was nothing we could do or say that could make up for their loss. Things like that. But it started the reconciliation process, which continued the next day with the mediation of a local cleric chosen with Amal's help.

Eventually it boiled down to compensation. I tried to explain to New York what a disaster something like this represents for the family in strictly material terms, the fact that these two young men can't be the family's breadwinners now. I emphasized that if the usual UN rules were applied, there would be revenge. New York got back asking what payment I would recommend, and I said about $25,000 for each brother. They wrote back that this was "above the going rate." What? Was I supposed to go around collecting bids? I told them that if they didn't pay up right now, the family could kill ten Irish guys and with the UN rate of $80,000 per UN fatality, how much was that going to cost? Finally, after six months of painstaking negotiations, we paid up and the Irish added some money, too. Even a traffic accident in those days became a conflict issue because there was no law and order, but this is the kind of thing outsiders never notice.

§ § § § §

Thankfully we all arrived home safely, in no small part due to the brilliant leadership on behalf of those in authority. Again, no criminal charges were ever pursued against Comdt. O'Donnell, and his actions were never made public. Not only was what he did criminal but also he put the lives of every soldier in the battalion at risk. Being a soldier, you have to keep your tongue in check, but in today's military theatre he would not have got away with it.

6

Home Once More to a Changing Ireland

Back home things were changing. John Hume and Gerry Adams from SDLP and Sinn Fein were having talks, and there was a sense of optimism that something was in the air. The economy was picking up, with massive infrastructure development, motorways, and construction, and of course the Galway races were buzzing.

Every July, Galway was the place to go; we had been going there for years as a family. It was a cheap week: we would stay with this woman in Francis Street, just behind Jurys Hotel. She had a young lad with Down syndrome, who was a handful for her; he used to always say to her, "Ma, I am going up the town with the B&Bs." Toward the end of the week we always got him something, and after hearty food and a clean bed it was nearly impossible to pay her fairly; you nearly had to force the money on her. It's funny that every year it was the same faces going back to her. In those days, it was possible to make a profit from a week at the races, and then around 1991 the landlady of the B&B phoned to say she was discontinuing the service. It was only to be expected; Galway had changed and was now much more expensive. The races took on a whole commercial facelift, but with a price.

The Lebanon experience down over the years, coupled with ongoing border duty, was taking its toll on married life. Some lads were hitting the bottle, but gradually you could see the figures adding up, people whom you would least expect. I know the mantra of separation, violence, drink abuse, etc., but this was not the case, and years later, it was diagnosed as post-traumatic stress disorder, which the army did not recognise. In 2011, we conducted a poll of those personnel who served in Lifford and found a 35 per cent rate for divorce and separation, a figure that would be found alarming in any other walk of life. That concerned all ranks from officer down to private soldier. In later years, after leaving the army, guys who stuck with it through thick and thin for the sake of the family eventually cracked and packed it in. I am not a doctor, so I cannot diagnose them, but it is without doubt that the impossible position those men were placed in had contributed to the condition.

To give an example, some years ago, I travelled to Poland for dental treatment, and then spent a day at the Auschwitz concentration camp. While returning to Krakow on the coach, I felt depressed, and I returned to my hotel room and fell to a bottle of Jameson Whiskey. The more I drank, the madder I got. There was only me, the bottle of whiskey, and Pope John Paul II in the room and because of the Catholic Church's implicit involvement with the Nazis, I let all hell break loose. I awoke early next morning, and shocked with what I said, I went to 7:00 a.m. mass, in case my Easyjet plane would be picked from the sky on my return to Ireland. Three months later, I had to go back, and a friend of mine, Paul Madden from Strabane, travelled with me. He did not drink. I had no intention of revisiting the concentration camps, but Paul went. I said nothing to him but observed his depression on return, and he hit the drink. In the mid-nineties, the "army deafness" claims of civil action were taken by individuals before it became an epidemic, where everybody claimed and was encouraged by ex-officers who became solicitors. The earlier claims got up to £80,000; some of them were never past the firing ranges; as we used to say, they were never outside the gate. I fired an 84-mm antitank gun when under fire and with no hearing protection from inside an enclosed building, after which I could not hear a thing for three days. When I went for the army deafness, the doctor told me for a man of forty years, my hearing was 100 per cent. The army and the Department of Defence relented to the formation of a union, called PDFORRA, which was set up for the welfare of the soldiers. It had limited power and anyway the damage was done; going overseas now was a means of getting away from it all, from the barracks, from the routine, and, in a sense, getting away from the family. They were getting bigger, going into their teens, and coping with all that was a bit much. Six months in Lebanon was a far better option.

I applied to serve with the Seventieth Battalion and was selected, the same routine once again. Comdt. Tom Creaton was to be the company commander, we arrived in Lebanon, renewed again with all the people we knew from before; they knew in advance those who were coming, so the *shi* was pouring as we sat and caught up on things over the last two years, who was dead, who was killed, the usual checkup. Bad Bob's, our old canteen, was gone, and every unit wanted its own identity, and so the Seventieth set about having its own. We got a good welcome from position 41 and gate 12, two IDF artillery positions, east of Houla village. They were firing into our area every night for the first six weeks, and we spent a lot of time in the bunkers. First-timers to Lebanon Privates Ferghall and Danny McLaughlin were getting their baptism of fire along with Private John McBrearty. The platoon officer was Lt. Browning, with whom I had a major blow-up in Mullingar. Sergeant Tony Grehan was the platoon sergeant, and we had done the same NCO course together; Private Jerome Hannigan was another first-timer. The CO became known as "Groundhog"—if there was a shot fired anywhere, he had us in the bunker, so getting posted to Post 628a was a blessing and a break from the routine in the camp. I was post commander along with Corporal Mick Whelan as my second in command, and the post had three shifts.

I think I became famous in Lebanon for one thing, which was burning the post to the ground. The weather was getting colder; and winter in Lebanon could be harsh. The old heaters were the diesel drip-fed, Damascus heater. I was just after taking over from Sergeant Titch Hewitt, a neighbour from my youth in Athlone. The elevated post was the operations centre, the ammunition store, and the nerve centre of the post; at any given time, there would be at least two people in the post. Private Jerome Hannigan had bought a big video camera and had it up on a tripod, making a film of the lads firing snowballs. The radio called in a radio check, and when I reached over for the handset, I accidentally knocked over the dodgy fuel filter that fed the fire. In an instant, the fuel spilled and caught fire, and in milliseconds, all four of us on duty were out the door and the place blazing. I don't know why, but I ran back in to retrieve the GMPG (machine gun) and within seconds, para flares, live ammunition, and everything were exploding. With everybody accounted for and in safe cover, the video camera running, we could do nothing but watch it burn to the ground, along with my Steyr rifle. The DFF in the adjoining compound called stand-to, starting up their tank, thinking we were under attack. When they started the tank, they used it; with no radio communication, I went over to the DFF to borrow a 77 Radio set from them, which we used for the night to maintain communications. The next day the company commander, along with Captain Quinlain, the second in command, arrived with equipment to restock us. Some two months earlier, the medical aid post in battalion headquarters was burned to the ground along with 650 medical records. A fire officer was to be appointed in every company to prevent a repeat. Comdt. Creaton and Captain Quinlain called me into the dining room. There was no doubt they were trying to set me up for the fall. I pointed out that fire extinguishers were supposed to be checked regularly, with the CO_2 canister being replaced and the extinguishers stencilled and dated. I also noted that the ones on post had not been changed since 1978. It was a different ball game now, as they realised they were the ones in trouble. Comdt. Creaton implored me, in the interest of company *esprit de corps,* to be economical with the truth to the investigating fire officer. I told him to take away the old extinguishers and replace them with new ones and that way I would not have to lie.

The next day, the fire officer came up from Naqoura. When he was interviewing me, he asked why I did not use the extinguishers. I told him, as post commander, I considered the situation to be too dangerous to allow anyone near the fire. On playing back his recorded tape, Jerome Hannigan's tripod for his camera was hit by a round. A month or so later, Comdt. Creaton summoned me to his office, he read out the fire officer's report, which stated, but for the foresight of the post commander, serious injury or death would have occurred had the use of fire extinguishers been applied. Both Comdt. Creaton and I came out smelling of roses. "I owe you one, Reg," he stated. Too right he did.

Another incident of negligence that I am sure was papered over was the shooting of Corporal Carthy, serving with B Company in the village of Attiri. Around Christmas, my section was sent to the Black Hole in B Company area to help out with their duties, as they had a large group travelling home for Christmas. Private John McBrearty approached me about having a bottle of vodka to take in the bottom of his kit bag, and I told him to go ahead. We arrived in the Black Hole and were met by the post commander, a Sergeant Jimmy Deeneen, who is now the sergeant major in Collins Barracks in Cork. Jimmy was on his second trip, and never in my life had I met anybody like him; he was a total control freak and had a record book for everything. Something told me he was related to our Seanie; for example, you would not get the rations we were getting in a hotel. But because we were behind the lines, Jimmy decided to conserve food supplies, so we would eat pack rations every other day. To put that in perspective, it was akin to having Pedigree chum. Even for Christmas day, we had one large turkey and a massive ham for fourteen men, and the ham was sacrificed to the freezer. After Christmas dinner, we were all sitting back and this character from Kilkenny was having a laugh, when he told Jimmy he had a bad dream the night before. The DFF had come down from their compound and taken over our camp and held all of us prisoner. He didn't mind that; it was the fact they got the leg of lamb in the freezer. That was the way it was. We only had to put up with it for ten days, but those sad bastards had him for six months. Christmas Eve we were off duty at 6:00 p.m., and our next shift was 6:00 a.m. on Christmas morning. John McBrearty and I were sleeping in a two-man billet, and we decided to have a wee drink. Some five years earlier, back in Lifford, a young Second Lt.

Gosling got really up my nose, to where I reached a point of no return and
dished out one of the worst rollicking I ever gave any man. It was madness on
my part, but the lecture wasn't lost on him for the remainder of his term in
Lifford. During our stay in the Black Hole, I don't think a work detail such as
my crew from Lifford worked as hard as I can remember for Deeneen. I told
the lads to knuckle down, as we were here for only ten days. Back to the billet
with the door tightly closed against entry, John and I got stuck into the vodka
and Coke, reminiscing about Prior United football club, the good and the bad
footballers, fags, and drink. As we were on at 6:00 a.m., we could not afford
to get slouched. A gentle tug on the handle of the door indicated that someone
wanted in. The evidence hid, I asked who was there.

"Sgt Deeneen," he shouted, as he entered the room, which was like a gas
chamber from the cigarettes. "Did I leave a pouch under that bed?"

Like the teacher's pet when nothing could be unearthed, he left; it was
obvious what he was looking for. John said to me, "Deny everything, he can't
prove it."

The next morning as we were having breakfast at 5:30 a.m., Sgt Deeneen
confronted me. I wouldn't give him the pleasure and told him, "Do your
worst." If it went ahead, it was a charge. Later I was informed that he reported
the matter to Captain Gosling. I pondered if this was the same Gosling from
Lifford to whom I referred earlier. Later that day, the SISSU APC came out
from Haddata, and I saw Deeneen explain to Captain Gosling at a distance.
They then proceeded in the direction of my billet, so I stood outside with my
beret on. As they reached a twenty-metre limit, Captain Gosling stopped. The
same thought must have entered his head about my name, when he told to
Deeneen not to go there, turned, got into the APC, and left. The remainder of
the vodka was passed onto the crew of a Mecava tank parked along with two
others outside the Black Hole, a somewhat welcomed gesture by the Israelis.

In the village of Attiri was a component of men with the platoon sergeant
whose brief was to monitor all DFF activity within the village. The SOP for
such activity was to report and for a SISSU to be dispatched from company
HQ and collect patrol from Attiri to go into the village and monitor the situation. On this occasion, the report was made to company HQ, and the platoon
commander, Captain Gosling, gave the order for the patrol to be dispatched on
foot and to RV with the SISSU in the village. The occasion was that a half-
track vehicle commanded by a lieutenant in the DFF had entered the village
from the direction of the cuckoo's nest compound. As the patrol rounded a
corner, the DFF opened up with heavy machine gun fire, wounding two members of the patrol and killing the patrol commander, Corporal Carthy. On
observing the firing, the SISSU returned fire, killing the DFF lieutenant. Now
why did this happen? Pure negligence. The DFF was aware of our SOPs, and

on seeing the personnel on foot, assumed them to be Hezbollah disguised as UN personnel. It was simple—they had used this disguise before, and the DFF were taking no chances. Was this avoidable? Was anyone ever charged for negligence? I think not; it was just another example of the unnecessary loss of life. That was the only fatality that occurred with the Seventieth Battalion, and the reason I can be so sure was that a medic who was severely traumatised from that incident was sent out to the Black Hole with as much Almazda beer as he liked to drink, and it was he who told the truth. One has to ask why he was not sent to hospital for treatment. The coming and goings of the Seventieth were much the same until we had the tour of duty completed.

One incident requires mentioning. My shift at Post 6–8 in Shaqoura was coming to an end, and the first chalk of the Seventy-First Battalion was in position. I was returning on the third chalk home, one last sixty-hour pass in Israel booked for that Friday. The night before, some lads returned from the canteen the worse for wear, and among them was Private Jerome Hannigan, who had been a bit lippy in front of the new guys. I detailed him to go to bed, when he started to be insubordinate, really bringing any dirty washing out, and a bit of it was personal. Without further ado, I whacked him one, leaving a deep cut just above his eye. The next morning, I was gone on the convoy for Naqoura, changed into civilian attire, and about to head for the border. Corporal Sean O'Leary from Lifford had a plum job in Naqoura; he came up to me to say that Lt. Browning had phoned down to say my sixty-hour pass was cancelled and I was to return to the AO. "Sean, you never seen me," I said and to the border I skipped. On returning, I was put on open arrest and travelled up unarmed in the car of Comdt. Kieran Spollen, who went to school with me. He asked what happened and remarked that I never changed. Of course, I knew who squealed; it was Mick Whelan—once a military policeman, always one. On my return to Brachit, Lt. Browning sent for me and proceeded to give me a rollicking, like only a Cork man can. When he was finished, I said it was summary justice to decide my fate, without even giving me the chance to air my side. He was a little embarrassed and allowed me my say. I told him that I had three choices in dealing with Jerome: I could have arrested him and put him in Gallows Green prison; I could have charged him, which would have no doubt had an influence on his future military career; the third choice, I took. That was the end of that. Jerome is still serving as an NCO as I write.

7

Another Tour of Duty Over

After the month's leave, we returned to our unit for more war stories to be told. Prior School military base was like everything else—it was evolving, with new clothing, camouflage, and kit, and of course, new personnel through promotion. Time was never routine, and it took almost a month to readjust to the way things were. Like every organisation, our daily life was perpetuated with the untimely death of a member, none expected and some of them characters who were moulded in heaven. There was Corporal Hugo Rooney, died of heart failure at only thirty-three years; Private Tony Heraty, killed in a car crash; Private Charlie Murphy, aged thirty-eight years, died from a brain haemorrhage; Private "Poundies" Crawford, aged thirty-eight, died from a heart attack; Captain Kevin McIntyre died in his early fifties from cancer; Private John Devenney died as a result of a car crash; Private Colm Curran, late fifties, from a heart attack. Sergeant Tony Hannigan died at age forty-eight from a heart attack; his brother-in-law, ex-Sergeant John Crawford, died a short time later from a heart attack at fifty-two. Earlier in 1979, Private Philsy Crogan died from a swimming accident in Lebanon, aged only nineteen years. Corporal John McGlinchey died in tragic circumstances; ex-Private Johnny Tierney died in his mid-fifties from cancer; other younger members to die were Corporal Ainsley Catterson and Private Danny McLaughlin, both in their early thirties from cancer. Long-serving member of the FCA, ex-Sergeant Hughie McCormack died in his early sixties, and ex-Corporal Michael Coyle in his late thirties, in tragic circumstances, and finally a much-loved ex-company commander in Lifford, Comdt. A. J. Kiely, who died from cancer in his early fifties. Of course, there were many more from Rockhill and Finner Camp who died young while serving in the Twenty-Eighth Battalion, which only compounds the issue. In most cases, when in service, those personnel were accorded a full military funeral, drawing elements from all over the Western Brigade. It generally knocked the stuffing out of you. Turmoil—or should I say, organised turmoil—is the one good thing about the army; just like Carlsberg, nobody does funerals better. Army life is like no other. When working with an element of men, you were concerned about each and every one of that element; from the innermost personal level right up to the professional level, you knew everything about the individual. It was simple, as these guys were carrying loaded weapons and were under your control; you had to be a psychoanalyst 24/7.

That was a responsibility placed on each and every man. We were working under pressure both professional and domestic, which at times could be a lethal combination, so managing the situation was a fine art. Looking back over the years, there were personnel who managed to slip through the net, and, instead of making life better, they just compounded their issues and eventually were brought to book.

In the early nineties, things politically were gathering momentum in the north of Ireland, and there was a sense of optimism that parties were talking, the British and Irish governments were talking, but as a soldier, while aware of these issues, you didn't take your eye off the ball. Adventure training, social get-togethers, and the annual barbecue were introduced—the barbecue being the main event of the year—and, as the qualified tent-erecting NCO, I would go to Athlone, get three big marquees, and erect them for the event. That was one day you did not want to be on duty, as it became of the biggest social events in the town of Lifford, with crowds up to four hundred attending. The food was fit for Monte Carlo. Public relations were a vital tool of the army, and all ill feeling that may have been there in the beginning, when the army was setting up base, was now long gone. The annual athletics day for the children of the soldiers was another event, and the various Christmas functions were other occasions to look forward to. Then all were amalgamated, the privates and the NCOs with the officers, to an outdoor venue, such as Jackson's Hotel or a hotel in Letterkenny.

One year, the IRA created the first human bomb by tying a civilian worker into a van on a British Army base, laden with high explosives at a border crossing near Derry called Coshquinn. We were called out on patrol to assist the gardai, myself and another NCO called Corporal Kevin Keegan. It would be fair to say that at this stage everybody did not get on like a bed of roses in such cases; duties were staggered, so that your paths did not cross. It was a small percentage, but on this day I was with the wrong man; when we reached

Bridgend, he remained with his men in a land rover on the main road, and I was on an elevated site or back road with my crew. It was a cold day, and, it being a long shift, I had two-in and two-out rotation in place, so that a man could get warmed up in the land rover. Both vehicles had radio communications, and at about 2:00 p.m., the radio operator in Lifford informed us that the company second in command was leaving camp to visit our location. I knew it would take him thirty minutes to get here, so there was no panic. Keegan left his post about three to four hundred metres from me to come up and inform me of something I already heard. His attitude was meandering to say the least, and when I told him to fuck off back to his own position, words were exchanged, and in a flash of anger, I head butted him. He went back to his position and threatened to have me relieved. The patrol was called back to camp at about 5:00 p.m., and I was arrested by the military police. It was the night of the company Christmas dinner, which was being held in a hotel in Letterkenny. I phoned my wife and told her I was being held up, that I would be out at 8:00 p.m. and to run a bath. The military police interrogated me up to 8:45 p.m., and I denied all knowledge of said incident. I arrived home to a cold bath, quickly got ready, saying nothing to the wife, and got a lift to the event by a fellow corporal, Paddy McGlynn, and his wife. Keegan did not attend, but all the officers were there, including the battalion commander and the priest as guests. On making my entrance, one of the lads jumped up and shouted, "How's the head, Reg?" That was my cover blown.

Two years or so later, another mission opened up in Iraq, but it was a plum posting for military police and a few other ranks in administration, worth ten times the allowance for a tour to Lebanon, so I thought it was time to get an administration course done. I applied for a mess administration, accountancy, and auditing course that lasted three weeks in the school of administration in the Curragh Camp. A total of twenty students attended, with fourteen of us finishing the course. It was very interesting throughout and was of immense help later in years, when I retired and went into business. But all the courses in the world meant nothing, if your face didn't fit. We were still in an era where the nod was stronger than the wink, but I was to learn the reason years later from Kyran McGinley, who retired as a captain and went on to do a law degree and had offices in Letterkenny. One day while walking down the street, he called me from an upstairs window; I was drawn into his offices and directed to his chamber. It must have been five or six years since I had seen him at Poundies Crawford's funeral. He wanted to know how I was getting on and asked about others' welfare. While having a coffee, I put forward a question. Why, even with admin courses and all in my favour, why was I not considered for one of the plum jobs in all my trips to Lebanon? He leaned back in his chair, like a real solicitor, and asked, "Do you not know?" and then paused. "The company commanders going overseas had the pick from the manpower list, and your name was always first chosen." I reflected on that statement, and as I look back now, that consideration by my previous company commanders meant more to me than all them plum jobs in the AO.

8

My Fight for My Final Tour to Lebanon

That consideration could not be applied to the last company commander I was to serve with overseas. His name was Comdt. Gerry Aherne, and he was lumped with me whether he liked it or not. The famous IT of 1994 (physical training test) was introduced to the army. It was a physical fitness test to be applied across the board and had different levels according to age, and you had to have it passed annually to apply for overseas service.

Comdt. Kiely sent for me one day and asked me if I would go down to Letterkenny in my own time and do some work for him, for which I would be paid. God be good to him, a great officer, fond of his golf, a good judge of the equine breed on the track, and liked his pint. He was married to ex-Comdt. Boyle's daughter, who was a nurse. All of those things he was, but a gardener he was not. It took me two full days to get his place sorted out; having pride in my ability, I left every weed killer, fungicide, and pesticide box or bottle to one side and only billed him for what he owed. One day in the camp he thanked me for a good job and told me to bring the bill to him after the 11:00 a.m. coffee break. I knocked on his office door, bill in hand, and he shouted for me to come in. I saluted him and presented him what I considered a fair bill. He leaned back in his chair with a look of shock and remarked, "I hope there is a lawn mower in the garage when I go home, at this price." When he saw my reaction, he said he was only joking and reached for his chequebook. That was our Tony Kiely. A number of days later, he said he wanted commission on my earnings as he had got me a job with one of his neighbours. It was a massive Leylandi hedge, on which I cut off one of my fingertips. I spent three days in hospital, and because there was some blood circulation it rebounded, but in hindsight it would have been better if it was taken off.

The IT 1/94 fitness test came up within weeks, but I could not partake. I had applied for service overseas and done the fitness test in July. The names came out in August, but there were vacancies for about four NCOs and not enough volunteers, so they started to promote private soldiers into "acting corporal" rank. Of course, all the talk was about me. I must have shit the nest. I applied to see the company commander, Kiely, who informed me that I was top of his list going from Lifford, and that I should take the matter up with the battalion commander. Enough said.

To THEA/9 THRough.
THE GOC.
THE O/c 28TH BN
the O/c A/coy. Sir I Submit this my Redress of Wrongs
against Lt Col Keane O/c 28TH BN under Section 114
PARA 2.

In Early May when the Vol/Proforma came out I Vol for
overseas Service with the 74th BN. On the Initial List my name
wasen't Selected; In Early June I Received an Injury to my
Left hand which Rendered me on E.D. On the 29th July Dr Kerr
BN MO. Returned me to fulltime Duties; ~~and~~ at that point I learned
Some NCO's at BN level had withdrawn their Name's from the Initial
List; I then approached the Coy 2I/c Capt O'grady and later the
Coy Comdr Comdt Kiely to have my name forwarded to COMD Manpower,
as a Volunteer, as it was apparent their was a Shortage of NCO's
for C/coy 74th BN. As I had been unable to undertake the ITIR
94 Earlier due to my Injury while on Ed, It was Imperative I
get the test done, however my Coy COMDR informed me it was
BN Policy that at the Initial Nomination Stage only people who had
completed the afy test were being forwarded to Athlone CMP.
though I had been Nominated by him to Unit HQ, this was
BN Policy. When the Sub Unit formed up for o/sea's training at 28th
BN Level 3 HQ, one from my own Unit was promoted A/sgt° through
pure frustration I then applied for an Interview with the G.O.C.
to air my Grievance, really during his visit to Mil Post Kffford on
the 8th/10th /93. The G.O.C. Either misread or otherwise the Brief
before him but he was under the Impression that I had been
on E/D & Continual WD up to that point I asked him about
the GTIR 94, and his Reply was that It did not prohibit any
man's Nomination but the test had to be Successfully completed
before leaving for the mission area; my Interpretation was if
a man was Selected and if he had not already undertaken
the test he could then prove his Calibre & fitness. I found
that Contrary to what was Unit Policy, and therein applied
for an Interview with the BN Comdr on the following Day.
I was granted the Interview in the presence of Capt McGahon
on the 4/11/93

Lt Col Keane Informed one that Irrespective of other Units or otherwise Policy; No person in the 28th Bn who had not completed the test, was forwarded in Name to C. M. P. and therefore wouldn't be Considered for o/seas Service; I knew this to be an untruth and Requested that he give one his findings in writing pursuant to Para 11 B Section 114 AT, at which point he Reluctedly told me he would.

I officially completed the R.T. & T.H. on Sept 23 and would have done likewise at any time beforehand had there been any Effort by my Bn HQ to Inform C. M. P. that I was available for overseas. The Reality is that 9 Ptes were promoted A/Cpl Paid and yet to Compound personal trauma further, 1 week before the Departure of Chalk 3 74 Bn a fellow NCO Cpl O'Leary S. from my own Coy was asked if he wanted to travel n/sgt to Naquira; his Name was forwarded to C. M. P. and then onto Enlisted personnel in Dublin, without any IT & T.H. This all took place prior to my Interview with the Bn CO/DR. 5 weeks have Elapsed since my Interview with Lt Col Keane, and In order to Protect my dignity as an NCO I want the Issues herein Investigated against Lt Col Kane under the following Sections AT Part I Para 4, & PARA 5; Para 11 B Section 114 AT.

I would very much appreciate the findings of your office to be conveyed to me in writing under the Relevent act PARA 11 B Section 114 AT.

Essectional Points:
Injury cleared up 29th July.
UN Medicals No 17th Aug,
Sub Unit Training 22nd Aug. 28th BN.
2 A/Cpls Promoted Spirit Level.
C/coy 74th Bn form up M.D Sept.
a Total of 9 Ptes Promoted A/Cpl Paid

I am Sir
No 826929
Cpl Sumner S
A/coy 28th Bn.

16ᵗʰ Mar. 1994.
To The O/c A/coy 28ᵗʰ Bn.

Sir
I wish to make Enquirie's about
a Redress of Wrong, that I Submitted on the 16ᵗʰ Dec
1993. The Matter was forwarded from Bn HQ on the
21ˢᵗ Jan to 4ᵗʰ Bdg, when it failed to Resolve itself.
I find after Some Three Month's, that The Spirit of
DFR A7 is not being complied with, as I to Date
no Effort has been made, to Inform me of the finding:
or The outcome if any to Date?
Due to the present Situation
I find myself Compromised in my Working
Environment.
I am Sir
№ 826929

J. Sumner O/c.

Telephone (0902) 92631
Telex   53178 HQWC
Fax   (0902) 94296

Headquarters,
Western Command,
Custume Barracks,
Athlone.

07 April 1994

Cpl F.P. Sumner
28 Inf Bn

REDRESS OF WRONGS APPLICATION

1.   I am directed to state as follows ;

      a.   GOC W. Comd has carefully examined all aspects of
           your application for Redress of Wrongs. He has
           paid particular attention to the points outlined
           by you and to the investigation which was carried
           out by Lt. Col Molloy.

      b.   Within the terms of the Defence Act 1954 and
           Defence Force Regulation A7 as they relate to
           Redress of Wrongs, GOC W. Comd is of the opinion
           that you have NOT been wronged in that no right of
           yours has been infringed.

2.   If you are not satisfied with the determination made by
      GOC W. Comd, you may have your application forwarded to
      higher authority. Please indicate your wishes in this
      regard.

J.J. QUILTY
LT COL
ADJT W. COMD

Copy   :   OC, 28 Inf Bn
           Comdt J. McKEOWN

12TH APR 1994

To O/C 28TH BN,
THROUGH O/C A/COY 28TH BN,

Sir; With Regard to the
Instruction given to me by Compt McKeown
Ref: My Redress of Wrongs; I do not Except
the G.O.C, w/cotrd findings, and therefore I
Wish This matter to be forwarded to a higher
authority as per Regulation 114 (2) Defence
act 1954.

I, am Sir   No 826929

        J Sumner Cpl.
        A/Coy 28TH BN,

15th May
To Bn Comdr 28th Bn.
Through O/C A/Coy 28th Bn.

Sir
I Submit this my query Regarding my Redress under Section 114 A7 which was Submitted on the 16th Dec 1993.
To Date the Redress has undergone Investigation up to A/G's level. While Serving with the 76th Inf Bn UNIFIL, I was Informed In Writing of the A/G's Decision. I Instructed Lt Col Skinner O/c 76th Bn to have my Redress forwarded to the Minister pursuant to Section 114; that was on the 29th Nov 1994; to Date I have never been Informed of Subsequent action. I would be Obliged if you could get an update on the Situation for me.
I am Sir
No 826929
J Sumner, Cpl.

To O/C 28TH BN   23RD Aug 1994.
THROUGH BN ADJ
   "   PLN OFFR No6PLN UNIFIL

         Sir I Submit This my Query
Regarding my Redress Under Section 114 & A7
Which was lodged with Enlisted Personnell
Section; AGs Branch; on the 25TH APR 1994 by the
Command ADJ; To date I have not been made
aware of any Ruling Regarding the Matter; As
I prepare for oversea's Service with the 76TH BN
I would rather feel more into the job at hand
if this Matter was Resolved, as I do not wish
to be dealing with the Issue Emotionally, and
on that Basis I would appricate if you could
make whatever Enquiries Nessessary that might
Expediate the process.

                I am Sir

           No 826929   F Sumner   Cpl.

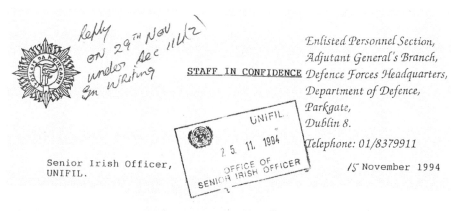

Enlisted Personnel Section,
Adjutant General's Branch,

STAFF IN CONFIDENCE *Defence Forces Headquarters,*
Department of Defence,
Parkgate,
Dublin 8.
Telephone: 01/8379911

Senior Irish Officer,
UNIFIL.

15 November 1994

UNIFIL
2. 5. 11. 1994
OFFICE OF
SENIOR IRISH OFFICER

APPLICATION FOR REDRESS OF WRONGS
826929 CPL SUMNER, F. - C COY 76 INF BN (PARENT UNIT 28 INF BN)

Sir,

1. I am directed by the Adjutant General to inform you that on consideration of the complaint submitted by Cpl Sumner ,he has ruled that Cpl Sumner has suffered no wrong within the meaning of Section 114(2) of the Defence Act.

2. The contents of the Chief of Staff's directive entitled "Physical Fitness for UNIFIL Personnel - October 1993 - TI 1/92 " precluded unit commanders from nominating personnel who had NOT completed Test 1 of TI 1/92 for overseas service in October 1993 with UNIFIL (74 Inf Bn, 29 IRCOMP, UNIFIL MP COY,and HQ and FMR personnel).

3. Cpl Sumner should now be informed of the Adjutant General's ruling on his application for redress of wrongs and the contents of para 2 above. Under the terms of Section 114 of the Defence Act, Cpl Sumner may require the Adjutant General to report on the matter of his complaint to the Minister. Please ascertain Cpl Sumner's wishes in this regard and inform this Section as soon as possible.

B Kenny Capt
p/s D. J. REIDY
COMDT
OIC ENLISTED PERSONNEL SECTION

Copy to: GOC Western Command

☎: (01) 771891

FAX : (01) 377993

TAGAIRT.
(Reference): 3/22411.

AN ROINN COSANTA
(Department of Defence)

COLÁISTE CAOIMHÍN

BAILE ÁTHA CLIATH 9
(Dublin 9)

Your Ref: S/M/R.

27 April, 1994.

Messrs. David Wilson & Co.
Solicitors,
Raphoe,
Co. Donegal.

RE: 826929 CORPORAL F. SUMNER - 28 INFANTRY BATTALION

Dear Sirs,

I refer further to your letter of 22 February, 1994 in connection with the above-named member of the Permanent Defence Force.

I have been advised by the military authorities that Corporal Sumner has submitted an application for Redress of Wrongs under the terms of Section 114 of the Defence Act, 1957. His application is being considered in line with normal procedures and he will be advised of the outcome in due course.

Yours sincerely,

DENIS G. GLAVIN,
HIGHER EXECUTIVE OFFICER.

APPLICATION FOR REDRESS OF WRONGS

826929 CORPORAL F. SUMNER

'A' COMPANY, 28 INFANTRY BATTALION, LIFFORD.

Having fully considered the above application I rule that Corporal Sumner has suffered no wrong calling for redress within the meaning of Section 114 of the Defence Act, 1954.

MINISTER FOR DEFENCE

14 June, 1995.

OIFIG AN AIRE COSANTA
(OFFICE OF THE MINISTER FOR DEFENCE)
BAILE ÁTHA CLIATH 9
(DUBLIN 9)

29th June, 1995

Dr. James McDaid, T.D.,
Dail Eireann,
Dublin 2.

Dear Jim,

Thank you for your representations on behalf of 826929 Corporal Frank Sumner, A. Coy., 28 Infantry Battalion, Lifford, Co. Donegal regarding a Redress of Wrongs.

I am making enquiries in relation to this case and I will write to you again as soon as possible.

Kind regards,

Yours sincerely,

SEAN BARRETT, T.D.,
MINISTER FOR DEFENCE

Dr. James McDaid, T.D.

Pearse Road, Letterkenny, Co. Donegal.
Tel : 074/25132 (Constituency Office)
074/21652 (Home)

DÁIL ÉIREANN
BAILE ÁTHA CLIATH, 2.
(Dublin, 2).

Tel : 6789911 (Dail Eireann)

Corp. Frank Sumner
A.Coy 28th Inf. Btn.
Lifford.
Co. Donegal.

July 5th 1995

Dear Frank,

I have been in contact with the Minister regarding your enquiry and I attach herewith his reply.

I shall get back to you again as soon as I have further word from him on the matter but if there is undue delay don't hesitate to get in touch with me.

Many thanks.

Yours sincerely,

Dr. James Mc Daid T.D.

The battalion commander was Lt. Col. P. J. Keane, renowned throughout the battalion as a bit of an eccentric. My only dealings with him were when he was second in command of the battalion; it was generally considered that he was a bit naff. I went in to his office with a rock-solid case that I thought required only a phone call to the manpower office for them to correct. The platoon was not formed up yet, so how simple could this be? When I entered the office, saluted, and stated my case to him, he told me to apply for the next trip, and that was that. When I pointed out to him that the administration of the unit was a joke, it was all-out war, and I told him that I was applying to the minister for defence for a redress of wrong, which was my entitlement. This is considered a last resort for a serving soldier and a decision not to be taken lightly. It was known in the past that such applicants had their military career cut short; however, on this occasion I felt on safe ground. The next eighteen months were interesting, as it states within the Defence Forces regulations that a reasonable time frame be applied, as the process has to go through a number of stages, first to the command (now brigade) OC, then on to the adjutant general (now deputy chief of staff), and then on to the minister for defence with the total time allowed laid down as six months. However, my application took two years. I remember Comdt. Kiely sending for me; what I write now, I don't like to, but to the memory of this colossus of a man, I think to serve him otherwise would be unjust. I entered the room to discover him very upset; he pointed out that he would be the one to suffer. He was much stressed and broke down; to see tears coming from this man nearly broke me. I decided there and then to withdraw my case for redress, but Kiely was having none of it. "You will go the whole way with this," he ordered. That was one of the worst days that I ever had in the Prior School military camp, but this was a point of principle, and Kiely was all about principle. There were not enough Tony Kielys in the army.

Events developed at every stage. The first was I had to go to Finner Camp to have a meeting with a Lt. Col. Sean McKeown, an officer whom I knew since he was a lieutenant. He was the first officer in charge of Ballyconnell military post in County Cavan. We talked about several issues, and it was obvious his role was to mediate. I was offered everything from serving in Iraq to promotion, but nothing could be put on paper and I thought of Kiely and declined. The next stage was Comdt. Andy Kilfeather offering me the next trip, which I declined as it was a summer trip and did not suit me, as my new second career in horticulture was now firmly in pole position. There comes a time in your life when enough is enough, but I was not quite ready yet.

Time passed, and the fitness test came around again, so off we went over to Rockhill in Letterkenny in the back of a truck. I knew the training officer and told him not much point in me doing the test when I could not get to serve overseas, having done it the previous time and being refused. I again applied for overseas service just for the heck of it and was selected. It was now clear that they were bending over backwards and breaking the rules, as I was not qualified, not having done the fitness test. August came, and off we went to Finner Camp for the predeployment training and then on to Mullingar as the normal schedule for the training. Lt. McNally, based in Rockhill House in Letterkenny, had a fitness issue, being on the generous side of chubby. Sergeant Tony Grehan, who did his NCO course with me, was selected as the platoon sergeant. We went through the now-normal motions of the training; it was a virtue having some first-timers, as it meant the training was not repetitive. As an NCO's instruction is an art of communication and we were dealing with a now more-educated client in the younger soldier, the average recruit now entered the service with at least leaving cert standard of education; indeed, some had university degree standard, which meant that it was easier to get through to them, and we also had to know what we were talking about.

Comdt. Gerald Aherne was the company commander; he was based with the Sixth Battalion in Athlone but had spent his earlier career based in the Defence Force Headquarters and on promotion to commandant rank was posted to the Western Command in Athlone. Danny Wall was the company sergeant, and he had also done his NCO course with me. He told me that this commandant had never worked with troops before and was a hated figure in Athlone Barracks. He was charging men right, left, and centre, so, armed with that knowledge, I was going to make sure that all *t*'s were crossed and all the *i*'s were dotted. We were able to put together a good crew, but as always we had our reservations about a couple of guys. I think I travelled to Lebanon on the first chalk out. Having got there, I was again on the ground renewing old acquaintances. People who were now like family welcomed us back, fed us, and brought us up to date with life in Lebanon.

My heart was no longer in the job, but professionally I knew what I had to do; nonetheless, I was determined to exact a response for my redress. After all, I was an NCO with more than twenty years of service who played by the rules, and I was not prepared to allow those same rules to protect incompetence. This is borne out by letters and correspondence from the command OC right up to the minister. I had reached a point in my mental state where I questioned everything. I went back to the early days, back to the Seoige Joyce issue, and replayed in my mind every second of the time and the rumour mill over the years, and again I came up with the cover-up syndrome, but why? An old friend of mine, Lt. John Picard, who served in Lifford for a while in 1976–78, was a bit of an "enigma" in his own right. John had his own tribulations during his military career, but on one occasion he was in charge of a group of men from the Eastern Command in Dublin that were up in Donegal doing adventure training in Rockhill for a ten-day period. On conclusion of the training, they all went to the "Golden Grill" night club in Letterkenny for an end-of-course "night out." There was this particular guy, who was an international athlete and had only recently joined the army. This guy excelled in all "fields" of the military. The platoon sergeant that night remarked to John Picard that he was the best that he had seen in his career, to which "Picard" replied, yes, but when the army finds out about him, he is in trouble.

I began to take a deeper interest in Lebanon: the geopolitical arena was somewhat muddy; Hezbollah was now the only power in the south, with a massive power base in Beirut and the Bekaa Valley region; and the Lebanese army was reconstituted and deployed in the south, working along the UNIFIL lines. Conscription was a way of life, and some of my friends from there found themselves offering up eighteen months in the line of duty, and they hated it. At least our soldiers are volunteers, which takes me back to my first involvement in military life.

As I was from a garrison town, with my father and grandfather both involved in the military, it was often the norm to try to enlist from fifteen years of age onward, and as I was not getting much encouragement at school from the Marxist Brothers, off to Dublin and Collins Barracks I went. It was a little late in the day, and the barrack orderly sergeant took me in, got me fed, and bedded down for the night. The next morning I would be medically examined, sworn in, and kitted out for military recruit training. There were three soldiers in the room, armed with Gustaf submachine guns, waiting around; this was part of army life. Waiting around for what was termed on a need-to-know basis as the heart of the famous arms trial concerning Charles J. Haughey, Neil Blaney, and an army officer named Captain Kelly. It's a wonder that Frank Sumner was not in court as well. After I played the military card game Don for a few hours, about midnight, Captain Kelly, as I now know him, entered the room along with the barrack orderly sergeant, detailing the men to follow them. He enquired as to whom I was, and then said, "Bring him along," probably wanting to impress me on my first day. I was willing and able, and, to make a long story short, we loaded three trucks full of guns, and I was then escorted back to my room. In the small hours of the morning, the drivers returned, but I was not to know the significance of that night until much later.

The next day it was off to Cathal Brugha Barracks in Rathmines, Dublin, to commence training with the Second Motor Squadron. As I have mentioned in the first chapter, after three months I had enough, and I did a runner back to Athlone. I could fudge a storyline with my father for about two weeks or so, and then I had to make provision to re-enter the military life, this time in Mullingar. Enlisting under the name of my uncle, Tommy Egan, things in the

Ninth Platoon were going along good; this was better than in Cathal Brugha. I was roused when somebody thought I knew much more about weapons than I should have for such a raw recruit. The military police investigated, and I was arrested and returned to Cathal Brugha Barracks, where I spent five days in the guardroom. Years later, I knew what it felt like to be locked up in the H Blocks. A Sergeant Walsh, who got his stripes from his qualities in the boxing ring, was the platoon sergeant; he walked me to the rag store and detailed me with his fist to get dressed. It was then orders in front of Lt. Col. "Bull" Callaghan, who was officer commanding the Fifth Infantry Battalion. The charges against me piled high, and he literally ran me out of Dublin. Years later, I was to hand over an Honour Guard to him when he was lieutenant general and force commander of UNIFIL in Lebanon. I eventually reenlisted in 1973 after the aforementioned sojourn in the UK and completed the training as previously outlined. We had thirteen men left, and we passed out on July 13, 1973, and on that day, I believe I was born to be a soldier.

Back to Lebanon. The battalion commander, Lt. Col. Jim Shreenan, sent for me on a Sunday afternoon. The battalion headquarters in Camp Shamrock was quiet, and this meeting was low-key. He was a good man, was Col. Shreenan, and went on to achieve the top job in the army of chief of staff. He informed me of the adjutant general's finding on my redress, and the matter was then forwarded to the minister for defence. Not a lot was happening in our area of operations in Southern Lebanon, as Hezbollah was up to its neck in it in other areas. It was time for me to organise a Mingi run to the Israeli town of Nazareth; after all, one had to keep up contact and maintain my price base. At this time, I knew Comdt. Creaton (whom I mentioned earlier) was the provost marshal with the military police in UNIFIL headquarters in Naqoura, so it was time to pull an ace out of my sleeve. Armed with the knowledge that he was on leave in Ireland, I organised six border manifests, and with military precision I went to Camp Shamrock, the battalion headquarters, on a Sunday to get Comdt. Delaney, the battalion adjutant (he was stationed with me back home in the Twenty-Eighth Battalion), to sign and stamp my necessary documents. The next day it was off to Naqoura to get the stamp of the acting provost marshal. On knocking on the office door, the reply came to come in, and sitting behind the desk was this Norwegian colonel. Now, they were not much up on protocol, so raising my right leg, giving one hell of a bang and the finest salute you ever saw, I informed him that Comdt. Creaton told me to bring them down for signing. He asked if I was sure; when I reassured him this was the case, he signed and stamped my documents.

So six cases went across the border and the goods delivered to Nazareth, causing a healthy profit of $5,000; the only expense was $50 a man to my helpers and hostel accommodation in Tiberius. I was careful never to sell to an Israeli citizen. Tiberius was some spot, usually used by officers when going on leave. Natayna and Nahariah were the towns that the enlisted personnel visited while on local leave. A great weekend we had and then back to the bacon; routine followed routine, until it was time again for another sixty-hour local leave pass. We were allowed two local passes during the tour, along with the home leave; however, this one was to be a banana skin. We approached the Israeli border, and a first-timer, Private Gerard Doherty from Castlefin, was with me. A Polish military policeman was on duty, and it was 12:20 p.m. on the Jewish Sabbath, and nothing was allowed across the border after noon. With broken and bad English, he kept saying, "*Chevaz, chevaz,*" trying to indicate it was the Sabbath. He then proceeded to search our cases and confiscated all the goods. He issued me a blue ticket, which I could redeem in the military police headquarters camp of Camp Martin in Naqoura for the return of the goods. The damage was done; some days later, the military police arrived in Brachit Camp. We were on duty in Post 642, when the order rang out that Gerard Doherty and I were wanted in camp. The company sergeant of the military police and a sergeant were to interview Gerard Doherty first; they had him in for three hours, and the look on his face as he came out indicated where I stood. It was lunchtime; I would not be required until after midday. They were out to make an example, as a lot of smuggling was taking place, and the Israelis were not a happy lot about the issue. If this could be nailed down on me, it was repatriation and possible court marshal and maybe even discharge.

The military police called me in; they were confident of a quick kill. Comdt. Aherne was also sitting in. It started like this: "Corporal Sumner, where were you in Israel on your sixty-hour pass?"

I enquired, "Were the Israeli authorities looking for me, or was a warrant out for my arrest?" When they replied no, "Then it's none of your business where I was," was my reply. Things were not going good, and it was time to pull the only card left. "I am not prepared to make a statement, except only in the presence of Comdt. Creaton, and I would like you to take a note to him to that effect."

The company sergeant agreed, informing me that he had all the time in the world, but that I would be on a plane home very shortly. Comdt. Aherne interjected that this delaying tactic would be to no avail, but I had to hold out, as it was my only hope. So back I went to Post 642. I was on duty 6:00 p.m. to midnight that night; while heading over to the cookhouse, I gleaned an insight into what opinions some people had about me. Corporal Micky McGahern and Lt. McNally were really having a gloat at my demise, but I was prepared to hold on. The next morning at 8:00 a.m., Lt. McNally was at the main gate, with the guard lined up, awaiting the arrival of the company commander. I was up the camp and I could hear by relay my name being called, so, donning my beret, I approached with a salute.

"Corporal Sumner, I don't know how high up your influence goes, but Comdt. Creaton rang this morning to say that all charges against you were dropped." Comdt. Aherne got back into his land rover, banging the door as he retreated back to the camp. McNally's face fell, and in a very diplomatic way, I advised him to stay out of my face for the rest of the trip, lest he wanted a transfer to Spike Island, and that was the last time I had direct dealings with him for the remainder of the tour of duty.

I was in the Black Hole with Henry Brady from Downpatrick, a sergeant with the Sixth Battalion platoon and post commander. Rumour had it that the CO was writing up very bad personal reports on the NCOs in the company, and everyone felt it was a betrayal of trust, insofar as to the work that was carried out over the six-month tour. I knew he was not great when earlier he tried to block Corporal Pat Ryan from applying for a sergeant's vacancy back in his home unit in the First Battalion in Galway—he made the remark that he would not even have recommended him for an NCO course. Sure enough, he arrived out to the Black Hole to give his opinion on us one and all; the lads' faces said it all as they came out. After a knock on the door and a "come in," I duly closed the door behind me, and with an about turn I rendered the CO a salute; after all, it was the rank that I was respecting. "Sit down, Corporal Sumner. I am about to read out what I have considered my opinion of your performance over the last six months," and off he went. I have heard of bad reports, but what my ears were taking in bordered on crazy. He pushed the paper toward me to sign, which was proof that he had read it to me.

"Under no circumstances will I sign that. This is a psychoanalysis of me over the period. I have never been in your company for more than fifty minutes over the period of the six months," and I went on to give him my opinion. "I will sign it only in the presence of the battalion commander."

He got up from the table, gathered his papers, went out the door with a bang, and left the camp. Brady called me at five o'clock that evening and said I was wanted in camp by the company commander. *A night in the canteen,* I thought, so in I went and knocked on his door. I entered his room—a fairly cluttered room, I might add. I thought, *if this was my room, it would be a different story.* He was definitely in a new mood. As I sat down on his invitation, he said that as a result of my long service in the rank, he was prepared to rewrite the report. As he read it out to me, it was hard to believe it was the same person as four hours earlier, and I had no problem in now signing this report.

9

Finishing with Military Life Was Now on My Mind—but Not Lebanon

My mind was pretty much made up at this stage. It was time to pack it in. I felt having given twenty-three years' good service that the house of cards was coming down on me. Just because I stood up for a principle, a process that should have taken no more than six months was now bordering a span of two years. As we rolled out the last few weeks, I was in Shaqoura, Post 6–8, and within the same building that we occupied lived a family that I used to visit in the evenings for *shi.* I knew them down over the years—Hassan, his wife, and two children. Hassan was a businessman who travelled over the whole Middle East and Africa. In his late thirties, he had a fourteen-foot python snakeskin adorning a wall in his living room at an angle of forty-five degrees. I don't know how much I offered him down over the years for this skin—maybe as much as $500, but to no avail. We always had very intelligent conversations and at times were joined by the local religious sheik; he spoke fluent English, as he was educated in Detroit, Michigan. It was through him I developed an interest in Islam. They were very good people. I learned from the sheik that Shias would recite the Lord's Prayer with a Christian. Hassan knew it was my last trip and invited me back the night before I departed. It was tradition for them to offer a *cadou* (present) to you before you left for home, and as we said our goodbyes, promising to stay in touch, Hassan handed me this plastic bag.

"For you, friend," he said. It would have been bad manners to inspect the bag in his presence, but when I went back to my room I found that in the bag was the snakeskin.

The Lebanese people really did appreciate what we were doing for them; they felt safe on our watch. UNIFIL in truth did keep the different factions apart, and it was everyone's wish that the country would return to normal. It was hard to imagine the Iranian Hezbollah were very big throughout the country. Factions within the PLO were trying to break out from the refugee camps that were surrounded by the Lebanese army. The Syrian Army controlled Beirut and the Bekaa Valley region. There was a hung government trying to legislate, and there was always outside interference—the Arab League, the United States, and the EEC, all of them trying to come up with initiatives, and so the saga went on.

Back home it was a matter of establishing any changes in the chain of command, using one's leave and spending our hard-earned money on the plans you shelved for nine months. My wife, Sheila, was heavy in the final stages of her last pregnancy, and I was at hand for the birth of our son, Aaron, a situation at the time for which I was never prepared. So back home now with the new baby, it was a school run every day for the other four siblings; with the house full of kids, the place was never dull, and I used my military skills in a refereeing format. Everybody was happy, and then one day a near neighbour, a fellow soldier called Sixteen McManus, called to say that the new second in command in the camp, Captain Mick McGeehin, wanted to see me. Of course, he did not know what it was about, but that was him—he would say that anyway whether he knew or not. The next day I headed into the camp; my leave from the UN was nearly up, and I had already applied for twenty-one days' annual leave to give Sheila a break, which would take me up to the school holidays. So I knocked on his door and entered. I had never met the man before; he was native to Donegal. Coming from Letterkenny, he had the look of a man who was forewarned, as he sat behind the desk, enquiring about my wife and the new baby. He was only the messenger, and I knew that. He said I had been selected by the battalion to go to Athlone on an NCO refresher course and that my annual leave was cancelled. A thousand thoughts ran through my mind. This was a course introduced a number of years earlier for personnel who were embedded for years in offices and had lost touch with, let's say, the word of command. Here I was standing, having instructed officers and NCOs, been fully operational at home, and with six tours of duty in Lebanon with UNIFIL behind me, so it was obvious what was happening. The knife was being sharpened, and I could feel it touching my back. It would be only a matter of time before the battalion commander, Lt. Col. P. J. Keane, stuck it in with all the power he could muster in his right arm. "You're to report to the CQMS in the morning for joining instructions before heading to Athlone." Still dazed as I was, he meekly asked, "Have you any problem with that?" Anticipating a barrage of abuse, he gathered himself tightly in the chair for the reply.

"Tomorrow," I reply. "No problem, sir, 10:00 a.m., no problem."

Somewhat shocked and relieved with my reply, he dismissed me. The one thing you needed as an NCO was to be fast on your feet at thinking; as I walked to my car in the car park, a thousand issues were resolved. The next day as I walked in the gate, Orderly Sergeant Gabby Fitzgerald, who had transferred up to Donegal from the Army Ranger wing in the Curragh some years earlier, was slagging me. I went to the medical aid post and reported sick. I attended the local surgery and was seen by Dr. Martin Coyne, a man about the same age as myself. I informed him of my plans and asked for his assistance with time off; when he heard my story, he agreed to assist me, so back to the camp I went. When Gabby enquired as to how I got on with the doctor, I told him I got eight over fifty-two in the heavy role, meaning that I got eight weeks off, and so the course was set. I had decided to open a garden centre in Strabane, across the border from Lifford in County Tyrone. John, my eldest son, was studying horticulture in Green Mount College. I had all the materials to get started; now the plan needed to be executed. I worked day and night at the project, employing Danny Shields, RIP, an ex-soldier from many years earlier. He was a local contractor with a pair of hands like shovels. Danny could do anything and not rip you off. Doctor Coyne kept me going with time off during the summer. The P. J. Keane issue was never resolved, as he was promoted to colonel, but I was not prepared to let go. I went to Doctor Jim McDaid, a local TD who was in the opposition at the time and told him the background, and he said he would make representation on my behalf. On June 14, 1995, Minister for Defence Sean Barratt, TD, issued a decree letter (see Appendix) making one finding and another letter dated June 29 (see Appendix) making a different finding. That said it all for me. I think at that point I made a subconscious decision to revisit the whole Seoige Joyce case, but at the same time tried to set up my business, and everything else had to go on the back burner (see Appendix).

Doctor Coyne had run his course with me, so I had to make myself available to the army doctor, Gerry Kerr. I always felt that being straight with somebody was better, so again I made my case to him. I had to be sure this project was going to work, as with a young family, I had no recourse if things went wrong. My first line to Doctor Kerr was, "How many times in your career as an army doctor have you seen me?" to which he agreed that I was one of the better performers. Of course he knew my history with the battalion commander, Lt. Col. P. J. Keane, so whether out of sympathy or otherwise, he kept me going along on sick leave with full pay. There were very genuine men in the army, and nobody liked to see someone get hurt or abused. By now I was well ahead with my plans for the garden centre, and instead of opening in March 1996, we were stocked, registered, and ready to trade by October 1995. Work was coming in thick and fast. I was not drawing down an income, as I was intending on drawing down my unemployment benefit once I had left the military, to give the business every chance. I was employing five people along with myself. Some lads were happy for you, seeing things as a success; on the other hand, you had spiteful types who no matter what field of work they were in would always be spiteful. Some of them I employed at landscape projects when they were off-duty from the army. The *Derry Journal* newspaper carried a centre-page spread editorial on the garden centre, pictures, the lot with me in it, and a certain NCO in Lifford sent it to army headquarters, making a complaint about me. Yes, it was hard to believe that I had employed him at one time. He was later to make a drunken enquiry one night at a function in the camp about where I got the money to start the garden centre. I replied, "Do you remember the job in Dungiven that we done? Well, that man paid me in Sterling money, when I had quoted him in Irish punts, which was an extra 30 per cent, and he gave me one hundred pounds to buy you a drink, which you weren't able to drink. That's where I got the money," indicating to him that I knew more than he thought he did.

My time was up; it was time to be boarded out, and I travelled to Finner with a tear in my eye. Finally I was leaving, and emotions swelled my eyes, thinking of those gone over to the other side, the characters from all over Donegal. It was like leaving holy orders. As I entered the office of the Command Medical Officer Lt. Col. Moriarity, who was in charge of the medical board and did five overseas tours with me, he welcomed me and enquired about my general health. Doctor Deeney, a captain, interrupted by saying, "Sir, this man is running a garden centre in Strabane," to which Moriarty replied, "We are not here to discuss his wealth; we are here to discuss his health." He proceeded to ask if I had applied for the VER (voluntary early retirement), which was a scheme introduced to offload personnel who were not performing operational duty. I replied, "I don't fit into that category, sir." (This scheme meant an extra £25,000 on top of normal gratuity.) He told me to have my application forwarded to his office; he was extending my sick leave for a further three months until the VER scheme came through; and I would be then finished whichever came first. Deeney nearly fell off his chair. Col. Moriarty then got up, shook my hand, and wished me all the best for the future.

As I arrived back in Lifford and proceeded into the company office to inform them about the CMO's decision, you could see the faces drop. My timing could not have been better with the start of the peace process in Northern

Ireland. Gerry Adams, John Hume, Albert Reynolds, and David Trimble were involved in talks about peace, the lot of them singing from the same hymn sheet, and when there was a slip up, there was always an Irish or English government minister at hand with the toilet roll. That's the way it looked to me—kids let on the loose, and when they did not get their own way, they sulked, and then Drumcree came along. I ask the question now, looking at it from the outside, but what did people in Europe, the United States, and the Middle East think? Now some fifteen years later, we have some semblance of normality, and thankfully most of those who were archenemies have grown up, spit the dummy out, and are acting like adults. The lines in the sand have been kicked up. We had the Nobel Peace Prize awarded to John Hume and David Trimble for their efforts. I am a recipient of the Nobel Peace Prize, as it was awarded to UNIFIL, and all men and women who served in the Lebanon were awarded a medal to reflect this; therefore, I have something in common with both of them.

Strabane is a funny town, mostly Catholic, with a strong Protestant influence in the town and the surrounding district. The name Sumner comes in handy in a place like Strabane, because they would not have a clue which foot you kicked with, and it's funny—my grandfather was a Protestant and my grandmother was a Catholic. I had a very open mind and needed to, to gardener both communities. Such is business, and thankfully I managed to do that.

There were two things Lebanon and Northern Ireland had in common at this time: talking and plenty of it. A Lebanese national named Hariri, who left Lebanon as a teenager and travelled to Saudi Arabia, had amassed a fortune only to be second in the wealth stakes to King Fahad of Saudi. He decided to come back to Lebanon to rebuild it; as they say, money talks, but this man was genuine about rebuilding the country and relationships among all factions of Lebanese society. I had the privilege to witness this first-hand. The Lebanese people referred to him as Mr. Lebanon; he donated $365 billion of his own wealth to the rebuilding of Lebanon—$1 billion for every day of the year. This figure today could be in multiples of twenty times as much. He ordained an Irish engineer as his prime architect, a person I had the pleasure of meeting in 1997. Likewise here in Northern Ireland, money was being poured into the peace process, but again, as an observer, it was clear that the political patriarchs were looking after their own backyards. To make a simple comparison, John Hume's city of Derry was transformed from a ghetto to a modern European city. Down the road in Strabane, some fourteen miles away, they got a new school and an Asda supermarket. Maybe a little of the same was happening in Lebanon.

In January 1997, while I kept in touch with friends in Lebanon, Fadi, Issam, and Hassan Farhat regularly phoned me and asked when I was coming out. I turned around one day and walked to the travel agent in town, which was packed with people booking their summer holidays. As I stood at the back, this assistant caught my eye and asked if I needed help. "Can you book me on a flight to Beirut?" As if in tandem, everyone looked around to see who this nutter was. It was an occasion I was looking forward to. It had been less than three years, but I was mad to get back. Lebanon had that effect on me, almost a terminal effect. I had to organise a visa, so I phoned the embassy in London, and they enquired who I was and what my interest in Lebanon was. After informing them of my details, it was just a matter of calling into Kensington Palace Gate Street, and twenty minutes later I had my visa. I had to stay overnight in a hotel in Heathrow. Seventy-five pounds was the tariff in 1997, which was expensive then, and for the likes of me, opulence was the state of the place. I was up at 4:00 a.m., bath and down for breakfast, which was self-service. There were these guys piling their plates with enough to feed ten men (*greedy bastards,* I thought). On checking out at 5:00 a.m., I handed in my room card, only to hear the desk assistant ask me if I wanted to settle my bill. I told him that I had last night, to the interjection of "Breakfast, Mr. Sumner." I reached for the loose change in my pocket as the printer totalled my invoice. The calm voice stated, "That will be twenty-eight pounds, thank you." This was capitalism at its best.

I flew with Cyprus Airways, which is, I have to say, one of the best airlines I ever travelled with. When you asked for a drink, they left the litre bottle of whiskey with you. In Larnicia, Cyprus, we landed, and there was about a two-hour wait for a connecting flight to Beirut. So after climbing to about 25,000 feet and a direct descent, I think the flight was twenty-five minutes in total. So here I was back in Lebanon at last, but on a different level. Little did I know I was coming down with an infection, hence all the whiskey in trying to suppress it. In through emigration, my passport was checked, and two men in civilian attire beckoned me toward a room; it was Syrian secret security, wanting to know why I was travelling to Lebanon. Luckily, I had my old UN ID card with me, and I told them that I was meeting friends, Fadi and Issam Farhatt, who were at the airport waiting for me. After an exchange in Arabic, which seemed heated at times, they allowed me through. I asked Fadi what the conversation was about, and Fadi dismissed it by referring to them as "stupid Syrian bastards." As we travelled through Beirut, the sheer semblance of what a civil war was will forever be etched in my mind. The Green Line was just a disaster zone with every building raked with tank, missile, and heavy machine gunfire on both sides of the road. I had never seen this before, except on video. This was the nearest to a living hell I ever experienced, and to mark the occasion I had landed on the first day of Ramadan, the Islamic period of fasting, which lasts for one month. Now, as I was a guest of Fadi's family for ten days, I had to act fast.

After all the introduction and translations, as Fadi's mother, Miriam, and father, Ali, did not speak English, we had *shi,* and then it was time for bed. I was in an apartment in downtown South Beirut, a massive built-up area controlled by the Shia Hezbollah. At 4:00 a.m., with dogs barking and the sound of what seemed like thousands of women and children whining and crying, I was wide awake. Heavy in the chest from my infection, I beckoned Fadi to get up and go for a walk; it was daybreak, after all. Fadi's father was a captain in the Lebanese police, so it was obvious that he informed our protectorates of my arrival and my proximity to the glorious spiritual leader, Sheik Mohamad Hussain Fadata, who lived on the next block. Because of the fast, there was no morning coffee, but I was more intent on finding a pharmacy. We left the apartment and started to roam the streets. It was amazing that at 4:30 a.m. the sun was up, and even in January it was twenty degrees Celsius. People were everywhere, most of them looking at me as if I was either a Martian or a day release from the local mental institute. Travelling around the block, the power left my legs when I saw a checkpoint manned by uniformed Hezbollah fighters, M16 fully kitted out, maybe six or seven of them. It was obvious they were protecting this massive complex with more satellites and aerials on a building than I had ever seen before. The looks on their faces seemed to indicate that they already knew of my existence, and they nodded for us to pass through. Fadi whispered, as we passed Fadata's house, "Some house." At about 5:30 a.m., we came upon a pharmacy. The guy could speak perfect English, and he prescribed a course of antibiotics for a five-day period, along with Ventilin tablets to relieve the congestion in my chest. Great, no prescription, no doctor; my time in Beirut was organised chaos. I went to the Imperial Hotel in Hamra, which is central Beirut, and I was able to organise a ten-day stay for the price of five, allowing me to stay with Fadi's family every other night, doing Ramadan and getting off my head the other nights, which was quite an experience as I look back on it now. Fadi used to take me to East Beirut, which is generally Christian.

The Flying Geese was a pub renowned for use by the Irish soldiers; that day, there were about twenty-five Dubs who were there on a sixty-hour pass. It was just my luck, I thought, *just keep out of the way and let them be to themselves.* Unfortunately, this was not to be the case; two of them in their forties, with shaved heads, studs, and earrings in the left lobe, tattooed from head to foot, were taking a keen interest in me at the bar. I knew if things got out of hand, it would be the twenty-five of them whom I would be faced with.

One of them by the name of George approached me, asking me about my nationality.

"Irish," I said.

"You're not Irish."

I reached for my passport, something I carried with me at all times, lest I be stopped by the Syrians, who were at every annex of the city. "There you are," I said. This guy was off his head; notwithstanding the amount of drink he consumed, I got the impression of drugs. "Listen," I said, "you are in Toulun, the village of A Company as I knew it three years earlier. I have been in Brachit and Haddata serving with UNIFIL," making a limited exposure of my army career. I did not go into the full number, rank, and name.

"You're CIA," he called out. This was getting ridiculous. Again I tried to reassure him that I was Irish. Then in a louder tone he said, "You're Mossad."

That was it, I had to act. The bar was full, mostly Arabs. The one person who would not have been asked for identity would be Mossad. Reaching for straws and an escape plan, I said, "George, do you know Martin McGuinness? Would you like me to organise an interview with him for you?"

Gone like a shot he was. Fadi suggested we leave, but I said no, let's have another drink. I could sense George's eyes biding down on me as he briefed his friend of his discovery. I glanced in his direction only to see his fixation of me quickly removed to an indifferent gaze elsewhere. A hairy moment, but nonetheless very diplomatically extracted from.

Fadi took me to see for the first time the Palestinian refugee camps of Sabra and Chatibla, policed by the Lebanese army; the men on the inside were not allowed out, only the women and only to beg on the streets. We have all seen beggars, but believe me this was something different. I learned a lot about Lebanon in those ten days; it was so historic to see everything that could not be seen during our service with UNIFIL. My time was punctuated every other day; first thing in the morning down to the local Starbucks for coffee and yesterday's *Daily Mirror* newspaper, glancing at the local Naomi Campbells, and then it was a planned trip somewhere with Fadi. Before, local Lebanese were restricted to their own areas, so at twenty-two years old, this was a new experience for him as well. The only intimidating area I was in was the Chouf Mountains, mainly populated by the Druze people, a religion I know nothing about, but they knew a stranger in their midst, so you did not hang around up there. Fadi took me down to Brachit, where I struck up old acquaintances. Comdt. (now promoted) Joe Gaffney greeted me at the camp and invited me in for lunch, and then out to Post 6–28 in Shaqoura, where I observed one of the McLaughlins from Lifford, gathering up cigarette butts with a sandbag. I walked up and tapped him on the shoulder, saying, "McLaughlin, pick it up a bit, you're not in Lifford now." As he turned around, I can safely say I have never in my life seen a person more startled. Having the crack again with the lads was once again my renewal; after all, I knew most of them. I suppose from their perspective I had to be a nutter. Where else would one go for holidays that did not have a swimming pool, bar, and the appropriate count of bikini-clad beauties other than Lebanon? One of the sights that will remain with me was a monument outside the Lebanese Ministry of Defence, about 100 to 150 feet high. It was a column of concrete about five metres square with every known weapon of war from an AK 47 to a Sherman tank.

Ten days goes by very quickly; it was totally different and a great experience, but it was time to say goodbye. I had seen a change and sensed a positive air in the country, because of Harrarri, the new kid on the block. As I said, I met this mountain of an Irish man recruited as the project engineer in Saudi by Harrarri. We had a few drinks together; I would put him at no more than thirty-five to thirty-seven years of age. He had to be special for his employer; I did get to see the fruits of his work in 2004 and 2005, and Beirut became some city.

I kept in touch with the Farhats by phone; it was always Fadi's ambition to travel to Ireland, but it was his cousin Fadi who eventually got a visa, for only three months. Fadi came to my home for a few weekends. He was working in a chipper in Athlone and attending Mary O'Rourke's clinic every week looking for a work permit; with her being the minister for education, you would think that she of all people could get the work permit organised. Fadi was in Ireland almost two years when he rang me to say he was coming up for the weekend and asked if I could collect him off the bus in Ballyboefy that Friday. Little did I know, nor did Fadi tell me, that he had handed over €2,000 to a girl from Athlone who lived in Derry, Northern Ireland, for a sham registry office marriage. The only thing I knew was I was to drop him off at the Guild Hall in Derry where he was meeting friends and he would see me that evening before getting back on the bus. After arriving back at the garden centre, about an hour later, I took a phone call from a solicitor in Derry; he was Fadi's appointed legal aid attorney. Fadi was now a guest of her Majesty and resident in McGilligan Prison in County Derry. I was travelling twice weekly to McGilligan visiting Fadi; his solicitor applied for political asylum to postpone any deportation. I had faxed every government minister, even the late Dermot Early, who at that time was in the army headquarters, but nobody could do anything. I even managed to get Mary O'Rourke's home number, and I phoned her on a Saturday morning. "What idiot took him across the border?" was her reply, and, for the want of it, that was the sum total of the Irish effort. Fadi had worked for the Irish since he was twelve years of age, cooking, cleaning, and general everyday work; now nobody gave a shit. He was incarcerated for seventy-two days, when one day a customer, Sam Martin, came into the garden centre.

Sam was a retired councillor here in the North of Ireland, a Unionist by tradition, but nonetheless a fair gentleman. He was connected to the very top. Sam remarked, "You seem very down and out," and after explaining Fadi's dilemma and the fact I was concerned he would self-harm, I asked Sam if there was anything he could do. I was really clutching at straws. Sam listened and said, "If you don't get a phone call in the next forty-eight hours, there is nothing that I can do."

I sensed a lifeline, no matter how minute. I thanked him, and Sam went his way. I don't think I charged him for what he came in for. The next day while out merchandising plants, the phone rang, and I ran in. "Strabane Garden Centre," I said.

A husky voice inquired, "Could I speak with Mr. Frank Sumner?"

"Who's that?"

"Ken McGinnis," was the reply.

"Ken who?" I said, at the same time realising the connection. I perked up as the conversation ratcheted up.

"I have arranged a pass for you with the governor of McGilligan Prison. I want you to go down and reassure that young man that his plight will soon be over. I am having a meeting with the Irish foreign minister tomorrow, and I would consider it most likely he will be released in the next few days." He then struck up a conversation about my past military career, as he was a major in the now-disbanded UDR. Today he sits in the House of Lords.

I travelled to McGilligan Prison to give Fadi the good news, but he was despondent and could not muster any hope. It really was an effort to get him to hold on and believe. Two days later, the PSNI removed Fadi from McGilligan Prison and handed him over to the gardai in Dundalk. From there he was given one hundred euros and a bus ticket to Dublin with an address to go to on arrival. His photo was taken, and within twenty minutes he was issued with his permanent work pass. Fadi built a lovely bungalow ten miles outside Athlone, where he is married with three sons.

As an ex-NCO, you were considered an honorary member of the NCO mess, so using the privilege kept you up to date with everything in the army, as if you never left. This was the case right up until the camp in Lifford closed in February 2009 under the government cutbacks as a result of the deep recession. Now the bond was severed. There was nothing greater on Christmas morning than going into the camp for the morning mass and then the bar, so December 2008 was bleak. The Irish Army finished in Lebanon in 2002 after Israel made a complete withdrawal. Hezbollah was now a working part of the government and the main military force in Lebanon. In May, under the cover of darkness, every last Israeli was gone from Lebanon, leaving their allies, the DFF, high and dry. Most of them, with no other choice, fled to Israel; others who wanted to remain in Lebanon handed themselves over to the Lebanese authorities, where they were sentenced to jail, only to serve a rehabilitant period. Lebanon now had jurisdiction right up to the international border, and Hezbollah families that had not met in more than twenty-five years became reunited. Commerce was reborn, and Southern Lebanon was to receive an injection of pace on the rebuilding of its infrastructure, roads, schools, and commercial business. People who had spent their entire lives outside the country were coming back in droves. Though the Irish withdrew after twenty-four years, UNIFIL remained and Lebanon was not out of the woods yet.

10

Strabane Garden Centre—an Uneasy Start and Micky Walker Rekindles Lebanon

Business was a new challenge, and as I built it up over the years, I was to learn fast that discipline outside in civilian streets is very much different to army life. Loyalty does not exist. My first two years were a partnership that went off the rails, costing me a lot of money to get rid of them. It reminded me of a saying my grandfather had, which was "the only ship that never leaves shore is a partnership." Then I had the unfortunate experience of bringing an ex-soldier into the business with me, as my son was still young. I needed a keyholder to look after things when I was out landscaping, which took me to Bunbeg, Dungloe, in west Donegal, and then as far as Birr in County Offaly, which was a one-off for my brother who had a restaurant in the area.

One night on entering Dooley's Hotel, I noticed about twenty ex-company commanders in civilian attire. All the eyes went skyward; no one wanted to be the first to speak. I asked for a glass of Guinness, when this voice from the rear called, "Barman, I will get that." He was the only one in uniform; it was Lt. Col. Tighe Crowe. All eyes descended from the ceiling, and one by one we all shook hands, now nothing wrong with any of them; it was just the officer thing. Tighe remarked about my van outside the gardai barracks, and he seemed to know a lot about me, even though he was now stationed in the Southern Command of the Army in Limerick. On enquiring about the volume of work I had down south, I told him I had two crews in Dublin working flat out all year; I could not have done more damage if I had thrown a grenade in the middle of them.

I had started to get suspicious about the staff member who was nearly two and a half years with me. Things did not seem to add up, so I brought a loss adjuster in one week when he was off. I was shattered at the top end of the scale. He had salted away £130,000 at the bottom end of the scale, and it was over £85,000. It's fair to say neither of us can be seen in the same parish alive at the same time.

A number of years ago, maybe in 2006, a guy called Micky Walker from Rockhill House called into the garden centre (see photo). He had served with me during the ill-fated Forty-Ninth Battalion and was Hughie Doherty's best friend. Micky served with me again with the Fifty-Ninth Battalion, the one and only guy I knew who was preoccupied with the events of April 27, 1981. Everything he said made sense and did happen. Micky was not going to allow this to slip into the annals of history. When he left the army, he applied to the Department of Defence for all records of the case under the Freedom of Information Act. On May 26, 2004, and June 9, 2004, as per letters (see Appendix), it is clear, under the act, that all records were not released. Micky passed all those records over to me, and they vary from

the letters from senior officers to diplomats and ministers. Having examined the records many times and placing them against the facts on the ground from that day, it is inconceivable that so many well-trained officers could come up with the same theory. I will attempt to set out in three stages why we should argue against the theory that has remained the only avenue pursued by military authorities. (See Appendix.)

Firstly, the so-called Iron Triangle was a massive area controlled by the PLO. Its area was from the city of Tyre on the west coast to Beauford Castle in the east. The crusader castle, well sighted, controlled vast areas within its range, the whole way south toward the Israeli border on the west coast, within five kilometres of the border. There was a deployment of up to fifteen thousand PLO operating in this area, and before we go any further, this grouping was no IRA—it was a military unit, well organised, well equipped, with anti-aircraft capability, ground-to-air surface missiles, and a transport echelon. This is what the fourth largest army in the world invaded against in 1978, when it only pushed toward the Litani River. On its retreat, the PLO regained its position of strength.

Secondly, military planning, as with all armies the blueprint to all military operations, is TEWT (tactical exercise without troops). All armies use it in the form of a sand table with all military positions placed, showing strengths, weaknesses, and likely avenues of approach. On the other side would be enemy deployments, and all planning is adhered to by this means. So let's look at the plan from a PLO point of view. Let's say we want to take this observation post out and look at the options as a planner: would you deploy men over open ground where they would be exposed from the air and have been observed from the checkpoint, especially with the IDF in the skies, bombing surrounding villages, or would you send in a two- to three-man group in a car who could have done the job and made a hasty retreat without any exposure, all this if the observation post was strategic? Remember I said at the beginning of this story, on the morning after the PLO liaison officer with his UN ID card signed by Lt. Gen. Callaghan arrived at Dynater from Tyre by car, why did he not come up the wadi?

Thirdly, I would like to draw your attention to military documents that were based on reports made by the authorities in Lebanon at the time. To the best of my knowledge, no statements were ever taken from the personnel in Dynater on that day. On November 3, 1998, from DFHQ in Dublin, Comdt. O'Neachtain in public relations points out in a letter that the two men were posted. That's to imply they were taken to the observation post by a higher authority, normally an NCO. This is incorrect, as they walked down the road from Dynater House at approximately 8:00 a.m., a walk of approximately one kilometre. It also goes on to state they were visited at 1520 hours and that both privates were present. This is incorrect again, as there was an aerial bombardment going on where surrounding villages were being bombed by Israeli F-16 fighter aircraft. The SOP in such situations is groundhog, and the minimum security requirement would be the non-movement of personnel. This can be borne out by a memo from the director of operations, Col. Gerry McNamara, dated September 5, 2001, where he stated that on April 27, 1981, "there was considerable amount of air activity from the Israelis in that area." Comdt. O'Neachtain's letter goes on to further raise two points: (1) who was responsible for the kidnapping and (2) what was the fate of Joyce? These are the most important issues when the facts of these points are not presented properly. How can we ever deduce what really happened to Joyce?

Another issue I would like to draw to the reader's attention is maybe there is someone about whom the highest authorities might like to make a statement at a later stage. While Dynater remained under the control of the Forty-Ninth and Fiftieth Battalions, from my knowledge, the Ghanaians were in it for one tour of duty. After that, there was no further UN presence in the village, though the political situation had changed after the 1982 invasion by the Israelis, wherein most but not all PLO were removed from the area. The question that has to be asked is why did Dynater become so much less strategic? Here I would like to mention a letter from Eamonn Lafferty, the president of PDFORRA, the army union, to Mr. Michael Smith, TD, minister for defence, dated September 21, 2000 (see Appendix). Lafferty, within the letter's reference to a situation, says, "You may be aware of a situation, which developed some years ago when the Joyce family did not wish to have any further interaction with the Defence Forces on this matter." Could the department explain that, or does the Joyce family now know something that the rest of us don't? I have listed the facts throughout; again, I want to further another fact. In some correspondence, it's stated Private Joyce may have been injured and died of his wounds at a later stage. This is not true. Again, it's stated Private Doherty was shot three times in the back. He was not; he was shot once in the back, and then two rounds were fired into the back of his neck, with scorch marks on the skin, indicating a shooting from close proximity to finish him off. As I asked in the beginning, why have we not had an enquiry where all persons present on the day be called to tell their side of events? I think that's more important now after the current minister for justice and defence, Mr. Alan Shatter, TD, apologised to the families of Corporal Fintan Henehan, Private Mannix Armstrong, and Private Thomas Walsh after twenty-five years for negligence by the Department of Defence.

A guy from Cork called Gerry Conroy, who had retired from the army as a corporal, set up a travel agency that specialised in tours of a military background, the likes of the Fields of Flanders, First and Second World War sites. He was now advertising in the army monthly magazine *An Cosantóir* with an organised tour to Lebanon, a ten-day trip costing about €1,300 with places being sold for up to fifty personnel. He had raised money for the Tibnin Orphanage, and he organised wreath-laying ceremonies, a ministerial dinner, and a Lebanese medal presentation, which was a big day organised in the town of Shaqoura on behalf of the government.

The crew were a typical motley group, and Sheila eventually relented and came along. Others included the widow of Gregory Morrow (murdered at Tibnin Bridge) and her partner, John Joe from Cork, now deceased (I believe he was a Congo veteran), and many others whose names I cannot remember. The lord mayor of Limerick also travelled—in total about thirty people. We spent three days in the south, and the remainder of the time was spent in Beirut as a base travelling north to Tripoli and the Bekaa Valley. This was interesting, as I had not been to this part of Lebanon before.

The days of the tour were long and hard but enjoyable. On one occasion, we were visiting the presidential palace. The coach was parked up, and Gerry gave an estimated time of departure to allow us to be back on the bus. Everywhere in Lebanon is on a hill, and this day the bus was at the top of one. John Joe, a man in his seventies, was struggling to get to the top. We were all outside the bus having a smoke when this guy from Cork said to me, "John Joe is related to Jesus Christ, you know."

"What?" said I.

He says, "With a pair of feet like that, he could walk on water."

I just laughed as John Joe had the biggest I had ever seen, must be size fifteen, maybe even sixteen.

Every night there was an organised event at some restaurant, with Lebanese music and belly dancers. The tour had a full schedule with breaks for shopping in Tyre and Beirut. It was great to meet old friends and to know they were doing well. On the day of the medal presentation in Shaqoura, I never seen such a turnout—half of Southern Lebanon was there, hundreds of schoolchildren, a band, elements of the Lebanese army, the UN, and some serving Irish army personnel. There were TV cameras and stages, and the governor of Nabitiyiaa made the medal presentation. The hospitality shown that day would have taken tears from a stone; there was no doubt how much they appreciated our service.

A day in Balbeck in north Lebanon was a great experience. We saw old ruins predating the Roman Empire. How they survived the Middle East conflict is remarkable, and one could see how Lebanon in the future would be a great tourist attraction.

Back home again after our ten-day excursion, everyone had enjoyed themselves and thought the trip was very good value for the money. Gerry asked me to keep in touch and to promote the event in Donegal for him for the following year.

11

The Boom Years Now in Full Swing

I was building a new house, a dream project; my business was booming, and landscape work was full throttle. A customer of mine by the name of P. J. Doherty was giving me good work. He owned the Cruit Hotel in Gweedore, and I had worked for him on a previous occasion. As a self-made millionaire in the construction industry, he was no man's fool; obviously I had impressed him with my application to the job, so a lot of work was coming in from him and his son, Hugh Martin. I couldn't make half of myself, so I organised my son, John, to be the project manager, handling events on the ground. By this stage, I was travelling to Italy to purchase directly from the Italian nurseries and a guy called Franco Covelli from Pistoia, the nerve centre of Italian nurseries. I was importing some class plants. I think at the time I became specialised in the unusual and mature plants, and people came from all directions to buy from me.

The house was nearly finished and needed to be furnished. There was only a certain amount I could take from the old bungalow; the rest had to be bought—you could say a complete new fit out. Ireland was booming, and so was the price of everything to buy, so I hatched a plan to travel to Beirut with Gerry Conroy. I had been talking to some friends in Lebanon and realised I could purchase everything I needed and ship it back to Ireland, so I made my plans. Nigel Brown, who was Protestant and in a long-term relationship with my sister-in-law, expressed an interest in the trip. He had served in the UDR, a regiment in her Majesty's service; not withstanding that, I did not want to be responsible for him. I passed Gerry's details to him, and lo and behold he made the booking, so come May 2005 we were heading to Lebanon. I briefed Nigel of the likely setup and informed him of my purpose in travelling. We travelled from Belfast to London and met up with the main group of travellers before we boarded the plane to Beirut—only this time there was a sense of anxiety.

Just five days earlier, the prime minister, Mr. Hariri, and six of his body-guards had been killed by a roadside bomb. Tensions were high, as here was a man who had rebuilt Lebanon and especially Beirut and had become known to thirteen different groups in Lebanon as Mr. Lebanon. He was trying to shake off the shackles of Syrian domination and rid Lebanon of outside influence; this approach would make the task of uniting the indigenous population an even easier task. Lebanon was a theatre that had Israeli influence within certain Christian groupings, Syrian influence within the PLO and the mainly Sunni Muslim groupings, Iran with its ability to payroll the Hezbollah, and nowhere in the world can escape the US greenback and its influence. This was one of the biggest events in Lebanese history and one that was not going to go away. You could sense it in the people, the air of despair, the feeling they were going to be led down the road once again of civil war. Make no mistake about it, not since 1975–76 had one issue ever been seen as more serious than the events of that week. Hariri's death had repercussions all over the world; here was a man who, before he entered politics, could stride into the French president's office uninvited. This was the situation for Lebanon: old men declare war and young men fight it. Behind the scenes, ordinary citizens from university graduates to mechanics from all sides were gathering to see if there was some way they could avert the inevitable. A rally was organised, calling for all foreign forces, in particular Syria, to be removed from the country.

Gerry Conroy was anxious about the upcoming events and the current situation as it then was. A friend of mine from the south of the country came up to Beirut to help me get the furniture organised. Nigel was not too fond of Gerry's attitude, so he wished to stay in my company. My friend Ali knew where to take me in the east of the city—Furniture City, a building about fifteen storeys high. It started with bathroom fittings at the top, with electrical goods at the bottom. I spent the first day viewing and pricing. It seemed great value for the money, and then I was to organise the shipping. I had filled a container with everything I needed for the house, including an American top-loading washing machine and tumble dryer, and the whole load, including the shipping, cost £10,000, a savings of more than 60 per cent.

The massive rally in Martyrs' Square was organised for the following Saturday; in the meantime, it was off to view the bomb site. My God, I had never seen anything like it in my life. Through the length of the entire street, about eighty metres wide with a depth of thirty metres, lay the mangled remains of about six SUVs and the services of electricity and water and sewage spewing everywhere. There was a police cordon around the area, but it didn't stop the crowds gathering to look on in awe. It seemed like we were there for hours trying to take in the enormity of the situation. Eventually we moved away from the site, as a drink and something to eat were now on the agenda. Right along the promenade was the Hard Rock Café; it seems like there is one in all big cosmopolitan cities. The opulence of the place was surreal, with iced glasses and Budweiser; Kentucky-fried chicken was complimentary, and the beer was still cheaper than back home but more expensive than the local downtown bar. The barman, I had gathered, was Druze, and in perfect English he informed us that Bin Laden owned the pub, which was another bit of nostalgia to add to the event. When I enquired as to who would want to kill Hariri, he told me elements from within were blaming the Syrians. But he went on to further reveal that the prime minister had spent almost $1 million on sophisticated electronic and computerised jamming devices, manned by an engineer in his extended bomb-proof Humvee, and that the only people who could bypass the equipment were the people who invented it, namely the United States. It seemed like they were trying to have a go at everybody now that they had kicked ass in Iraq. With Syria being controlled by the Bathist Party, the same group that ruled Iraq, it would be opportune to stand up for a small country like Lebanon and hit Syria for its occupation.

Anyway, Saturday had arrived early. Gerry briefed everybody at breakfast that he had been advised by the local police and intelligence units that it would be best for us to be outside the city for the day. With that, he decided to take everyone to Sidon, Lebanon's second largest city, for the day; however, I had other things to do, and so Nigel decided to remain with me. The rest got on the bus, looking back at the two of us as if we were mad to remain in Beirut, and maybe we were.

Later in the morning, we could view the crowd coming into the city, all heading in the same direction, in the thousands, carrying Lebanese flags and the flags of every militia in the country. It was as if the country was locking down. Nigel and I decided to have a few beers and relax, which was better than the get up on the bus, get off the bus scenario. The crowds were now swelling, and along our way came five female students dressed in Western attire. They stopped to enquire of our nationality and invited us to attend the rally. I declined, as I felt this was a Lebanese day and a Lebanese issue, but they were having none of it, adorning us with the regalia that everyone was wearing, a sash and a flag. Now, with Nigel being a Protestant, I quipped, "That's the nearest you will ever see of me wearing a sash," and so off we went, with the girls very happy with their new converts. Martyrs' Square was the arena; I had been there in the evening before to view the grave of Hariri, which was some sight in itself. There were thousands who came from every corner of the country to pay their respects, being ushered by police and stewards, with a queue of about eight deep and about three hundred metres long. With only a limited amount of people being allowed in at a time, Nigel was not too keen on the idea, but when I was there I wanted to be part of the moment. Eventually, as we reached the crypt, which was very open, I observed the prime minister's final resting place adorned with lilies like I had never seen before, and on the opposite side lay six other graves with large framed photos of the six bodyguards killed along with him; all looked like fine young men, and their graves also were adorned with flowers. I don't know why, but I got a sense that this was a defining moment.

Back at the rally, Nigel and I were making plenty of new friends. We were in the square from about noon until 5:00 p.m. There were free water stations all over the place, a very large stage with several key speakers, large TV screens like we would see at concerts, positioned at key sites, and TV crews from all over the world. There were up to one million people in Martyrs' Square on that day. The speeches were about reconciliation, but the main focus was the withdrawal of the Syrian army, and the next day the Syrians were gone. Lebanon learned one lesson that day; people power was better than all the weapons in the world.

So with my business completed, we joined in with the rest of the tour, which turned out as a repeat of the previous year's trip. One night at the bar I overheard Irish accents, and, after I introduced Nigel and myself, I discovered that they were a film crew from the Irish TV channel TG4, in Lebanon to make a film about the story of Private Seoige Joyce. I was intrigued and decided to say nothing as tongues get loose with the effect of alcohol. They had with them as an advisor a retired lieutenant colonel who was based in the Irish HQ camp, Camp Shamrock, at the time of the incident back in April 1981 as a signal officer. Now, as I listened to the same rhetoric being spewed out as it had down over the years, I felt it only right when I got the film director in the toilet to brief him of exactly what happened on that fateful day. Somewhat shocked and in a sense of disbelief, he asked if I would partake in the film, to which I replied, "Definitely not." I don't even like having my photo taken, let alone taking part in something for the television, and anyway I was heading for a visit to Chiam Prison the next day. I wished them all the best with the shoots.

Off to Chiam, which was an old Lebanese garrison barracks converted to a prison by the Israelis during their occupation. It was now in the hands of Hezbollah, which had transformed it into a museum. After an admission charge of five dollars, I received a DVD showing the Hezbollah attacking IDF compounds during the occupation, a Hizi scarf and a tape, and then there was the guided tour. This was a prison one could end up in without a trial, and one such person was a girl of eighteen who was lifted in one of the villages in 1981. Her detention consisted of twenty-three hours of every day in a cell six feet long, four feet wide, and five feet high. She was released by Hezbollah in 2002, with severe osteoporosis; she was five feet, ten inches. Other cells were larger, occupied by five or more prisoners, mainly male. Their conditions did not live up to the Geneva Conventions' standard, let alone any standard. There were torture rooms, and we were advised that there were between three and five hundred poor mortals incarcerated at any one time. I thought of the Holocaust and how anybody could ever do such acts to another human being, let alone an Israeli. Feeling worse for the experience, we headed back toward Tyre city, calling at the famous Gate Twelve. Ali asked if I wanted to see it. It was actually in Israel but bordered by Lebanon, and when you drove up, there was a triangle of roads at the point, divided only by the breadth of a turning area. On the left side was a highly reinforced elevated Israeli position with aerials, satellite dishes, and mobile security cameras. Behind this was a very large security fence that ran the length of the border between the two countries. Just across the road was a compound occupied by the Hezbollah, adorned with the same materials, and then just up the right-hand side was a UN post occupied by the Indian Army contingent. We got out of the car, watched by all the elements. This was like a scene from the film *Dodge City;* this was the place that rained down on us in the Irish area of operations with their artillery 155 shells that caused us so much grief and damage. We could see it from our positions, so to be standing there in the flesh after all these years made me feel like going over to the Israelis and giving them a piece of my mind, but I diplomatically decided against this idea.

"Come on, Ali," I said, "Let's get the fuck out of here. It gives me the creeps."

As we headed down to Tibnin Bridge, having called into Brachit to see old friends, there was an UNTSO land cruiser parked up, with Comdt. Paddy Ryan on the road, as if he were waiting for me. We stopped, got out, and shook hands.

"Reggie, I heard you were out again," he said, making a joke about having a secret woman out here.

"I wish," I said.

He then mentioned the TG4 film crew and literally told me in a nice way not to go on film.

"I have no intention," I said, keeping the conversation jovial. It was time to go for a drink, so we said our goodbyes.

Paddy Ryan had served in Lifford Barracks for a time, and he was on a two-year stint with this observer group covering the Middle East. As we made our way down toward Tyre city, I paused in my mind. How did he know that I was in Chiam and why? It was obvious the retired officer made contact with him; this maddened me, and on reaching the hotel I told the film director that I was now interested. He told me that he would use me, but what he could show was subject to a censor. I don't think the retired officer was impressed.

Off we headed to Dynater. It was almost twenty-four years since I had been there, and I could not believe the changes—massive new buildings and a new mosque that was constructed from black polished granite. It was obvious that a lot of wealth had since poured into the town. On this occasion, due to expansion, we were able to reach the observation post by walking just about one hundred metres. One had to be careful still, as the Israelis dropped thousands of cluster bombs during the 1982 invasion. The area was a little different, with mature olive trees planted by the land owner, so it took me a while to figure out ground orientation, but not so for the ex-officer. He went straight into his script. I thought, *How strange this was for a man who was probably never there before.* After rechecking—and not withstanding that I did not want to embarrass him—I pointed out his mistake, which was about fifty metres out. Again he pointed out the likely area where the armed elements came from, and it was at this point I preferred my tactical awareness against his. The TV crew did not know what we were talking about, but got the gist of it. I said it would have been impossible for them to approach from that direction without being seen, and if the two lads on the OP had seen them from a distance, they would have reported it and made a withdrawal from their position either under instruction or from their own merit. This visit to the area only reinforced my military opinion that the gunmen made their approach from the rear and hence the village; as we stood on this plateau, our eyes commanded the area for up to two kilometres all around, except to the rear, where there was a restricted view down to one hundred metres. Anyone forward of the position would have been picked up long before they reached the OP. Many military writings over the years point to a sandbag position; however, no such construction was ever there. Previous duties had gathered stones and rocks to build a defence structure that could be used from the prone position. Another factor was that I was involved in the search of the area forward of the position, and on returning toward the OP no one could figure out how the two lads would not have seen an approach. Again, department letters state that Private Doherty was shot three times in the back, and in one letter it states he was shot three times in the chest; however, forensics found—and the platoon commander, Lt. Hugh Carthy, who identified the body, told me—that Hugh received one shot in the back, had staggered eleven paces, and collapsed. Though the shot was fatal, he was still alive, and the assassins fired another two shots at close range into the back of his neck, as there were scorch marks or powder burns on his body. I can assure you that Private Doherty would have been highly alert or on the ball, in military speak. He was standing doing his job; he was young, focussed, and a well-trained soldier. Nobody was going to creep up on him, and, as I stated earlier, with the aerial bombardment going on in the area at the time, the PLO was not going to break its cover as its members would surely know that, with the heat-seeking technology that the IDF had, their movement would have been spotted by the F-16 jets. On the other hand, Amal from the village would have felt more comfortable, as the IDF knew it was a UN OP, and, as such, any movement from the village would have been picked up or seen as a UN patrol. So one has to examine the events that took place during the Forty-Eighth Battalion's tour of duty in Lebanon. There were three civilians shot behind the mosque in Brachit, and two males found in the wadi between Brachit and Byjhoun, with their hands tied behind their backs and shot in the head. Where were they from? Had they any association with Dynater? If what I state is the truth, then serious questions need to be answered.

12

Business Is Flying, and China Is Calling

I arrived back from Lebanon and had to get on with my life. An old friend, Austin Rouse, who sadly has since passed away, was well known in Strabane as a session musician and regularly came along to the garden centre. On one occasion, he commented on the TG4 programme, which had been aired. I told him what had taken place and how the programme was edited. "Write a book. You would be well able to do it," he said, and that comment spurred the idea in my head.

We were into 2006, and January is always a dead month in garden centres, so that's when I started writing. I got about seventy pages of notes done and then had to shelve it again due to work commitments in the office. Forget about the writing after that.

The year 2006 was my best year in business since I started out in 1995. We were looking at different options to invest in for the following year. My son, John, kept insisting on the idea that I get on a flight to China with a view to buying garden machinery. We did not at this stage have the Internet in the office, but I knew from the trade that Guangzhou was the place the Canton Fair was held, a big international trade show for the industry. A mate of mine, Seamie Boylan, who had been there several times, advised me to go at a different time, so the plan was put in place, and with flights and hotel booked I headed off.

§ § § § §

At this parallel, I must go back to Lebanon, back to Dynater, and examine the tactical deployment of troops to OP 622a. Let's imagine half a horseshoe facing outward, the ridge on the left as the high ground, surveying the plains and the wadi below it. Dynater was to the rear of the shoe, and along the shoe was the military police headquarters called Gallows Green. This had access from the rear to high ground. Further along the shoe was the village of Harris, which was in the Dutch contingent area of operations. There were several locations within Harris that would have given an even greater area for observation. At this stage, we have to look at UNIFIL operations. The decision to man these OPs would have been taken at the highest level of authority and passed down to the battalion level and onto company level, so somebody was responsible for sighting this OP. If you are going to isolate two private soldiers, you reduce the risk to their exposure at all times in assessing the situation; the points to note would be (1) the distance to back up and the reaction time and (2) their accessibility and cover. In any of the areas I pointed out, there were all of those things, but in Dynater, we had a civilian population between two men and their reinforcements back at platoon headquarters, an obstacle of almost one kilometre. At any time, that population was capable of cutting off the OP, so from a planning point of view it was a disaster waiting to happen. If a student on an NCO course made such a decision, he would have been returned to his unit as a failure, so then did the sighting of the OP have anything to do with the final military report on the murder? I tend to think it more than muddied the water; I am convinced a lot of questions would have had to be answered, so we can conclude the investigation that followed was always going to be flawed.

Robert Fisk, a world-renowned journalist based in Beirut for thirty years to cover the Middle East troubles, wrote an article for the *Defence Forces Review 2008,* which can be searched for on the Internet. In it, he rightly reviews the Battle of Attiri and goes on to write an article on the Doherty and Joyce tragedy, from the information he gained from the Irish. It's obvious to the reader that he did not go into investigative mode, as he would not have been familiar with the area. He goes on to state that he made enquiries with the PLO in the Beirut area and was met with a wall of silence. He mentions that in 1982, during the invasion by the Israelis, the IDF recovered the skeletal remains of a human body from a deep well and, fearing it may have been the remains of a missing IDF soldier, took it away for forensic testing, but, after discovering it was not the remains they were looking for, ploughed it back into Lebanese soil. The IDF was aware of Joyce as missing, and it would have been good propaganda for them to have handed over the remains to the UN if it could have been proved that the remains were indeed of Private Joyce. This would have shown the Israelis in a good light, so that raises the question, was there ever a skeleton found?

§ § § § § §

January 2007 I was in a plane flying over Amsterdam on an eleven-hour flight to Beijing, and after the in-flight meal and with four seats to myself, I reached into my pocket and took one of the sleeping pills that Austin Rouse gave me before I left. Hell, these were strong, as I never heard a thing for nine hours, when the cabin crew member shook me and advised me to prepare for landing. I was excited, arriving in China, at fifty-one years of age. Never as a child or in my adult life did I ever imagine being in China. From going through the process of gaining my visa from the Dublin embassy, I knew I was going to have a different experience than, say, going to Spain. The aircraft descended, and the landscape was bleak and dark brown, with not a blade of grass to be seen, trees arching in the wind, and the place totally bare and black. We hit the runway, here at last, and were removed by bus to immigration, where I never saw so many uniformed personnel. They were ever so strict; if they placed you in a position and you moved a step or two, left or right, they were over with you and physically put you back in place. I thought, *This was going to be a long two weeks.* Beijing was arctic cold. After clearing immigration, we then were bussed back to the same plane. It was then a further two-and-one-half-hour flight to Guangzhou. Such a stark difference this was from Beijing: the trees full of leaves (they never shed their leaves), the grass lush green, and a nice temperature of twenty-six degrees. I got a taxi and headed for the Canton Hotel, which ironically was in Beijing Street. Such luxury I had never seen for the value of the money paid, about twenty euros per night.

The first day was familiarisation, getting to know that quarter of the city, and then heading to the business centre of the hotel to organise an interpreter for fifty dollars per day. I briefed him as to what I was looking for—machinery manufacturers. He went home to peruse the Internet, arrived the next morning at 8:00 a.m., and off we went by taxi across the city. By midday, I was becoming frustrated by his efforts; he was taking me to every kind of sweatshop you could think of, so on realising that I was not happy, he had one last throw of the dice, and we arrived in Zhonzen. Now this was the real deal, a factory assembling garden machinery using real Honda engines. On a guided tour of the factory, they showed me the machines and their performance capabilities. They knew nothing about me, only that I was buying a container, with the view to setting up distribution in the UK and Ireland. This story line would ensure that I got the best machinery and spare parts. I had the business done in two days, shipping organised, money transferred, and my container due to port at the end of February or early March. I spent many an hour back at the hotel, working on the profit margins from the invoice that I was given; if all went well, this was going to be a piece of good business. Why had I not thought of this years earlier? I found the Chinese people very warm and excellent hosts. On realising that I had packed no shaving razors, I asked one of the management at the factory to get me some, and he went out and bought me a new electric razor and would not take any money for it. Shopping in China is not straightforward; if you go down one street and the first shop sells shoes, then all shops on that street sell shoes. I had almost eight days to take in the views and social life of this metropolis, throw in a bit of shopping, go for a few Chinese head massages, and then it was time to return home. I felt I had broken new ground, and a few excursions to China would make me financially secure. The return journey was by the same route, same routine, and the same four seats; I was that fresh when I arrived home. I drove my Jeep up home from Dublin, with presents for one and all, and the storytelling kept the air of conversation fresh for a few weeks. That spring was very busy, and I had met a new friend in China, a journalist named Lydia Chen, who was e-mailing me frequently and looking after my business with Zhonzen. I had bought a laptop for my son, which was in a Chinese programme, and she adjusted it to an English programme. That is how we met, and there was nothing else to it, other than she was a lady. My container arrived on March 15, and we set about merchandising, advertising, and selling. Business was frantic; I was selling about six machines a day, and I had in stock lawnmowers, long-reach hedge cutters, and different models of trimmers. Everything was going well. We were busy, and the summer went in very quickly. The downside of the garden centre is that a lot of capital is invested in stock; this reflects the quality of the business, but it never gets any easier. As my grandfather once said, "There no such thing as handy work."

On to 2008, the start of the recession. At first we did not notice too much, but it was everywhere when you turned on the television. The banks were in trouble, but we strived on as we mere mortals were the working bees. The weather was working against us, so any slowdown was attributed to that. I had now sold out all the lawnmowers but still had a fair supply of other machinery, and the thought of going back to China was mulling in my head. I was keeping an eye on the economy, and as the eternal optimist I could not see the breakdown of the economy on the scale that was to happen. One Saturday morning as we came to the end of the year, I realised my turnover was down considerably on the previous year; as we entered 2009, innovative and new approaches were needed. After all, people would still be looking after their gardens. However, it was more of the same—terrible weather and stock was being managed on a more sensible level: if I didn't have it, then I didn't have it. I still wanted to turn things around; it's a bit like the proverbial hole in the bucket—you have to plug it. The area bank manager was in one morning as a customer, asking how business was.

"It's crap," I said. "You are the very man in the right place to advise me. I am thinking of putting all my eggs in the one basket and going back to China. What would you advise?"

"Well," he said, "forty per cent of businesses have no access to cash, and the other sixty per cent has half sitting on the fence and the other half reinvesting in their business, and I think they will be the winners at the end of the day."

That was good enough for me, so China it was. I started to plan for the end of the year. I reflected on the idea of taking my eldest son out to show him the ropes, as I wouldn't always be available to travel. I spent a lot of time on the Internet, checking out nurseries in China and the logistics of importing plants, and I engaged with the Department of Agriculture and Rural Development. At first, I found them to be very helpful regarding Paysto Sanitary certificates, etc. Then I sourced nurseries in the Guangzhou district. I was bringing the plan together. It was at this point a friend of mine, Paul Madden, suggested that he would like to travel for the experience, and so a date was set for November, as it would be quiet in the garden centre. The planning, visas, and travel arrangements were all acted on, and this time the flights were via Paris to Guangzhou. Paul was excited about the trip, but I had reservations. John, my son, was keen, and I realised this was the first time I would travel with him as an adult anywhere.

We arrived in Guangzhou at a hotel based on economics, called the Silver Swan—not in the same class as the Canton, but still a four-star in Irish terms. It was like letting a kid into a sweet shop regarding John; he had loaded €1,100 on to my credit card. The exchange rate was about nine hundred Chinese dong to one hundred euros, which was a lot of money; with careful planning, it would last about three days. I gave him nine hundred dong, and the next morning he asked me for more, as how could I expect him to survive on forty-five euros a day? He had no concept of the exchange rate; after striking up a relationship with a young girl on the first day, it was obvious it was a pure waste of time bringing him out. He tried over the course of the two weeks to show an interest, but he really didn't care. I was grateful for Paul's presence, as he wanted to see the country and live the Chinese experience. In Zhonzen, there were some changes; the two partners had parted ways, and it looked like one had taken the manufacturing element with him. What was left was distribution and, yes, improved product. In 2007, I had bought seventy lawnmowers with a 5.5-horsepower Honda engine, but they were push-type. I did sell them but would have sold four times as many if they had been self-drive. My 2007 mower was retailed at £269, but the customer would have been prepared to pay one hundred pounds more for the self-drive model. So I was faced with the choice of three self-drive: a twenty-inch 5.5 HP, a twenty-two-inch 6.5 HP GXV Honda, and a twenty-three-inch aluminium 6.5HP GXV. The difference in the first and last was nearly double the price. I was impressed with the first mower, so sixty of them would have been good business. John made a big issue out of things, so for a quieter life I ordered twenty of each. Again, I was also interested in tractor mowers and ordered ten of the 15HP mulcher type. We purchased an array of machinery, including electric for the urban market, and again the process took two days to complete everything. Mr. Zhong said he would see us again on the evening of our departure. Searching the Chinese Internet, which is firewalled from the West, I was able to download the information I needed regarding the nurseries.

I made contact with Tom Che, who was the owner of Greenworld Nurseries. In fact, he was an agent who had perfect English. He arrived at the hotel and picked me up for a two-hour drive out of town to the nursery world. The Chinese have a policy of conglomerating all business together, like I said about the shoe shops. This was a massive area, with mouth-watering plants. After initially discussing the logistics of importing—the dormancy of the plants, the temperature-controlled container, light, and travel time—I was satisfied this was a deal worth making. We spent two days scouring, and I was conscientious of hardiness, so all specimens were chosen on that basis. Again, I looked at the profit margins, which were so exciting. During our tour one day, Tom had to go back to his office to sign off on some forms and asked if we minded. I said not at all, so we went back with him, and about thirty minutes later four Italians emerged, shocked at our presence. It was obvious they had been doing this for years and then forwarding the stock into the UK and Ireland. Paul looked at me; a business plan was already being hatched in my mind. If I could organise *en masse,* multitasking with Irish nurseries and garden centres, the flow of containers into Ireland and take a commission, while tying Tom Che down to an agreement, this would be a money cow. Everything was arranged, and I felt Tom was a good guy.

We spent the remainder of the trip going on day trips and going to an Irish pub called the Paddy Fields, where the food was top cuisine; after all, I wasn't very fond of the local food. Paul, on the other hand, would eat anything; I saw him eating frog legs, which was enough for me. It was time once again to return home, and my head was full of ideas, as this was all about commerce. Mr. Zhong came that evening to the hotel to personally see us off, giving us the use of his driver to take us to the airport.

My experience of the two trips to China was of a communist country with a capitalist system that allowed wealth to grow, but there was a high level of poverty. The one thing was everybody worked hard. Back home from a successful trip, it was down to business. I had a book or catalogue printed, did the pricing, and got in contact with every garden centre in the country, and times were going to be exciting. Christmas was on top of us, and we suffered a horrendous winter with heavy snowfall and severe frosts that destroyed the Christmas trade, but there was 2010 to look forward to. I was ever the optimist. However, January and February were also very poor months, and shipping around the world was slow and delayed. Things every day seemed to be getting worse, manufacturing and the construction industry were disintegrating, and the mortgage system and banking were imploding. Great Britain and Ireland were basket cases, with unemployment going through the roof, but *surely,* I thought, *if we get a good summer, we might be able to arrest the situation.* Garden trade magazines were spewing out the rhetoric that we were recession-proof. My first container arrived in early April. The department was in contact and would have to examine the load, even though I had the necessary certificates. *No problem,* I thought, but with it being high season it was imperative that all plants were removed from the container and potted up as quickly as possible.

Now, before I go any further, the department has inspectors that visit garden centres every year to check plant quality and passport numbers. Usually, when they arrive, they appreciate a well-run establishment, and the visit is normally diplomatic. I have to say, over the years, I met some fine people; however, as my army experience taught me, you always run into a bollocks along the way. About 2006–7, this guy arrived one day, produced his ID like this is *Hawaii Five-0,* and proceeded to check literally everything in the garden centre. He came twice a year, so if you can imagine one hundred bollocks all wrapped up in one, that was him. The morning after the load arrived, he and his supervisor proceeded to take soil samples, and after laboratory testing they discovered nematodes they could not identify. To put it into layman's terms, there are bacterial nematodes in all soil, Chinese and Irish, and they are, in part, responsible for keeping the soil and plants in a healthy state. They decided to put a detention order of three months on the plants, which meant I could not sell them, and in some cases required a root wash with bleach, which at that time of year would be detrimental to the plants. This particular guy, twice if not three times a week, came around the centre, checking and counting everything—a total disaster of an individual.

The machinery came in shortly after this. Now customers were looking for a cheaper machine, maybe one they could push. "Retail is detail," they say. No, it's a science that has not been fully understood yet. Things were not improving; after investing €70,000, I needed a return on my money. July was now on us and no great shakes were occurring, so I decided to run an auction.

People came from everywhere, and it bolstered the turnover for August, so I went for another one in September. By October, I came up with another initiative.

It was a hard year; life at home on the domestic front was becoming a disaster, as Sheila spent more time in Manchester with our daughter, Sarah, and I felt the sons were not interested. After all, they were picking up €200 plus on the dole, and, to be honest, I had lost heart with them. Patrick would make himself available to me if I needed to get away for a day.

13

The Boom Is Gone Bust, and a Break in Vietnam and Cambodia

Paul Madden kept enquiring as to where we would go this year. I needed a break, just to get away from it all, so I suggested Vietnam, but he balked. "Why not?" I said. After all, I knew nothing about it, other that it was once a war zone, so it had to be interesting. I then suggested North Korea. "You mad bastard, we might get in there, but we would never get out again," he said, so the notion of Vietnam and Cambodia was born.

We both looked it up on the Internet and it looked good, so we booked our visas online, as well as the hotel—Kelly's, in district one. The flight was £600 return and the hotel cost €20 a night, so we were all booked and ready to go. Our flight took us from Belfast to London, and then on to Doha in Qatar, a nine-hour flight, with a two-hour stopover followed by a seven-hour flight to Ho Chi Minh City, formerly Saigon. It was a buzzing city, so different from China, with clean air and a temperate climate.

I had broken my glasses two days before I left, and it was important that I have them repaired the morning after we arrived, so after breakfast, having taken instructions from the receptionist on where to find an optician, I set off to find the shop quite close by. An optician in his late sixties with a modern office, he beckoned me toward this machine and carried out an eye test, and then repaired my glasses while I waited. Paul advised me to get another pair, as they were so cheap, so I ordered a Japanese frame called Kenzo that would cost £600 at home, plus a set of new lenses and two wings for another pair. All this for the total cost of sixty-three pounds. Yes, you could not spend money in Vietnam.

Ho Chi Minh City is a major tourist hub in South East Asia, mainly for Australians and Scandinavians since the country was reunited in 1975, and, like China, it was a communist country but very capitalistic. It had a growing export trade, and for a country that suffered so much during the war, it was twenty years ahead of the West. So much history to explore, with travel groups on every street, day trips to anywhere and everywhere, the Mekong Delta, the Thui Chee tunnels, and so much to do in our three weeks that we spent the first three days planning and getting to know the city. Paul and I were enjoying each other's company, and I had long grown to admire his determination as a result of having a prosthetic leg from the knee down. You would never know it, though occasionally he would get a welt on the joint, slowing him down. Our first day trip was up the Mekong Delta; this was a lesson in waiting on the greatest guerrilla warfare group the world had ever seen, so it was imperative that I got a book on Ho Chi Minh, which I read to understand his thinking. Remember, we are talking about an army that killed more than fifty-five thousand US troops. Compare that to the loss of 4,500 over a nine-year period in Iraq, which puts the magnitude of that theatre of war into perspective. As we travelled up the main river, it was amazing how industrious the river was. A whole people lived on the river as their home. We reached the Mekong Delta, with its sprawling jungles and narrow waterways making it very difficult to navigate, which would have exposed the Americans to great danger. *It's no wonder they were on drugs,* I thought, *as they would have been sitting ducks.* As we moved further inland toward the tunnels, guided by a guy called Donald, whose father was a captain in the South Vietnamese Army during the war, he told us he had mixed emotions about the war, but continued to point out the prowess of the Vietcong. Because of the soil structure in that area, the engineering of literally whole communes below the ground connected by the narrow tunnels made it very hard to detect them.

There was a tourist tunnel constructed the same way, but just a little larger to accommodate the Caucasian build, with an exit every twenty metres in case you needed to get out. I was just after opening a can of beer when the guide decided to go down the tunnels. It was only a hundred metres, and, as I was just behind him, I was not going to leave my beer behind. I was feeling the heat, and it was a struggle, but I was not going to be the first to get out when everyone in the party knew about my military past. As we ascended at the end, they were all gathered around with their cameras soaked from sweat, and I held up the can and said I never dropped a bit of it.

The ingenious traps that were set in the jungle by the Vietcong rendered a lingering and painful death to the victim. They even made sandals from tyres with the threading on the sole indicating you travelled in the opposite direction from the way you came, and because the Vietcong were integrated with the local communities and village life, the Americans resorted to getting people to take off their shoes to see if they had any sandal markings on their feet to identify the Vietcong. Even cooking underground was an art of science; they had a ventilation system that released the steam and smoke from anthills about half a mile away.

Returning to Ho Chi Minh City on the Saigon River was something; I could imagine myself as part of a US unit operating in the area. It was a no-brainer, and they hadn't a chance. We also visited the war museum and the presidential palace. It became very clear to me that, with boots on the ground, the Vietcong controlled two-thirds of the country during the war, and the republicans only had a shaky foothold, because the Vietcong operated behind enemy lines. Staying at the hotel used by mostly Asian guests, it was obvious some of them were English-speaking. I observed a gentleman in his seventies who lived in the United States. We exchanged words, and it transpired that he was a captain in the South Vietnamese Army but had evacuated to the United States in 1975. It was not until 1998 that the Vietnamese government allowed ex-pats to return, and he had been back every year since 1998. One morning in the foyer of the hotel, I was waiting for Paul to come from his room, because we were about to head down the city. I was dressed in a T-shirt, shorts, and flip-flops. This man was going out to the city wearing a heavy overcoat with the hood up, and I could just see the whites of his eyes. It appeared that even thirty-five years later, for whatever reason, he needed to protect his identity. I felt this was mad.

The backpackers' area of Ho Chi Minh City was a sociable place to go, and you could get accommodation for six dollars, so it was popular with the tourists. There was never any trouble, and we never saw the police. I thought that strange, until sitting in the bar one night with four local fellows sitting across from us, drinks in hand, this guy pulled up on a motorbike. Before you knew it, they were on top of him, guns, handcuffs, and IDs checked, and they literally stripped the bike to the last bolt—all of this in the open. It was obvious to us that he was some kind of a drug dealer, and these guys had his cards marked. The one lesson that I learned there and then was the police were very active and could be sitting beside you talking and listening. The other thing about Vietnam was the tailors. I went in on a Wednesday for a fit. I selected the cloth, cashmere wool, and design, and ordered three tailor-made shirts, a pair of slacks, and the suit. "Come back Friday," was the reply. The total order cost me $110, about £70. The following March, Noel Graham, the guy who looked after me in Lebanon with the minibus during my tour of duty with the Fifty-Second Battalion, died. I put the suit on for the occasion; it was the biggest funeral in Mullingar for quite a while, since Joe Dolan's. I was like Don Corleone.

Back to Vietnam…after the first week into the trip, I had not a care in the world. I can never remember being so relaxed, with lovely people and a lovely country, and everything was dirt cheap. What a contrast to the belligerence in Ireland. These people were happy, and it rubbed off on me; they liked us, were happy to promote their country, and were also God-fearing. The religion was mostly Buddhist, which meant that there were temples all over the place, some ancient and very ornate. I couldn't help but visit them, and it was obvious from their devotion that Buddha is the same God to them as ours, so heaven will be full of Vietnamese as well.

It was time to organise phase two of this trip, a four-day visit to Cambodia, so off to the travel agent. It cost me $178 (£112) for coach travel, three nights in a four-star hotel, all meals, and entry to the national parks. We were collected at 5:00 a.m., and off we went on the long journey to the border, all Vietnamese on board with us, as well as the captain, who was back on his yearly visit from the States. Paul and I were the only two Europeans in the bus. I had bought *Day Zero,* a book about Pol Pot and the Khmer Rouge, their rise to power, and the atrocities they committed in Cambodia between 1975 and 1979, but this trip was much more. We stopped at about 8:00 a.m. for breakfast at a roadside eatery run by a local family. Paul stuffed himself, I had a can of beer, and then it was off again to the Cambodian border. It cost us twenty-five dollars for the visa, the whole process similar to entering any country, and then back on the bus on the Cambodian side and off we went.

Our first stop, which was yet another eight hours away, was Angkor Wat; this journey was punctuated with at least another three breaks, each lasting forty-five minutes, usually at a filling station or restaurant where toilet facilities were available. Cambodia was so different from Vietnam. It was poor, the landscape flat and covered with rice fields, the houses on stilts with thatched roofs and very basic facilities, and a water buffalo tethered at the front, usually lying in a murky pond. All the houses were by the roadside, and the roadways were just one straight line for hundreds of miles. I don't think we ever went around a bend, and if we did, then I cannot remember. On one of our stops beside a filling station, there were communal gathering points, and there might have been up to two hundred people hanging around, either waiting to be picked up or just having been dropped off at their destination, so it was a place for traders to do a lot of business, sell food, and barter. I lit up a cigarette, only to observe Paul with our coach load and others taking video clips and photographs. *What's he up to now,* I thought, as I meandered over. There was a farmer with a large woven basket filled with about two hundred tarantulas about the size of your hand, and Paul had them crawling on his face, head, and chest. "You're mad—they are killers, called the black widow. What are you at?"

"Don't worry," he said, "I've seen it on TV. The farmers catch them in the fields and pull their venomous teeth out; they are then sold as a delicacy." My first impression was who was the maddest, the farmer or Paul? "Come on, try it," he said, but not likely. Even the Vietnamese wouldn't try it, but that wasn't the end of it. They were then deep-fried and sold for pennies, and Paul ate them as if they were McCoy's crisps.

"You dirty bastard," I said.

He replied, "They are gorgeous." With the frog legs in China and now the spiders, he was a minicelebrity with everyone, especially the crew we had on the bus.

I didn't like all this undue attention. Back on to the bus for another straight line of miles, I returned to my book, occasionally looking out at the countryside, trying to put the faces of the victims onto the pattie fields. It was hard to comprehend such things could have happened in my lifetime; the world just seemed like one big war zone. We finally arrived at Angkor Wat, a national park, with temples going back in time. I think they are one of the wonders of the world; the carvings and the art, cut out of stone, in themselves were amazing, and the crowds were massive, even at this late stage of the evening. I took it all in but was tired. We were twelve hours on the road, and I needed a sleep. Next, it was off to dinner; needless to say, Paul got stuck in to it. I will refrain from describing Paul's eating habits from here on in. After the dinner, it was back to the hotel, a massive five-star hotel. It was time to get a few hours' sleep; we had a double single room, shower *en suite,* and after a few hours of a lie-down, it was time to explore the town. Vietnam was cheap, but Cambodia was ridiculous; a pint of tiger beer worked out to about twenty cents. The people were different from the Vietnamese, somewhat darker in complexion, but still very welcoming. We fluttered about for a few hours, but it was an early start again in the morning, and after a long first day we got a *tuc tuc* (taxi) back to the hotel. We were up in the morning at six o'clock, and after a coffee I decided not to go on the tour, as the thought of "get up on the bus, get down off the bus" was a little too much for me to contend with. After all, I had my book to finish, and I felt like just walking around this famous town on the stroll. Paul and the rest of them left, and I just meandered down around the streets, book in hand. I visited all the temples and eventually at about 11:00 a.m., I found this niche café and bar; I asked for a beer and the waitress handed me two ice-cold bottles of Miller beer. The temperature was in the low thirties, so there was nothing nicer than a cold Miller beer to cool you down. I really got stuck into the book, occasionally glancing outward, looking at a mother with her three children keeping in close contact to her, as if she was the only protection they had, and an old man stooped from the years of heavy labour, his stare fixed in another world, the lines on his face an encyclopaedia of life. It was making the content of the book come alive, and I knew the next day I would visit the killing fields. This was secretly hidden from the populace of the Western world. As I read on, I found it incomprehensible that worldwide people would have tolerated such extermination, but then the media was blocked out of Cambodia by Pol Pot. Or was it just that this poor country was so irrelevant? Whatever the reason, the clock could not be turned back. Several bottles of beer later and realising there was a menu in front of me, I decided to eat. Now this was where they made their money. I decided to order a cheese and ham omelette, and this came with the best bread I ever had eaten. This was followed by more bottles of Miller. I must have been there now for about five hours, and the book was now finished. I thought I would head back to the hotel and wait for Paul and the others to return. I had a good idea what I had spent in the café bar, so I called for the bill. I thought this would be around twenty dollars, but to my astonishment, it was six dollars, so I gave the waitress a nice tip. Paul had completed a course of malaria tablets two weeks prior to our departure, after having five different injections. I did not bother as I had enough needles in me during my military career. He thought I was mad. At this stage, Paul was suffering from diarrhoea and vomiting; I don't know if it was the spiders he had eaten or what. He returned that evening, and we talked about our day in the main. After showering, it was down to "Beer Street." I had brought with me to Vietnam four bottles of Powers whiskey, just in case there was a short supply here. I need not have bothered, as there was plenty. Beer Street was like one big block of pubs and restaurants; it was happy hour all night long, and with buy one, get one free, I kid you not, it has to be the cheapest place on the planet to eat and drink. The *tuc tuc* back to the hotel was the most innovative piece of engineering I had ever seen; it was a Honda fifty motorbike with a buggy attached like a horse and cart. After day two and on to breakfast the next morning, the tour left, as they were not taking in the killing fields, like us. I had a pair of shorts on and the flip-flops, and Paul looked down at my right foot and asked if the two red bite marks on my foot were mosquito bites. I said, "Yeah, but they are dead."

"What do you mean, they are dead?"

I replied, "They just flew up straight and crashed into the wall. They must have had alcohol poisoning." We had a good laugh; Paul was a little preoccupied with malaria and whatnot. I said, "If you die, you die."

We made enquiries as to the killing fields and were told they were about seven to eight kilometres outside Phnom Penh, so we got a *tuc tuc* and headed off. As we approached, the driver indicated to the area by pointing his finger, a smile indicating he had something to be proud of. It was as if he himself didn't fully understand the issues. We knew this was a sacred place, and a solemn feeling engulfed everybody, with nobody talking as we approached the admission desk. A paltry sum of two dollars was the fee. Nobody spoke, and we were held until such numbers were available that merited the use of an English-speaking guide. Eventually, one was available, a woman about forty-five years of age who brought us to an area where she outlined the events from 1974 to 1979: the underhanded methods they used, the secrecy of how they used the killers, before they were killed themselves. The Vietnamese invaded in 1979 and defeated the Khmer Rouge, establishing the Cambodian government; it was then that the killing fields were discovered, after opening three mass graves that held the bodies of more than five thousand mortals. When they realised how many people were buried there, they decided to allow the remainder to stay in the final resting place allocated to them. They then erected this massive monument, reaching more than fifty feet tall and housing the five thousand skulls that were dug up. Everywhere we now walked had revealed bone matter and clothing, due to soil erosion, which meant you were literally walking on top of the dead. It was very eerie. We were invited to go into the monument at the start of the tour and took our shoes off as a mark of respect. Paul, with digital camera in hand, took pictures of everything. In we went, Paul snapping away, and I had just about entered the building, when what I can only describe as the most incredible feeling overcame me. It was unreal and very disturbing. I turned to Paul and said I was going outside. I left and lit a cigarette, looking back, wondering what happened, but put it down to emotions. After all, I had just read a book on all the issues. Paul emerged from the building with a broad smile, saying, "Don't tell me you're afraid of a few skulls."

"No," I replied, trying to explain the sensations and feelings I had, but he just brushed it off.

We finished the tour after about three hours, and I was about five hundred metres from the monument, waiting with Paul for the *tuc tuc* to arrive. Both of us were in bad form, discussing the Khmer Rouge, when I experienced a sensation, just as I had when I was in the monument. I said to Paul, "I'll be back in ten minutes."

"Where are you going?" he asked.

"To take some photos on my phone," I replied. I did not even understand myself, as I am not a photo taker. I prefer to remember, but here I was, doing something that just wasn't me.

Paul was eager to get away, as we had learned earlier from the driver that there was a firing range just outside the city, where you could fire anything from a machine gun to a rocket-propelled grenade, and the target was a cow;

how mad, but he was raring to go. A few days earlier, we had been on a firing range in Vietnam, run by the army. My preference on that day was firing an M60 heavy machine gun, by single shots. Having had twenty-four years of range firing practice behind me, killing a cow by RPG was not top of my priorities.

He protested, "I have all the photos you need; I will e-mail them to you."

"I'll be back in ten minutes."

"You are a mad bastard," Paul uttered, and off I went.

Taking off my shoes, I entered and proceeded to take maybe ten to twelve shots from my mobile phone. I was calm, and there was a sense of peace, not like before.

I returned to Paul and the *tuc tuc* driver, and off we went to a school that Pol Pot had taught in, as he was a schoolteacher in his earlier life. We headed down the road in the direction of the city, but the traffic started to build up and slow us down. It soon became chaotic, and even a manoeuvrable vehicle such as the *tuc tuc* was in gridlock. I pondered the thought that if there was a population of eight million and Pol Pot had murdered 25 per cent, then at least 50 per cent must be here in Phnom Penh, that put paid to killing a cow.

The school was turned into a state prison, and we spent about three hours there, looking at the thousands of photographs of the victims, each with a serial number, like the Second World War all over again. The skulls were horrible, and to think that when I was enjoying myself to the sounds of David Bowie, Mud, ABBA, and all the rest, this was happening in Cambodia. At least the Germans gassed their victims, but these poor beings were tortured to death. It was at this point that I didn't question if there was a God—I literally engaged in an argument with him. We were finished at the school, which was smack in the middle of the city. Back in the seventies, the outside population was not around to hear the screams, as they were all in the pattie fields as Pol Pot removed everybody from urban areas. All the pain resonated by echo, from empty wall to another.

We had a long day; the appetite was not there for food. We had that long journey the next morning for the border and back to Vietnam, so we went back to the hotel, and, with it being eight hours ahead of GMT, it was Saturday, and I wanted to get the English football results. Sitting by the TV, I poured myself a strong Powers whiskey. Paul was over on his bed with the prosthetic leg off for relief, all his money on the bed, sorting out the Cambodian from the Vietnamese currency, and of course, the dollars. Then the sensation that I experienced in the monument once again overcame me; it was weird, almost controlling. I reached for my phone and, without making a conscious decision by myself, started to scroll through the photos of the skulls that I had taken earlier. Now, wait for it, when I came upon this image, a spirit field of about one metre square engulfed me, and I was in a state of paralysis for about thirty seconds. I felt the presence in the room, not threatening. Just like flicking off a light switch, it was gone, and it felt as if I had regained my senses. Still glued to the image before me, I shouted, "Paul, get over here."

Whether he realised or not that something of magnitude had happened that he could not comprehend, he immediately, less the prosthetic leg, hopped over to my chair to view the image before him. "Holy fuck, that's mad."

"Paul, that's the face of a forty-three-year-old female doctor," I said.

"How do you know that?" he asked.

"She was here," I said. We pondered for hours trying to figure how the image got into the phone; we blew the image up until it fragmented, but in the end, as Paul said, it is what it is. This was mad. I knew I had felt different sensations while feeling my way through all that took place in that hallowed and sacred ground; after all, I was only human and would have expected anybody to have had the same feelings. In the immediate aftermath, I didn't have a clue, but I knew this was a phenomenon that meant something. I was preoccupied by the whole experience.

The killing fields was an experience I will never forget, starting with the introduction of the guide who told us her story as a victim, held with her uncle and cousin, the tears running down her face as she told us of their escape to the jungle, leaving her family behind and having to hide out there for months. That was some introduction, and what she witnessed after that is indescribable. I thought of putting it into print but have decided not to, for with every word written, it would be the same as resurrecting each and every death all over again. What's important is that we know it happened and learned from it, but then again we are only human, so it's likely we won't.

The next morning we were leaving Cambodia behind us. It was an interesting experience, but the innermost feeling was that it wasn't up there with Vietnam. Heading back on the bus was the same routine, up on the bus and down from the bus. I showed the image on my phone to everybody on the bus, and it freaked some of them out. We arrived back in Ho Chi Minh City to a monsoon; I had never seen rain like this. We were glad to be back; it was as if we had adopted the city as our second home. Back at Kelly's Bar, they were glad to see us back, and then a shower and off to an Irish pub called O'Sullivans, which was just around the block. There were plenty of Irish working in the city, in banking, teaching, and God knows what. This pub served traditional Irish meals; it was just alright, but not up there with the Paddy Field. There was always good music every night; it was a Western experience, which was nice to drift into every now and then, especially the draught Guinness.

We were into our last week, and down at the Buffalo Bar on the backpackers' trail, we met this guy from Australia in his early fifties, who was out here teaching and liked his drink. A nice fellow, but I got the impression he wasn't too dedicated to his profession, just like the type you see in every job who's just there marking up time. We had them in the army, a breed that just exists. We talked about Cambodia, and I showed him the image on the phone. He was amazed, but he did give me a bit of good advice: he told me to lock the phone away, not to use any computer software out here, and to download the image onto a USB memory stick when I got back home, in case it was accidentally deleted. That I did.

For me to say that I had the best three weeks of my life is an understatement. I had discovered a country where, if I could get rid of everything I owned, I would have no hesitation in relocating for the rest of my life. We did too many things, so much that paper would not reflect the craic, and so it was time to depart. We were leaving with the sense that, yes, we will be back, and then off to the airport, which was just a short journey.

Three hours before check-in, and Paul was observing me, buying coffee, and trying to use up whatever Vietnamese currency we have left. The bags were checked in, and Paul was still watching me; I did not realise, but as long as I can remember, and I have been all over the world, I am the worst passenger on an aircraft that one could ever meet. I have to have a half bottle of whiskey in me before I board the aircraft. I am okay once I get up there at thirty-five thousand feet and relaxed at the landing, but for take-off, you don't want to be sitting next to me. Still, Paul said nothing; we walked through the airport, past the bars, and then it was time to board. We were taxiing down the runway when Paul blurted out, "You know you don't have a drink in you."

Calmly, I replied, "I don't need one," and tapped my phone in my jeans pocket. "The lady in the phone has to get to Ireland, and so will I." The aircraft hurtled down the runway for take-off, and, for the first time in my life, my fear of flying was gone. I have flown on at least six occasions since, and it remains the same—the fear is gone.

The next peculiar thing that happened was when we were making the connecting flight from Heathrow Airport in London to Belfast. As I mounted the front step from the staircase on to an Aer Lingus aircraft, I turned to go into the cabin, and down on the left-hand side, about twenty seats back, I recognised this individual. Though I had never met him in person, he was eyeballing me, to the extent that when somebody in front of me to put something into the overhead storage space, he leaned out to watch me. I thought, *Why the hell is he looking at me? I don't even know him.* It was the knowledge you had when you knew somebody was watching you. As I approached him, he looked up and said, "How are you? Where are you coming from?"—something you don't say to a complete stranger.

Reaching out my hand and without any protocol, I said, "How are you getting on, Pat?" It was the very outspoken, ex-communicated, self-declared Bishop Pat Buckley. I said, "I am coming from Vietnam and Cambodia." It wasn't as if I had a suntan; I could easily have been coming from Camden Town in London. "I have something in my phone to show you."

"Sure, we will see it in Belfast," he replied. This is not the kind of conversation you strike up with a complete stranger. We landed in Belfast, and Pat got off with his briefcase in hand. He was a day tripper to London for a meeting, I guess. I proceeded to collect my luggage, and, as everyone knows, it can be thirty to forty-five minutes waiting for the luggage to appear on the conveyer. By this time, I had forgotten all about Pat Buckley, but, to my surprise, he was waiting by the front exit door of the airport. "You have something to show me," he said.

"I have, and you won't ever see anything like it in your lifetime."

He looked at the image on the phone and asked me to e-mail it to him, as he wanted to show it to his parishioners. I said I would, but asked if he could explain how the image came into my phone. He went on to say, "On the first occasion, you went to the monument. This soul came at you too fast, and your innermost self and soul rejected it; that's why you experienced the sensation and feelings you had. It's funny you say she's a forty-three-year-old doctor. She had the power of hypnosis, so much so that she was able to lure you back to the monument on the second occasion, and when you felt the presence in the hotel room, that was her, making her identity known to you through your subconscious. She is in your phone for a reason, but it is nothing evil." That was at least reassuring for me. "It will manifest itself to you at a later date."

14

Home with My New Inner Feeling

Back home and once again it's a horrendous winter, worse than the previous year, with temperatures down to minus eighteen Celsius. It was prolonged from December right through January and brought all kinds of hardship. It totally pulverised business; the losses mounted up. I had lost about £100,000 in stock, and a lot of the Chinese imports were gone, including indigenous stock. We spent all spring dumping; it was a nightmare. Value in stock, even unsold, gets stronger in value, but this was a tsunami to the industry by any standards. Again we were preparing for the new season with all our energies focussed on the year ahead. The gains of previous seasons were all but wiped out, and we were never going to regain, but at least if we had a good summer, we might start trading back up.

The damage throughout the country indicated that we could have a bumper year, but we had not factored in the following points: (1) people had come through the worst two winters running in living memory and they were not going to replace their losses, in case the same thing happened again the next winter; (2) the recession was now at the "mouth face"; and (3) yet again we had another terrible summer of weather. It reminded me of a couple that we had met in Vietnam; as I can recall, they were from Cork and were in their early thirties. Two years earlier, they packed in their secure full-time jobs, sold their house, and went to travel the world. To me, the whole project sounded mad, but, as I reflect, they would be likely be unemployed by now and living with negative equity. They were young adventurers, and, more importantly, their decision turned out to be the right one.

I was still engrossed with the lady in the skull. What could it mean? Was it a warning? I searched my mind for all possible meanings. Then one day, my mind made the connection between the eye in the skull, which was a person lost to her family and friends, and Seoige Joyce, who was lost to his family. Both of them in the theatre of war, both of them lost forever—it was then that I realised I had abandoned my promise to try to get the truth out about that fateful day in April 1981. The next day I searched the office; it had been five years since I first started to write all this. The amount of writing I done—was it lost? Thrown out? I didn't know. Eventually I found it and resolved to finish it. Here I was revisiting the past. I went on to the social networking site Facebook to try to make contact with Hugh Carthy, the platoon commander from many years ago. I got in contact with him and told him of my intention and ambition to write the book and asked him if he wanted to make a contribution. I am still waiting, but that has made me even more determined. I went on the Internet to do some research and see what information I could get.

The one man in UNIFIL who was more important than even the force commander, as they came and went every couple of years, was a man by the name of Timur Goksel, whose appointment was to last for twenty-two years of permanent service. A Turk by birthright, he was with UNIFIL as the press officer, but his real role was as Mr. Fix-it. He had direct contact with the powers in New York. Now retired, but still living in Beirut, he had given an interview to a reporter about his time working for UNIFIL. I found it remarkable. He spoke of all groupings and his relationship with them; he placed certain emphasis on the PLO, the Burj al-Shamali refugee camp in Tyre, and their relationship with UNIFIL. The two main PLO groups in Tyre were Fatah, controlled by Yasser Arafat and the PLFLP, headed by George Habash, who was in exile in Damascus. They were controlled by two Jordanian officers, who with their Sandhurst training had strong control over the groupings. Timur remarked that Arafat, due to his ego and the fact he was on first-name terms with the force commander, considered UNIFIL a friend. This I experienced myself during my time in Tyre in 1981–82. This was transition time in Lebanon, and a lot of things were up in the air. The PLO was a thorn in the foot of Israel; the Shia in the south felt more cut off and adrift from the authorities in Beirut; and there was a mood for change. A group of students in the town of Nabataea formed an alliance and created the Revolutionary Justice Organisation, which was the forerunner to Hezbollah, a group that was against any foreign troops occupying Lebanese soil. This is borne out by events in 1988, when Col. William Higgins of the US Army was kidnapped and executed. One has to remember whose company he was in; he was with Daoud Daoud, the second-most senior figure within Amal. He had reassured Col. Higgins, yet his stature was to mean nothing. I have included two docu-

ments from Timur Goksel to support this, which outline the innermost work-
ings of the UN, how it treated him as a senior advisor, how he was Mr. Fix-it
who rode the diplomacy horse to the very limit. He dealt candidly with the
murder of the Higzassi brothers in Haddata, as I outlined here earlier. There
was a threat of reprisals for up to ten Irish soldiers for the murders, and Timur
called the chief of staff, a Norwegian major general, and suggested they visit
the family. The general was somewhat nervous; they went to the family and
were made unwelcome. Because Timur was Muslim himself, he was able to
engage the family, and after apologising and accepting that UNIFIL was in the
wrong, he offered the family $50,000 as compensation or blood money. They
accepted this, and the threat to the Irish was removed. As he says, "We have
an axiom that says, 'if they want to get you, they will.'" On returning to
Naqoura , he telephoned New York to brief them on events, and the people he
was dealing with strongly objected to such a sum of money been paid to the
family. Timur replied, "Well, just let them murder ten Irish soldiers then;
thereafter, you will have to pay their families $85,000 each." I am sure you
can do your math on this one; the family was paid. It was at this juncture that
I did my own sums: if a soldier died, his family at that time received £25,000
to £30,000; even in death, the government was making money. Some partici-
pating countries gave their soldiers the full allowance, such as Norway and
the Dutch in our time. The Irish government made $8 million a year on the
back of two rotations of Irish soldiers; so little wonder is it that the truth is the
first casualty in war. Timur once said, with UNIFIL, there had to be "giving
and taking," so who can investigate whom?

I have no axe to grind. When you enlist in the defence forces of your country,
you do so as a volunteer. You learn to respect authority the whole way up, and
when that abandons you, you soon realise what the word "enlisted" means. I
have copied my discharge book, beginning on page viii, to show that my service
was considered exemplary on discharge. When you examine the whole process
of April 1981, it was more about protecting the officer cadre and those who
were upward bound. They were more like film directors than military strate-
gists; the one obvious difference between the famous Jadiville Jack and these
commissioned planners is they had real choice. How would Major General
Murphy feel now? How do I feel now? Let's be straight—failed. Failed, just
like the Catholic Church that failed us all. What a waste of time; it was all about
privilege.

As I previously stated, I started writing this in 2006, just after the TG4 programme was on air, and then after thirty to forty pages, I discarded it in the
office jumble of paper. Now, I am not a natural at this writing game, and after
all, who am I to influence the very core and vertebrae of government? We all
know how it works. Look at the McBrearty case here in Donegal.

Let's say I have worn the T-shirt. I once fell afoul of the gardai for standing up to a bully. I got preliminary justice, and he was transferred, but for two years my life was made hell. I was in court on gun charges and, as a result, sentenced to a month in prison, which I appealed and eventually won, but not without cost—a few thousand pounds and two years of acute anxiety. In the end, the system will get you.

So how does the truth work? Look at the promises made at our election times. We hear "we will give you this and that" only to later find, once elected, it can't be done. That's the system we live within, so I ask again, how can we ever get the truth? Transparency, it's called. It took twenty-five years and many battles by the families of Armstrong, Walsh, and Henehan before the minister for justice and defence, Mr. Alan Shatter, eventually acknowledged that the Department of Defence was negligent. Will this same man now stand up for the others I have mentioned in my writing? Will he stand up and admit that it was more than likely rogue elements within the village of Dynater who were responsible for the execution of Private Hugh Doherty? Will he admit it was more than likely that Private Seoige Joyce was alive for a period after the abduction and eventually killed? Will he admit that placing those two young men, two private soldiers, in such an isolated area contributed to their deaths? Will he admit that the follow-up operations were useless, due to the proper briefings not being adhered to? Will he admit those last hours for Private Joyce were torturous, seeing and hearing his rescuers miss the cue? Will he admit that Seoige is buried in Dynater? Will he admit that the same PLO that opened a HQ in Dublin and hailed by the late Minister Brian Lenihan had nothing to do with the abduction and death? Will he admit that the post-mortem on Hugh Doherty conflicts with all the department reports? Will he admit that everything was a cover-up to protect the reputation of the officers who served in that theatre, thereby making the Department of Defence very negligent, to say the least? Will the Department of Defence finally admit that no soldier serving his country and the United Nations was ever interviewed or asked to make a statement about the events on that fateful day?

I was really amazed, shocked even, and emotionally drained with my experiences in the killing fields. There was no justice for those people—the haunting image on my mobile phone. All year I wondered what this has meant, searching my mind for reasons. Was it trying to tell me something? I worked through 2011, making the same effort as I had in every previous year of business, but watching everything getting destructively worse within our economy. People were losing heart, and going to the pub was now a mission. Gone was the laughter and the banter; the faces were now glazed over, looking at the pints before them, having a sip, and putting the glass back in slow motion, as if it was their last. The unemployment, bank bailouts, the arrival of the IMF, the "men in white suits" was the term used, to take over the running of our country. *Jesus,* I thought, *can this get any worse?* Look at the next generation of people—they are not even bothered about getting out of bed in the morning, as they get €200-plus every week in social welfare just for lying there watching the TV as guests of their parents. Now where was this autocratic government machine that could change "orange into green," that could go before the TV cameras and tell us all what we wanted to hear—anything, I say, anything but the truth? It was then that I realised what the "eye" meant. It was not just about Seoige, but Hugh Doherty as well, who is lying in a cold grave in Conwall graveyard, just outside Letterkenny, County Donegal. Now these two men should be down in the pub this present time, but they are not. So will all those then stand up when they are at church service receiving the Eucharist or whatever is their sacrament—stand up for the sake of the truth, or do they care? I think not, and I think you all know by now the reason—the money factor—and if it was to be proven down over the last thirty years of negligence, then all those families would have been remuner-ated by the hundreds of thousands and not by the meagre sums that they were given, as the next of kin. There surely would have been enquiries set up, costing thousands of euros, and, indeed, careers would have been destroyed. No, we were paid lip service, and that is why I dedicate this to Hugh Doherty and Seoige Joyce, two young men, just twenty-one years of age, who trusted the organisation they served to look after their welfare. What young fellow now would not want that job? Little did they know that morning back in 1981, in April, in the spring of our year, as I told Hughie "to fuck off," that this indeed was going to be the case. So I ask, would you walk down that road, if you knew?

As we conclude with all the events of April 27, 1981, let's look at the board of inquiry findings carried out in 1983, headed up by a then Col. V. Savino, who ironically was the Irish contingent commander in the UN headquarters base in Naqoura, Southern Lebanon, in 1981. He was appointed by the adju-tant general at the time to head up the inquiry. Though I deal with his issues in a different format to the sequence of his findings, I nonetheless exploit the deception. Firstly, the aerial bombardment; he stated that this took place in the city of Tyre at approximately 1730 hours. Why? He could have checked with UNIFIL operations, which would have logged all the reports in the daily inci-dent journal as they were sent in from all the contingents operating in that immediate area. The aerial bombardment went on from 1400 to 1630 hours on a village three to four kilometres due east of Dynater, which is quite a long way from Tyre. He stated that there was a VIP at Post 622D at 1500 hours, but no UN transport would be allowed to move during such intense Israel activity. He goes on to reprimand Sergeant "Mossey" Scanlon and Captain Herbert for not visiting Private McLaughlin, who was on sentry duty on the rooftop, but the facts are that the whole of the Irish platoon based in Dynater House were on the roof for the duration of the bombardment. He then goes on to slight the company signal operator back in company headquarters for not reporting the breakdown in the line of communications between company headquarters and platoon, but I have it from a good authority that the company signaller reported the communications breakdown to the company second in command of the Forty-Eighth Battalion, Captain Christy O'Sullivan, but what action he took is not dealt with in the report findings. He further goes on to say that each man based at Post 622 (Dynater House) made a statement about the events of the day, when in fact, more than thirty-one years later, none of the fourteen personnel ever made a statement, and I suspect that neither did the company signaller. Again he pointed out that the platoon commander posted the two privates that morning and read them their orders for the post. I can categorically deny that, as I observed the two privates on that fateful morning leaving Post 622 and walking off in the direction of Post 622D on their own accord.

His summary of the execution has all the hallmarks of a theory set in stone, of a candidate who was returned to unit from an NCO course. He was of the opinion that the PLO element moved into location under the cover of darkness and remained under cover until 1600 hours the next day, because of all the activity that was going on at the OP. But why would such a unit expose itself for that length of time in an area controlled by Amal, a sworn enemy? If it was a theory of any credibility, would they not have moved at the first opportunity? Further to that, the OP was so isolated that they would have had the run of themselves. Is it credible that they would have moved a captor with extra weapons and radio communication equipment out over open ground for four to five kilometres at a time with such high tension in the air, lest we give no credit to the PLO for their sense of military awareness? His assertion on the impact of the first fatal shot to Private Hugh Doherty also conflicts with the forensic reports of the day. He stated that Private Doherty was bending down in an effort to use the radio when he was shot, which would have resulted in him dropping there and then. In fact, Private Doherty took a shot in the back and then managed to move eleven paces in his military instinctive search for cover before he collapsed, whereby his killers fired two more rounds into the back of his neck, as observed by the Platoon Commander Lt. Hugh Carthy when he went into the Tibnin hospital to identify his remains.

And, finally, how fitting that the military police, on the following day when investigating the site, recovered a set of orders. Now, that was everybody covered, or were they?

Indeed, I can ask this question of the military—have we reached the day when the average soldier, with a heavy 77 set radio on his back, along with his personal load, carrying equipment (PLCE), his rifle, ammunition, and food

rations, in over thirty-degree weather covers 1.5 kilometres in fifteen minutes? Even with the modern kit of today, it would take more like forty-five
minutes, bearing in mind that they would have to move and be tactically
aware. I think if I was in such a situation, I would have gotten out of the VIP
car that was supposed to have been there and walked it to give me a true
reflection of the distance that I could enter in a report.

§ § § § § §

The following is a re-creation of the report dated August 27, 1982:

Office of Adjutant General
Army Headquarters
Parkgate
Dublin 8
27 August, 1982
Col. V. Savino
D/OPS
U.N. BOARD OF INQUIRY INTO DEATH OF PTE DOHERTY AND THE
DISAPPEARANCE OF PTE JOYCE 49 BN UNIFIL
1. The above Board of Inquiry is considered inadequate and it has been
decided that a further investigation is desirable to fill in the obvious gaps. You
have been nominated to undertake this investigation.
2. Your investigation should be directed to reporting on and obtaining all data
required by the following terms of reference in all cases relevant to the date of
the above occurrences.

 a. (1) Who was the Pl Comd i/c at Post 6.22 and Post 6.22D?
   (2) What personnel were on duty at Post 6.22 on 27 April 1981? And
   what was the nature and duration of this duty in each case?
 b. (1) Obtain and comment on adequacy of all orders governing the
   operation of Posts 6.22 and 6.22D on the relevant date.
   (2) Were these orders complied with by all those concerned but particularly by those referred to at (2)a above? If NOT indicate
    (a) to what extent they were NOT complied with? and
    (b) the responsibility for non-compliance in each case?
   (3) Attach copies of all relevant orders as exhibits to your report.
 c. (1) What systems of communication were available at Posts 6.22 and
   6.22D on the relevant date?
   (2) Were these systems effective and adequate? If NOT to what extent
   were they ineffective and/or inadequate and who was responsible for
   same?
 d. (1) Why was there a failure in communication between Posts 6.22 and
   6.22D from 15.40 onwards on the relevant date?

(2) Why was no action taken in relation to this matter until 18.30 hours?

(3) Should action have been taken in relation to this matter prior to 18.30 hours? If so

    (a) What action should have been taken?

    (b) Who should have taken this action?

    (c) When should it have been taken?

    (d) Who were responsible for a failure to take action?

e. (1) What was the distance between Posts 6.22 and 6.22D?

    (2) Is there visual contact between Posts 6.22 and 6.22D?

f. (1) Obtain copies of all incident and other reports made by the personnel on Posts 6.22 and 6.22D for the period 270800 April 1981 and 280800 April 1981. (Attach these documents to your report)

(2) Obtain copies of unit journal entries at Posts 6.22D, 6.22, Company and Unit headquarters for the same period. (Attach these documents to your report.)

(3) Report on the evaluation of these reports at Platoon, Company and Unit Headquarters, with reference to any incident which could have been connected with the matter being investigated.

(4) Did any other incidents occur in the area of Posts 6.22 and 6.22D on 27 April, 1981 which were relevant to the matter under investigation but which were NOT logged and reported? Should these matters have been logged and reported and if so who was responsible for a failure to so log and report them?

g. Obtain relevant statements from the following personnel

    (1) O.C. 48 Bn

    (2) O.C. 49 Bn

    (3) Comdt. Downes

    (4) PL. Comd 6.22

    (5) Pte Russell

    (6) Pte Reilly

    (7) Lt Carthy

    (8) Duty officers at Company and Unit Headquarters

    (9) Any other personnel who were present at Post 6.22 during the relevant period whether on duty or otherwise

h. Report on the system of supply to Post 6.22D as it operated during the relevant period.

i. Report on the system of supervision, inspection and relief of Post 6.22D as it operated during the relevant period. Did this conform to orders in that behalf?

j. The evidence before the Board of Inquiry indicated that Pte Doherty
was shot 3 times. Three Kalashnikov shells were found. 13 (7.62
shells) were found.Were these in respect of rounds fired by Pte
Reilly? What significance if any has this to the disappearance of Pte
Joyce?

k. Any other matter arising during the course of your investigation which
you should report and any recommendations you may wish to make
with particular regard to the operational procedures applicable to the
relevant posts.

1. The Provost Marshal will arrange to provide you with any assistance
you may require for the purpose of obtaining any statements or other
documents required but this should not prevent you from interviewing witnesses yourself where this is necessary.

W. Prendergast, Major General
Adjutant General

*(This letter is a re-creation of the original letter in its exact format; as it is
from 1982, it was typed from an old-style typewriter from that time and the
typist used poor military writing.)*

§ § § § § §

So on examination of the facts before you, even the most amateur or novice
of police cadre, let alone the military police, would firstly preserve the scene
of the crime and then take statements of every person who was based in
Dynater (Post 622) on that day, whether on duty or not; that would be the minimum to garnish any sort of inquiry or investigation.

From every government or department document within the book, it
becomes obvious that this was not done, so we have a situation where every
report is punctuated with statements that read "it is believed" or "it is thought"
and that is backed up over the years with transmissions such as "detailed
searches" and "inquiries" were carried out. Yet the very basics are missing
from the very beginning, and no one thought, *Hold on here, a very big part of
this jigsaw is missing.* It begs belief that over thirty years this could happen.
What was Captain F. E. Dwan, a trained military police officer, doing for
eighteen months? Even if it took ten years for it to be highlighted, then I am
sure all personnel would have had as clear a memory as I have today. Imagine
my statement regarding the young man I mentioned who approached the
checkpoint that day and spoke in French with Hugh Carthy. He would have
been twenty-two to twenty-four years of age. Even after ten years, he could
have collaborated that in fact Private Joyce was being held in the village. For

historical purposes, even today, he would be forty-two to forty-four years old, more than likely still living in Lebanon, and were he to be tracked down, it would put to bed all the "it is believed" or "it is thought" syndrome that surrounded the disappearance of Private Seioge Joyce. But the real question here is, why was this not done? Somebody has the answer; when the time comes for that, please don't start with "It's more than likely."

PERSONALITY OF THE MONTH

Col. V.F. Savino
Chief Military Personnel Officer

Col. V.F. Savino – Chief Military Personnel Officer

The devastating events of World War II, death and destruction to life and property could have served as enough evidence to dissuade many a man from taking up soldiering as a career at the time, but not the young Irish man named V.F. Savino, now in his C.O.s

In spite of all the odds, he enlisted in the Irish army immediately after the second World War as a cadet in the Irish Military College in Curragh, County Kildare. Two years later when he earned his commission with the rank of a 2/Lt, he had his first postings to the fourth Infantry Battalion of Ireland where he served his early years in the military as a platoon commander in Cork.

For three years he was the weapons platoon commander in the southern command. Those were the times of the long bayonets. In the early fifties, he got back to the cadet school, but this time, as an instructor. After three long years he had qualified as a staff of the military college where he served for two years.

From the year 1959 to 1962, in Dublin, he was staff officer in the Quartermaster General's Branch of the Irish Army Headquarters. He was in the Congo (ONUC) as Assistant Chief Military Personnel Officer in 1962. At the end of his tour of duty, he was again found among the staff of the QM back in Ireland.

His next tour of duty with the United Nations took him to Cyprus where he served as a staff officer in the Q Bn HQ. Before then he had successfully gone through the mill of the command and staff course in Ireland. A year later, he returned home. As if enough was not enough he was assigned to yet another UN duty tour. This time to serve with UNTSO. He was Ops officer at one time, and officer in charge at Kantara Control Centre at Rabah in Sinai at another. When he returned to Ireland, he was made a rifle company commander and was also head of the Irish Army Public Relations Office for a period of five years. Later, he had another appointment as OC of a Border Battalion. In 78/79 he commanded the second Irish Battalion to UNIFIL.

At the end of this first UNIFIL tour of duty, he was given the appointment of Executive Officer of the second Infantry Brigade in Dublin, Ireland. On his second tour of duty with UNIFIL in 1980 he was appointed Deputy Chief of Staff. He held this appointment until April this year when he relinquished that post to take over the responsibilities of the Chief Military Personnel Officer of UNIFIL.

Col. Savino has great interest in all aspects of physical education. He is a keen sportsman and has represented the army in many games, among which were rugby, cricket and gymnastics. He also likes mountain walking as a past time.

He had since said farewell to UNIFIL for a happy re-union with his family.

CAUTION WHILE DRIVING DURING INCLEMENT WEATHER

Below is a directive issued by the Chief Administrative Officer, Mr. Erik Andersen, on the above mentioned subject for the information of all UNIFIL military and civilian personnel:

"With the onset of the rainy season all personnel are cautioned to exercise extreme care while driving on wet and slippery roads. This will include, but not necessarily be limited to, reduction of speed to suit any road condition at any given time.

It should be borne in mind by

DRIVE WITH CARE TO EARN UNIFIL'S DRIVING DIPLOMA

all concerned that after a long dry season, accumulated road dust, combined with the residue from exhaust fumes, and rain water will create a slippery layer on the roads which will tend to cause vehicles to skid even at low speeds.

It is requested that all personnel pay strict attention to this warning".

Findings

(Re-created verbatim from Col. Savino's findings)

1. Capt Kieran Herbert was the Pl Comd i/c post 6/22 and 6/22D. Although he was a member of 48 Bn, and his replacement LT Carthy was present, he still retained comd because 49 Bn had NOT resumed op control.

2. Some members of No 5 Pl "C" Coy 48 Bn had been repatriated but had been replaced by the incoming PL of 49 Bn so that the PL was up to strength. All men present were on duty at all times as is the norm on active service.

3. Copies of the orders for posts 6/22 and 6/22D are attached as exhibits "F" and "G," and were adequate.

4. The orders were complied with.

5. Copies of relevant orders are attached as exhibits.

6. Posts 6/22 and 6/22D were in communications by PRC "77 radio set." Post 6/22 was in contact with "C" Coy HQ by radio and by land-line.

7. Communications were adequate although it would have been desirable to have a second system, i.e., a land line. This was however NOT considered feasible because of the fact that 6/22D was occupied by day light only. Although the radio network was generally reliable there is evidence to show that, on the day preceding the events at 6/22D, there was interference on the net so that "C" Coy used a relay station to contact Bn HQ in TIBNIN. Such interference is NOT uncommon in difficult terrain and in adverse weather conditions.

8. Bn SOP's required a system of radio checks every hour, on the hour. This is a routine well known to all radio operators and users, and this procedure is practiced at home. The sentry on duty on the roof of post 6/22 understood that he was to contact his outpost 6/22D every 15 minutes and states that he made his last contact with 6/22 at 1340 hrs. In any event there was a Bn and Coy check at 1600 hrs., but from then on the radio man on the roof at 6/22 failed to contact 6/22D.

9. It was NOT until 1745 hrs. that the sentry on the roof at 6/22 informed anyone that he was unable to make contact with 6/22D. The sentry, PTE MC LOUGHLIN, then informed his relief, PTE CRONNOLLY, of the situation. In a normal situation the OP party would have left their loc at 1730 hrs. to return to 6/22. The land rover, driven by PTE RUSSELL, left 6/22 for DYAR NTAR to pick up the two men at 1800 hrs. When they did NOT arrive PTE RUSSELL returned and informed the Pl Sgt, SGT SCANLON.

10. PTE McLOUGHLIN should have reported his failure to contact 6/22D to his Pl Sgt immediately after he failed to make contact at 1600 hrs. The "C" Coy HQ radio-operator PTE TWOHIG was listening to McLOUGH-LIN trying to contact 6/22D but took NO action other than to warn Pte McLOUGHLIN that he would waste his batteries, and should call less often. Both men showed a lack of awareness by their inactivity. The Pl Sgt SGT SCNLON should have made sure that all was really "OK" when he visited the sentry. From 1700 hrs. onwards the ISRAELI bombing of TYRE distracted all the radio operators as they sent and received reports on the attacks.

11. The distance between 6/22 and 6/22D is 1.5 kms. However, such is the difficulty in proceeding from the village of DYAR NTAR to post 6/22D that a time for the walk could be reckoned at 15 mins.

12. There is NO visual contact between the two posts as the village of DYAR NTAR intervenes and 6/22D is on a reverse slope from 6/22.

13. There was NO report, other than routine radio checks made from post 6/22D during the entire three weeks, that it was in existence, NOR are there any reports logged in 6/22 on the matter. The entire post incident events were handled by OC "C" Coy and OC 48 Bn.

14. "C" Coy Radio Log for 27 April 81 is attached as exhibit "M" and Bn Logs for the 27/28 April 81 (Exhibit "H"), 28/29 April 81 (Exhibit "J") and 29/30 April 81 (Exhibit "K") are attached.

15. The actions taken by all the Commanders concerned, in the wake of the events at 6/22D, were commendable and correct.

16. In his evidence PTE BARRY O'REILLY states that he heard a local from the village of DYAR NTAR complain to the Post Comd CAPT HER-BERT that there was PLO in the village. At that time CAPT HERBERT had set up a checkpoint on the road at post 6/22. CAPT HERBERT says that he took NO action because any vehicle coming from DYAR NTAR would have to pass through the checkpoint and be searched. There is NO other way a vehicle could enter DYAR NTAR as it is on a spur and is unapproachable, except on foot, from any other direction. This fact only came to light when the investigation commenced. However, it may have been a ruse by the villagers to apportion blame to the correct source without incriminating themselves.

17. Statements were taken from all those listed and from others as suggested.

18. Each morning on going on duty, the men involved carried food and drinks with them to 6/22D. At lunch time further food was brought down and they were visited by the Post Comd of 6/22. All other stores were carried

down in the morning and the main meal was eaten in the evening on return to 6/22.

19. Each morning the Pl Comd went to 6/22D with the duty men and briefed them in situ before returning to 6/22. The post was visited during mid-morning by the pl comd, and again at lunch time when the food was brought down. There were also visits from time to time by officers from the Coy HQ. This was an adequate system of check and visitation. The duty was of over nine hours' duration which was long but NOT unusual for IRISHBATT posts.

20. PTE O'REILLY states that he fired fifteen (15) shots as a warning when he found PTE DOHERTY's body. He was hopeful that PTE JOYCE might be hiding nearby and would hear and answer his shouts and/or the shots.

The shots fired by PTE O'REILLY had NO bearing on the disappearance of PTE JOYCE, SO D/Ord has stated that KALACHNIKOV rounds could NOT be fired from an FN rifle.

(Below is Part Five of the report, under the heading as shown.)

OTHER MATTERS

I visited Post 6/22D, now abandoned, on SAT 23rd April 1983. I was accompanied by the Pl Comd Post 6/22 and by C/S COYNE MP PL 53 Bn who had been a member of the investigating team from the UNIFIL MP Coy in NAQOURA in April 1980. The scene was almost as when the incident occurred, and the time of day, and of the year, the weather conditions were almost identical. The scene was tranquil and almost idyllic. The raised voices of people working in nearby fields, and of shepherds, and of people in the nearby villages were clearly to be heard. Despite reports to the contrary there is NO evidence of bombing in the TYRE area on that day until 1703 hrs. on the evening in question. I am convinced that a number of local people, including the two hunters and the boys present during the VIP visit, were witnesses to the subsequent events at the OP. The two hunters may have even been used as a decoy by the killers.

A view over the terrain to the front (i.e., to the WEST) from Post 6/22D leads one to believe that it would have been almost impossible for an armed group to cross the terrain without being seen by two trained soldiers who would surely have reported such activity by radio. PTE JOYCE had performed the duty at 6/22D several times before and in the three weeks that the post had been occupied there had been NO report, from the observers, on any suspicious activity.

The post was established by OC 48 Bn as a result of pressure from UNIFIL HQs Staff Offrs who wanted observation over a wide area of the so called "IRON TRIANGLE." In spite of his reservations about establishing the post in such an isolated location OC 48 Bn did so in order that OC 49 Bn could take over a "going concern" rather than have to set up the post with personnel who did NOT know the area and who would NOT be well versed in OP procedures. The original concept of an NCO and two men for the post was shelved because of the shortage of NCOs.

Although there was NO report of armed element activity by the OP during the three weeks of its existence there is always the possibility that the AEs manning their positions in the "IRON TRIANGLE" area felt threatened by the observation afforded by Post 6/22D. There is NO doubt in my mind but that the perpetrators of the murder of PTE DOHERTY and the abduction of PTE JOYCE were in an ambush position from an early hour of the 27 April 1981. Whatever their motivation, we have evidence from a shepherd and from a local boy that there were armed men to the SOUTH of the post on the afternoon of the events. It is possible that the two soldiers on duty had relaxed their vigilance after the departure of the VIP party and that they were caught unawares by the AEs coming from their left rear, i.e., from SOUTH EAST of the OP. A study of the photograph, taken while the VIP party were being briefed, shows that the "77" radio set was on the ground at the rear of the OP. A reconstruction of the incident leads me to believe that PTE DOHERTY was shot as he was bending over to try to send a warning call to 6/22. It would NOT be possible for him to have wounds, where he had them, unless he was in a bent position as his killer was standing above and behind him. It was NOT possible to judge where PTE JOYCE was when the shooting took place, but as a book and the orders were subsequently found to the WEST of the OP it is likely that he was forward of the post when the incident occurred.

The time which the fatal shooting and abduction occurred is indefinite. The VIP party which visited the OP departed for TIBNIN circa 1500 hrs., and the M.O. Capt T.D. McNAMARA is of the opinion that PTE DOHERTY died before 1700 hrs.

As the two men should have made a radio contact with Post 6/22 at 1600 hrs., and as PTE McLOUGHLIN who was on sentry duty on the roof of 6/22 says that he thought he should contact them every 15 mins, it is likely that the murder took place nearer to 1600 hrs.

The delay in realising that something sinister had happened at Post 6/22D after 1540 hrs. can be explained by PTE McLOUGHLIN's inexperience and lack of common sense. He was undoubtedly preoccupied with the air attack from 1700 hrs. onwards. PTE McLOUGHLIN appears to be a soldier of limited ability and intelligence and is largely inarticulate.

He was newly arrived and was on his first duty on the roof of Post 6/22. It is ironic that he and PTE DOHERTY tossed a coin to see who would have choice of duties, i.e., the roof or 6/22D. If PTE McLOUGHLIN had chosen 6/22D the incident might have had a different outcome.

When PTE McLOUGHLIN failed to make contact with 6/22D he should have called his Pl Sgt, SGT SCANLON and told him of the situation. SGT SCANLON was present all afternoon and says that he visited PTE McLOUGHLIN several times and was told that all was "OK."

SGT SCANLON should have taken more care to ensure that when he visited his sentry on the roof from time to time to check that all was really in order.

CAPT HERBERT as Post Comdr at 6/22 was also remiss in NOT visiting and speaking with the sentry, especially as he was so inexperienced. Both Post Comdr and Pl Sgt were in 6/22 during most of the afternoon.

The signaller at Coy HQ in AS SULTANIYAH, PTE TOUHY, should also have taken more intelligent action when he heard PTE McLOUGHLIN repeatedly call 6/22D and get NO reply.

The concept of establishing an OP on overseas service should be founded on a number of factors NOT least of which is that OPs in general should be mutually supporting. Post 6/22D was isolated and undermanned and probably would have been equally effective located in a building on the WEST side of the village of DAYR NTAR.

I can recall that there have been, over the years, numerous occasions when UN Ops have been over-run or simply taken over by members of the protagonists. UN SOPs require to be highly visible during daylight hours, i.e., painted white where possible, flying the UN flag and with the letters "UN" boldly painted for all to see. At night, a light is mandatory. If OPs are in contact with each other by radio or land line, and are in sight of each other it should be possible to obtain support when there is a threat.

It is significant therefore that, at two OPs which were NOT "mutually supporting," i.e., 6/22D and latterly TIBNIN BRIDGE, there were incidents of major moment.

The scenario which could be painted of events at 6/22D on the date in question is as follows:

The OP when set up by OC 48 Bn at the insistence of UNIFIL HQ was to be "a window" into the "IRON TRIANGLE." It gave a good view into the PLO stronghold especially over "Hill 420," which was a heavily fortified position. The PLO factions probably decided to eliminate the OP by surprising the two occupants disarming them and taking them and their equipment to their HQRS nearby, before commencing negotiations for the dismantling the OP.

The group sent on the assignment, moved early in the morning of the 27 April and lay up, undetected by UNIFIL pers, in a position to the rear of Post 6/22D and on the SOUTH EAST side of the OP. The constant going to and coming from the OP during the day precluded any move before late afternoon, when they finally approached the OP. The two men on the post were possibly in a relaxed mood after the VIP visit and were caught unawares. When challenged, PTE DOHERTY tried to make a radio call from the radio which was on the ground and was shot three times in the back by the man on the high ground behind him as he bent down. This is the only sound explanation for the path the bullets took through the body. The attackers then took PTE JOYCE and all the equipment with them back to their position. PTE JOYCE'S subsequent movements are a mystery. Despite reports of his being taken to BEIRUT and being killed there, there is no evidence to support this claim.

Reports from local DFF sources that he was killed and his body burned in a cave within the "IRON TRIANGLE" would seem to make more sense. Subsequent reports on his movements may well have been "red herrings." However, until his remains are found and identified there is NO proof that he is NOT alive.

I have made arrangements for the MIO and MP Offr of 53 BN to carry on the investigation, and I had meetings with the Leb Army IOs to enlist their help in the matter.

There does NOT appear to be any motive for the murder of PTE DOHERTY by PTE JOYCE. PTE JOYCE was, by nature and by background, a quiet and withdrawn individual. He was known to be frugal and careful with his money. When PTE O'REILLY and party went to Post 6/22D their intension was to borrow money from PTE JOYCE whom they knew was sure to have some on hand.

PTE DOHERTY was only one week in LEBANON and was comparatively unknown to PTE JOYCE. As this was his first duty at Post 6/22D there was hardly a chance of PTE JOYCE and PTE DOHERTY getting on each other's nerves.

PTE DOHERTY appears to have been shot by three aimed shots from a KALACHNIKOV. The cases from these rounds were located by the Mil Police and sent for forensic examination to the UNIFIL MP Coy at NAQOURA. They are NOT to be found NOR is there any report on the extant.

SO D/ORD has certified that he is satisfied that the bullets that killed PTE DOHERTY could NOT have been fired from an FN Rifle.

This seems to eliminate PTE JOYCE as PTE DOHERY'S killer.

Two tragic incidents which took place at about the same period and in the same general area must also be adverted to as they indicate that other UNIFIL contingents were subjected to the same cynical and brutal treatment.

On the night of the 18/19 Jan 1981 three SENEGALESE soldiers were shot to death, at close range, by unknown killers at an OP to the NW of the "IRON TRIANGLE." The three men were killed by 9mm rounds, fired at short range, probably from pistols. No motive could be established for these killings. The OP was approx. 10 kms from Post 6/22D. On the 19th June 1981 two FIJIAN soldiers, taken prisoner after an ambush in the FIJIBATT area, were shot to death by their captors probably in the vicinity of the village of MAZRAAT AL MUSHRIF, which is 4 km from Post 6/22D.

From these accounts it can be seen that the incident at 6/22D was NOT an isolated one but was part of a pattern of murder committed against UNIFIL troops in the "IRON TRIANGLE" area.

RECOMMENDATIONS

1. The matter of the investigation into the disappearance of PTE JOYCE must NOT be allowed to die. Until such time as his remains are located and identified, there will always be a doubt about his fate. Enquiries from all possible sources, including the Leb Army, Israeli Army and local people and their leaders, should be pursued by successive IRISH IOs and MPs in the hope that some light may be thrown on the whole affair. D/Ops should be tasked with keeping up the pressure on IRISHBATT to continue the search, and the contacts made must be kept, and even harassed for information.

2. Operational briefings prior to departure from home should labour the importance of establishing Ops only where there is visual contact with other Ops, and Ops should be opened only when Commanders are satisfied that they can be garrisoned in sufficient strength to maintain their safety. The relevant UN HQ must NOT be allowed to over-ride the Bn Comds view on this matter.

3. There must be continuing efforts made to ensure that personnel selected for overseas duty are of good quality in every way. They must be physically and psychologically ready for duty, and be of a calibre that guarantees survival in difficult and demanding situations.

(The above report is re-created from the original report word for word. It was typed up in military writing, hence the overuse of capital letters. Any spelling mistakes or lack of punctuation is left is as.)

§ § § § § §

In 1980, while the Forty-Sixth Battalion was serving in UNIFIL, C Company was involved in a gun battle with the DFF in the village of Attire. During this battle, a young boy was shot dead by the Irish troops; his uncle was Mohamed Bassi, a militia leader with the DFF, who issued a fatwa that many Irish would die because of the death of his nephew. As a result of this threat, all travel to the enclave was banned; however, soon after at battalion HQ one morning three officers serving with UNTSO (UN observer mission) had to travel to the manned observation post called OP Mar, which was deep inside the enclave. Someone in high authority of the battalion sanctioned for Privates Barrett, Smallhorn, and Kennedy to drive these officers, which, as outlined earlier, resulted in two of these young men losing their lives and the lucky escape of Private Kennedy, who was seriously injured. Mohamed Bassi had his photo displayed on every UN Post as wanted for murder; however, aided by the Israeli authorities, Bassi was able to get out and immigrated to the US city of Detroit. Years later, his place of residence was revealed to the Irish government by UN personnel, who have an extradition agreement with the United States, but this never happened—never was sought, most like, so the verdict here is "gross negligence."

The tragic endings of Pte. Doherty and Pte. Joyce, with whom I started out in this book from my first tour serving with the Forty-Ninth Battalion, are of startling importance. Firstly, the sighting of the OP was very poor planning, leaving no backup to two isolated private soldiers; someone in a high authority made this decision. The follow-up procedure after the tragedy was inadequate, as someone in a more important position than the local "Mouchhter" should have been requested to keep a watch over what was happening around the village during the search period and allowed for a much more thorough search of the buildings within the village of Dynater. This theory of the PLO involvement was a cover-up for poor military planning by our officers—so again this was "gross negligence."

On to the tragic circumstances that occurred on Tibnin Bridge during the Fifty-Second Battalion, when three of our troops were shot dead by one of our own, Private McElevey. Now, Private McElevey should never have been allowed to serve overseas in the first place; perhaps he should never have been allowed to serve or indeed join our defence forces had the proper vetting procedures been in place. I wish to point out here that much more thorough procedures and checking of personnel wishing to enlist were introduced immediately after this. This again was poor planning by our leaders and leads to another case of "gross negligence."

On we go to the Fifty-Ninth Battalion and the death of the young officer Lt. Angus Murphy. As outlined earlier, the mine sweeping exercise was carried out every morning at 0630 hours from the village of Attiri. This mine sweep was of negligible use to our UN personnel and only benefited the IDF/DFF. Our HQ was given several warnings by the personnel laying the mines and roadside bombs to cease the mine sweeps; however, this was ignored and the Amal personnel were ridiculed. Soon after, this young officer lost his life from a roadside bomb during a mine sweep, and, to compound the whole issue, the procedure of mine sweeping was stopped with immediate effect. Again, we question our military planners and the result once more is "gross negligence."

On now to the Sixty-Fourth Battalion, where we lost three fine young men in Corporal Fintan Henehan, Private Mannix Armstrong, and Private Walsh. Yes, in platoon and company posts, defensive positions have to be built and strengthened from time to time. God only knows how many gabions I built during my service overseas. The stone was always collected from an old quarry approximately seven hundred metres away from Post 616 on the road to the village of Aljourn; however, the commander(s) in this situation sent these young men along a road that every dog in the street knew was mined. They drove over the road in an empty truck and were returning with a full load of stone when they hit a tank mine and got blown to bits with their load of stone. Personnel who served with this battalion will now know that some twenty-five years after the event, the minister finally admitted the negligence, so we have our answer to this one—"gross negligence."

A year later, the Sixty-Sixth Battalion had an incident; but this time it was not the Irish who were the victims—it was the Higzassi brothers. They were murdered on our watch, thereby endangering the lives of every soldier in the battalion. The consequences could have been horrendous. Verdict—"man-slaughter."

Next it's the Seventieth Battalion, Corporal Carthy, and B Company. As outlined, here if the SOPs had been carried out to the letter, then this man would probably still be alive today. Verdict—"gross negligence."

Now, there were several other fatalities in Lebanon, a lot of them in circumstances that I am not privy to, but I can account for fourteen during the various times that I served there. The Irish government in those days made $8 million every year after the soldiers were paid from the serving Irish contingent, so after twenty-three years that adds up to $184 million. Some contributing countries to UNIFIL, like Norway, Holland, and, I believe, Sweden allocated the full pay to their serving soldiers, so we certainly got the very short straw. Let's consider this: the government got $85,000 from the UN for every casualty resulting in death, and then factor in the government's findings into each and every death where the families received an average payout of IR£30,000, which is about half of what they received from the UN. Consider this: if proper investigations were carried out into the cause of every death, then what would the consequences have been? The first victim would have been our officers' careers, maybe even court martials—now we couldn't have that, could we? The only positive point, if there was to be any, would have been that proper procedures would have been put in place as a result of a comprehensive inquiry, and then, as far back as the deaths of Privates Smallhorn and Barrett in 1980, a lot of other lives would have been saved. I would like to close this paragraph by saying that the first victim in war is the truth. How much of the $184 million would the Irish government have retained if civil cases had been taken by the families as a result of all these deaths? Sure, Jesus, what sort of career would I have had? I'm thinking there would have been promotions all over the place. Comdt. Gerald Aherne, OC, C Company, Seventy-Sixth Battalion, once pulled me up on a technicality where I retorted, "Practice makes perfect," and his reply to me was, "Perfect practice makes perfect." Now as I write this down, he has been promoted to the rank of brigadier general, officer commanding the Fourth Western Brigade, but I might have been his boss as the chief of staff.

So what should the public glean from such a work? Firstly I would like to make a couple of points. To be a soldier, what makes a soldier; the public perception would be totally different from the real thing. When I joined the army in 1973, the Vietnam War was in full swing, Northern Ireland was getting flared up, the Middle East was a cauldron, and, of course, we had the ongoing Cold War. All of this added to making a conscientious decision to join the army, a decision to try to make the world a better place, though, as a soldier, I was trained to kill. However, the emphasis was always to preserve life. I often reflect and compare a novice going into the church and a guy joining the army; one was going to serve to save souls and the other was going to serve to save lives. The question I asked was which was more important? I also often think of the British soldiers coming to Northern Ireland. They were welcomed initially with open arms; those young guys came to help, but decisions about application politics and everything attached to forward planning put them in a very different situation. The guy who squeezed the trigger on Bloody Sunday, is he guilty? Not bloody likely. It was the machine that turned him from a pacifist to the killer he was trained to be. He could equally have been the saviour. "Soldier" is one of the most conscientious professions on the planet, but it is garnered and supervised by a privileged grouping rather than a properly trained cadre that has passed man-managed skills and proper military training and evaluation. They wanted to send me on a NCO refresher course, yet, when on a command ranger course, a young lieutenant from my own unit could not strip down a 9-mm Browning pistol, which was his personal weapon. This was after been commissioned following two years of training in the military college in the Curragh Camp, so it begs to suggest that at all costs they were to be commissioned. Not in all cases—but it only takes 10 per cent of that to slip through the mill.

I have never known a soldier who was redundant in his abilities to sort things out; he was a born diplomat, so the era of privilege has to come to an end. It has to an extent since I left the forces. Now we have a defence force of which Lieutenant Picard once said, "When the army finds out, he is in trouble."

As a practising Catholic all my life, with no doubt in my mind, the message proclaimed by the clergy was the truth, the whole truth, and nothing but the truth. I did start to examine my conscience with my involvement in Lebanon; my fascination with Islam was more investigative than anything else, so I pursued a course of action over the years that drew comparisons, even to the extent of reading the Koran twice, as you have to, because it's very repetitive. Then, with the scandals besieging the Catholic Church worldwide over the last five years, I questioned my ability to carry on. I then realised everything was a smokescreen. How could the God I knew have anything to do with this, the most heinous evil that could be inflicted on a child? I recalled the words of Jesus: "Suffer little children who come unto me." The silence from the remainder of the clergy, who continued to practice and preach, not one prepared to question, chastise, or punish his immediate authority—this proved to me that canon law was superior to that of God's law, and so I protested in the only form I know—total abstinence. I will take my chance with God's mercy. A similar trait runs through the spine of the military organisation—cover-ups and denials, the inability to question or raise issues for fear of castigation. Things today no doubt have improved with technology, the computer age, the sat navs, etc. Nonetheless such an organisation, which I was proud to serve in and still very proud of today, should have the spleen to put its hands up and admit its failings; otherwise, it can never go forward. The Irish Defence Forces is respected worldwide for the professional approach to peacekeeping duties, so let it now have the power of its own convictions, and finally admit that they got it so wrong.

I am, sir, 826929 Corporal Frank Sumner.

Epilogue

This book tried to give an insight into the working lives of soldiers, who through their careers literally put their lives on the line for whatever country they serve. It gives an insight into married life within the defence forces and the sacrifice most families endure, but, more importantly, it craves for the truth to be told.

Today, the Irish Defence Forces has extended its UN missions to countries such as Eritrea, East Timor, Bosnia, Kosovo, Liberia, and Chad, and indeed has now returned to serve with UNIFIL in Lebanon. They are much better equipped and trained than ever before, which is a credit to all the experienced NCOs and soldiers who have carried forward their experience from the earlier years in Lebanon.

Around thirty thousand soldiers have served in Lebanon over the twenty-three years that the first UNIFIL mandate ran from 1978 to 2001, many of them with multiple trips behind them. I served with the Forty-Ninth, Fifty-Second, Fifty-Ninth, Sixty-Sixth, Seventieth, and finally the Seventy-Sixth Battalion. I wanted to acknowledge through this book the many good officers and senior NCOs with whom I had the pleasure to serve my twenty-three-plus years in the PDF. I left the army with very good discharge papers, and my discharge book (LA 89) is copied as an insert, just as proof to the reader that I have no ill feeling or sour grapes arising from my service, other than those matters that I have dealt with.

This book is in no way intended to cast a slur on any one individual or to undermine the professional approach that is the *pro quo* of the Irish Permanent Defence Forces.

I would also like to thank Paddy for his skills in formulating and typing this book and indeed his memory of the previous thirty years, despite his many adventures in Africa, from Eritrea, Liberia, and Chad, and having endured the many bad days as a result of the weekly intake of the mind-destroying tablet Lariam, the cheap alternative for the enlisted personnel of the defence forces. His memory, he tells me, is enforced through his love of a "good drop of red wine" the hour before bedtime.

While, historically, thirty-one years seems like a long time ago, and it may help with time to forget things, let me reassure you that every minute of it is as if it was yesterday.

Today, Privates Seoige Joyce's and Hugh Doherty's spirits crave from beyond the grave for the truth to be told, if for no other reason than to have a wrong put right. It was my pleasure and, more so, my duty to set the record straight.

The state has a duty to look after its employees. It has a responsibility to ensure it discharges these responsibilities to the highest standards, thereby giving the maximum protection to the individual.

Where it fails to do so, it should be held liable, and if it can't give the answers, it should admit its failings. To close off, I wished to state the reality of life. Therefore, I rest my case and let the reader of this book marry up all my findings with the situation we now find in the Ireland we have today, and think about all the self-serving politicians who will seek re-election in either local or national election in the not-too-distant future and all the want-to-be officers of the defence forces who will receive their promotion based on their political alliance, rather than on their ability. Indeed, this one fact alone may be the reason why we as a defence force lost too many of our comrades, as a result of their negligence.

Photos—Lebanon, 1981

168

A Group of soldiers await meal time - probably a Bar-B-Q in Tyre Barracks - May 1981

A resupply of water with the driver taking some shelter from the midday sun - May 1981

The Irish catching some leisure time in the 'Med' behind Tyre barracks- note the suntans are coming on

Two 'Fiji' Soldiers on sentry duty outside Tyre Barracks (A long way from home)

Enjoying a soccer game in Tyre Barracks - June 1981

Corporal Joe O'Brien with the Company Clerk in Company Office complete with Typewriter

Troops getting briefed prior to Guard Mounting in Tyre Barracks in May 1981

Two UN 'Stores' trucks leaving the main entrance to Tyre Barracks in May 1981

Irish UN Soldiers get ready for a Patrol in May 1982 - Note Helmets and Body Armour

Corporal Joe O'Brien gets some 'Weapon Training' from the Lebanese Army - 1981

A group of Soldiers relaxing in Tyre Barracks - June 1981

The 'Doctor' along with Lt Hugh Carthy, local 'Mingi Man' and Corporal Joe O'Brien

Frank Sumner with Joe O'Brien - 1981

Private Brian Foster and Corporal Frank Sumner

Frank Sumner and Hugh Carthy in 1981

Micky Walker in background with local child - 1981

Appendix A—Report By U.N. General Secretary on Hostilities, Period December 1980–June 1981

UNITED NATIONS

SECURITY

COUNCIL

Distr.
GENERAL

S/14537
15 June 1981

ORIGINAL: ENGLISH

REPORT OF THE SECRETARY-GENERAL ON THE
UNITED NATIONS INTERIM FORCE IN LEBANON

(for the period from 12 December 1980 to 12 June 1981)

CONTENTS

81-15293

/...

172

172

S/14537
English
Page 2

INTRODUCTION

1. The present report contains an account of developments relating to the functioning of the United Nations Interim Force in Lebanon (UNIFIL) for the period from 12 December 1980 to 15 June 1981. Some of the information contained in this report was submitted to the Security Council in my special report (S/14407) of 16 March 1981 on the incidents which occurred at Al-Qantara in the Nigerian battalion sector. The purpose of the present report is to provide the Security Council with a comprehensive picture of the activities of UNIFIL in pursuance of the mandate laid down by the Council in its resolutions 425 (1978) and 426 (1978) and extended or reaffirmed by resolutions 434 (1979), 444 (1979), 450 (1979), 459 (1979), 467 (1980), 474 (1980) and 483 (1980). The last extension of the Force's mandate, as decided by the Security Council in resolution 483 (1980), was for a period of six months, until 19 June 1981.

2. The activities of UNIFIL from its inception up to 12 December 1980 are outlined in my periodic reports on the Force to the Security Council (S/12845, S/13026, S/13384, S/13691, S/13994 and S/14295).

I. COMPOSITION AND DEPLOYMENT OF THE FORCE

A. Composition and command

(a) Composition

3. The composition of UNIFIL as of 15 June 1981 was as follows:

Infantry battalions

Fiji	628
Ghana	377
Ireland	601
Nepal	430
Netherlands	810
Nigeria	696
Norway	688
Senegal	561

Headquarters camp command

Ghana	99
Ireland	51

Logistic units

France	738
Italy	34
Norway	143
Sweden	144
Total	6000

S/14537
English
Page 3

4.   In addition to the above personnel, UNIFIL is assisted by 67 military observers of the United Nations Truce Supervision Organization (UNTSO). These observers are under the operational command of the Force Commander of UNIFIL.

5.   During the period covered by this report, the Nepalese battalion, which had been withdrawn from UNIFIL in May 1980, began rejoining the Force as of 1 June 1981. The Ghanaian contingent, which had been reinforced to take over the area previously controlled by the Nepalese, is being reduced accordingly.

(b) Command

6.   The present Commander of UNIFIL is Lieutenant-General William Callaghan. He assumed command as of 15 February 1981, replacing Major-General Emmanuel A. Erskine, now Chief of Staff, UNTSO.

(c) Rotation of contingents

7.   During the six months covered by this report, all contingents have carried out rotations, with the exception of the Nepalese, which is rejoining UNIFIL.

(d) Casualties

8.   During the period under review, 15 members of the Force lost their lives and 49 were wounded. Of the fatalities, 8 died as a result of hostile actions (see para. 41 below) and others from accidents or natural causes. Of the injured, 24 were wounded as a result of hostile actions and the others in accidents.

9.   Since UNIFIL was established, 62 members of the Force have died, 31 of them as a result of firing and mine explosions, 22 in accidents and 9 from natural causes. More than 100 have been wounded in armed clashes, shellings and mine explosions.

(e) Discipline

10. The discipline, devotion and bearing of the members of UNIFIL, as well as of UNTSO military observers assigned to the Force, who have continued to serve in difficult and often dangerous conditions, reflect credit on themselves, their commanders and their countries. Their self-restraint in the face of hostile action deserves special recognition. A case in point was the unprovoked attack on the Nigerian platoon headquarters at Al-Qantara by the de facto forces (Christian and associated militias), when the soldiers of UNIFIL and members of the Lebanese army unit withstood intense shelling for several hours, incurring numerous casualties without firing back, as such action would have entailed the risk of hitting innocent civilians.

B. Deployment

11. A major change in deployment is being brought about by the return, as of 1 June, of the Nepalese battalion, which had been withdrawn in May 1980 and temporarily replaced by an additional Ghanaian battalion (see S/14295, para. 11).

S/14537
English
Page 4

The Nepalese battalion is again being deployed in the northeastern sector, and the Ghanaian battalion-North is being withdrawn.

12. In order to prevent infiltration by armed elements (mainly the Palestine Liberation Organization (PLO) and the Lebanese National Movement), UNIFIL redeployed some of its units and established additional check points and observation posts as necessary. Further, in order to check incursions into the UNIFIL area by the de facto forces, patrol activity was increased, as were measures for the protection of those villages most prone to attack by the de facto forces, such as Brashit, Al-Qantara, Yatar and Shaqra. Additional defensive steps had to be taken to protect the Force headquarters in Naqoura following a hostile demonstration on 7 April, which nearly became a riot (see para. 49 (ix) below).

13. UNTSO military observers, organized as Observer Group Lebanon (OGL), continued to man five observation posts (Lab, Hin, Ras, Mar, Khiam) along the Lebanese side of the 1949 Israel-Lebanon armistice demarcation line (ADL). In addition, six UNTSO teams assist UNIFIL in the performance of its tasks. There is a team based in Metulla (Israel), which serves as liaison with the Israel Defence Forces (IDF) in that locality and with the de facto forces; a team based in Tyre, serving as liaison with local representatives of PLO, the Lebanese National Movement and AMAL (Lebanese Shi'ite armed organization); and four mobile teams whose functions are to prevent and investigate incidents.

14. The present deployment of UNIFIL is as follows (see annexed map):

(a) The Force headquarters is located at Naqoura;

(b) The Senegalese battalion is deployed in the northern part of the western sector, with its headquarters at Marakah;

(c) The Fijian battalion is deployed in the southern part of the western sector, with its headquarters at Qana;

(d) The Nigerian battalion is deployed in the northern part of the central sector, with its headquarters at Tayr Zibna;

(e) The Dutch battalion is deployed in the south-western part of the central sector, with its headquarters at Haris;

(f) The Irish battalion is deployed in the south-eastern part of the central sector, with its headquarters at Tibnin;

(g) The Ghanaian battalion is deployed in the eastern part of the central sector, with its headquarters at Kafr Dunin;

(h) The Nepalese battalion is deployed in the western part of the eastern sector, with its headquarters at Blate;

(i) The Norwegian battalion is deployed in the eastern part of the eastern sector, with its headquarters at Ebel es-Saqi;

S/14537
English
Page 5

(j) The headquarters camp command, composed of Ghanaian and Irish troops, is based at Naqoura;

(k) The French logistic component is located at Naqoura;

(l) The French engineer company is located at Al Hinniyah;

(m) The Norwegian maintenance company is located in the vicinity of Tibnin;

(n) The Italian helicopter wing is based at Naqoura;

(o) The Swedish medical company is located at Naqoura;

(p) Observer Group Lebanon is based at Naqoura;

(q) A guard detachment is stationed in Tyre barracks. This 45-man unit from one battalion continues to be drawn on a two-week rotation basis from all infantry battalions in the Force;

(r) The military policy company is based at Naqoura; it functions throughout the UNIFIL area of operation and outside it as required.

15. The Lebanese national army unit, under the operational control of the UNIFIL Commander, was increased in strength from 617 to 1,350, all ranks. Its headquarters is at Arzun; subunits are attached to UNIFIL battalions in the western and central sectors. In January, an infantry platoon was deployed in Tyre barracks, and, subsequently, other subunits have been deployed in Al-Qantara, Al Qulaylah, Abbasiyah and Dayr Qanun. They are increasingly involved in patrolling and in manning observation posts and check-points jointly with UNIFIL.

16. A Lebanese engineering company, 130 strong, has been stationed at Arzun and is working on improving existing buildings and the construction of shelters. It will also undertake projects for the benefit of the civilian population in the area of operation. A Lebanese medical team of nine, led by a doctor, has joined the staff of the Tibnin hospital.

17. During the period under review, relations between UNIFIL and the Lebanese Internal Security Forces (ISF) were significantly strengthened. In addition to ISF personnel assigned to UNIFIL check points, ISF has started to carry out independent patrols within the UNIFIL area and has organized mobile check points, always in close co-ordination and co-operation with UNIFIL. ISF also assists UNIFIL with special investigations of mutual concern and is making an important contribution towards restoring law and order in the area.

176

S/14537
English
Page 6

II. ADMINISTRATION AND LOGISTICS

18. During the period under review, UNIFIL experienced administrative and logistic
difficulties for a variety of reasons. Those difficulties, and the efforts to
remedy them, are set out below.

A. Accommodation

19. Efforts continued to implement the UNIFIL prefabricated building programme and
to improve facilities at UNIFIL headquarters and in the battalion areas. However,
some troops still have to be accommodated in tents, and the number of such troops
will increase with the return of the Nepalese battalion. An extensive fencing
programme to protect the headquarters compound was completed. Additional efforts
are now being made to reinforce physical security throughout the area of operation
and, in particular, in the forward areas.

20. Contractors were engaged to build the Norwegian battalion petrol station at
Ebel es-Saqi and to install a 4,000-litre-capacity kerosene tank, with protective
walls, at the Irish battalion petrol station in Tibnin. Contracts were made for
asphalting 5,850 square metres at the Force forward headquarters in Al Hinniyah and
in battalion areas. Contracts were also entered into for the following essential
jobs at Naqoura headquarters: building of an ammunition magazine and the repair of
four warehouses for the French logistic contingent; installation of armoured
electrical power telephone cables; installation of four fibreglass water-tanks;
and asphalting of areas totalling 5,575 square metres of the headquarters compound.

B. Communications

21. The installation of the communications equipment, acquired from the stocks of
the United Nations Emergency Force (UNEF) is now nearly complete. All battalions
have been equipped with teleprinters, and, with the temporary exception of the
Fijian and Senegalese battalions, all have also been provided with dial telephones.
The generator and radio workshops required for maintaining the newly acquired
equipment have been completed. Owing to the expansion of the Naqoura camp, the old
electrical grid proved to be insufficient. New generators and distribution systems
were installed by UNIFIL during the current mandate.

C. Logistics

22. Logistic support for UNIFIL continues to be provided by a headquarters
logistic branch, a French logistic component, a Norwegian maintenance unit, a
Swedish medical company and an Italian helicopter wing. A welcome development was
the arrival of a Ghanaian engineer platoon.

23. During the period under review, financial constraints and delays in delivery
time for supplies and spare parts affected logistic support to the Force. For
instance, petrol consumption had to be restricted at a time when the Force was

S/14537
English
Page 7

seeking to increase its operational capability. Special measures had to be taken
in an effort to alleviate those and related difficulties and the situation is
being kept under careful review.

24. In my report of 12 December 1980 (S/14295, para. 21), I informed the Security
Council of the efforts undertaken by the UNIFIL administration and of the progress
made in enlarging the purchase of supplies from Lebanese sources or through
Lebanese ports. This policy has continued, and in spite of recent developments in
the area, which caused irregularities in the delivery of essential commodities,
procurement from Lebanon has been maintained at a high level.

25. Fresh food has been supplied from Lebanese sources, except for the units in
Naqoura, which are supplied from Israel. Dry and frozen food rations continue to
be obtained from Cyprus. Certain supplies from Cyprus and elsewhere have been
routed via Haifa, particularly during periods of closure of the Beirut port.

26. The unserviceability of equipment is now such as to place a strain on the
operational capacity of the Force. The fleet of vehicles, mostly contingent-owned,
comprises more than 40 different makes and 80 models, some of them 20 years old;
this has created serious maintenance problems. Unfortunately, plans to use
maintenance facilities in Lebanon (see S/14295, para. 21) failed to materialize.
UNIFIL has therefore started an emergency programme aimed at reaching an acceptable
maintenance level in the near future.

27. In order to lessen UNFIL dependence on costly generators, a study was made,
in conjunction with the Lebanese Electricity Authority, to determine where a
combined local network/generator electric system could be installed. The matter
has been followed up with the Lebanese Government, as has the question of the
maintenance and improvement of the roads in the UNIFIL area of operation. The
water supply is not entirely satisfactory, and efforts have been undertaken to
improve it at headquarters and in battalion areas.

28. During the period under review, the French engineering company defused 160
shells, mines and grenades, and neutralized 187 cluster bombs. It also cleared
20,000 square metres of mined ground and destroyed 4,000 rounds of small-arms
ammunition. Its works and plant platoon moved 58,840 cubic metres of earth,
levelling sites for prefabricated buildings, shelters, septic tanks and roads.

29. The UNIFIL hospital at Naqoura continued to provide health services to Force
personnel. In conjunction with the battalions' medical centres and in the absence
of other facilities, it also continued to treat the local population as required.
During the period, the out-patient clinic had a total of 5,084 patients - 3,070
UNIFIL personnel and 2,014 Lebanese civilians. In the same period, the hospital
admitted and treated 422 patients - 274 UNIFIL personnel and 148 Lebanese civilians.
The operation unit of the hospital, in its two operational theatres, performed 269
operations - 189 cases of minor surgery and 80 cases of advanced surgery. A total
of 1,449 x-ray examinations were performed. The hospital dentist treated 1,643
patients.

S/14537
English
Page 8

30. As in the past, UNIFIL personnel or Lebanese civilians wounded in the area as a result of shelling or accidents were evacuated by UNIFIL helicopter to the hospital at Naqoura. During the period under review there were 55 medical evacuations, 47 of them by helicopter and 8 by ambulance. The services of Rambam Hospital in Haifa remain available for emergency cases which cannot be treated at the UNIFIL hospital. In this connexion, appreciation is reiterated to the Israeli Government for the assistance provided by Israeli health authorities for the treatment of wounded UNIFIL personnel, especially at Rambam Hospital. During the period under review, UNIFIL medical personnel intensified contacts with the Lebanese authorities in connexion with both the upgrading of medical services for the population in the area and the use of hospitals in Tyre and Saida for the referral of civilian cases.

31. The Italian helicopter wing transported a total of 2,588 passengers, including seriously wounded and sick persons. In some emergencies, flights had to be undertaken at considerable risk to the helicopter crews and hospital personnel involved.

III. FUNCTIONS AND ACTIVITIES OF THE FORCE

A. Guidelines and terms of reference

32. UNIFIL continued to operate in accordance with the guidelines set out in my report of 19 March 1978 (S/12611) on the implementation of Security Council resolution 425 (1978) which was approved by the Council in its resolution 426 (1978). According to that report, UNIFIL was envisaged as a two-stage operation. In the first stage, the Force was to confirm the withdrawal of Israeli forces from Lebanese territory to the international border. Once that was achieved, UNIFIL was to establish and maintain an area of operation. In that connexion, the Force was to supervise the cessation of hostilities, ensure the peaceful character of the area of operation, control movement and assist the Government of Lebanon in ensuring the return of its authority in the area.

B. Co-operation with UNTSO

33. UNTSO military observers of OGL continued to assist UNIFIL and to co-operate in the performance of its tasks under the institutional arrangements described in my reports of 12 January 1979 (S/13026, para. 14), 12 June 1980 (S/13994, paras. 26 and 27) and 12 December 1980 (S/14295, para. 26).

34. During the period under review, the only change in the operational assignments linking UNTSO and UNIFIL was the formation of an additional team to operate in the sectors of the Norwegian and Ghanaian/Nepalese battalions.

35. In my report of 12 December 1980 (S/14295, paras. 27-29), I informed the Security Council of the meeting which took place in Naqoura on 1 December 1980 between Israeli and Lebanese representatives, under the chairmanship of the Chief of Staff of UNTSO, in relation to the efforts to reactivate the Israel-Lebanon Mixed

S/14537
English
Page 9

Armistice Commission (ILMAC). In its resolution 483 (1980), adopted on
17 December 1980, the Council called "on all parties to continue such efforts
as are necessary for the total and unconditional implementation of the General
Armistice Agreement". Accordingly, I instructed the Chief of Staff of UNTSO to
pursue actively negotiations with the parties and, as a first step, to make
arrangements for another meeting as soon as possible. Throughout those efforts,
the Israeli authorities continued to maintain their position that ILMAC was no
longer valid, and the Lebanese authorities continued to uphold the view that the
Armistice Agreement was still in force and that ILMAC should be reactivated. The
Chief of Staff of UNTSO sought to convene another meeting under his chairmanship
in early April. While that did not take place because of recent developments in
the area, efforts towards the reactivation of ILMAC will be resumed at the
earliest opportunity.

C. Contacts with the parties

36. During the period under review, contacts with the parties concerned were
maintained both at United Nations Headquarters and in the area, with a view to
further implementing the UNIFIL mandate. In this connexion, it will be recalled
that the Security Council, in its resolution 483 (1980), requested that I "take
the necessary measures to intensify discussions among all the parties concerned,
so that UNIFIL may complete its mandate". As a practical arrangement, I requested
Mr. Iqbal A. Akhund, who is serving in Beirut as Co-ordinator of Assistance for
Reconstruction and Development of Lebanon, to establish contact with the Lebanese
authorities and representatives of various groups concerned, including PLO. The
purpose of those contacts was to promote better understanding and support of
UNIFIL and to build support for further efforts to fulfil the UNIFIL mandate,
including the strengthening of the Lebanese Government presence, both military
and civilian, in the south. Those contacts were intensified and widened when
Mr. Brian Urquhart, Under-Secretary-General for Special Political Affairs, visited
the region from 7 to 17 April 1981 at my request. In the course of that visit,
Mr. Urquhart had wide-ranging discussions with the leaders and senior officials
of Lebanon and Israel. In Beirut, he also met with leaders of political groups
and with the Chairman of PLO.

37. General Callaghan and his senior staff have been in continuous contact with
the parties on matters regarding the deployment and functioning of the Force. To
that end, they have continued to meet at regular intervals with high Lebanese
officials in the ministries concerned and, particularly, with the Army Commander.
In the area of operation, negotiations and consultations have been held by members
of UNIFIL with the various armed groups, as required, to ensure the smooth
functioning of the Force and to reduce the risks of confrontation and armed
clashes. Contacts with the various armed groups have generally been undertaken by
UNIFIL headquarters staff, through OGL military observer teams and through contacts
by the battalion commanders. The battalion commanders have investigated local
violations of the cease-fire and all other situations involving incidents which
might have led to hostile activities within the UNIFIL area of operation.

180

38.   As in the past, the headquarters of ILMAC in Beirut has functioned as a liaison office for UNIFIL and provided valuable assistance to the Force.   The services of the Director of the United Nations information centre in Beirut, Mr. Samir Sanbar, have continued to be most useful to UNIFIL.

39.   In Jerusalem, General Erskine, Chief of Staff of UNTSO, and his senior staff have maintained contact with the Israeli authorities, as necessary, on matters pertaining to UNIFIL.

S/14537
English
Page 11

D. Situation in southern Lebanon and activities of UNIFIL

40. The situation as of 11 December 1980 was described in my last periodic report (S/14295). After examining that report, the Security Council, on 17 December 1980, adopted resolution 483 (1980), in which it renewed the mandate of UNIFIL for a further period of six months and reiterated its commitment to the full implementation of the UNIFIL mandate throughout its entire area of operation up to the internationally recognized boundaries, according to the terms of reference and guidelines as stated and confirmed in the relevant Security Council resolutions. In spite of intensive efforts made both at United Nations Headquarters and in the field, the basic situation has remained essentially the same as last reported. During the period under review, the activities of armed elements (mainly PLO and the Lebanese National Movement), the de facto forces (Christian and associated militias), and IDF in and near the UNIFIL area of operation continued and, on occasion, intensified.

41. I regret having to report that, during the period, UNIFIL again suffered fatal casualties. On 10 January 1981, a Fijian soldier was mortally wounded and later died as a result of fire by armed elements; on 16 March, three Nigerian soldiers were killed by fire directed at their position in Al-Qantara by the de facto forces. Earlier, during the night of 18/19 January, three Senegalese soldiers were found murdered at their post in the vicinity of Barish; on 27 April, one Irish soldier was murdered and another was missing from an observation post in the vicinity of Dayr Ntar. In the last two instances, despite intensive investigations, it has not been possible to determine the identity of the perpetrators, and, to date, the missing Irish soldier has not been located.

(a) Incidents involving armed elements

42. Armed elements continued their attempts at infiltration into the UNIFIL area of deployment but on a lesser scale than during the previous mandate period, in part, because of increased patrolling and surveillance by UNIFIL. UNIFIL patrols continued to apprehend or prevent groups of armed elements from entering its area: 5 such groups were stopped during the second half of December, 13 in January, 11 in February, 4 in March and 7 in April, 12 in May and 10 in early June. Repeated attempts were also made to enter the UNIFIL area or to move within it by individuals who were armed or in military uniforms or refused to have their vehicles searched. Those individuals were stopped at UNIFIL check-points and their weapons confiscated. There were 36 such denials of entry during the second half of December, 99 in January, 67 in February, 62 in March, 66 in April, 83 in May and 77 in early June. In certain instances, tension developed at the check-points because of the refusal of individuals to co-operate with UNIFIL. Those incidents were usually resolved through firm but restrained handling by UNIFIL troops, who, when the situation warranted, drew on the assistance of the liaison officers of the groups involved.

43. In my last periodic report, I referred to the establishment of two new positions by the armed elements in the Senegalese and Fijian sectors (S/14295, para. 36). Continued intensive efforts by UNIFIL to have those positions removed have not yet proved successful. Armed elements have sought to relocate certain of their positions and to increase their presence with additional positions

in the Fijian, Senegalese and Dutch sectors. In this connexion, the PLO
leadership has stated that it has had to relocate positions for defensive reasons.
At the time of reporting, certain of the positions have been evacuated, and
intensive efforts to have others removed continue. Pending the settlement of these
questions, UNIFIL has increased its surveillance of the remaining positions, with
a view to ensuring that they are not used for tactical or hostile purposes.

44. Although the number of incidents involving armed elements in the UNIFIL area
remained comparable to those in the previous mandate, certain groups have shown an
increased reluctance to co-operate with UNIFIL. Some of the more serious incidents
involving armed elements and UNIFIL personnel are outlined below:

    (i)   On 21 December, armed elements opened fire with rocket-propelled grenades
and other weapons against two Fijian positions south of Qana.

   (ii)   On 25 December, a UNIFIL helicopter flying to Tibnin to evacuate an
injured civilian came under machine-gun fire from positions near the
Rashidiyah refugee camp.

 (iii)   On 10 January, armed elements fired at the headquarters of the Fijian
battalion. As mentioned in paragraph 41 above, a Fijian soldier was
killed as a result of that firing.

  (iv)   On 16 January, armed elements fired on a UNIFIL helicopter in the area
of Jabal Kabir. The Force Commander was aboard the helicopter.

   (v)   On 20 January, armed elements opened fire on a Fijian position after
being denied entry into the UNIFIL area.

  (vi)   On 30 January, armed elements fired rockets from the Fijian sector after
forcing their way through a check-point.

 (vii)   On 1 March, armed elements fired at the headquarters of the Fijian
battalion, one rocket-propelled grenade impacting on the signal store.

(viii)   On 29 May, a check-point manned by Fijian soldiers came under intense
fire from armed elements following the denial of entry to two men who had
refused to have their cars searched. In a prolonged exchange of fire,
a Fijian soldier and at least one armed element were wounded. Fijian
personnel contained the situation using minimum force. Later in the day,
the leader of a local group apologized for the incident.

  (ix)   On 4 June, two members of the French contingent attached to UNIFIL
headquarters were forcibly detained by armed elements near the village
of Dayr Qanun in the UNIFIL area of deployment. They were released in
the evening after having been maltreated and threatened with execution.

   (x)   On 11 and 12 June, an armed element check-point east of Kaoukaba stopped,
in one case by firing, Norwegian vehicles and held UNIFIL personnel
hostage in retaliation for petty matters. In both cases, UNIFIL personnel
were released following intensive negotiations.

45. During the period under review, various UNIFIL positions and personnel came
under close fire by armed elements. A total of 42 such incidents were recorded

S/14537
English
Page 13

throughout the period. There were also several serious incidents of harassment of
UNIFIL and UNTSO personnel by armed elements. Those incidents occurred for the
most part in areas where the members of the various armed factions were trying
to increase their presence and met with UNIFIL opposition. Certain of the
hostile actions by armed elements took the form of arbitrary detention of personnel,
hijacking of vehicles and stealing of weapons, ammunition and personal property
of the soldiers and unarmed observers. A typical such case occurred on the night
of 24 May, when an ambulance of the Swedish medical company, carrying a sick
Irish soldier, was stopped by armed elements on the road to Tyre and allowed to
proceed only after protracted negotiations. Such actions have been firmly
protested.

(b) Incidents involving the de facto forces

46. In addition to its headquarters in Naqoura, UNIFIL has established 16 positions
in the enclave. Further, the five observation posts, originally set up ty UNTSO
in 1972 in pursuance of a consensus of the Security Council, have been maintained
and are manned by UNTSO observers of OGL, which is under the operational control
of the UNIFIL Commander. During the period under review, the de facto forces
continued to oppose and prevent further deployment of UNIFIL in the enclave.

47. There was no change in the restrictions on freedom of movement of UNIFIL and
UNTSO personnel within the enclave. Thus, UNIFIL personnel could move in the
enclave only on Mondays, Wednesdays, Thursdays and Fridays for resupply purposes,
and UNTSO observers could move only on Mondays and Thursdays for logistical
purposes and only on the main road. The restriction on the observers' freedom
of movement greatly hampered their operational capability and limited their
ability to observe the situation in the border area. UNIFIL and UNTSO are pursuing
their efforts to remedy the situation and to enable the observers fully to
discharge the responsibilities entrusted to them by the Security Council.

48. As indicated in my previous periodic report (S/14295, para. 43), the de facto
forces had established encroachments in the UNIFIL area at Bayt Yahun, Blate,
Ett Taibe, Jabal Basil and Rshaf. They no longer occupy the position at Jabal Basil
and, at the end of April, they removed their tanks from the positions at Bayt Yahun
and Rshaf. Efforts are continuing to have the remaining encroachments removed.

49. Harassment of UNIFIL and UNTSO personnel, as well as the Lebanese army
personnel serving with the Force and the local population in the UNIFIL area,
continued during the period under review: there were also violent incidents
involving the de facto forces and UNIFIL personnel. Some of the more serious
incidents are outlined below:

(i)   In the night of 17/18 December, the de facto forces blew up houses in the
Dutch and Irish battalion sectors. Three people were killed and four
seriously wounded in those actions.

(ii) On 1 February, the de facto forces fired on an Irish foot patrol in the
village of Ayta az Zutt.

(iii) On 9 February, the de facto forces attempted to kidnap a 16-year-old Lebanese boy from the village of Majdal Zun. After exchanges of fire with Dutch soldiers who were manning a check-point, they fled, leaving the boy behind.

(iv) On 15 February, a patrol of the de facto forces, using a half-track, tried to force its way through a Dutch position near Shihin. There was an exchange of fire, after which the patrol withdrew.

(v) On 13 March, following threats by the de facto forces against the stationing of one platoon of the Lebanese army in Al-Qantara, a Lebanese army doctor, two army medical assistants and a driver were forced to proceed in their ambulance into the enclave, where they were temporarily detained.

(vi) On 16 March, the de facto forces fired approximately 60 mortar and tank rounds on the village of Al-Qantara, resulting in direct hits on the headquarters of a Nigerian platoon. Three Nigerian soldiers were killed and 20 wounded; 4 Lebanese soldiers and 10 civilians were also wounded. This incident was the subject of a special report (S/14407). On 19 March, the President of the Security Council made a statement on the situation on behalf of the Council members (S/14414).

(vii) On 27 March, the Irish battalion prevented the abduction of a 16-year-old Lebanese boy by the de facto forces near Brashit.

(viii) On 5 April, a Dutch listening post near Majdal Zun came under machine-gun fire from a de facto forces position west of Al Bayyadah. A Dutch armoured personnel carrier received some direct hits, and mortar rounds impacted within 80 metres of the Dutch troops.

(ix) On 7 April, the de facto forces organized a demonstration at UNIFIL headquarters in Naqoura. A group of men, some of them armed, accompanied by women and children, forced their way into the compound. Television crews and journalists were allowed by IDF to come to the scene from Israel to report on the demonstration. Only the self-restraint of the UNIFIL headquarters defence team prevented a violent escalation of the incident.

(x) On 26 April, an ambulance of the Swedish medical company, en route to Tyre barracks to evacuate a seriously ill UNIFIL soldier, came under fire from the de facto forces check-point north of Naqoura, despite prior assurances of safe passage.

(xi) On 30 May, a de facto forces half-track attempted to force its way past an Irish check-point between Bayt Yahun and Brashit. The attempt was prevented by the use of an Irish armoured vehicle, in spite of machine-gun fire by the de facto forces.

50. In the period under review, there were also many cases of firing at or close to UNIFIL positions. There were 22 such cases in the second half of December, 40 in January, 30 in February, 56 in March, 61 in April, 26 in May and 21 in early June. In some cases, the fire was returned by UNIFIL personnel. Such incidents pose a serious security threat to UNIFIL personnel at all times.

51. Attempts at incursion by the de facto forces into the UNIFIL area were mostly in the form of patrols sent into areas contiguous to the enclave. The most serious of those, were an attempt in February to move to the village of Zibqin in a combined patrol with IDF personnel, which was blocked by the Dutch battalion, and another to the village of Brashit, using an armoured personnel carrier and two civilian vehicles. In the latter case, the de facto forces fired at Irish personnel, who, in the end, were able to block the move.

(c) Exchanges of fire across the UNIFIL area

52. During the period under review, there were heavy and frequent exchanges of fire between the de facto forces in the enclave and armed elements stationed in the Tyre pocket and north of the Litani River. On a number of occasions, IDF personnel joined the de facto forces in the firing. These exchanges of fire took place over and across the UNIFIL area of deployment, but on occasion shells fell near UNIFIL positions. In this connexion, it is important to underline the relationship between those firings and other acts of violence which occurred outside the UNIFIL area of operations (see para. 59 below). The most serious exchanges of fire were as follows:

(i) During the night of 18/19 December, there were heavy exchanges of fire affecting areas both to the west and to the north-east of the UNIFIL area. The de facto forces fired some 400 rounds, and armed elements fired approximately 55 rounds. On 19 December, 26 rockets fired by armed elements impacted in the Norwegian and Ghanaian sectors, and one Norwegian soldier was seriously wounded.

(ii) Shelling was light during the first half of January. However, a heavy exchange of fire, initiated by armed elements, took place on 23 January, mainly in the north-eastern sector. On 28/29 January, another heavy exchange, covering all sectors, was recorded. On that occasion, the firing was initiated by the de facto forces. On 29 January, following an Israeli air raid, armed elements fired 8 rockets into Israel, followed by 6 more on 30 January.

(iii) On 11 February, the de facto forces and IDF again exchanged heavy fire with armed elements. On 22 February, in conjunction with an IDF ground operation against targets north of the Litani, the de facto forces and IDF fired 300 artillery, mortar and tank rounds. Armed elements artillery later returned 180 rounds, mainly towards the Marjayoun area.

(iv) On 2 March, following an Israeli air raid, armed elements fired into northern Israel. That was followed by another Israeli air strike.

Shelling was also initiated by the de facto forces and IDF in the north-eastern sector and spread rapidly to the western sector and lasted until the next morning. Armed elements responded by firing 64 rockets in the western sector, with many impacting in Israel. On 14 and 22 March, there were brief exchanges in the north-eastern sector between the de facto forces and armed elements. On 27 March, the de facto forces, later joined by IDF, fired heavily to targets north of the Litani. Armed elements artillery responded an hour later. The exchange was resumed on the night of 28 March by the de facto forces; both sides fired close to 200 rounds each. On 29 March, the de facto forces resumed fire in the morning, firing more than 100 rounds by late evening. Armed elements response was limited to 30 rounds. On the fourth day, 30 March, the de facto forces started shelling Chateau de Beaufort. From noon on 30 March to the early morning of 31 March, the de facto forces and IDF fired approximately 340 rounds towards targets north of the Litani. In that exchange, armed elements fired 205 rounds towards targets in the enclave. On the same day, there was also an exchange of fire in the western sector, in which Israeli gunboats were involved.

(v) On 3 April, firing was initiated by the de facto forces in the eastern sector, with armed elements responding four hours later. The de facto forces also fired to the vicinity of Rashidiyah camp on that day. On 4 April there was another heavy exchange, initiated by the de facto forces, later joined by IDF. In the eastern sector, the de facto forces and IDF fired 400 artillery, mortar and tank rounds; armed elements fired 300 artillery and mortar rounds and 19 rockets. In the western sector, the de facto forces started shelling the Tyre area; the armed elements response came an hour later. By midnight, the de facto forces had fired 50 artillery rounds, and armed elements had fired 80 rockets and 10 mortar rounds towards the enclave. During the day, artillery, mortar rounds and rockets fired from both sides impacted close to Norwegian, Dutch and Fijian positions. Firing continued throughout 5 April but at a lower level. On 6 April, there was a minor exchange of fire initiated by armed elements.

(vi) On 8 April, the de facto forces and IDF fired approximately 30 rounds, to which armed elements responded with 11 rounds to Marjayoun. On 9 April, armed elements initiated the firing at night, and the de facto forces and IDF responded shortly thereafter. By the early hours of the next morning, the de facto forces and IDF had fired close to 650 artillery, mortar and tank rounds, and armed elements artillery close to 440 rounds. On 9 April, Israeli gunboats fired naval artillery into the Tyre area. On 10 April, armed elements fired rockets into Israel; that was followed by an Israeli air attack and a limited exchange of fire in the north-eastern sector. That same night, armed elements fired 19 rockets towards El Qlaiaa, to which the de facto forces responded with 31 mortar rounds.

(vii) On 17 April, armed elements fired 15 rockets, 6 of which impacted in the northern area manned by the Ghanaian battalion. On 18 April, there was

S/14537
English
Page 17

another exchange of fire, which was initiated by armed elements. During that exchange, both sides fired approximately 60 rounds each. On 19 April, a minor exchange was initiated by the de facto forces in the north-eastern sector. The same day, in the western sector, armed elements initiated rocket firing into the enclave. At one point, Fijian soldiers fired warning shots over a mobile rocket launcher which had been moved into the UNIFIL area, forcing it to withdraw. The de facto forces responded with 27 artillery and mortar rounds, some of which fell close to Fijian positions at Al Qulaylah.

(viii) On 20 April, in the western sector, armed elements fired 44 rockets towards the enclave. Fire was later returned by the de facto forces and IDF. That night, 19 more rockets were fired in the same sector, with many impacting in northern Israel. The same day, firing in the north-eastern sector was also initiated by armed elements and lasted from 0730 hours until midnight. A total of 250 artillery and mortar rounds and rockets were fired, with some impacting in northern Israel and close to UNTSO observation post Mar. The de facto forces and IDF responded at noon and fired 450 rounds. The day also saw a series of Israeli air strikes north of the Litani over a period of six hours.

(ix) On 21 April, armed elements initiated the firing and fired 10 rounds in the course of the day. The de facto forces and IDF responded with approximately 230 rounds. In the western sector, the de facto forces and IDF shelled the areas of Ras al Ayn and Rashidiyah.

(x) On 24 April, in the early morning, there were exchanges of fire between Israeli gunboats and the coastal positions of armed elements. At night, firing in the north-eastern sector was initiated by armed elements. They fired about 110 artillery and mortar rounds and approximately 100 rockets into the enclave. The de facto forces and IDF responded with 140 rounds of artillery and mortar.

(xi) On 25 April, armed elements opened the shelling: 24 rockets fell into the Ghanaian and Norwegian battalion areas and 38 into Marjayoun. The de facto forces and IDF responded one hour later with 185 rounds of artillery and mortar. On 26 April, the de facto forces and IDF responded with 125 rounds.

(xii) On 27 April, there were intense hostilities. Firing in the north-eastern sector was initiated by the de facto forces and IDF in the morning and lasted until the early hours of the next day. Approximately 800 artillery, tank and mortar rounds were fired by them. During the same period, armed elements fired approximately 340 artillery and mortar rounds and rockets, with some rockets impacting in Israel. In the western sector, on the same day, armed elements fired 41 rockets, most of them falling into western Galilee. In that sector, while the response by the de facto forces was limited, IDF shelled the Rashidiyah area. Also on that day, Israeli jets conducted heavy raids against the Tyre pocket and other targets north of the Litani.

188

S/14537
English
Page 18

(xiii) On 29 April, the de facto forces initiated the firing in the eastern
sector, joined by IDF shortly afterwards. They fired 150 artillery and
mortar rounds; armed elements responded with 40 mortar rounds. In the
western sector, 12 rockets fired by armed elements impacted in Israel
and drew heavy fire from the de facto forces and IDF. Firing continued
in all sectors throughout the night.

(xiv) On 4 May, the de facto forces and IDF fired close to 300 rounds of
artillery and mortar in the north-eastern sector. The response by armed
elements was relatively limited. Heavy firing ceased on 6 May but was
resumed on 13 May, when the de facto forces, later joined by IDF, fired
150 rounds of artillery and mortar. Again, armed elements response was
limited. A brief exchange of fire occurred on 17 May in the north-
eastern sector.

(xv) On 18 May, the de facto forces and IDF fired 64 artillery and mortar
rounds. Five 155-mm shells fired from the enclave, east of Ett Taibe,
impacted near the Lebanese battalion headquarters at Arzun. Armed
elements response was limited. On 19 May, the de facto forces and IDF
fired 72 rounds from eight positions in the north-eastern sector, and
armed elements responded with 4 mortar rounds. On 20 May, 21 rounds
were fired from the enclave, and armed elements returned 6 rounds during
the night. On 24 May, 66 rounds were fired from the enclave.

(xvi) On 25, 26 and 28 May, armed elements initiated the firing in the north-
eastern sector, but the situation did not develop into heavy exchanges.
On 29 May, IDF shelled north of Khardala with a total of 37 artillery and
mortar rounds; armed elements returned fire with 27 rounds.

(xvii) In the first 15 days of June, shelling was relatively low. On 2 June,
the de facto forces and IDF fired more than 70 artillery and mortar
rounds, with no return fire. The same pattern continued on 4 and 6 June
but on a lesser scale.

53. Throughout the period, I and my senior advisers, as well as the Commander of
UNIFIL, were in touch with both sides, with a view to bringing those very heavy
exchanges of fire to an end. On 1 May, I once again appealed to the parties to
exercise restraint and instructed General Callaghan to make every effort to achieve
a cease-fire.

(d) Activity of IDF in and near the UNIFIL area of operation

54. The activities of IDF in and near the UNIFIL area of operation further
increased during the period under review. UNIFIL and UNTSO raised the matter of
IDF activities repeatedly with the Israeli authorities.

55. The presence of IDF personnel inside the enclave remained at a high level
during the reporting period. IDF gun and tank positions were developed and
observation positions established. IDF personnel were regularly sighted in various
localities in the enclave. On 25 December 1980, IDF personnel killed five armed

S/14537
English
Page 19

elements and blew up their ammunition and equipment in an incident at Wadi al Ayn in the enclave. On the basis of reports by UNIFIL soldiers who were in the vicinity, UNIFIL issued a press bulletin, stating, among other things, that the IDF soldiers had piled the bodies on each other and detonated an explosive charge on top of them. That was denied by the Israeli authorities. In view of the controversy that arose, I established a board of inquiry to look into the matter. The Board concluded that there was no evidence to support the account contained in the UNIFIL press bulletin. It was of the view, however, that the UNIFIL soldiers had reported in good faith what they thought they had seen. In making public the findings of the Board on 10 February 1981, I expressed regret that the UNIFIL bulletin contained what proved to be an incorrect statement of the facts. I also instructed the Force Commander to review UNIFIL reporting procedures.

56. While the movements of IDF personnel were generally confined to the enclave, there was a serious incursion by them into the UNIFIL area of deployment on 1 April. On that occasion, IDF personnel entered the village of Tulin in the Nigerian sector, blew up three houses and kidnapped two persons, who were eventually released on 12 May. In that incident, one Lebanese army sergeant was killed when a house near which he had taken cover was blown up. During the incursion, there was a brief exchange of fire between IDF and a combined Nigerian and Lebanese army patrol.

57. There were numerous violations of Lebanese air space by Israeli military aircraft and of Lebanese territorial waters by Israeli naval vessels. UNIFIL observed 159 air and 38 sea violations in the second half of December, 191 air and 92 sea violations in January, 222 air and 91 sea violations in February, 225 air and 127 sea violations in March, 281 air and 84 sea violations in April, 302 air and 90 sea violations in May and 144 air and 41 sea violations in early June. Pilotless reconnaissance flights over and north of the UNIFIL area, which had decreased during the winter months, increased notably from the beginning of April. There was also an increase in IDF helicopter activity over the UNIFIL area, especially over the western sector.

58. IDF also conducted a number of air operations against targets north of the Litani and adjacent to the UNIFIL area. In particular, locations were hit in the Tyre pocket, in the area north of Kasmiyah Bridge and near Chateau de Beaufort.

(e) Other incidents in the area affecting UNIFIL

59. In a situation as complex as the one in which the Force must operate, incidents occurring in the region outside the UNIFIL area of operation and involving various armed forces and groups inevitably have a bearing on developments in the UNIFIL area. During the period under review, there were serious outbreaks of violence in various parts of Lebanon which have compounded the problems facing UNIFIL. There are repercussions on the work of the Force whenever there are shellings of northern Israel or explosions and other actions inside Israel or in the Israeli-occupied territories for which Palestinian organizations claim responsibility; the same can be said about the shelling by the de facto forces of targets in Lebanon, such as Sidon, outside the UNIFIL area of operation and about military operations carried out by the IDF, including air and sea attacks. Such

190

S/14537
English
Page 20

incidents have been brought to the attention of the Security Council and/or the
General Assembly by the Permanent Representative of Israel (S/14297, A/35/783,
S/14316-A/36/57, S/14322-A/36/62, S/14328-A/36/72, S/14355-A/36/88, S/14394,
A/36/122, S/14398, S/14403-A/36/127, A/36/130, S/14409-A/36/132, S/14427-A/36/169,
S/14438-A/36/186, S/14448-A/36/211, S/14449-A/36/212, A/36/219, S/14454,
S/14476-A/36/235, S/14492-A/36/292); the Permanent Representative of Lebanon
(S/14307, S/14354, A/36/87, S/14381, A/36/109); and the Permanent Observer of PLO
(S/14435, A/36/217, S/14470, S/14507-A/36/310). In addition, a number of
communications on the subject have been addressed to me by PLO.

E. Humanitarian activities

60. During the period under review, UNIFIL continued to carry out its humanitarian
activities in close collaboration with the Governor of South Lebanon and the United
Nations Co-ordinator of Assistance for Reconstruction and Development of Lebanon.
UNIFIL also continued its co-operation with United Nations programmes, particularly
UNICEF, in a number of activities aimed at improving the social and economic
conditions for the population of the area. Special efforts were made to restore
and upgrade water, electricity, education and health services, the distribution of
food supplies and the rebuilding of schools, houses and roads. The humanitarian
section of UNIFIL assisted on several occasions in resolving cases of kidnapped
villagers.

S/14537
English
Page 21

IV. FINANCIAL ASPECTS

61. By its resolution 35/115 A of 10 December 1980, the General Assembly authorized me to enter into commitments for UNIFIL at a rate not to exceed $12,180,500 gross ($12,060,166 net) per month for the period from 19 December 1980 to 18 December 1981, inclusive, should the Security Council decide to continue the Force beyond the period of six months authorized under its resolution 474 (1980) of 17 June 1980. Accordingly, should the Security Council renew the UNIFIL mandate beyond 19 June 1981, the costs to the United Nations for maintaining UNIFIL up to 18 December 1981 will be within the commitment authorized by the General Assembly in its resolution 35/115 A, assuming continuance of the Force's existing strength and responsibilities. Appropriate financial provision will need to be made by the General Assembly at its thirty-sixth session in respect of periods after 18 December 1981, if the period of extension determined by the Security Council goes beyond that date.

V. OBSERVATIONS

62. Since I reported on UNIFIL to the Security Council on 12 December 1980, developments in Lebanon have commanded the increasing attention of the international community. These developments and the heightened tension which has accompanied them have underlined the importance of UNIFIL as a conflict control mechanism in a particularly sensitive area of the Middle East. Indeed, the complexity of the problems in the region and their interrelationship have had a profound bearing on the work of the Force.

63. Since its establishment, UNIFIL has encountered serious difficulties in fulfilling its mandate. I regret that the parties have not so far found it possible to extend to the Force the full co-operation that it requires. Despite the calls of the Security Council, this situation has persisted during the period which is now coming to an end.

64. Thus, the Force has continued to be faced with attempts by armed elements to infiltrate personnel and weapons into its area of operation and has almost daily had to deal with such incidents, sometimes at grave risk to the safety of its personnel. Armed elements have also sought to relocate certain of their positions in the UNIFIL area, stating that their actions were defensive because of the danger of attack. For its part, UNIFIL has made strenuous efforts to prevent infiltration and to contain such activities. Difficulties have persisted, however, in spite of the fact that the leadership of the PLO has renewed its assurances of co-operation with UNIFIL and has assisted in defusing tense or difficult situations.

65. To the south, the de facto forces have continued to resist further deployment of UNIFIL in the enclave held by them. Restrictions relating to freedom of movement of UNIFIL and UNTSO personnel in the enclave have also continued to complicate UNIFIL operations. In the UNIFIL area of deployment, while one encroachment has been removed and tanks have been withdrawn from two other encroachments, four positions are still maintained by the de facto forces. These forces have also

S/14537
English
Page 22

sought to harass the local population in the UNIFIL area of deployment. Following the grave incident which occurred in March 1981 (see para. 49 (vi) above), intensive efforts were made both locally and at the diplomatic level to prevent the recurrence of such incidents. While these have been avoided, it is essential to keep in mind that the mandate of UNIFIL in relation to the remainder of its area of operation, now controlled by the de facto forces, remains to be fulfilled.

66. Since the de facto forces are known to be supported and supplied by Israel, close contact has been maintained with the Israeli authorities at all levels in an effort both to secure further progress in the implementation of the UNIFIL mandate and to reduce incidents between the de facto forces and UNIFIL. Such incidents have been reduced in recent weeks, with the assistance of the Israeli authorities. However, these authorities, citing overriding considerations of national security, have not, as yet, extended to the Force the degree of co-operation necessary for the fulfilment of its mandate.

67. During the period under review, the activities of the Israeli forces in and near the UNIFIL area of operation increased. Encroachments along the international border and a high level of Israeli military activity within the enclave continue. In addition, Israeli forces have repeatedly violated Lebanese air space and territorial waters and have, on many occasions, launched attacks against targets in Lebanon outside the UNIFIL area. These activities, as other violent incidents in the region, inevitably affect the task of UNIFIL by making even more difficult the efforts of the Force to secure and maintain a cease-fire between armed elements to the north and west of its area, and the de facto forces and Israeli forces to the south. Indeed, there have been extremely heavy exchanges of fire over and across the UNIFIL area. I have been particularly concerned with this aspect of the Lebanese situation during the recent weeks of greatly heightened tension in the region and have made constant efforts to reinforce the cease-fire in southern Lebanon, with a view to avoiding any incidents which might have the effect of escalating the over-all danger of conflict in the area.

68. Despite the many difficulties which it has had to face, UNIFIL has continued in its endeavours to consolidate its position and, in co-operation with the Lebanese Government, to strengthen and make more effective the Lebanese presence, both civilian and military, in its area of operation. The strength of the Lebanese army in the south was increased by more than 700 during the period under review and now stands at 1,350, all ranks, which the Lebanese Government points out is within the limit of 1,500 allowed by the 1949 General Armistice Agreement between Israel and Lebanon. This is a significant development, particularly at a time when the Lebanese Government is dealing with most serious crises in other parts of the country. I wish to pay special tribute here to the support which the Lebanese Government has been providing to UNIFIL. It is also important to note that the population in the UNIFIL area is living and working in relative quiet and has recently increased with the arrival of relatives and friends from other, more troubled regions of the country. Civil administration is gradually being restored, along with education, health, water, electricity and other services. The collaboration between the Governor of South Lebanon, the United Nations Co-ordinator of Assistance for Reconstruction and Development of Lebanon and UNIFIL has continued and intensified, with a view to expediting the programme of activities for the benefit of the civilian population throughout southern Lebanon.

S/14537
English
Page 23

69. In the course of the current reporting period, the Chief of Staff of UNTSO has continued his efforts towards the reactivation of ILMAC, in accordance with Security Council resolution 483 (1980). Though recent developments in the area have prevented progress, these efforts will be resumed at the earliest opportunity.

70. Although the Force has not yet been able to fulfil the mandate in the way intended by the Security Council, I have no doubt that its presence and activities in southern Lebanon are an indispensable element in maintaining peace, not only in the area but in the Middle East as a whole. It would, I believe, be disastrous if UNIFIL were to be removed at the present time when the international community is witnessing with acute anxiety the tensions and conflicts in this vital area of the world. For these reasons, I find it necessary once again to recommend to the Security Council that the mandate of UNIFIL be extended for a further period of six months. The Permanent Representative of Lebanon has informed me of his Government's agreement to the proposed extension. In doing so, he has submitted a letter dated 16 June 1981, setting forth the views of his Government concerning the renewal. The text of his letter is attached to the present report.

71. In making this recommendation I wish to renew my appeal to all concerned to co-operate with UNIFIL in its task, to exercise restraint and to review policies which militate against the fulfilment of the mandate entrusted to the Force by the Security Council. It remains my view that all the parties concerned must observe strictly the cease-fire called for by the Security Council and avoid actions which inevitably lead to violent reactions. Likewise, a determined effort must continue to be made on all sides to render possible the consolidation of the UNIFIL area by the removal of positions that have proved to be provocative. It is essential that the parties desist from challenging the authority of UNIFIL and from using its area for hostile acts against each other. It is also necessary that they take reciprocal steps progressively to reduce their armed presence in the area.

72. In conclusion, I wish to express once again my deep appreciation to the troop-contributing countries for their support and co-operation in this essential peace-keeping operation. I wish also to pay tribute to the Commander of UNIFIL, Lieutenant-General William Callaghan, and his staff, both civilian and military, to the officers and men of the contingents of UNIFIL, as well as the UNTSO military observers assigned to the area. They have continued to carry out their important tasks, often at great risk, with the highest courage and dedication. They are indeed a credit both to their countries and to the United Nations. I wish also at this time to express my sincere appreciation to Major-General Emmanuel A. Erskine, for his outstanding performance as Commander of UNIFIL for nearly three years, from the inception of the Force to mid-February 1981. Finally, I should like to pay special tribute to the memory of those soldiers of UNIFIL who have given their lives in the cause of peace.

194

ANNEX I

Letter dated 16 June 1981 from the Permanent Representative of Lebanon
to the United Nations addressed to the Secretary-General

1.   As the Security Council is about to meet to examine the renewal of the mandate
of UNIFIL, the Government of Lebanon wishes to express its deepest gratitude to you
personally, and, through you, to members of the Secretariat, to the Commanders and
staff of UNIFIL, to the officers and soldiers of the various contingents and last,
but not least, to the troop-contributing countries and friendly Governments for
their efforts in preserving international peace and security in our country and
beyond.   The sacrifice of human lives for the cause of peace in the ranks of UNIFIL
will forever be remembered by Lebanon as a challenge for us all to do our utmost in
fostering the ideals of liberty and international justice embodied in the United
Nations Charter.

2.   My Government feels a particular commitment towards UNIFIL since we have been
able to meet part of the challenge and deploy substantial contingents of the
Lebanese Army, under UNIFIL command, in UNIFIL's area of operation as a major step
in fulfilling the objectives of Security Council resolution 425 (1978), and the
ensuing resolutions: the return of Lebanese authority and the restoration of
Lebanon's sovereignty.   Given the present tragic conditions in Lebanon and the
grave difficulties which our Government is confronting, our efforts in the south
will no doubt acquire a particular importance.

3.   Pending your report on the activities of UNIFIL, I am instructed by my
Government to draw your attention and the attention of the Security Council to
Lebanon's attitude when the present mandate was extended by resolution 483 (1980).
On 15 December 1980, the Government of Lebanon had submitted to the Secretary-
General and to the Security Council a memorandum (S/14296), discussing problems
that should be approached in a practical manner, so as to enable UNIFIL to implement
its mandate in the totality of its area of operation, up to the internationally
recognized boundaries.   We had quoted amply from your own report of 12 December 1980
(S/14295) to underline the importance of the role of UNIFIL, as well as the
difficulties and obstacles it was encountering.   We had also referred to Security
Council resolution 444 (1979) of 19 January 1979, repeated a number of times
since, by which the Council

   "Reaffirms its determination, in the event of continuing obstruction of the
   mandate of the Force, to examine practical ways and means in accordance with
   relevant provisions of the Charter of the United Nations, to secure the
   full implementation of resolution 425 (1978)".

4.   In our memorandum of 15 December 1980, my Government expressed its desire that
the renewal of the mandate of UNIFIL be accompanied by a number of dispositions
designed to enhance the Force, articulate its deterrent capability and review
even the methods of definition of the "area of operation", so as to render the
mandate more credible, more effective and more implementable.   Not only are the

S/14537
English
Annex I
Page 2

adverse conditions under which UNIFIL operates rendering progress difficult,
hazardous and, indeed, limited; there has also been a distinct and declared
tendency on the part of Israel to broaden the scope of its so-called "pre-emptive"
attacks in a manner that threatens the safety of UNIFIL, its very existence and
the very significance of its role as a peace-keeping force.

5.   I am instructed by my Government, once more, to ask from the Security Council
that the renewal of the mandate for another term should accent the interim
character of the Force by creating the objective conditions of its success, within
an immediate time-frame and according to a phased programme of action. The
Government of Lebanon feels compelled to ask that the renewal be accompanied by
efforts as discussed in this and in previous memoranda. Only such a disposition
will enable us all to overcome the present status quo, avoid an ever expanding
state of war and attain significant progress for the full implementation of
resolution 425 (1978) and its clear objectives.

6.   When, therefore, the Council renews the mandate of UNIFIL, we request that
the resolution should embody a clear reference to conditions stated above.

                                        (Signed)   Ghassan TUENI
                                                   Ambassador
                                                   Permanent Representative

196

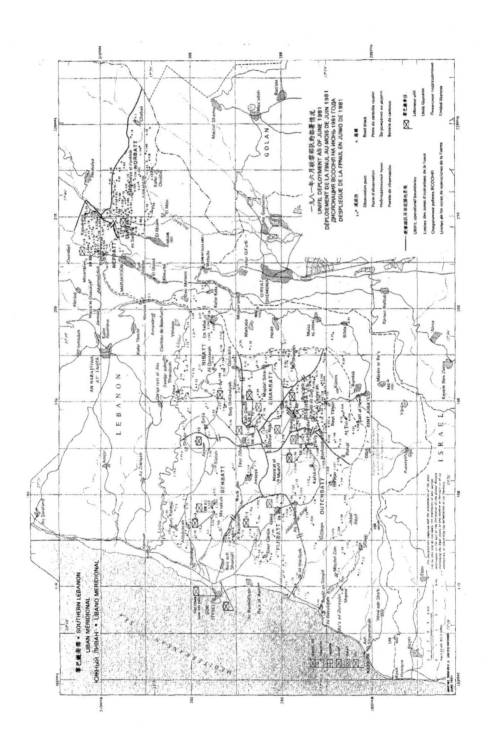

黎巴嫩南部 • SOUTHERN LEBANON
LIBAN MÉRIDIONAL
ЮЖНЫЙ ЛИВАН • LIBANO MERIDIONAL

一九八一年六月联合部队的部署情况
UNIFL DEPLOYMENT AS OF JUNE 1981
DÉPLOIEMENT DE LA FINUL AU MOIS DE JUIN 1981
ДИСЛОКАЦИЯ ВСООНЛ НА ИЮНЬ 1981 ГОДА
DESPLIEGUE DE FPNUL EN JUNIO DE 1981

Appendix B—Update on the Abduction of Kevin Joyce

<u>PRIVATE KEVIN JOYCE - 46 BATTALION - MISSING</u>

On 27 April, 1981 an observation post at Dayr Ntar near As Sultaniyah in the Irish Battalion area of operations was manned by Pte. Hugh Doherty and Pte. Kevin Joyce.

The soldiers were tasked with observing movement of vehicles and personnel in the area.

WATCH

When they failed to return to a scheduled pick-up point at 1800 hrs that evening a patrol was sent to the observation post where they found Pte. Doherty dead from gunshot wounds. Pte. Joyce was missing. The two soldiers' equipment - 2 Fn rifles and ammunition, 1 radio set, 2 flack jackets and 1 set of binoculars - was also missing.

Medical evidence indicates Pte. Doherty died instantly from 3 gunshot wounds to the chest. Three spent cartridges were found at the scene of the incident. An immediate search of the area around the post was carried out but nothing else was found.

It is assumed that Pte. Joyce was abducted by the attackers who are unknown. The abduction of Pte. Joyce was investigated at the highest diplomatic levels. The resources of UNIFIL at all levels were used (including the use of tracker dogs) in the conduct of searches of the area and meetings with and questioning of people. Military observers with UNTSO, familiar with the terrain and population of the area, as well as units of the Lebanese Army and Police assisted with the searches. PLO and IDF sources also co-operated with the investigations.

198

The Department of Foreign Affairs made extensive enquiries into the disappearance of Pte. Joyce via the Permanent Mission in New York, through the United Nations in New York to UNIFIL, through other missions in New York via the Irish Embassy in Beirut but to no avail. No motive for the attack has been established and the perpetrators have not been identified.

While all efforts to locate Pte. Joyce were unsuccessful, the Force Commander UNIFIL was not prepared to say that he should be presumed dead.

In January 1984 in response to an enquiry in the case the Force Commander stated that since the disappearance of Pte. Joyce every possible lead had been followed but there had been no indications that gave hope of finding him alive or to give hope of providing early and firm information regarding his possible whereabouts.

In 1985, an officer of the Military Police was assigned full-time to investigating the disappearance of Private Joyce. The investigation was conducted over a period of 19 months but failed to establish conclusively whether or not Pte. Joyce was still alive.

In May 1988, the military authorities received a final report from UNIFIL which concluded that Pte. Joyce was killed on 27 April, 1981 in the vicinity of Dayr Ntar. The family of Pte. Joyce now accept that he is dead and it has, accordingly, been decided to post him missing, presumed dead, with effect from 27 April, 1981. The appropriate entitlements have been paid to his next of kin.

R7155L

Appendix C—Mr. U.N.I.F.I.L.

"MR. UNIFIL" REFLECTS ON A QUARTER CENTURY OF PEACEKEEPING IN SOUTH LEBANON

AN INTERVIEW WITH TIMUR GÖKSEL

On 19 March 1978, three days after Israel's first invasion of Lebanon reached the Litani River, the United Nations Security Council (UNSC) unanimously passed (with two abstentions: Czechoslovakia and the USSR) Resolution 425 calling on Israel "immediately to cease its military action" and to "withdraw forthwith its forces from all Lebanese territory." The resolution also decided the creation of an interim force in southern Lebanon "for the purpose of confirming the withdrawal of Israeli forces, restoring international peace and security and assisting the Government of Lebanon in ensuring the return of its effective authority in the area." With a mandate of six months, the first troops of the United National Interim Force in Lebanon (UNIFIL) arrived on 23 March.

Under U.S. pressure, Israel withdrew its own forces from Lebanon by October 1978. But because it turned the border zone over to right-wing Lebanese Christian auxiliary force (later named the South Lebanon Army or SLA), Israel was seen as remaining in effective control. As a result, UNIFIL's mandate under UNSC Resolution 425 was repeatedly renewed and extended.

Israel's area of occupation greatly expanded following its second invasion of Lebanon in June 1982, which pushed all the way to Beirut. Though Israel pulled back from the Beirut region that autumn, for the next three years it occupied the entire southern part of the country up to the Awwali River just north of Sidon. After completing a phased withdrawal in June 1985, Israel retained a 10- to 20-km wide "security belt" along the border with a salient jutting northward encompassing the town of Jizzin—about 10 percent of the country. In May 2000, Israel withdrew from south Lebanon entirely and the SLA was disbanded, but UNIFIL remained because its mandate had not been entirely fulfilled since the Lebanese government's "effective authority" had not been returned.

While the boundaries of Israel's occupation shifted over the years, UNIFIL's area of deployment never changed. From the outset, it was limited to the areas Israel occupied in 1978: Lebanon south of the Litani River except for the "Tyre pocket," where the PLO in 1978 had been strong, and the border strip where Israel's proxy the SLA was ensconced. The UNIFIL area was divided into a number of sectors where some nine to ten national contingents contributed by UN member states were deployed, each based in villages or towns in the area it was assigned to patrol. The national contingents, though under the direct command of their own officers, were under overall UN command. Though the composition of the force changed over time, there was nonetheless considerable continuity, with national contingents of a number of countries remaining in south Lebanon, patrolling the same sectors, for many years. UNIFIL troops were assisted by the UN Observer Group Lebanon, a unit of some fifty men from the UN Truce Supervision Organization set up in 1949 to monitor the armistice lines. Almost all the UN observers, like the UNIFIL staff officers lived in Israel. By contrast, the UNIFIL national contingents, both troops and officers, lived in the south Lebanese villages where they were deployed.

Until Israel's full withdrawal from Lebanon in May 2000, the size of the UNIFIL force varied over the years, reaching as high as 6,000 but mostly remaining around 4,000–4,500. Following the withdrawal, the UN temporarily raised the authorized limit to 7,900, but when the area remained calm and the anticipated atrocities did not materialize, UNIFIL was gradually reduced to 2,000 and remained at that level through the summer 2006 war. As that war ended, the UNSC on 11 August unanimously passed (without abstentions) Resolution 1701, which "enhanced" UNIFIL, raising its authorized force strength to 15,000 and expanding its mandate.

With UNIFIL—the new UNIFIL—very much in the news following the summer 2006 war between Israel and Hizballah, JPS decided to interview the man most closely associated with the "old UNIFIL." Timur Göksel, who had been with the UN information office in Ankara, Turkey, joined UNIFIL as its press officer and spokesman about six months after its creation and remained with the organization for the next twenty-four years—years that saw not only Israel's invasion and two major incursions, but also the height of PLO power and its obliteration, the birth and development of the local resistance after 1982, the waning of the powerful Amal movement and the rise of Hizballah. Because of Göksel's long association with the interim force (where individual tours of duty rarely exceeded a few years), his familiarity with every village and hamlet south of the Litani, and his personal acquaintance with all the leading players, he has frequently been referred to as "Mr. UNIFIL" or "Mr. South Lebanon." In 1995 he became UNIFIL senior advisor as well as spokesman, confirming the political and mediating roles he had exercised from the outset. Since his retirement from UNIFIL in 2003, he has taught conflict management and other courses at the American University of Beirut and continues to visit south Lebanon on a regular basis.

The interview took place at the end of November 2006 in one of Göksel's favorite Beirut hangouts, the Café de Prague, formerly the Rose and Crown bar where foreign journalists congregated during the early years of Lebanon's civil war. The immediate background to the interview was the assassination of a young cabinet minister, Pierre Gemayel (son of Lebanese ex-president Amin Gemayel and nephew of Phalangist leader and assassinated Lebanese president Bashir Gemayel), raising tensions and exacerbating the standoff between the government of Prime Minister Fuad Siniora, backed by a Sunni-Christian-Druze coalition, and the opposition led by Hizballah, but which itself had Christian and Druze components. With rumors abuzz about the impact of the deteriorating situation on the new UNIFIL forces, still being deployed a the time, the interview was interrupted several times by journalists and others seeking Göksel's take on the unfolding events: he seems to have remained an unofficial spokesman for south Lebanon and popular with journalists not only for his knowledge but for his colorful speech and shoot-from-the-hip frankness. The interview, which took place on 24, 26, and 27 November 2006 over serial espressos and in clouds of cigarette smoke, was conducted by Linda Butler, associate editor of JPS.

Butler: Everybody is talking about the new UNIFIL and the fact that it can use force. What did the original UNIFIL's mandate say about the use of force? How far could they go?

Göksel: Look, like all peacekeeping forces, the original UNIFIL had the right of self-defense. Most people don't realize that self-defense includes using weapons against those who are trying by force to prevent you from carrying out your mandate. There is a wide latitude in "self-defense" for using force, if you want to use it.

So it wasn't that the original UNIFIL was emasculated or lacking a mandate. The problem is not what's missing on paper, but what's possible on the ground. UNIFIL in 1978 was given these powers, but who was going to back you up? Could you count on the international community to send in a force to help you? Was there some semblance of local authority to provide support? No. So basically you were given this wide mandate but told you were on your own.

The difference today is there's a longer menu of reasons that the new UNIFIL can open fire—they're spelled out in detail. And of course now the Lebanese national army is on the ground. The absence of that army or any other legal force was the major cause of the original UNIFIL's perceived failure. But the flip side of that backing is that the new "enhanced" UNIFIL that is supposedly so "robust" can't do anything without the okay of the Lebanese army. When the old UNIFIL deployed in the south in 1978, we didn't ask anybody for anything because there was nobody to ask, so we did what we wanted—within the "rules of the south," of course, the local customs and practice, and with a healthy dose of realism. What the new force has going for it is that the international community is more involved, and the sponsors of the new UN resolution are completely committed to it.

Butler: But wasn't that the case back in 1978? Wasn't there strong backing, especially from the United States, for UNSC Resolution 425 calling for Israel's withdrawal and creating UNIFIL?

Göksel: That backing was pretty short-lived, and while the United States was the driving force behind Resolution 425, its real motivation was not to solve the Lebanon problem but to buy time to save the Egyptian-Israeli peace initiative opened by [Egyptian president Anwar] Sadat's visit to Jerusalem a few months before. If Israel had been allowed to stay in Lebanon, the Barbara Walters–inspired Sadat mission would be finished. And after the usual foot dragging and delays, Israel did leave south Lebanon, at least technically. The UN certified the withdrawal. It's true that Israel's Lebanese proxies, the militia of Sa'd Haddad, remained. The whole thing was a gimmick, but that's what the Americans wanted and they got it.

Actually, there was a lot of opposition to the creation of UNIFIL from UN officials. They said it wasn't doable to have a peacekeeping force in south Lebanon, that there was no state, that it was a civil war situation, that the force would be left to the wolves. They were overruled, but it was because of this opposition that the force was called "interim." The Americans pushed the resolution through by saying "no, no, this is just for the very short term, so let's call it an interim force, it will be out in one year." So UNIFIL was created and then everybody forgot about it. And there were a number of mistakes made at the beginning that UNIFIL never stopped paying for.

Butler: For example?

Göksel: The decision to put UNIFIL headquarters in Naqura, right on the Israeli border, and to have the UNIFIL civilian employees and staff officers living in Israel—I myself lived there for twenty-two years. This made us hostages of Israel and its proxy, Haddad's South Lebanon Army. 1[*] The fact that all these UN people had to cross into Lebanon every day meant that Israel or the Haddad people could just close the border at will, for no reason. "The border is closed, you can't go to work." Okay, you don't go to work. Or they close it in the evening, and you can't go home. The Israelis of course were very happy to have these hundreds of UN families spending money in Israel. Plus, because Lebanon was in a state of war, most of UNIFIL's official purchases were from Israel also. So it was very lucrative for Israel. But this didn't change their attitude to the UN.

Butler: Who made the decision about the headquarters at Naqura and the staff living in Israel?

Göksel: It was a UN decision. Obviously, it was not possible for the headquarters to be in Israel, the occupying country, but the officers wanted it close enough to Israel so they could play tennis, have a beer, and that sort of thing. None of them wanted to be confined to the village of Naqura—Beirut after all was inaccessible because of the civil war. Of course there were good excuses for not locating it elsewhere. The Lebanese government had suggested the barracks in Tyre, for example, but the Palestinians didn't want UNIFIL moving into what was basically their logistical and command center and they argued that because that area—the so-called "Tyre pocket"—had not been occupied by Israel in 1978, the UN couldn't take it over. The UN agreed. Tyre wasn't all that safe anyway, but they could have chosen some village that would have been both safe and beyond Israel's control, except most such villages lacked infrastructure and conveniences. So they hit upon Naqura, which had once been the UN crossing point between Lebanon and Palestine. That was the first and most serious in a long series of mistakes at the beginning.

Butler: What were some of the others?

Göksel: There were some concessions that shouldn't have been made. For example, as I just mentioned, when UNIFIL was established the Palestinians insisted that the UN couldn't move into areas Israel had never occupied. Besides the Tyre pocket, there was another smaller area to the east that had not been taken—there was a concentration of Palestinian bases there and I guess the Israelis didn't think it was worth the losses they would have had to incur to capture it. So the Palestinians argued that they had the right to keep those bases—I think there were about sixteen of them—smack in the middle of what should have been the UN zone. The UN agreed. A big mistake. So this area east of Tyre, south of the village of Juwayya, became the "Iron Triangle"2[†] where UNIFIL couldn't enter. The Palestinians agreed that we could control access to the Iron Triangle and prevent entry of all but humanitarian supplies, food and such—in other words, no weapons. But come on! There were hundreds of ways to get to those bases and no way to control what went in.

The Israelis never let the UN forget that concession, and they insisted on getting a similar deal for their own guys, the Haddad militia, who were deployed in this wide strip all along the border. They claimed Haddad was independent—analogous to the Palestinians. Excuse me? Haddad gets a salary from the Israelis, he's supplied by them, armed by them, clothed by them, takes his orders from them—it was an auxiliary force! But using this claim of independence they didn't allow the UN to take up the entire border area. The UN went along. That created a lot of problems for us because these guys were always trying to encroach on UNIFIL areas, and not just to extend Israel's control but also, it should be said, to expand the areas where they themselves could "tax" the local population. There were a number of clashes between us and the SLA over the years, and a number of UN soldiers got killed. In any case, the UN had accepted the deal and it became an established fact. One of the inherent weakness of any multinational command—which is always worse in a UN command—is that the contingents make local deals with the forces on the ground, without telling headquarters. These later come back to haunt you.

But beyond the mistakes, it has to be said that the whole UN peacekeeping idea is prone to miscalculations. Whatever the manuals say, there are no fixed rules—it's all very local, you have to play it by ear. It's very difficult to take any collective action. There are these nine or ten separate national contingents. Everyone goes through the motions of being under UN command. We have these terrific parades, so colorful, so spit and polish, in perfect formation—I love them! But do you think any of those contingents will take orders from the UN when the going gets rough? Basically, they all do their own thing. It's worse with this new "robust" UNIFIL because no less than twenty-nine countries have contingents. So a young cabinet minister gets assassinated in Beirut the other day3[‡] and all of a sudden there's talk of some of the contingents being pulled out. *Ya habibi*—what's the connection? Is it so easy to give up UN peacekeeping?

But that's the way it is. You don't really control the national contingents. For starters, no one trusts the set up at UN headquarters in New York. There are 100,000 peacekeepers all over the world, and they're managed by a couple of bureaucrats who have never served in an army in their lives and who specialize in not offending anyone. Nobody's going to entrust their soldiers to these guys. Plus if the situation on the ground gets ugly, New York doesn't want to hear about it. The less you refer unpleasant issues to them, the happier they are. And there are bound to be unpleasant issues: when UNIFIL came in 1978 they had no idea about the local dynamics, who the Palestinians were, what the Israelis were all about. They thought relations with the Israelis would be easy because they thought they were Europeans and because their army had such a legendary reputation. They got over that pretty quickly.

So UNIFIL was thrown into this environment where there was no state, no army, where there was a triple war going on, where you had all these Palestinian groups, all these Lebanese groups, you had the Israelis, you had their SLA proxies. So this is where you send these nice UN soldiers with their light rifles and tell them not only to survive but to fight these characters when necessary, with absolutely no support from anybody. If you ask me, that original UNIFIL that everybody's denigrating so much was a lot more "robust" than this one that can't even put up a checkpoint. I mean, the presence of the Lebanese army makes everything so safe and easy for the UN. Somebody gets a flat tire and they call in the army to fix it.

Butler: Explain what you mean by a triple war going on.

Göksel: Well, there was the civil war "south Lebanon version," the civil war "Beirut version," and the cross-border Palestinian-Israeli war. The Palestinian-Israeli war was pretty straight forward, but the alliances and stakes in the two civil war versions differed. The parties that were allied to each other, at least nominally, in Beirut—i.e., the Palestinians and Shi`a—were fighting each other in the south, where it was an internal war for turf, not ideological; even the Christian-Muslim dimension had already quieted down by the time we got there. In the version up north, in Beirut, it was the so-called Islamo-Palestinian-progressive alliance against the mainly Christian forces.

That was the environment, in a nutshell. You are a UN force, you are told to keep your area peaceful. So if armed Palestinians come into your area, you're supposed to disarm them and hand their weapons over to the national authority because it's a national sovereignty issue. But excuse me, where's the national authority? So you're told to turn them over to the PLO liaison officer who signs for them, and you say "please don't let your guys come into our area again," and he says "yes yes," you kiss, you have a cup of tea, and it's all very friendly. And then ten days later you stop another Palestinian patrol and confiscate their weapons, you check the numbers and you find it's the same weapons, back again.

Butler: It's that easy to confiscate their weapons, just like that, no fuss?

Göksel: That's why we had a lot of clashes—weapons are crucial to a man's honor in our parts. People got killed on both sides. UNIFIL took a lot of casualties—about 270 dead over the years and out of that about 100 were killed in action. That's a very big number, and most of those were in the first years. Whether these confiscations were friendly or turned nasty depended partly on which Palestinian faction you were confronting. If it was Fatah it was usually pretty friendly, because we were on good terms with their leaders. Besides, they had a bunch of good former Jordanian officers in the Tyre area with a degree of control over their men.

But there were fourteen different factions, Palestinians plus their allies. I know because one of the first tasks the force commander assigned me when I first came to UNIFIL—even though I came as the press officer, not a political officer—was to make an inventory of all the groups we had to deal with and who was affiliated with whom. Which gives you some idea about how much at sea we were at the beginning. And in the course of my investigation I discovered that there were no less than three "Arab Socialist Unions"—basically Lebanese gangs who hire out their services to any group willing to pay, which in those days basically meant the Palestinians. To show how surreal it was, one day I'm in Tyre and there's this fellow behind a big anti-aircraft gun waving at me and he runs over and kisses me. It turns out he's from Turkey, one of these guys from the southeast who come without passports to Lebanon to find work in construction or something. He's just a kid and hasn't even done his military service in Turkey and has never fired a gun in his life, but someone asks him if he knows how to fight and he says sure and the next thing you know he's a gunner with some gang with a sexy name like Arab Socialist Union. I mean, is that real?

Butler: Tell me how these disarmaments—the difficult ones—might be carried out.

Göksel: Let me give you an example. There was a serious case in a place called Wadi Jilu, east of Tyre. The Fijians, who are good soldiers and take their mission seriously, were in charge of that area, which was on one of the main access routes to the Iron Triangle, which meant that there were always problems with the Palestinians. The Fijians see these guys placing heavy weapons, recoilless rifles, in the hills overlooking their area, and get nervous. They deploy their troops, the Palestinians bring in more fighters, and a serious confrontation develops. The UNIFIL force commander asked me to see if I could do anything. I said "Hey, I'm just the press officer," but he said I was the only one who could talk to the Palestinians without starting a war. So I went to Wadi Jilu, with the new deputy force commander, a general fresh from Europe, and some American officers from the UN Observer Group in Lebanon. These Americans were good military men, top notch professionals mostly—some had been combat officers in Vietnam and some even knew Arabic. We went there as a team.

The Fijians had tried to call the PLO liaison officer, but he was unavailable—they all become unavailable in these situations. The Palestinians involved turned out to be the Popular Front [for the Liberation of Palestine], George Habash's PLFP. They had a very tough commander there, Major Nur. He was a legendary fighter. Even the Israelis respected him. I don't know what became of him. Anyway, we had a kind of *High Noon* scene from an American Western in the middle of that three-road junction: I'm in the middle of the road, my guys behind me, and the Palestinians are on the other side, armed to the teeth and pretty ferocious looking, five-day beards and all—I think they hand pick these guys or keep them in reserve for these encounters, for intimidation. I'm waiting for Major Nur to come out so we can talk, and I tell my general, who is very nervous—this is his first day out—"Don't interfere. This is my show." Meanwhile I tell my Americans to get a fix on where the weapons were, so I can use the information to impress Major Nur at the right moment.

He comes out, very angry. So I act angry also. We're both talking tough because that's the way you do it, you don't back down at the outset. Things seem to escalate and my European general is nudging me, "Please, please, be polite!" I ignore him. The intimidation works on foreigners and newcomers, but I know the style: I'm a Turk, this is my part of the world, too. Nur knows and I know that we are not going harm each other, but we have to create this public show, right? I know that he can't lose face with his men so I will give him that. He's saying this is a Palestinian area and Lebanon has given them the right to operate freely there to recover their lost country, and so on. I escalate: "Major Nur, you are an experienced fighter, so obviously you know how to read maps." "Of course," he says. I say, "Habibi, this is Lebanon. Palestine is that way. You have no right to put your guns here." I thought our new deputy commander was going to faint, but the Americans knew the game. Meanwhile they had whispered to me where the weapons were and I said to Nur: "You have one recoilless rifle there and one machine gun there and another there, etc." He asks how I know and I reply, "Look, I am a simple Turk, but I did my military service and I can see those things. Why don't you just remove them?" For the face saving, I agreed to let them be removed the next morning. The Fijians were worried, but I said, in front of Nur and his men, "Relax. If Major Nur says he's going to get them out tomorrow morning, he will. He's a man of his word." Our European general was quite shaken by the encounter and I told him, "Look, this is not Europe. We have a different lifestyle here, a different way at looking at problems. I'm not against your style, but this is the reality here. If you try to impose your ways, it won't work."

That's why peacekeeping with all the nice civilized meetings doesn't always work. Outsiders just don't get that this region has been here for thousands of years and has its own time-honored ways and you can't just impose your ways and expect it to work. Anyway, I ended up with a commendation for my conflict management at Wadi Jilu and possibly saving UN lives.

Butler: Is this kind of, shall we say, difference of approach pretty standard?

Göksel: Oh yes, in all kinds of situations. For example, let's say a UN official kills somebody in a traffic accident. It happens. So what is the reaction from UN headquarters? "We'll send our insurance adjuster and he'll take care of it." Uh, excuse me, you kill a nine-year-old boy and you think the family is going to wait around for your adjuster? If an honorable reconciliation process does not begin immediately, this kid's family is going to take their guns, stop you on the road, hijack your vehicle, whatever. But the UN mindset is to send an adjuster who tries to put the blame on the victim to save his company money. One thing I succeeded in doing was to bring the *sulha* process4[§] to UNIFIL. Sometimes I wished I hadn't because I ended up spending most of my time doing what gets the fancy name of "conflict management." I had no idea that I'd later be teaching it as a university course.

Actually, some of these cases can get pretty serious. I remember an incident in Haddatha village, which was in the area patrolled by the Irish. The Irish were very outgoing, probably the most beloved soldiers in the south, but a couple of them got into a quarrel with some Amal guys and two brothers were killed. This was in the late 1980s, when the Amal movement was the dominant force in the south, and these brothers were from a large militant family that would wipe out the whole Irish contingent if something wasn't done. A nightmare situation. I immediately contacted Nabih Birri, the head of Amal. I said "*Ustadh*, I need you. This is a very serious case. We cannot have bloodshed. I know you don't want that." He says "Of course not." So he sends me his deputy, the highly respected Dr. Ayoub Humayed, to take me to visit the family. On his advice I took the UNIFIL force commander, a Swede at the time, along. When we got to the house the other brothers and the relatives all grabbed their guns—if Humayed hadn't been with us, who knows what would have happened? But because of his intervention, we were able to pay our condolences. All we could do was say how terribly sorry we were, that something had gone very wrong, that the Irish fellows had nothing against them, that there was nothing we could do or say that could make up for their loss. Things like that. But it started the reconciliation process, which continued the next day with the mediation of a local cleric chosen with Amal's help.

Eventually it boiled down to compensation. I tried to explain to New York what a disaster something like this represents for the family in strictly material terms, the fact that these two young men can't be the family's breadwinners now. I emphasized that if the usual UN rules were applied there would be revenge. New York got back asking what payment I would recommend and I said about $25,000 for each brother. They wrote back that this was "above the going rate." What? Was I supposed to go around collecting bids? I told them that if they didn't pay up right now the family could kill ten Irish guys and with the UN rate of $80,000 per UN fatality, how much was that going to cost? Finally, after six months of painstaking negotiations, we paid up and the Irish added some money, too. Even a traffic accident in those days became a conflict issue because there was no law and order,

but this is the kind of thing outsiders never notice. Today UNIFIL has a much easier role, because the Lebanese army is there. I mean, the UN is in a luxury position now, very robust with luxuries.

Butler: You really like that word "robust."

Göksel: It kills me. I feel insulted by it and hope this new force never finds itself in our situations. At least nobody is shooting at them—I can't even count the times I've come under fire myself. The original UNIFIL had a lot of shortcomings, but come on. What angers me is that the international community is not more grateful to the Indians and Ghanaians and others for staying the course during this thirty-three days war last summer. That was true peacekeeping. I mean these guys stood their ground under fire, they helped the people when they couldn't even get their own food or supplies. And now you read in the papers that the UN troop contributing countries are on high alert because this unfortunate young cabinet member got assassinated in Beirut. Excuse me, what is the connection? The countries are calling for withdrawing their troops. Hey, what happened to the robustness? I mean, if they think of leaving because of a situation that is totally irrelevant to the UN, what's going to happen if one single soldier of this robust force gets killed? We had tens of guys killed and nobody said a word, but now, I'm just dreading the day one of this new force gets killed. You have to wonder what all those ships are doing off the coast of Lebanon. You don't need that armada to patrol Lebanese waters—four gunboats would be plenty. Obviously, they're there to get their soldiers out fast, if need be.

Butler: Let's talk more about UNIFIL's early days. For example, its relations with the various parties on the ground.

Göksel: They all paid lip service to the UN, especially the Palestinians were very good at that. We had liaison arrangements with them, mainly through the UN Observer. We dealt with Yasir Arafat, not with the various factions. The PLO loved the recognition they got from the UN. Actually, at the beginning, even our dealings with the various Lebanese factions—the Lebanese National Movement groups5[**]—went through Arafat. The force commander had been told that Arafat was the address not only for all the Palestinian groups but also for their Lebanese allies, and the UN went along—it was easy for us, and it made sense since these guys were being paid by the PLO anyway. But little by little it became clear that it wasn't working all that well. Arafat had insisted that he could deliver but when things got tough he would disappear—on the one hand he said he controlled these guys but then all of a sudden he'd claim they were undisciplined elements he had nothing to do with. Make up your mind!

But besides that, there was the issue of dignity. The Lebanese groups wanted to speak for themselves. What really changed the situation was when Amal and the Palestinians began to clash seriously as of 1980, peaking in 1981. One day Amal came to us and said "Don't approach us through the Palestinians anymore, or we won't talk to you. Talk to us directly." I said fine. So we start looking for a liaison officer and we found Daoud Daoud, a teacher in the Burj al-Shamali technical school, who spoke English, a very pleasant and ethical type. It turned out that we were from the same university in Turkey, and we became good friends. He became Amal's liaison to UNIFIL. Amal really defended UNIFIL, I mean they actually fought for us. At first we didn't understand, but it turned out that just before he disappeared in 1978, Imam Musa Sadr6[††] made a statement saying that UNIFIL soldiers should be treated like Lebanese, like Amal. And they stuck to that. Amazing. Amal today is only a shadow of what it was in those days, when it was an incredible grassroots movement. Today Hizballah has taken over that role.

Butler: Did you have similarly good relations with Hizballah?

Göksel: First of all, Hizballah wasn't even on the scene at that time—they emerged years later. In any case, relations with Hizballah were always tense. Most of the Hizballah guys weren't from the south and had no idea who these UN guys with blue berets were or what we were doing in Jabal `Amil.7[‡‡] They thought we were Zionist imperialist agents and couldn't understand why we had such good relations with the people. Amal tried to help in the early days, but we just couldn't reach these guys. I had to constantly seek them out in coffee shops, the village mosques, or Husayniyas8[§§] just to keep the peace between us. Things got better when Shaykh Hasan Nasrallah took over in 1992, but that's another story.

Butler: What about relations with the Israelis?

Göksel: We had a proper liaison system with them, which was easy because it's a regular army, but relations were not all that good or friendly. The Israelis were always deeply distrustful of the UN and mostly they didn't distinguish between the organization and the individuals connected with it. The relationship was based on common interest. We needed them to survive and we were useful to them not only because of the economic benefits but also because by talking to the UN guys crossing the border every day they got priceless information about south Lebanon.

I personally got on with most of them, but there were always problems with various UNIFIL contingents. UNIFIL officers tend to have very different notions of military protocol than the Israelis, who like to project this brash tough guy image and pretty much ignore courtesies taken for granted elsewhere. A lot of UN officers couldn't handle that. Another problem was that some countries were treated with kid gloves, being offered tours and benefits in Israel, and others were treated with contempt. Some contingents felt abused and in some cases we intervened and tried to cut off the direct contact between them and the Israeli army.

It wasn't only the courtesy issue. Israel's proxy, the SLA, was a big problem. The UN forces hated the way the Israelis used these guys against the UN and the local population. Some of these SLA characters, especially ones who weren't from the south, were real lowlifes and UN soldiers tended to equate the SLA with Israel. Israel always protested that and it's true that the SLA behaved much worse than the Israelis. But the fact is the SLA was totally dependent on Israel, totally obedient, and Israel did not make any real effort to rein them in. This definitely affected attitudes toward Israel. For example, the Dutch were Israel's best friends in Europe when they were first deployed in south Lebanon, but after six months the whole contingent had become thoroughly anti-Israeli, mainly because of Major Haddad and his merry men. Also the Norwegians, who are big on these social science surveys, used to have their soldiers fill out questionnaires before they arrived in the south. Coming in, it seems that their views about Israel were about 80 percent positive, but after six months it was down to 15 or 16 percent. I think this was pretty typical. The Israeli Foreign Ministry knew this was a problem and for that reason hadn't wanted the Dutch to be part of the UN force in the first place. But in south Lebanon the Israel military ran the show—they basically had their own foreign policy.

Of course the Israelis couldn't care less about what the Nepalese or Fijians or the third world contingents in general think, unless they're buying Israeli weapons. But they do care about the Europeans. That's why I was happy that the UN had the brains this time to include big European countries in the new UNIFIL. That's the only thing that can put the brakes on the Israelis, even if it won't stop them. Because the Europeans have the political clout that certainly the third world troop contributing countries don't have and even the UN as an institution doesn't have. Of course the Israelis will still try to "show who's boss," but they'll have to think twice before taking on countries like France, Italy, or Spain.

Butler: You already talked about liaison relations with the Palestinians. But what about the personal interaction between them and the UN forces?

Göksel: Relations were very good with the Palestinian civilians, and friendly and correct with Fatah, especially at upper levels. Palestinians can be very charming—this is their big advantage—and they really won over the UN people. They had excellent relations with the American UN observers. As I said, some of these Palestinians were ex–army officers themselves, so they had a military background in common. The Americans all lived in Nahariya in Israel. They would work in the field for a week, and then they'd have a week off with their families. In their week in the field they had free access to the refugee camps, they saw the suffering of the people, they saw their schools, their charity work. At Christmas the UN guys would buy all their presents at the handicraft center of Burj al-Shamali refugee camp near Tyre. There was an instinctive sympathy for the Palestinians, no doubt about it. The Israelis couldn't understand this sympathy or the close personal relationships between some of these officers and the Palestinians. Of course, contrary to what the Israelis kept saying, this sympathy never translated into active support of Palestinian armed struggle or anything like that. Israel always accused us of being pro-terrorist, first that we were pro-PLO, then we supposedly became pro-Amal, then pro-Hizballah. They always think you have to be on somebody's side.

Butler: Picking up on your reference to the fallout between the Palestinians and Amal. What can you say about the deteriorating relations in the south and possible mistakes the Palestinians made?

Göksel: First of all, the Palestinians were such a diverse group that they were uncontrollable. As you know, Arafat liked to scatter power, conveniently claiming that the PLO was a democratic movement so you couldn't dictate to anyone, but that meant lack of discipline. Apart from Habash's PFLP, all the other groups violated every rule in the guerilla book about how to deal with the local people. The Habash people were the only ones that maintained dedicated local support, because they gave back. Long after Palestinians were kicked out of south Lebanon as a military force, the PFLP still paid the salaries of the Lebanese who had worked for them. Unbelievable. But more than that, they gave help, they provided medical services, they showed concern for the people, while in the end most of the others were just using their guns to push people around.

Of course there were good Fatah people, especially the former Jordanian officers I mentioned, who were disciplined, smart, ethical. We were very comfortable with them. There was one guy in particular, Colonel `Azmi al-Saghayer, commander of the whole Tyre region. He had a limp. If the war between the Palestinians and the Shi`a didn't start sooner, it was largely because of him. A real disciplinarian and a very brave man—a legend, in fact. He was killed in the few days after Israel's 1982 invasion; he never left his fighters. I thought highly of him. I'll also never forget Colonel Abu Ahmad, the PLO's top liaison to the UN. But a lot of them were pretty much good-for-nothings hanging around, making the rules as they went along, lying through their teeth to cover up for themselves, and doing everything to please the *ra'is* so he wouldn't cut their salaries or rein them in.

So inevitably the local people began to react to the bullying, the protection rackets, the excesses. They were saying things like "How can you be so ungrateful? You fought your wars from here and our people have been driven to the slums of Beirut. And this is how you pay back?" Meanwhile, growing Shi`i politicization meant that Amal was growing, getting better armed. So it was inevitable that they would clash with the Palestinians. By 1981 the fighting had gotten serious. A few months before Israel's 1982 invasion, we actually had to put a UN force in between the Palestinians and Amal in Hannawiya village, near Qana—that was a first in UNIFIL's history. I should mention that most of the foot soldiers in the south, including in the Palestinian groups, were Shi`i—there weren't enough Palestinians to go around—and as Amal became stronger the Shi`i fighters began defecting to Amal.

The real problem with the Palestinians was that there was just too much money coming in from the Arab countries in those days and absolutely no accountability. So they bought all kinds of useless weapons for millions and millions of dollars. When Hizballah buys something, you can be sure it will be 100 percent used. Because they have a plan, they know what they want and they buy their weapons accordingly, on a limited budget, because they also have to feed their people, give them medical help, run their schools. The Palestinians didn't have those burdens because UNRWA provided for the refugees, so everything went for the guns. This is where they went wrong. And this encouraged the huge waste. I remember when my father, a retired air force pilot, came to visit me from Turkey. I picked him up in Beirut and on our way south we got stuck in Sidon, where the Palestinians were celebrating Fatah Day—3 January. We're sitting in my UN car watching this long Fatah parade, hundreds of brand new Mercedes trucks all with anti-aircraft guns. My father's saying "Wow, the Turkish army doesn't have anything like this! What are these guys going to do with all this?" I said, "They go shopping with them, they pick up girls with them."

Butler: How sad.

Göksel: Yeah, so much for show. Instead of bettering the lot of the refugees, they kept buying. In the hills of Aichiya in the east, they dug this huge tunnel under the mountain to use as their ammunitions depot. The only thing they didn't do was put up a big neon sign saying "Here are our guns and ammunition." When the Israelis invaded in 1982 the first thing they did was head straight for Aichiya. It was too risky to cart these explosives stuff away, so they blew it all up. I heard the explosion 60 kilometers away in Naqura. The whole mountain. After that the Israelis began to make off with the booty. From my office I could see the whole thing, these long convoys of Israeli flatbeds piled high with Mercedes cars, Nissan Patrols, much of it in the original packaging, anti-aircraft guns. They took everything to Israel. They financed some of that war with the booty.

Another problem with the Palestinians was they had no sense of security. They were always visible. Everybody knew where they were, because all these competing factions and their Lebanese extensions were all sitting in their clearly marked camps with the boss's picture plastered all over and flags and checkpoints at the entrance and so on, so when the Israelis would wake up some morning and feel like going on a bombing raid, they didn't have to hunt around. In contrast, look what happened in this summer's war with Hizballah. The Israelis, with all their military intelligence, sophisticated technology, satellites, drones, spies, agents, didn't know where to find them so they took out their frustration by bombing bridges near the Casino du Liban in Maronite territory north of Beirut. With the Palestinians they had it easy. You want to take out the Palestinian ammunition dump in Beirut? You go bomb the stadium near Fakhani, the PLO headquarters: you know the weapons are there because the whole world knows the weapons are there.

Now, the Palestinians of course had a serious, built in problem, and nobody knew it better than Arafat. He said, "I know that people from my organization are reporting to the Israelis, but this is the price we pay for occupation." And it's true—if a guy's family is under occupation in Palestine it's easy to turn him around. All you have to say is "That brother of yours in jail won't get out for the next twenty years unless you provide us with such and such, but if you do he'll be out next week." Or your father ends up in jail. You want him to stay in jail? You get the message. You do this or your family will pay the price. The Israelis do that beautifully, of course, which is why they were able to infiltrate, and still do, the Palestinian structure.

Butler: Tell me about the June 1982 war, from what you saw. For starters, hadn't there been a cease-fire?

Göksel: Yes, for almost a year. The Palestinians were not violating it at all—even the Israelis admit that. But Sharon was itching for a fight and already by spring had mobilized his troops and massed them in the north. Everyone knew something big was going to happen—the U.S. television networks had positioned their crews in Beirut by April. Even the brand new CNN sent someone. So when this Israeli ambassador got shot in London,9[***] even though everyone knew the faction was anti-PLO, the Israelis jumped at the chance and sent in this massive force. The most serious resistance they got in the south was outside Tyre at the Burj al-Shamali camp. These were mostly young kids—the Israelis called them the RPG kids, because they kept popping up and firing these RPGs and that sort of thing. They did not fight like an army unit, which is why they gave the Israelis some trouble. The Palestinian leadership had these pretensions of having a regular army, which was a suicidal mistake. I mean, when your foe is the Israeli army, there's no way you can match it, so why make this army structure? But Arafat loved being able to say "I have brigades, I have regiments." Habibi, if you have brigades and regiments they can be wiped out in two hours! Guerillas are the ones who can escape and keep fighting.

Anyway, the Israelis ran into serious resistance at `Ayn al-Hilwa camp, near Sidon. But that was rather easy to bypass since it was on the side, so they simply shot their way through Sidon and pushed on to Beirut and took care of `Ayn al-Hilwa later, with much destruction. They had practically no further resistance until Khaldeh, south of the Beirut airport, where they were confronted by Palestinians backed by Amal. So it was a bit of a cakewalk, really. The Israelis said they were surprised at how easy it was. They shouldn't have been surprised. I mean, they sent in more than 4,000 tanks and armored vehicles, the whole air force, navy, about 90,000 soldiers—against 3,000 or 4,000 Palestinians. It was unbelievable, a case of overkill if there ever was one.

Butler: What about UNIFIL? Didn't it try to block the advance?

Göksel: Like everybody else, the UN knew the Israelis were going to invade or do something and the instructions from New York were: do as much as you can, but don't sustain casualties— basically, you're a peacekeeping force, you're not equipped or mandated to resist an invasion. These were the typical kind of loose instructions you get from New York in a situation like this—that's the way it works in the UN system.

The force commander at the time was William Callaghan, an Irishman. On 6 June he was called to a meeting with the chief of staff of the Israeli Army, General Rafael Eitan, at his Nazareth headquarters. When the location was changed to Safad, we knew there was going to be an invasion because Safad in those days was the forward headquarters of the Northern Command. Callaghan was supposed to call us at Naqura with the codeword "Rubicon" if the invasion was on. He called us at 1000 hours, and at 1035 the invasion began.

All the UN battalions had already been told to find some way to try to block the Israeli advance if and when they invaded. Everyone tried to do something. The Norwegians proposed blowing up the entry roads without engaging the Israelis. The force commander didn't like that idea so instead they blocked the narrow roads in the village of Shaba` with their Land Rovers, but the Israelis simply bulldozed them out of the way. The Irish piled up concrete blocks at the entry roads in their area, but these were pulverized in short order by Israeli tank fire. The French had just arrived as a battalion, and there was a story going around at the time about a French sergeant blocking the way of an advancing tank near the village of Kantara, I think it was. The driver of the tank, who obviously was a nice guy, stopped. The sergeant climbs on the tank and says, "You cannot enter, this is a UN zone," and the Israeli says "OK, you stopped me. But look what's behind. How are you going to stop that with your pistol?" And the sergeant sees this whole column of 152 tanks and that was that. On the coastal road you had the Dutch—that was where the Israelis first entered, near the Hamra bridge. Six Dutch soldiers tried to stop the advance with their obstacles, but they ran out of obstacles after causing damage to the first two tanks.

So everybody did something, nothing very big, but something. Could we have done more? Perhaps, but at the end of the day, the most you could do as a peacekeeping force was maybe delay them ten or fifteen minutes. Because these guys, coming in with this unbelievable force, were determined to go to Beirut and certainly weren't going to allow a tiny UN peacekeeping force to stand in their way. We could have done a little more to save more face for the UN, but the bottom line was that you couldn't stop it.

Butler: Wasn't there something about the Nepalese contingent resisting the invasion?

Göksel: That's a famous story, but everyone has it wrong. There was a Nepalese position halfway across the Khardali bridge east of Marja'uyun10[†††]—the bridge was blocked anyway, with minefields on both sides. The Israelis came and said we want to pass to encircle the Beaufort castle and reach Nabatiya through there. And the Nepalese said "No, no, you cannot pass." The Israelis didn't push too hard because the bridge was right under the Beaufort castle, so they would have come under fire from the Palestinians who were defending it. So when the Nepalese said they couldn't pass, the Israelis said okay, we'll come back tomorrow. The Israelis did come back the next day and the Nepalese again lined up across the road and wouldn't let them pass, and again the Israelis didn't insist because the Palestinians were still holding out in the castle. When it finally fell after three days and the Israelis needed the bridge, they just bulldozed the UN position out of the way, cleared the mines and that was the end of the UN resistance there. But we got a lot of mileage from a PR standpoint about the Nepalese heroically standing their ground. Of course we didn't elaborate on the circumstances—the fact that the Israelis hadn't pushed—and it became a kind of legend about the Nepalese standing up to the Israeli army. So that was a legend that the UN created, actually. Perhaps I am bit guilty in that one.

Butler: Without much resistance from the Palestinians and their allies, where did all these deaths come from? The figures are something like 18,000.

Göksel: If you follow Israeli warfare history, you understand why there were so many. The Israeli army is rich. They never skimp on ammunition. When in doubt, they bring in the air force and just bomb away, and in a densely populated place like Lebanon a lot of people die. Actually there was fierce resistance in a number of places. I just mentioned Beaufort castle. It took the Israeli army three days of fierce fighting to take it and then only after they called in their air force when they had lost a few men—six, I think. They bombed the place to rubble. A lot of Palestinians were killed in that battle. Large numbers of people were also killed in all those places where the Palestinians had bases, which were bombarded relentlessly. Around Beirut the Dahiya area in the southern suburbs, the Palestinian camps of Burj al-Barajneh, Sabra, and Shatila were hard hit. 'Ayn al-Hilwa camp in the south suffered heavy casualties. In the eastern sector, the clashes were mainly with the Syrians. The Israelis had an easy run in the Biqa' valley at the beginning, but as they got closer to the Damascus highway, the Syrians began to stiffen up and stopped them.

By the time the Israelis laid siege to Beirut, it was clear that the aim was not to stop rocket fire into Israel, which in any case had stopped for almost a year, but to get the Palestinians out of Lebanon altogether and to change the map of the Middle East. They succeeded in part in the next months, but they couldn't get out of Lebanon because things didn't go as planned. "Their man" Bashir Gemayel was assassinated in September 1982—though already it was clear that once he was elected president of Lebanon he was not going to be an Israeli stooge—but then with U.S. help the Israelis pushed through the famous 17 May 1983 Israel-Lebanese "peace" accord. A capitulation agreement, actually—I don't understand to this day how anyone who could claim to be an American diplomat could have negotiated such a thing and expected it to work. But some Lebanese went along with it, and for a moment the Israelis thought they had Lebanon wrapped up. Except, guess what? The Americans who brokered the deal forgot to consult with the Syrians! Amazing. Even at the time the mistake was obvious. But that's another story. The upshot was that all Israel's plans for Lebanon collapsed. They didn't move out of Lebanon, but pulled back to the Awwali [River] line immediately north of Sidon. And south Lebanon became their prison.

Butler: Did the resistance in the south begin right away?

Göksel: No, not right away. For the first few months, the Shi`a were quite happy with the situation because the Israelis had broken the Palestinian military hold over the south. Except that the Israelis didn't leave. Suddenly there were all these lines people were not allowed to cross and restrictions on movement. You began hearing things like: "The Palestinians are gone. So why are the Israelis still here? Why can't we cross the Awwali River and go to Beirut?" The Israelis alienated more and more people, made more and more enemies, and the reaction set in. Already in the western sector there was Amal, and in the eastern sector the Lebanese Communist Party, and so on. But the resistance was slow getting organized—it wasn't so easy because the Israelis came with all their intelligence apparatus, Shin Bet, and they had allies in the south. In addition to the SLA already there, they brought in the Lebanese Forces11[‡‡‡] to open offices. They also had collaborators in the Shi`i community.

The turning point was Ashura day of 1983.12[§§§] Nabatiya is the center of the Ashura commemorations, which are always very highly charged. And just as about 50,000 people are pouring out of the mosques, along comes this Israeli supply column right through the middle of the crowd. These soldiers had orders not to enter Nabatiya that day, but they were reservists not known for their discipline, they got lost and couldn't care less. "Ashura day? So what?" So they drove into that crowd with six or seven armored vehicles and the people went crazy, attacking the convoy with chains and knives. The Israelis panicked, abandoned their vehicles, got up on the rooftops, and opened fire. They called for help and the Israeli army had to come in with a massive force to extract them. It could have been a lot worse: I think only two people got killed and fourteen or fifteen wounded—Lebanese, of course—but it changed everything. The Shi`i clerics had been advocating civil disobedience against the Israelis but until then it hadn't gained momentum. But this incident pushed even the moderate clerics off the fence and the leading clerics of the region (Sunni as well as Shi`i, by the way) issued a fatwa proclaiming that the sanctity of Ashura day had been violated and calling for a defensive jihad against the Jewish occupiers. I told the Israelis, "Guys, you are in trouble." I had told them early on that the Shi`a were going to turn against them, but they laughed it off. After all, the Israelis know best, and they knew that the Shi`a were their friends. It took them a while to begin to get the message.

Butler: Was Hizballah involved in the resistance from the outset?

Göksel: Hizballah was born in the Biqa`, the Baalbek area, and didn't start moving into the south until late 1983. By that time there was already the makings of a strong local Islamic resistance there. Around Nabatiya, in the village of Jibshit, there was this charismatic, dynamic young shaykh, Raghib Harb, a firebrand type, who organized this amazing group of local kids called the Islamic Students Union. They were organized in five- or six-man cells in the villages and they were giving the Israelis a tough time. When Hizballah came south they wanted to assimilate the Union, but didn't make much headway. For a long time Hizballah wasn't accepted by the local people. Of course they were Shi`i and all that, but they were outsiders and people were suspicious. But after the Israelis killed Harb in February of 1984, most of his fighters joined Hizballah and that made Hizballah more acceptable locally.

Amal was still dominant and their relations with Hizballah, strained from the beginning, became worse and worse. One of the issues fueling the tensions was Amal's siege of the Palestinian camps in Beirut and the south, which began in 1985 and lasted two years—the so-called "War of the Camps." Most people think Amal was doing a proxy battle for the Syrians, who were not happy about the resurgence of Palestinian military power in Lebanon. In any case, many innocent people died in those useless battles, including poor Shi`a living in Palestinian shantytowns under attack. Hizballah was very much opposed to Amal actions and at times intervened on the Palestinian side, providing humanitarian support. Many in Amal were also unhappy about the battles and a number of them left the movement to join Hizballah. There's no doubt that the two-year siege of the camps set the stage for the open hostilities between Amal and Hizbullah that broke out in 1988.

An important source of tension between the two concerned their differing attitudes to UNIFIL and the UN Observer Group. In fact, these tensions were at the heart of the incident that triggered the actual fighting: the kidnapping and subsequent killing in 1988 of U.S. Marine Colonel William Higgins, head of the UN Observer Group Lebanon. A couple of days before the kidnapping he had been with my friend Daoud Daoud, the Amal leader, who assured him that he was safe in Lebanon, that he was Amal's guest, and so on. So Higgins's kidnapping and killing by a murky outfit calling itself the "Revolutionary Justice Organization" was deeply embarrassing for Amal. There are a lot of unanswered questions about the perpetrators, but it was widely believed that some of those involved had ties to Hizballah, though Hizballah has officially denied it. Anyway, Amal and Hizballah eventually reached a peace agreement, the famous Damascus accord of 1990 sponsored by Iran and Syria. This was a milestone, because after that Hizballah suddenly began coming out of the woodwork: all these people that you never knew were Hizballah—lawyers, teachers, doctors, whatever—now declared themselves openly. Actually, there was a clause in the Damascus agreement—put in at Birri's insistence—that UNIFIL was not to be touched. As a direct result Hizballah approached me and said, "Can we meet?" So we met in my office in Tyre. That was our first official contact.

Butler: It's interesting to hear that as late as 1990 Hizballah was just coming out, that Amal was still so important.

Göksel: Actually, the real turning point for Hizballah was not until 1992, when Shaykh Hasan Nasrallah became leader of the movement after the Israelis killed his predecessor, Shaykh Abbas Musawi, along with his wife and 5-year-old boy. Nasrallah was only thirty-two at the time—unbelievable. He was from the south originally; in fact he had started out with Amal. Almost immediately after he took over radical changes began to be introduced. For example, Hizballah had tried hard to impose religious strictures on the people. In Tyre, for instance, they said no card playing in the cafés and no beaches for women—even the guys had to wear long shorts down past their knees. Now, the Shi`a in Tyre are pretty cosmopolitan. They may donate money to Shi`i charities but they like to play their cards and go to the beach and have their beer. So relations soured.

The minute Nasrallah took over, Hizballah relaxed the "rules." The change was especially visible in Dahiya, Beirut's southern suburbs. If you went there in the late 1980s what you mainly saw was chadors and black all over. There were rumors that you got $100 a month if you wore a chador. Whether or not that was true, pretty soon it was about what you see today—a mix. Few chadors, some hijab, but like any other part of Beirut. Nasrallah obviously said leave them alone, let them wear what they want. And it was also under Nasrallah that these powerful welfare services really took off. One of the important things he did was to mobilize Shi`i women as volunteers—many of the social services are run by women. He liberalized the movement and of course that brought more supporters, more donations.

Butler: So this is when Hizballah definitively surpassed Amal?

Göksel: Yes. Another factor was that this was the period when the 1989 Ta'if agreement that ended the civil war in Lebanon was being implemented, in bits and pieces. All the militias were supposed to disarm, including Amal. Birri was the speaker of parliament—he couldn't be running a militia and parliament at the same time, right? So many young Amal cadres—at least the militant ones—moved to Hizballah. Now that Amal was in the domestic political game, its popularity plummeted. Birri monopolized patronage in the Shi`i community, so a lot of people got jobs through him, but it didn't stop Amal's decline. By the mid-1990s, Hizballah had reached the high level of popularity it has enjoyed ever since.

Butler: What would you say accounts for its popularity?

Göksel: To my mind, it's basically about the communal identity they promoted—even though the south also has Sunnis, Christians, and Druze, it's predominantly Shi`i. There's also Hizballah's image of incorruptibility in a country where corruption has become a respectable art form, and its resistance feeds into the Shi`i sense of dignity; if you don't understand the link between their idea of dignity and resistance, you'll never understand the Shi`a. So Hizballah gradually became an identity in the south. They have provided so much for the people over the years that even if you don't support them politically, you need them for their medical services, their social services. Hizballah has created this image—and it's not only an image, they deliver—that they care about the people. When something happens—a family goes bankrupt, falls on hard times, whatever—they're the address. No doubt there are cases when they can't do much, but if nothing else they *listen*, they show compassion, they come to visit, they follow up. So loyalty of the people is almost total.

Butler: Earlier you said that UNIFIL's relations with Hizballah improved after Nasrallah took over.

Göksel: That's right. As I said, he's from the south and was originally with Amal, so he knew UNIFIL. I mean, we were in his village, Bazuriyah. After he became head of the movement, we met and I told him: "Look, we don't have to like each other, but we don't have to shoot at each other either. We can talk." He says "Yes. That's what I want also." And he appointed an official liaison officer to UNIFIL for the first time. He said, "Any problem you have, find that guy." What also helped was Hizballah's changing composition, because increasingly the fighters were local guys who grew up with UNIFIL and so couldn't be as negative toward us as those who came from the outside in the 1980s. Since then, the relationship has been correct, but you can't say it's very friendly. There is still a wariness about foreigners.

Butler: Let's talk about this latest war, in July 2006. For example, how would you compare it to the other Israeli interventions you've witnessed?

Göksel: Well obviously, 1982 was a total, all-out invasion, with this massive force, the siege and occupation of Beirut, the goal of changing the political map of Lebanon and the Middle East. The July 2006 war was narrow in scope, primarily targeting Hizballah. It has a lot more in common with the 1993 Operation Accountability and the 1996 Operation Grapes of Wrath—all three were aimed at provoking the Lebanese against Hizballah—Israel said so openly in 1993 and 1996. Of course, this tactic has the opposite effect with the Shi`a, but that's another matter. Certainly the 1993 and 1996 incursions were limited compared to what we had last year. Israel had a hard time justifying them. They were meant to punish the Shi`a for the casualties being inflicted on Israeli troops in Lebanon, but the obvious response was: if you don't want your soldiers getting hurt, get out. In 2006, Israel got more international support for their actions not only because their best friend was in the White House, but also because there had been a border breach. That put them on more solid legal ground than in the 1993 and 1996 operations.

Butler: How would you compare the physical destruction of 1982 to 2006?

Göksel: It was much, much heavier in 2006. In 1982 the resistance was in the Palestinian camps: `Ayn al-Hilwa got pulverized, some damage in Burj al-Shameh. Most of the damage was in Beirut. There wasn't that much destruction the Lebanese villages because the Lebanese were not fighting. In 2006 the destruction in the south, in the border villages, was staggering. Of course the massive destruction had nothing to do with military considerations per se. It was more indicative of Israeli intentions. They didn't want the people to return to those villages, so they just wiped them out.

Butler: Do you think that decision to clear the border zone was made before the war?

Göksel: I don't think so. I think it came up after the Israeli army realized that Hizballah was not going to just roll over and surrender. At first they thought that an air operation and heavy long-range shelling would do the job and they wouldn't have to get their boots dirty. But it didn't work out that way, and I think that's when they came up with this idea of creating a *cordon sanitaire*.

The extent of the destruction also reflected the profound humiliation and embarrassment on the Israeli side—they just lost control and it became a kind of hysterical vengeance operation more than anything else. The fact that Hizballah had been building all these tunnels, bunkers, etc., for five or six years right under their noses—and this despite all their human intelligence, their balloons, their drones, their technical this and technical that—well, yes, this was humiliating. And the way Gal Hirsh, one of their star generals and the commander of the lead unit in the war, the Galilee Division—he's the one who recently resigned under criticism—comes to Bint Jubayl and declares it a liberated town, and the next morning eight Israeli soldiers are killed there. . . Wow! All these announcements that Hizballah's long-range rocketry is wiped out, that Bint Jubayl is liberated, that `Ayta al-Sha`b is cleared, and Katyushas keep falling in Israel all the while. These are all humiliations, making their reaction even more hysterical.

Of course all this is against the background of what many Israelis saw as the humiliating way they withdrew in 2000: for the first time, they left an Arab land under pressure without getting anything in return. And Hizballah kept that anger alive in various ways. Israel had hoped the border zone would be taken over by the UN and the Lebanese army, but instead they got Hizballah flags flying and taunting on a daily basis.

Also, even though Israeli intelligence was clearly not performing at its best, they still knew that Hizballah was building up a force. Historically the Israeli reaction to such a situation would have been to launch a preemptive strike, right? But they couldn't, and Hizballah rightly was boasting about having created a "balance of terror" that prevented Israel from striking for fear of its response. This is an equation the Israelis couldn't live with forever. I mean, Israel is a powerful military state and to have some nonstate resistance group telling you "Don't do that or we will do this to you"—come on! Something was bound to give and when the July operation took place, that was it. Some people say the Israelis were waiting for this opportunity and it's true that not long before the July war they had held military exercises premised on a clash with Hizballah. They had contingency plans like any army, but I wouldn't go so far as to say they were gearing up for an operation.

Butler: On the other hand, Hizballah, from what they say, didn't really expect the extent of the reaction.

Göksel: Yes, and that was unusually naïve of them. I usually think of the Hizballah leadership as being very smart, analytical, people who review developments, learn from their mistakes, are good students of their enemy, and so on. But here, they totally misjudged Israel's "tipping point," to use the cliché you keep hearing these days. Israel had just lost a soldier in embarrassing circumstances in Gaza, and now, two weeks later, you give them this blow on their northern front—a guerrilla outfit militia crossing the best guarded border in the world, killing a couple of their soldiers and kidnapping two others and getting away! Given Israel's domestic audience, the army's reputation, the billions in military spending, it could hardly sue for peace with an organization of 2,000 fighters. Despite all their analytical powers and sophistication, Hizballah just cannot understand the role of public opinion in a free society, because Israel *is* a free society for the Jewish people.

Butler: There was a lot of talk in this war about the failure to distinguish between military and civilian targets. What would you say about that, in terms of Hizballah and Israel?

Göksel: I would say look at the numbers. If you have 1,200 civilian and 200–300 military deaths on the Lebanese side (we don't know the exact number of Hizballah dead), versus 35 civilian and 150 military deaths on the Israeli side, I think that says it all.

Butler: But you keep hearing that Hizballah intentionally fired from civilian areas, making civilian deaths inevitable.

Göksel: Do you know Tel Aviv? The Israeli Defense Ministry is smack in the middle of a posh residential area of the city. Most Israeli bases are also in civilian areas. Go visit Kiryat Shemona. Towns grow toward military bases. So I mean, their deployment is no different from Hizballah's.

Look. This was a very asymmetrical war. Hizballah is not going to make Human Rights Watch happy. They're not going to sit around in open fields waiting for the Israeli army and air force in order to please Amnesty International. They're going to make use of the terrain, their own country, their own turf, to minimize their own casualties. Right? After they fire, they run into the nearest village. They don't necessarily fire *from* the village, they fire from *near* the village, usually. But of course you can play with photographs—the Israelis show a videotape of what looks like a rocket coming from a village, but it's coming from *behind* the village. That's what happened with that house in Qana, where all those people were killed and where the IDF initially claimed there had been firing from the house. In the end, they admitted that it wasn't true.

Butler: Actually, your mentioning Qana reminds me of the famous Qana incident in 1996, when the Israelis kept bombing a UN post and were later accused of having done so deliberately. And that makes me think of a similar incident in this last war, when a clearly marked UN post came under sustained fire. Didn't the UN secretary-general make a similar accusation this year, too, and then back down?

Göksel: You're talking about the shelling and air strikes against the UN observer post at Khiyam. Four UNIFIL soldiers were killed in those attacks. And yes, the secretary-general, under pressure, did back down somewhat from his initial statements. But I personally don't think the attacks were deliberate in the sense of targeting the UN per se. In a way, it's worse: the Israelis just didn't care. I mean, they knew those UN guys were there. The base was very clearly marked and they'd been hitting close to it all day, they'd been repeatedly warned. But they had their own agenda and if a couple of UN guys get killed, tough. It's the same mindset that led them to shell the Fijian battalion headquarters in April 1996, when more than 100 mostly women and children were killed.13[****]

Butler: But I don't see, in this latest war, what would be gained in pounding the Khiyam post.

Göksel: Simply that the UN post was about 100 meters from the famous Khiyam prison, which had become a museum of the Israeli occupation of the south. Hizballah had turned it into a kind of shrine of anti-Israelism and the Israelis wanted it gone. So they destroyed it, and because it was solidly built it took a while to completely level it, and a lot of what was around was leveled too. Also, Hizballah anti-tank units in Khiyam had made it impossible for the Israelis to advance toward the Biqa`. The reserve armored brigade the IDF had sent to clear the way performed dismally, by the way. One battalion left the battlefield without orders, another battalion commander resigned in the midst of battle, and the brigade commander was left alone in the field. Not a glorious chapter in the history of the IDF. So the Israelis, as usual, brought in the air force to do the job and if that means that some UN soldiers have to die, so be it.

Butler: Given the scale of the destruction, one would think that as time goes on there would be some impact on Hizballah's popularity.

Göksel: It's true that this is a risky time for Hizballah. People are expecting miracles from them again, and the scale of what is required is way beyond their capabilities. So far their support remains strong, but the longer reconstruction takes, the more questions will be raised: How did this happen? How are we going to get out of this? I think Hizballah is very aware of this.

Butler: So perhaps Israel's tactic of bombing the people until they turn against Hizballah is not so ill conceived.

Göksel: I don't see that happening. Asking questions, challenging, is one thing—actually turning against Hizballah is something else. To my understanding, the Shi`i community doesn't operate that way.

It's strange. The Israelis have an incredible amount of information about Lebanon: military, civilian, human, technical—in many cases they even know where individuals live. But with all this information, they don't really understand the place. They certainly don't get the Shi`a. These people have a very different sense of dignity that Israelis will never understand. Even the other Lebanese are just coming to understand it, slowly, from the Shi`i community's behavior during this last war. I mean, a woman loses her son, loses her house, and she's shouting, "We're for Nasrallah!" And she's not acting, they're not acting, that's the way they feel. They are not going to submit to that kind of pressure be it from the Israelis or internally here in Lebanon. There is a real communal identity now that wasn't there before. They were a feudal society, they were serfs, nobody thought about them. All that's over now and they have a political voice, which now is Hizballah. And guess what? They don't want to be marginalized any more.

Butler: Looking back over your more than two decades with UNIFIL, what do you see as its main accomplishments?

Göksel: Well, of course it did not accomplish the mission it was established for, which was to supervise Israel's withdrawal and assist the return of the Lebanese government, because Israel in effect stayed.

I think UNIFIL's biggest success, if you want to call it that, was its relations with the people. When UNIFIL came in 1978, nobody else was coming to south Lebanon. It was totally abandoned, like a ghost town. There were maybe 10,000 or 15,000 people there. In those days you could almost say that those who remained needed UNIFIL to survive. We had zero budget for humanitarian affairs, but we helped them in every way we could. We helped them with their schools; we provided their medical services—and excellent ones at that. I mean, if it was an emergency we would send you a helicopter. Some of the UNIFIL contingents—the Norwegians and Finns, for example—got their countries to mobilize their own national resources to assist in the south, because they liked the place, the people, the way the people expressed their gratitude.

Sometimes it came to a point—I smile when I think of it—that the local people would intervene to protect UNIFIL soldiers from the UNIFIL command. For example, if a soldier commits a serious offense, the only punishment we had in UNIFIL was to send the guy home, because discipline in UN peacekeeping is a national affair. And it sometimes happened that we would get a local delegation to plead for the soldier: "Please don't send him home, he's a nice guy! He came all the way here. Why don't you let him stay?" Sometimes the offense was against local customs, like getting a bit tipsy and behaving badly, having a traffic accident, getting into a fight, or whatever, and we would remind the delegation of this. But they would come back: "No, no. We forgive him, so why don't you forgive him also?" And the people helped us, too. Sometimes they would warn us of danger. When Hizballah first came and things were bad, for example, villagers would warn us when something was going to happen and where.

But the most important thing we did, I think, was give the people a sense of normalcy. The Lebanese government could not return to the south because the civil war was still going on. But even in these conditions, UNIFIL brought a sense of security. I don't think there's any doubt that UNIFIL played a big role in the bringing the population back—after a few years it was up to a half million. I think UNIFIL can take real pride in that.

Butler: What about the economic impact of UNIFIL's presence?

Göksel: Of course there were many economic benefits just by having us there and spending money. UNIFIL became the biggest employer in the south, and created a lot of opportunities for contractors and subcontractors. Our presence gave a big impetus to the famous Lebanese entrepreneurship: in any poor one-Mercedes village with a handful of dwellings, a laundry service and a market would suddenly spring up to cater to UN soldiers. I remember when the Norwegians were trying to put up a position on mountaintop, near Hibbariyah, which was inaccessible by road. They were tough guys and didn't mind, but they wanted to know how we were going to keep them supplied. A helicopter would be okay temporarily, but you need ground connections in the long run and who was going to build a road? One day we were up on this mountaintop, pondering the problem, when all of a sudden this old Lebanese guy appears from nowhere with his mule loaded with cassettes, cigarettes, Coca-Cola, and so on for the Norwegian soldiers. We couldn't believe it. We asked how he got there and he said: "I tell the mule that we are going to the mountaintop and he finds the way." So we marked the path and built the road following it. Actually, that's the way the Ottomans built roads in the mountains, they'd just follow the mule or donkey, who always find the easiest way. Anyway, that's the Lebanese sense of business. The UN soldiers could always tell when it was payday by looking outside and seeing floating markets popping up along the road, these Mercedes cars with their trunks open displaying their goods. I wouldn't go so far as to say that UNIFIL regenerated the economy, but it definitely helped.

Butler: So it seems that the first UNIFIL's legacy is not so much peacekeeping, but what you did for the people. Will the new UNIFIL build on that?

Göksel: It's too early to say. Certainly, in the beginning the mindset seemed pretty different. Somebody told them that they are a "robust" force, which means you get into big armored vehicles and drive up and down. When you go south now you see all these massive UN convoys and people say "Why do they need all this?" And it's true: UNIFIL is not an occupation force and they're not going to fight the Israelis or Hizballah, so why all this machinery? When I go to the villages and I ask what the problem is when people complain about "this new UNIFIL," they say, "They don't talk to us." That is what the people really want—they want you to walk around the village and say "Hi, how are you? How's the family? How's life?" They want you to give them a shoulder to cry on, and they have plenty to cry about now. That's what people expect of the new UNIFIL, because for twenty-eight years they got used to a different kind of UNIFIL, a friendly UNIFIL who shared their lives in tough times under very difficult circumstances. The new UNIFIL is not able to do that yet, but lately they do seem to be trying.

Interview with Timur Goskel—Another Angle

Interview with Timur Goksel
written by: Manuela Paraipan, 29-Nov-07

Timur Goksel is Former Spokesperson and Senior Advisor for UNIFIL.

WSN: How did you arrive in Lebanon?

TIMUR GOKSEL: I came for six months but it has now been 24 years.

WSN: You came originally for a specific period of time?

TG: Initially for 6 months. In those days with the war, it was different. UNIFIL now has a good time, although some complain about the old UNIFIL. Back in those days, UNIFIL was surrounded by wars – 3 or 4 at a time. Not surprisingly there weren't many people in the UN who wanted to come to Lebanon. It was difficult because we could not move around.

WSN: Where were you located?

Timur Goksel, Former Spokesperson and Senior Advisor for UNIFIL

TG: In Aqoura, which is 3 kilometers from the borders. There was Major Haddad, who was part of a Christian militia and Israel controlled the borders. It was their part of the country. It took us some time to realize that this is an open space used by all sorts of militias, but how do you get out? In 1982 it was the Israeli invasion and we said that we have to go, there was no reason to stay. We started to pack our office. The Security Council met and said that we have to stay. When I asked about the budget, they said no budget.

WSN: Why did UNIFIL stay?

TG: They said - and maybe it was a smart idea - that since the Israelis will leave one day and there will be a need for another UN force, why dismantle what we have only to send a new force later on? It costs too much. We were told to keep quiet, stay put and when Israel is out, we would take over again. It was an unusual situation. We were a peacekeeping force in an area that was totally occupied by a country that was not very friendly toward us. Very uncomfortable situation. We could not move around freely. We always had to be escorted by the Israelis. I refused to go anywhere escorted by the Israelis. If I wanted to go to Beirut I needed Israel's permission so I said that the day I do it, I would leave the country. It became a problem. They became a problem and I made it a problem. Then the Israelis started to get into trouble, not because of me so they forgot about us.

WSN: When did you hear first of Hizbollah?

TG. In 1982 or 1983, the name Hizbollah first appeared and the rest is history.

WSN: Did you have contacts with Hizbollah from the very beginning?

TG: At first no one knew who these people were. They came from the North, from Bekaa. It was a small, yet effective resistance. However, the resistance against Israel started with the cells of the Islamic Student Association in and around Nabatyeh. This is how it began. Few talk about those days. Nowadays everyone talks about Hizbollah. They were well organized, based on family relationship. The Israelis killed the Sheikh in 1984 because he became a nightmare for them. Going back to Hizbollah. The moment Hizbollah came to Southern Lebanon we had problems with them. They fought foreigners and we were foreigners, and they just could not understand why we were so friendly with the people of the South. There were casualties on both sides. We became a target for them. Southern Lebanese were always hospitable toward us and we had a good relationship with Amal, but these new guys did not know what to make of us. I decided that it was time to have a talk with them and find out more.

I went to Amal and asked them to introduce me to these people. Amal said that they were not important – only Amal was important. I told them, fine, you are, but they are killing us. It was serious and I had to do something.

I started to go to the villages where these people hang out. I went to the coffee shops. In Lebanon if you go to the right coffee shop, you're in business. They knew me from newspapers, from people. Being a Muslim made me more acceptable in their minds. I said, look I want to meet you guys. Why are you shooting at us? It was very dangerous. In mosques they were preaching against us, to kill us. I talked to a few of them and explained that we are peacekeepers. They asked, what's a peacekeeping force? This was a good question to ask. They wanted to know why in the middle of the war an international force came to the South? Why would you give up a comfortable life to come here and get shot at? For what, they asked? There must be something you want. They just could not understand that we wanted peace. They said we are Zionists - imperialist agents. I asked, am I a Zionist? They responded: Not you personally, but the force you are with. I told the commanding officers in New York that these guys were here to stay and would become a big problem if we didn't talk to them.

The UN is a very official organization. It is only now after decades that the UN is slowly realizing that not only is there a conflict between states in the region, but also there are non-state actors involved in this conflict and if you marginalize them, you are in trouble. Then the Embassy in Beirut was blown up, the marines were killed and New York said that we could not engage Hizbollah. This would give them recognition. I was told to go and talk to the people in Beirut. I went to Beirut to the foreign ministry and asked about Hizbollah. They asked, what is Hizbollah? They had never heard of it. They did not care about the rest and anyway they did not control anything outside the capital. The ministry had good coffee, but there was no government, no nothing.

WSN: What did you do afterwards?

TG: Finally, I talked to Hizbollah. New York said that if something went wrong, they wouldn't acknowledge they knew me. The first contact between the UN and Hizbollah was not a very happy experience as we did not agree on anything, but at least we were talking.

In 1988, an American officer was kidnapped and found killed. He was a good friend of Amal. Amal took pride in the fact that it protected the Americans and now this officer was killed. It was a big problem between Amal and Hizbollah at the time. The clashes ended with the accord. There was one stipulation regarding UNIFIL. Musa Sadr always said that UNIFIL was most welcome and we should be treated as guests. In 1992, the Israelis kill Musawi and Nasrallah was designated as the new leader at a young age. And what a smart choice the Iranians made.

After the agreement there was an almost immediate relaxation. We got a message from Hizbollah saying that they wanted to establish contact with my office. They sent a delegation. We agreed to forget the past problems. I told them that we don't have to like each other, we don't have to agree but we don't have to shoot at each other, either. I knew some of them personally and I was surprised to see them there. Personal relationships are very important and can open doors that otherwise would stay closed. If there is a problem, don't shoot, I said; come to me. They appointed a liaison officer to keep in contact. Again the UN said that I am on my own. I met Nasrallah. I explained that we wanted to help the people of Southern Lebanon. We didn't care about ideology. He could not give us an official blessing but there were other ways he that showed we were welcome there. It was never a warm relation, but it was a civil one.

There were very few incidents after 1992 and at that time Hizbollah become really strong in the South. They kept their promise. One thing changed in the South and the people don't realize it. This new generation of fighters grew up with UNIFIL. UNIFIL was not a foreign force for them. It was part of the landscape. The Lebanese, no matter what ideology they follow find it difficult to shoot their guests.

WSN: Has the UN admitted that there is dialog?

TG: No. Did you see my latest piece? I was in Germany last week and in the foreign ministry they seem to have memorized it. Some complained it was not positive. It is positive all right. As long as you are talking with these guys, then why don't you make it official?

What happens here is, if you don't admit that you talk to them and contacts are anyway as headquarters you don't know what they are talking about; the peacekeeping force is a strange thing. It's like humanitarian work with a gun in your hands. It's nothing else. So the countries don't want to have their soldiers killed. They want a quiet mission, get the money and go home.

Like with the Palestinians in the beginning. We made contacts with the local chiefs. The headquarters had no idea of what was going on. So you came one day and want to go to a place and you are told that you can't.

Why? We agreed with this or that person to stay away from their area and in return they help us out. Who made the deal? It's tricky.

This is why I insisted that at all meetings, a civilian from the UNIFIL headquarters would be present. The military did not like it, but we did it anyway. They wanted to feel they are in control and the generals think that there is this military code from one army man to another. But imagine you come from Ghana or Fiji and you talk with an Israeli general. To be generals, they have to be political animals first of all. Who are you to deal with these guys? They are masters of the game. The Israeli foreign ministry is a protocol agency. They deal with consular affairs and countries you never hear about. In all these years I did not go to the Israeli foreign ministry except for courtesy visits when I was invited. I always went to the army. They are the ones who can make life easy or impossible. The army has a very big say in how the country is run.

WSN: But it is still a democracy.

TG: It is a democracy for the Jews. I lived there 20 years, I know. But when it comes to security, army is first, no argument. Even in the press all guys are army men, reserve. Everyone important has some kind of tie with the army.

WSN: How do you see the mission of the new UNIFIL?

TG: UNIFIL today is in a very comfortable position because there is no war going on. All they have to do is to be nice to people. Initially an idiot came with the idea that this must be a robust force. So they came with guns and beautiful tanks. I like that. But for what? The main parties decided that they are not going to fight. So what are you there for? This is the US idea. To fight Hizbollah? Excuse me, but you cannot do it. You don't have the mandate and did you ask the Lebanese if they want you do to it? Now you are working in cooperation with the Lebanese authorities and army. Do they want to disarm Hizbollah?

WSN: There are many somewhat bombastic speeches about the new UNIFIL.

TG: They decided to come with heavy weapons and tanks and I kept asking if they were planning to use them. The French painted the tanks in white so they can be seen 10 kilometers away. There are 13 of them and they need permission from Paris to fire a gun. You are not going to fight Hizbollah or the Israelis. UNIFIL started to patrol the small villages with tanks. Many said and I said, don't do it. What are you doing with tanks on the streets? They look aggressive and funny and scare the children. Many reacted and the French put the tanks to the parking lot. This is unrealistic. It is important that the UN is here, just that they cannot do anything. A weak mandate, too many of them and too many countries involved.

WSN: Would a small force have been a better choice?

TG: You could easily cut it to half. Now it's peaceful and it's OK. You have ceremonies, special days, flags, parades and good food. This is what it should be. The trouble is that this is Lebanon and this is the Middle East. It can blow up. If it does how do you control 30 countries? This is dangerous.

They can't even talk to each other because of the language.

WSN: There is this barrier as well?

TG: They have cultural, religious and all kinds of other barriers and language is one of them. No two countries are the same. If you give them an order, each will understand it differently. Some may fight, some will ask their countries what to do and some will go back to the base and wait.

WSN: What is UNIFIL doing right now?

TG: They are building a peaceful environment for the people. The Lebanese are usually much faster than this. They faced many disasters and recovered fast. Now it's much slower than before. They fear that the conflict is not finished yet. All the UNIFIL countries understood that the most important thing is to do small projects for the people. Now they are organizing computer courses, football tournaments, playgrounds, they are teaching yoga in the villages.

TG: There was too much talk about it politically. This is always the case especially in democratic countries, because you have to create a certain background, to attract attention on the subject. The problem was that during this time the UN kept quiet. People asked, they shared our trouble since 1978 and now they will fight us? The idea of a strong, multinational force and not a UN force came out at the Saint Petersburg G8 summit in 2006. The Israelis loved it. I know many people in Israel; I have friends there so I told them that they should be careful that the UN is all they're going to get. Be nice to UNIFIL because nobody else is coming, I said. Why would any country send soldiers to Lebanon? To do what? What the Israelis could not do themselves so send in a multinational force or the UN to do it? It does not work like that. I remember the first day when this idea came out. I was on CNN or the BBC and they asked what I thought of it. Excuse me, who is coming? Look at Afghanistan. NATO is a military alliance that costs billions of dollars, the best armies in the world. They can hardly function as a military alliance on the ground. What should one expect then from the UN? Let me be clear. National interest comes first. Always. We have Turkish soldiers in Afghanistan. It is a big, expensive and good army but they are not involved in security. Why? Turkey said that it couldn't take part in it, that it has historical ties and other interests in the country. Twenty other countries are saying that, so what does one do? Compared with NATO, the UN is a Mickey Mouse organization when it comes to military missions. The men and women who are leading the forces are not from military. Some of them have never carried a gun in their lives. They are bureaucrats who have an army of hundreds of thousands under their control. Peacekeeping is not military. It's a hybrid. Until they find someone willing to come here and fight, nothing will change. And when they have found someone I want to know.

WSN: The impression right after the political speeches was that UNIFIL's mandate would be dramatically changed.

TG: They need the permission of the Lebanese army and government for whatever they want to do on the ground. They cannot do a simple security operation, not a single checkpoint without approval. The old UNIFIL had checkpoints where it wanted, since there was no one to ask. Of course there were dangerous times. It is important that now there is this strong European participation. Politically it is very important. Basically the mandate that is pages long states that UNIFIL cannot do anything without the express approval of the Lebanese government.

WSN: Can UNIFIL go to the Syrian border?

TG: Not with this mandate. And of course the Lebanese government has to invite the UN to do so. The Syrians said they don't want foreign forces at the borders with a country they have brotherly relations with. Hizbollah has also said that it doesn't want this. It is good that UNIFIL is here and that it is doing nice things on the ground for the people. That matters.

WSN: Thank you.

Appendix D—Propaganda at Its Best

As the patrol stood its ground one of the Amals suddenly fired off an anti-tank shell at the jeep. Private Riccardo Lucchesi, a Dundalk man on his second tour of duty in the Lebanon, was wounded chest.

The Amals unleashed a hail of gunfire and Private Patrick Mason of Shankill, Co Dublin was hit in the abdomen and Private Anthony Sheeran of Dunleer, Co Louth, was hit in the right thigh and hand.

Jeep

Two Privates from Dublin — Harold McQuaid of Harolds Cross and Patrick Murphy of Blanchardstown — were beside the jeep when the RPG shell hit and they were thrown to the ground in shock.

Commandant O'Don-

neil saw his men going down around him. He gave his troops orders to fire at will and they returned the fire.

"He had no option but to tell the men to open fire," said an Army spokesman in Dublin last night.

"He had to ensure the patrol didn't take any more casualties."

Flashed

The three wounded soldiers — and their two shocked comrades — were quickly evacuated from the killing ground and rushed to the unit's UN position.

A helicopter was called in to airlift them to the UN hospital in the southern border town of Naqoura.

Word of the attack was flashed back to Dublin. As officers began inform-

ing the wounded men's relatives of the shootings, the Tanaiste and Minister for Defence Brian Lenihan interrupted Dail proceedings to tell a hushed house of the attack.

Sinister

Amal chiefs in the area said they "regretted" the incident. They immediately ordered an investigation "to determine the reason for the clash".

The Amals normally have a good relationship with the UN force which numbers around 5,800 men.

They are led by Nabih Berri who has told them to hold their fire against UNIFIL forces.

Beirut

But the reaction among top Amals in Beirut was more ominous. A spokesman there said the clash could have come about because of what he called "personal reasons" but he refused to elaborate.

Last night the battalion feared of a reprisal attack. An "increased alert" order was given — and extra sentries and look-outs were posted.

WEAPONRY: A 81mm mortar perched outside a lookout post

COLLINS' OUTRAGE

FOREIGN Affairs Minister Gerry Collins had urgent talks with his Israeli counterpart yesterday.

He told him the EC "deplored the Israeli settled policy in the occupied territories."

But minister Benjamin Netanyahu denied Israel was pushing for new Jewish immigrants to settle in the region.

AT THE READY: Irish troops with Browning .5 heavy machine guns keep watch in the war-torn valleys   Pics: Commdt Patrick Walshe, rtd

231

232

11 Irish slain in killing fields of mayhem

IRISH Army chiefs have had to write "Killed in Action" beside the names of 11 men since the force began UNIFIL peace-keeping duties in the Lebanon.

The soldiers who died were:

Private Stephen Griffin, shot by a sniper on April 16, 1980

Private Thomas Barrett and Private Derek Smallhorse, both shot in the same attack on April 18, 1980

Checkpoint

Private Hugh Doherty, shot on April 27, 1981

Lieutenant Aongus Murphy — son of the current Adjutant General of the Army Major General F K Murphy — killed by a roadside bomb on August 21, 1986

Private William O'Brien, shot at a UN checkpoint on December 6th, 1986

Corporal Dermot McLoughlin, killed when an Israeli battle tank opened fire on a UN billet

Private Michael McNeela, killed by heavy machine-gun fire while manning a checkpoint on February 24, 1989

Corporal Fintan Heneghan, Private Tom Walsh and Private Mannix Armstrong, all killed in a landmine explosion on March 21, 1989

Heroes all

TWO more of our peace keeping troops were shot by Amal militiamen in the Lebanon yesterday.

A third was injured when an anti-tank round struck a jeep while his commanding officer was bravely trying to reason with the gunmen.

Thankfully this time army chiefs did not have to add their names to the eleven already "Killed in Action".

But in yesterday's brief clash two of the militiamen were fatally wounded when the Irish soldiers returned fire.

Ironically our brave soldiers were on a mission of mercy when the attack began at the village of Haddata, near Israel's self-declared security zone in South Lebanon.

Amal leaders later said that their actions had been based on a misunderstanding.

Some misunderstanding.

Our troops have done us proud with the UNIFIL force.

But how many more have to die or be injured before this troubled land finds lasting peace?

SEDMED

Seguridad y Defensa en el Mediterráneo

GOKSEL, Timur (2009) "UNIFIL: A crisis Management instrument in the Middle East", en SOLER i LECHA, Eduard y GARCIA, Irene, *VIII Seminario Internacional sobre Seguridad y Defensa en el Mediterráneo. Nuevos escenarios de cooperación.* Barcelona: CIDOB/ Ministerio de Defensa, pp. 111-115.

SEDMED
Seguridad y Defensa
en el Mediterráneo

www.sedmed.org

Este artículo es el resultado de la ponencia presentada en el VIII Seminario Internacional sobre Seguridad y Defensa en el Mediterráneo. Nuevos escenarios de cooperación, organizado en Barcelona por CIDOB y el Ministerio de Defensa el día 26 de Octubre de 2009.

UNIFIL: A CRISIS MANAGEMENT INSTRUMENT IN THE MIDDLE EAST

Timur Goksel

*Former Senior Advisor,
UNIFIL, Beirut*

This is not going to be an academic and properly organised lecture with emphasis on goods and evils of international organizations in conflict management and peacekeeping. Having worked 33 years for the UN, 24 of them in the Lebanese-Israeli conflict, I will freely share my experiences with you, without worrying about being politically correct. I am not after a UN civil servant anymore. I can name names now. I am already retired. I can't be retired again.

Because of time restraints I am not going to get into the fascinating history of United Nations Interim Force in Lebanon (UNIFIL), which was set up in 1978 following Israel's partial occupation of South Lebanon. At that time, the conflict was between Israel and the Palestinian Liberation Organization (PLO). Lebanon was in the midst of the violent civil war. Nothing was ripe for a UN peacekeeping force to be deployed in Lebanon. But, under severe US pressure, UNIFIL was created. It was actually the last UN peacekeeping mission approved in the Cold War era. PLO's military presence in Lebanon ended with the 1982 Israeli invasion. UNIFIL, which had come to manage the PLO-Israeli conflict in Lebanon, found itself trying to manage a new conflict, this time between non-state Lebanese forces and Israel. UN never thought what this radical change would mean for the peacekeepers in South Lebanon.

Israel did not abide by 1978 Security Council Resolution that set up UNIFIL and demanded Israel to withdraw. That happened only in 2000, not under international pressure but as a unilateral move under the pressure of the Lebanese resistance, mainly Hizbullah, and public opinion pressure in Israel. UNIFIL was subsequently reduced in numbers and its deployment was restricted to observing the Israel-Lebanese border.

Following the 2006 Israel-Hizbullah War, UNIFIL was expanded and made more "robust" by UNSC Resolution 1701 in a bid to ensure the "cessation of hostilities" between IDF and Hizbullah. EU troop contributions increased substantially, but this did not improve the efficiency or the robustness of UNIFIL II which, despite US/Israeli efforts to transform it into an enforcement mission, remained as a peacekeeping mission.

UNIFIL's expanded presence, especially the political clout it has acquired with the strong European participation has so far thwarted the resumption of hostilities. But, to that extent, there has been no serious political action to resolve the conflict and bring it to closure with determined US and EU action. This wishful thinking presupposes at least a modicum of European unity. Given the dominance of national interests over foreign policies of most EU nations, I am afraid it is bound to stay as wishful thinking. Consequently, either this UN force too will stay "interim" for an indefinite period or one day will be forced to helplessly watch the resumption of hostilities.

UNIFIL is not a solution, but a conflict management tool. It does not solve the conflict. But it is an essential tool that is worth every penny, most pennies anyway, spent on it. If nothing, it provides an instant, unique channel of communication between two countries that are technically at war. Since its very first days, UNIFIL prevented conflicts that could have erupted out of misunderstandings. Today officers of Lebanese and Israeli armies meet regularly under UNIFIL chairmanship to discuss all border problems. Look at the rhetoric raging in the Middle East and imagine what could happen if you did not have the UN in the middle talking to both sides.

There have been many instances when the Israeli army contacted UNIFIL to ask about suspicious movements near the border or to inform UNIFIL of an activity they would undertake that could be misinterpreted by Hizbullah. Hizbullah leaders in South Lebanon used to call me at my Haifa residence often to inquire about what saw as suspicious, hostile Israeli army moves.

Of course not to be ignored is the unheralded humanitarian services UNIFIL has rendered to this much neglected region of Lebanon. In 1978, when UNIFIL arrived, the area had a population of 15,000 people who had nobody looking after them. Within 3-4 years that population went up to more than 200,000, thanks to services and some semblance of security provided by UNIFIL.

When villages are populated, schools and businesses are open and life returns to normal, the likelihood of those areas to be used to launch attacks are minimal. Today, unlike the original force, which had no budget for humanitarian activities, UNIFIL has funds for quick impact projects and, especially, the European contingents mobilise significant funds from their home countries. One beneficial aspect of this is that the villagers who long gave up of state services are now learning to deal with official bodies instead of first running to the nearest non-state activist.

EU Member States, particularly France, Italy, and Spain, play a leading role in UNIFIL today. More EU contingents are likely to join. European commitment should not be discouraged because some UN bureaucrat will say "oh, we have too many Europeans, let's get some from other continents."

While EU troops are essential because of their professional background and the political clout they enjoy with the parties in this conflict, such deterrence only works as long as the parties to the conflict find that the current truce works to their advantage. EU troops have unfortunately also become high-profile targets for jihadist groups now operating with impunity in Lebanon.

236

These threats have prompted EU troops within UNIFIL to over-emphasise force protection, to the point of neglecting the real mission. Democratic countries with free news media and developed public opinions have become over sensitised to casualties they suffer in foreign missions. This, in turn, has been putting great pressure on their commanders to avoid casualties, sometimes by taking extreme measures to the detriment of the mission.

Although, in principle, these troops are under UN command and are not supposed to be taking orders from their national commands, in reality, they first report to their homes and regularly ask for permission for any action that remotely be risky. They take extreme and aggressive protection measures not to suffer casualties. They introduce electronic countermeasures against Improvised Explosive Device (IEDs). They minimise contacts with the local population, whose sentiments are ignored. They withdraw behind fortifications and barbed wire. Don't forget that these national commanders are evaluated by their home commands, not the UN. Their careers' advancement depends on what their own superiors think about them, not what the UN command thinks. Moreover, they are paid by their own army, not the UN. If the UN command, for whatever reason, does not act like a true field commander, who keeps track of what his units are doing, does not want to hurt feelings by taking corrective action and insists on being politically correct, what you end up with is a colourful and well looked after international force, with impressive parades but cut off from the people they are there to protect.

Worse are ineptness, inexperience and aloofness of the "supreme command" in New York. There is nobody there who will tell the field commands that what they are doing is wrong and is damaging UN credibility. There is nobody who will tell the commander in the field that they should stop being a prima donna and faux diplomat and instead be a true commander? Does anyone wonder who runs UNIFIL from New York today? Just ask. I am afraid at the first sign of serious trouble, national commands will take over and the international force will disintegrate.

This extreme risk aversion cannot be overruled by the UN command who would not want to be accused of not caring for the lives of the soldiers. As a result, friendly contact with the local population is ruptured. UNIFIL had always enjoyed the trust of the people who at times took risks to protect these foreign soldiers they saw as their guests. The best source of intelligence has always been the friendly villagers. Once you lose that trust, you are on your own. Original UNIFIL which had to survive on its own during heavy battles in its region was always very careful to respect local sensitivities and at times take risks to protect the people. I think the people have paid back generously.

Moreover, the technical countermeasures introduced, such as jamming devices against IEDs, etc., do not mean much in South Lebanon. Israeli army, certainly one of the most technologically advanced in the world, constantly developed such countermeasures but kept on sustaining casualties that eventually led to its withdrawal from Lebanon. The US military has a force about 5000 with separate command dealing only with IED's in Iraq and have spent billions of dollars to deal with that threat. Don't forget that one of the best protected Prime Ministers was

While EU troops are essential because of their professional background and the political clout they enjoy with the parties to the conflict, such deterrence only works as long as the parties to the conflict find that the current price works to their advantage.

killed in the middle of Beirut in broad daylight. In Lebanon, we have an axiom that says: "If they want to get you, they will".

Another disturbing product of excessive risk aversion is the danger it poses to the harmony within the force. While European contingents are taking series of protective measures, including severe restrictions on movement of their troops and cutting off their contacts with the local people, other contingents are trying to move around freely, visit and shop in villages. But, this is restricted by force-wide security rules. Soldiers come to Lebanon and leave without seeing Beirut. Rules imposed by the European units and their aggressive postures that turn the people against UNIFIL are severely resented by other contingents. This affects the cohesion and overall harmony of the force. There is a need for EU contingents with UNIFIL to be reduced. Downsizing would lower their profile and make their targeting more difficult, but will not reduce the political clout of the force.

> National commanders are evaluated by their home commands, not the UN. Their careers' advancement depends on what their own superiors think about them, not what the UN command thinks

EU national authorities should coordinate more closely with their UNIFIL counterparts when intervening in the local politics of Lebanon or even when making statements about UNIFIL. UN failed badly in giving public diplomacy support to the new UNIFIL and allowed the troop contributors a free hand to say what they want. The public acceptability of UNIFIL troops were compromised by foreign policy statements or blunders and some contingents were received by indifference, if not seen as a potential enemy. In peacekeeping, public perceptions are vital. You are not sending your soldiers to fight. So why are you talking as if you are?

The presence of 28 troop contributing to UNIFIL may seem like an ideal situation. It gives it an international flavour with troops from all continents and religious backgrounds, but it seriously hampers practical coordination and communication. It is UN's wishful thinking and ignorance of military culture to recruit troops from all over the world without taking into consideration the differences in quality, equipment, training and suitability of these troops for a complicated mission such as UNIFIL.

I remember a contingent that refused to send out night patrols because of their beliefs. Another refused to post officers at checkpoints because in their military culture that is not what officers do. They sit at the officers club and chat all day. At crisis times, language always was a serious impediment. Joint action on the ground was practically impossible. UNIFIL should consider reducing the total number of contributing nations, but UN headquarters is still increasing their numbers.

As in all peacekeeping missions, for UNIFIL too, composition of the force is paramount. Luckily for UNIFIL, UN had no problems in recruiting countries. A force based on the Mediterranean basin and European countries will have better acceptability, meet less hostility and achieve more respectability than troops from far continents. Cultural and geographical proximity are always strong force multipliers.

The true problem is these issues are hardly ever addressed by the UN, which is simply incapable of putting together, deploying and running a large force. Once the Security Council decides to set up a peacekeeping force, it becomes an administrative and logistical task for the UN secretariat. Where do we find the soldiers? How do we move them to the mission

238

area? How do we house and feed them? Minimal consideration, if any, is given to suitability of those troops to the mandate and the mission area. What are the parameters of our intervention? Will the mission require peace building? State building? Do you have the funds and the right staff?

Sadly still very much neglected is the internal cultural compatibility, the ability of such a diverse collection of civilians and military to work together harmoniously in a conflict zone.

At one point in not too distant future, Europe will have to get more intimately involved in the Middle East. It is not only the Arab-Israeli conflict and the oil we should be concerned with. The Arab nation state suffering from political incompetent governance, corruption, injustice and indifference to meeting the basic needs of the society is in danger of disintegration. Instead of trying to address the wrongs, we see more concentration of power in the hands of a few in the security regimes that dominate the region.

There are so many disconnects in our region between the rulers and their subjects, rich and poor, urban and rural, educated and illiterate. There is a new breed of Islamist, populist political leaders emerging in the Middle East to challenge the traditional, family based and usually corrupt regimes. The region is being flooded with new generation of weapons and military know-how in the hands of non-state groups. At the moment, their efforts are directed at challenging their ruling establishments and co-opting their heavily armed but generally incompetent military forces while slowly creating states within states.

At one point, these movements will dominate internal politics of their countries and will adopt Palestine as their key problem and that is when we will feel the impact of this regional conflict on international security. People are increasingly critical of autocratic regimes and pledge their loyalty to fundamentalist groups who care about their plight and hungry families. Basic and modest demands of the large segment of the society are not met. Worse is the sense indignity and humiliation that masses feel. The only help and compassion that the poor are getting are from Islamic charities and welfare units of groups such as Hizbullah and Hamas. Why are we surprised then when people declare their loyalty to politicians or groups instead of state institutions which have failed to perform their primary functions?

The lessons learnt from both UNIFIL and UNIFIL II, as well as two minor EU missions to Israel-Palestine conflict, should be analyzed before any large-scale EU intervention into the Middle East, particularly in Palestine. Any mission should have realistic objectives that help advance conflict management between the conflicting sides, in parallel to general initiatives aimed at solving the underlying political problems. If this does not occur, then all such operations will either become permanently "interim", such as UNIFIL, or face an embarrassed suspension right when they are most needed, as EUROBAM.

It is time for the EU and the Mediterranean countries to start thinking about these issues because rise in violent socio-religious movements is threatening the Arab countries, while more and more people believe that negotiations do not produce results but struggle does.

The lessons learnt from both UNIFIL and UNIFIL II, as well as two minor EU missions to Israel-Palestine conflict, should be analyzed before any large-scale EU intervention into the Middle East, particularly in Palestine. Any mission should have realistic objectives that help advance conflict management between the conflicting sides, in parallel to general initiatives aimed at solving the underlying political problems

TIMUR GOKSEL

EU troops should not be deployed to Palestine unless this action is perceived as impartial and there is a parallel, effective advancement of the comprehensive political agenda. For this to occur, we have to think of an EU with a united vision, which is not reluctant to use its considerable economic and political clout to resolve the conflict. It may well be the right time for EU to stop acting as a cash cow to the Middle East conflict.

Appendix F—Paper Never Refuses Ink

An Roinn Cosanta
Department of Defence

FOI/2004/18

Mr. Michael Walker,
Lake-View,
Crohyboyle,
Dungloe,
Co. Donegal.

26 May, 2004.

Dear Mr. Walker,

I refer to the request you have made under the *Freedom of Information Acts* 1997 and 2003 for records held by this Department in relation to the deaths of the Private Hugh Doherty and Private Kevin Joyce.

A final decision on your request was made by me today and I am pleased to advise that I have decided to part grant your request as to some records or parts of records . I have decided to refuse other records, should they exist, as they would not come within the scope of the Act, having been created prior to 21 April, 1998, the operative date of the Act insofar as such records are concerned.

I am attaching a schedule which shows the records that this Department considers relevant to your request. The schedule describes each record, and indicates whether the record is released in full, released with deletions or refused. Where records have been refused in full or in part, the schedule refers to the relevant sections of the FOI Act which apply. The schedule also provides brief reasons for the decision to exempt these records

This fee payable for the copies of the records is calculated on the following basis:

1. €62.85 in respect of 180 minutes of staff time to locate and draw together the records covered by your request @ £20.95 per hour

2. €4.52 in respect of photocopying costs @ 4 cents for each page of photocopying (there are 113 such pages to be released to you).

I understand that a refund of €5 is due to you arising from a recent request by you under the Freedom of Information Act (Our Ref FOI 12/04). The Department proposes to set off this amount against the fee in respect of this request. As such the total fee payable by you before the records can be released amounts to €62.37. The photocopied records will be sent to you within one week of the date that payment is received by this Department. Should you wish to pay the fee, you must do so within 8 weeks of the date on which you received this letter. This Department will keep the records available for an 8 week period.

240

An Roinn Cosanta
Department of Defence

FOI/2004/18

Mr. Michael Walker,
Lake-View,
Crohyboyle,
Dungloe,
Co. Donegal.

9 June, 2004.

Dear Mr. Walker,

I refer to the request you have made under the *Freedom of Information Acts* 1997 and 2003
for records held by this Department in relation to the deaths of the Private Hugh Doherty
and Private Kevin Joyce.

I have received your payment of €62.37 and I now enclose copies of the records in
accordance with the decision set out in the schedule of records issued to you on 26 May
2004. If you are not satisfied with this decision, you may appeal it by writing to the
Department's Freedom of Information Officer, seeking that the matter be considered by the
appropriate Internal Appeals Officer.

The address of the FOI Officer is as follows;

Freedom of Information Unit,
Press & Information Office,
Department of Defence,
Infirmary Road,
Dublin 7.

Note: Please ensure the envelope is marked **Internal Review**.

Please refer to this decision in your letter. You must make your appeal within 4 weeks
of receiving this letter, but the making of a late appeal may be permitted in appropriate
circumstances. The appeal will involve a complete reconsideration of the matter by a more
senior member of the staff of the Department and the decision will be communicated to you
within 3 weeks.

Yours sincerely,

P.P.Ciaran Murphy
Principal
Executive Branch

DEPARTMENT OF DEFENCE, INFIRMARY ROAD, DUBLIN 7.

AN ROINN COSANTA, BÓTHAR NA HOTHARLAINNE, BAILE ÁTHA CLIATH 7.

TELEPHONE: (01) 804 2000 FAX: (01) 670 3399 G:\Freedom of Information\FOI18-04issuedocs.doc

242

Oifig an Aire Cosanta
Office of the Minister for Defence

An Roinn Cosanta
Department of Defence

Mr Michael Walker
Crohyboyle
Dungloe
Co Donegal

11 May 2012

Dear Mr Walker

I have been asked by Mr. Alan Shatter, T.D., Minister for Justice, Equality and Defence to refer further to your recent correspondence in relation to the tragic incident involving Private Kevin Joyce and Private Hugh Doherty while serving with the United Nations Interim Force in Lebanon.

The incident occurred on 27 April 1981, during which an observation post at Dayr Ntar near As Sultaniyah manned by Private Hugh Doherty and Private Kevin Joyce came under attack. Private Doherty was later found dead from gunshot wounds and Private Joyce was missing. The Minister understands that the incident has been the subject of an investigation by a UN Board of Inquiry in November 1981 and an investigation by the Defence Forces in 1982.

Two inquiries were conducted into this incident, one by the United Nations and the second by the then Director of Operations for the Defence Forces, Col Savino. The Savino report identifies inadequacies in the conduct of the operation and in the location and manning of OP6/22D and makes recommendations in this regard. However, there is nothing in the report of either inquiry or in the document attached to your letter to suggest a recognisable increased threat to Irish or UN personnel at the time of this tragic incident. As such, the Minister considers that there is no reasonable basis to accede to your request for an independent inquiry into the circumstances of this incident at this time.

Yours sincerely,

VINCENT LOWE
PRIVATE SECRETARY
MINISTER FOR DEFENCE

Cuirfear fáilte roimh chomhfhreagras I na gaeilge

Bóthar an Staisiúin, An Droichead Nua, Contae Chill Dara
Station Road, Newbridge, Co. Kildare

Teileafón / Telephone: (045) 492000   Facsuimhir/Fax (045) 492007   R-Phost / E-mail: minister@defence.irlgov.ie   Láithreán Gréasáin / Web:www.defence.ie

Oifig an Aire Cosanta
Office of the Minister for Defence

An Roinn Cosanta
Department of Defence

26 June 2012

Mr. Michael Walker
Crohyboyle
Dungloe
Co. Donegal

Dear Mr. Walker,

I have been asked by Mr. Alan Shatter, T.D., Minister for Justice, Equality and Defence, to refer further to your fax received on 28th May 2012, in relation to the tragic incident involving Private Kevin Joyce and Private Hugh Doherty while serving with the United Nations Interim Force in Lebanon.

The Minister notes your comments that both you and others were present in post 6-22 at the relevant time and were not interviewed by Col Savino. As you will appreciate, in the absence of the main body of the Savino Report, it is not possible to determine who was interviewed or the considerations used to determine who was to be interviewed. However, if you have substantive evidence which would suggest that the findings in the Savino Report are flawed or which provides a reasonable basis for establishing a further enquiry into this incident, the Minister would ask that you consider now making a formal statement setting out that evidence and providing your version of the events surrounding this tragic incident. The Department can organise for you to make a statement to the Military Police. Alternatively, if you prefer, you could make a statement to An Garda Síochána or you could submit a written statement to the Department or directly to the Minister.

I trust this clarifies the matter for you.

Yours sincerely,

VINCENT LOWE
PRIVATE SECRETARY
MINISTER FOR DEFENCE

Cuirfear Fáilte Roimh Chomhfhreagras i na Gaeilge

Bóthar an Staisiúin, An Droichead Nua, Contae Chill Dara
Station Road, Newbridge, Co. Kildare

Teileafón / Telephone: (045) 492000 Facsuimhir/Fax (045) 492007 R-Phost / E-mail: minister@defence.irlgov.ie Láithreán Gréasáin / Web:www.defence.ie

Office of the Director of Operations,
Defence Forces Headquarters,
Parkgate,
Dublin 8.

5 Sept 01

MEMO

SEARCH FOR PTE KEVIN JOYCE (SEOIGH)

1. On 27 Apr 1981 Pte Kevin Joyce (21) and Pte Hugh Doherty (20) were manning an
    Observation Post (OP) near the village of Dayr Ntar in the Irishbatt Area of Operations
    in South Lebanon. The OP had a panoramic view of an area known as the "Iron
    Triangle" which was occupied by a number of armed groups which included the main
    Palistinian factions FATAH, PFLP and PFLP (GC). The duty of the two Privates was
    to observe ang activity and report to their HQ. On the 27 Apr there was a considerable
    amount of air activity by the Israeli Air Forces in that area. The last radio contact from
    the OP was at 1540 hrs and when the twwo soldiers failed to appear at the designated
    pick up point at 1800 hrs, the alarm was raised and a search party was formed. They
    found Pte Doherty's body at the OP, with three gunshots in his back. Pte Joyce was
    missing. Searches were carried out in the subsequent days, and a full investigation
    was conducted. No trace of Pte Joyce was found.

2. Successive Irish Battalions continued the search to no avail. In 1988 he was officially
    declared dead. It is believed that a Palistinian group was reponsible for killing Pte
    Doherty and abducting Pte Joyce who was killed shortly afterwards and buried
    somewhere near the area of the OP. In Nov 2000 the 88 Inf Battalion (Bn) reopened
    the investigation, the conduct of which was made easier by the withdrawel of the
    Israeli Defence Forces from South Lebanon and the consequent freedom of movement
    in the area. Various leads were followed on the ground and representations made to
    the Palistinian Authority through diplomatic channels. At all times it was stressed that
    the Irish Battalion and the Irish Government wished to recover Pte Joyce's body for
    humanitarian reasons only and had no interest in apportioning blame or seeking
    retribution.

3. In march 2001 contact was made with the leading members of the FATAH
    Organisation in Lebanon. The commenced an investigation and within a short time
    confirmed that Pte Joyce was buried in uniform close to the area from which he was
    abducted. They claimed that the FATAH group were not responsible but they were in
    contact with a man in Damascus who was involved in the incident who would point
    out the location of the burial place by early April. This did not materialise.

4. The 89 Inf Bn (current Irishbatt) continue to maintain contact with FATAH who claim
    to be still confident of persuading the man in Damascus to point out the location of the
    body. They also stress that they are under direct orders from President Arafat to
    resolve this case. Contact has also been made with representatives of the PFLP in
    Lebanon and the PFLP (GC) in Damascus. All contacts have expressed their

willingness to help. As Irishbatt withdraws from Lebanon in Nov 2001 there is a limited amount of time remaining in which to solve this case and every effort is being made to locate the remains of Pte Joyce and return them to his family in Inis Thiar in the Aran Islands.

OC Irishbatt feels that it would be very helpfull if President Arafat were to be thanked for his cooperation and assistance so far and that the urgency of the matter be impressed upon him given the limited time remaining.

G. McNAMARA
COLONEL
DIRECTOR OF OPERATIONS
05 Sep 2001.

Question No. <u>77</u>

To ask the Minister for Defence the position regarding the search for the remains of a person (details supplied) who has been missing in the Lebanon since 1980; and if he will make a statement on the matter.

DEPUTY SEAN RYAN

<u>FOR ORAL ANSWER ON TUESDAY, 15TH MAY, 2001.</u>

<u>REPLY</u>

On 27 April 1981, an observation post in South Lebanon manned by Private Hugh Doherty and Private Kevin Joyce of IRISHBATT came under attack. Private Doherty was later found dead from gunshot wounds and Private Joyce was missing. Some equipment was also missing. The attackers are unknown.

I wish to assure the House that efforts to obtain information on the whereabouts of Private Joyce have been ongoing since his

pq13772/01

disappearance. I have raised the matter with the Israeli Ambassador and, the matter has also been pursued by the Department of Foreign Affairs with the Palestinian authorities. During a meeting in the Department of Foreign Affairs in August last year, the then Palestinian Representative to Ireland, the late Dr. Youssef Allan undertook to pursue the matter with his authorities. The Department of Foreign Affairs has also asked the Representative Office of Ireland to the Palestinian Authority, Ramallah, to make inquiries with the Palestinian authorities there. The EU Special Representative to the Middle East Peace Process, Ambassador Moratinos has also been advised on the case by the Department of Foreign Affairs and asked for any assistance he may be able to provide.

During my visits to UNIFIL I have taken every opportunity to raise the issue both with Government and local representatives and with the Lebanese media. In addition, each successive Irish Battalion

Supplementary Questions

Q.   **Will the Minister give details of the circumstances surrounding the**

   abduction of Pte. Joyce?

A.   On 10 April 1981, IRISHBATT opened a daylight observation post near Dayr

   Natr village. This post was manned by two personnel. On 27 April 1981, a

   patrol was sent to the post when the two soldiers on duty there failed to

   rendezvous with scheduled transport. At 1855 hours the patrol reached the

   post and found Pte. Hugh Doherty dead from gunshot wounds. The other

   soldier Pte. Joyce was missing and remains missing since that time   Detailed

   searches and inquiries have been carried out since 1981 with no positive

   results. High level contacts through military and diplomatic channels have

   failed to locate Pte. Joyce. With the imminent withdrawal of the Irish Contin-

   gent from Lebanon in November 2001, the Department of Defence in

   conjunction with the Department of Foreign Affairs is redoubling efforts to

   locate Pte. Joyce and bring this tragic incident to a conclusion.

Q.   What recent efforts are being made by your Department in relation to this matter?

A.   As late as 27 April, 2001 my Department requested the Department of Foreign Affairs to pursue a number of specific avenues of inquiry, suggested by the Chief of Staff, through diplomatic channels. The Department of Foreign Affairs has confirmed that tit is actively pursuing the matter through its representatives in the region.

Q.   Would the Minister indicate what those inquiries entail?

A.   In view of the sensitive nature of this matter I am sure that the House will appreciate that I do not wish to go into any great detail at this stage.

CIARAN BRENNAN

90 New Cabra Road
Dublin 7
Ireland

Phone: 01-868 1145
Mobile: 087-2269 629
E-mail: ciaranbrennan@tinet.ie

28 October 1998

John Hanney
Press Officer
Department of Defence
Parkgate Street
Dublin 8

Dear Mr Hanney,

My name is Ciaran Brennan, a Dublin-based freelance journalist. I am attempting to write a story on the disappearance of Private Kevin Joyce in southern Lebanon in 1981. I thought that perhaps you may be able to help me with my investigations or that you may be able to put me touch with somebody familiar with the case.

Could you tell me the exact circumstances surrounding his disappearance?
Who was responsible for his kidnapping?
What efforts were made by the Irish authorities - military and political - to secure Private Joyce's release?
What, to your knowledge, was the fate of Private Joyce?
Has anything been done in recent years to determine the whereabouts and fate of Private Joyce?
If, as is most likely at this stage, Private Joyce is dead, have you any idea of the events surrounding his death and have you an idea where his remains may lie?
If Private Joyce is dead, has anything been done to bring his remains home to Ireland?
In the light of agreements being reached in the Middle East and a new climate of political co-operation, is the Irish government seeking to use this opportunity to find out what happened to Private Joyce and bring his remains home?

I understand that there may be sensitive military and political issues involved in this case. However, I would appreciate any help with which you could provide me. I am available to talk with you at any time.

Thank you for your help and for taking the time to read this letter.

Sincerely,

Ciaran Brennan

Teleton
Telephone } (01) 478 0822

Tek   J720

Tagairt
Reference }

AN ROINN GNÓTHAÍ EACHTRACHA
Department of Foreign Affairs

BAILE ÁTHA CLIATH 2
Dublin 2

Ms Mary O'Reilly
Executive Branch
Department of Defence
Parkgate
Dublin 7

27 January 1999

Dear Mary,

I attach a copy of a letter received from Mr Ciaran Brennan, a freelance journalist who is preparing an article about the disappearance of Pte Kevin Joyce in South Lebanon in 1981.

I would be grateful for your assistance in providing answers to some of the questions forwarded by Mr Brennan. A number of these questions fall partially within the remit of this Department also, but your Department or the Defence Forces may have supplementary material which would be of use, while specific reference to the efforts of your Department in this matter is also made.

Due to pressure of other work commitments, there has been some delay in responding to Mr Brennan's letter. I would be very grateful, therefore, if you could give this matter attention at an early date.

Yours sincerely,

Gareth McFeely
UN Section

Memo
John Hanney received information from Army Press Office sometime ago to reply to a direct inquiry from Mr. Brennan. He will send a copy of the letter. Informed G. McFeely that I would send him a copy.
MOR
29/1/99
reminder to Press Office (Hanney)
DFA call.
MOR
3/2/99

CIARAN BRENNAN

[handwritten: Gareth / any news on this / SOK 14/12 / 98]

90 New Cabra Road
Dublin 7
Ireland

Phone: 01-868 1145
Mobile: 087-2269 629
E-mail: ciaranbrennan@tinet.ie

[handwritten: Gareth. / Grateful for any material you can provide for reply — we will of course clear any drafts we do with your section before issue / Seán]

28 October 1998

[handwritten: Please acknowledge and send to U N side for draft reply SOK 13/11/98 30/10/93 (16)]

Declan Kelly
Press Officer
Department of Foreign Affairs
80 St Stephen's Green
Dublin 2

Dear Mr Kelly.

My name is Ciaran Brennan. a Dublin-based freelance journalist. I am attempting to write a story on the disappearance of Private Kevin Joyce in southern Lebanon in 1981. I thought that perhaps you may be able to help me with my investigations or that you may be able to put me touch with somebody familiar with the case.

I would like to know what measures have been taken by the Irish authorities to find out the exact circumstances surrounding his disappearance?
Who was responsible for his kidnapping?
What efforts were made by the Department of Foreign Affairs, Department of Defence and the Defence Forces to secure Private Joyce's release?
What, to your knowledge, was the fate of Private Joyce?
Has anything been done in recent years by the Department of Foreign Affairs or the Department of Defence to determine the whereabouts and fate of Private Joyce?
If, as is most likely at this stage, Private Joyce is dead, have you any idea of the events surrounding his death and have you an idea where his remains may lie?
If Private Joyce is dead, has anything been done to bring his remains home to Ireland?
In the light of agreements being reached in the Middle East and a new climate of political co-operation, is the Irish government seeking to use this opportunity to find out what happened to Private Joyce?
Has the department of Foreign Affairs been in touch with representatives of the Lebanese government, Syrian Government and the new Palestinian Aurthority to find out the circumstances behind Private Joyce's kidnapping. where he was taken and his ultimate fate?

I understand that there may be sensitive military and political issues involved in this case. However, I would appreciate any help with which you could provide me. I am available to talk with you at any time.

Thank you for your help and for taking the time to read this letter.

Sincerely.

Ciaran Brennan

253

Department of Defence

24 November, 1998.

Mr. Ciaran Brennan,
90 New Cabra Road,
Dublin 7.

Dear Ciaran,

I refer to your letter dated 28 October, 1998 regarding Private Kevin Joyce.

The military authorities have provided the following replies to your questions:-

Q.   Could you tell me the exact circumstances surrounding his disappearance?

A.   Pte. Joyce and Pte. Doherty were posted as sentries at a "listening post" called 6-22d near the village of Dyar-natar in South Lebanon on 27 April, 1981. The post was visited by Irish personnel at approximately 1520 hrs on that day. Both Privates were present.

At approximately 1800 hrs personnel arrived at Post 6-22d to relieve the two Privates at the end of their duty. The post was deserted and a search was conducted. The body of Pte. Doherty was found close to the post. Follow up searches were conducted over the following days and they failed to locate Pte. Joyce.

Q.   Who was responsible for his kidnapping?

A.   It is believed that the PLO are responsible for his disappearance and the killing of Pte Doherty.

Q.   What efforts were made by the Irish authorities - military and political - to secure Private Joyce's release?

A.   Intense efforts have been ongoing in Lebanon since his disappearance to determine his whereabouts. Contact was made with all the factions operating in Lebanon at the time and also with central government. No information as to his location has been forthcoming.

DEPARTMENT OF DEFENCE, INFIRMARY ROAD, DUBLIN 7.

AN ROINN COSANTA, BÓTHAR NA HOTHARLAINNE, BAILE ÁTHA CLIATH 7.   J11563

TELEPHONE: (01) 804 2000   FAX: (01) 670 3399   GTN: 7105   e-mail: defence@iol.ie

Q.   What to your knowledge, was the fate of Pte Joyce?

A.   It would appear that Pte. Joyce was abducted and killed a short time after his abduction.

Q.   Has anything been done in recent years to determine the whereabouts and fate of Pte. Joyce?

A.   The case regarding Pte. Joyce has NOT been closed. Efforts are made from time to time, in Lebanon, to establish his whereabouts.

Q.   If, as is most likely at this stage, Pte. Joyce is dead, have you any idea of the events surrounding his death and have you any idea of where his remains may lie?

A.   The events surrounding his death, to the knowledge of investigating officers, are outlined above. It is rumoured that his remains were dumped close to the village of Dyr-natar soon after his abduction.

Q.   If Pte. Joyce is dead, has anything been done to bring his remains home to Ireland?

A.   Ongoing enquiries into the location of Pte Joyce's remains continue and, if located, it is probable that efforts would be made to repatriate his remains.

Q.   In the light of agreements being reached in the Middle East and a new climate of political co-operation, is the Irish Government seeking to use this opportunity to find out what happened to Private Joyce and bring his remains home?

A.   This is a matter for the Department of Foreign Affairs.

I hope that this information is of use to you.

Yours sincerely,

JOHN HANNEY,
PRESS OFFICE.

255

Copy

March, 1999.

㉗

Mr. Michael D. Higgins, T.D.,
Dáil Eireann,
Dublin 2.

Dear Michael,

You asked me to keep you informed of progress in investigations in the case of Private Kevin Joyce (Caomhán Seóighe), who disappeared while on service with the United Nations Interim Force in Lebanon (UNIFIL) in April 1981.

As far as UNIFIL is concerned the case remains open and efforts continue in Lebanon to establish his whereabouts. Regrettably no new information has come to light.

During the course of my visit to the Lebanon in September last and the Taoiseach's visit there in January of this year we raised with local political figures the case of Private Joyce. We were assured by them that they would continue to do anything that they could to uncover the truth. Hopefully some information will come to light which will give some further lead in this most tragic case.

I will certainly keep up the efforts in relation to Private Joyce's case and I will continue to avail of every suitable opportunity I can to bring a resolution to the matter.

Yours sincerely,

MICHAEL SMITH, T.D.,
MINISTER FOR DEFENCE

256

QUESTION NO:____205____ *

To ask the Minister for Defence the number of Irish defence force members killed in action while serving overseas with United Nations ; and if he will make a statement on the matter.

- Seán Power.

* **FOR WRITTEN ANSWER ON TUESDAY, 3RD NOVEMBER, 1998.**

REPLY

Minister for Defence (Mr. Michael Smith, T.D.,): Thirty five (35) members of the Permanent

Defence Force have been killed by violence while serving overseas with the United Nations.

Seventeen (17) of these were killed while serving with the United Nations Operation in the

Congo (ONUC). A further sixteen (16) were killed while serving with the United Nations

Interim Force in Lebanon (UNIFIL) and two (2) were killed while serving with the United

Nations Truce Supervision Organisation (UNTSO) in the Middle East. One other soldier, Private

Kevin Joyce, who was serving with UNIFIL has been missing in action since 1981.

Question No:___86_____

To ask the Minister for Defence the number of United Nations missions in which the Defence Forces have participated; the number of members killed while serving overseas ; and if he will make a statement on the matter.

DEPUTY SEÁN POWER.

FOR WRITTEN ANSWER ON THURSDAY, 1ST JULY, 1999.

REPLY

Minister for Defence (Mr. Michael Smith, T.D.,) Defence Forces personnel have participated in

a total of 34 United Nations missions to- date. A total of 76 members of the Defence Forces have

died while serving with these missions.Thirty-six (36) of these personnel were killed or fatally

wounded as a direct result of a hostile action or act, perpetrated by an enemy, opposing armed

force, hostile belligerent or other party. In addition,one soldier, who was serving with UNIFIL,

has been missing in action since 1981.

Information note on Private Kevin Joyce (Caomhán Seoighe)

On 27 April 1981, an observation post at Dayr Ntar near As Sultaniyah manned by Private Hugh Doherty and Private Kevin Joyce of the Irish Defence Forces came under attack. Private Doherty was later found dead from gunshot wounds and Private Joyce was missing. Some equipment was also missing. The attackers are unknown.

The UNIFIL investigation into the whereabouts of Private Joyce has continued but there have been no indications of his possible whereabo   or to suggest that he is still alive. It has been speculated that Private Joyce was killed a short time after his abduction.

The situation in UNIFIL is that the case remains open. Efforts have continued to establish his whereabouts. On the assumption that he is no longer alive, ongoing enquiries into the location of Private Joyce's remains continue.

▇▇▇▇▇▇▇▇▇▇▇▇▇▇▇▇▇▇▇▇▇▇ Private Joyce joined the Defence Forces ▇▇▇▇▇▇▇▇and was stationed with the Western Command's First Battalion at Renmore Barracks, Galway.

▇▇

Plea to locate body of soldier

The Star

18th March

Plea to locate body of soldier

EAMON DILLON

DEFENCE Minister Michael Smith made a personal plea to local Lebanese leaders for help in finding the body of an Irish soldier missing for 19 years.

Private Kevin Joyce (2I) has never been found since an attack on his post in which his comrade Hugh Doherty was killed.

His disappearance is a sad chapter in Irish involvement in Lebanon the Army would like to close.

Chapter

In a private meeting with the local Muktars, Minister Smith asked that every effort would be made to help track downside young Galway man's body.

In April 1981, when Irish soldiers finally reached the outpost at As Sultaniyah, private Doherty was shot dead.

The position had come under attack from an unidentified Arab faction and to this day no group has claimed responsibility.

Despite an exhaustive investigation, Joyce's body was never found leaving the Army with an unwanted mystery they have yet to solve.

"Our investigations went on for four or five years. There was a full-time officer appointed to the investigation," said Army spokesman Coin O'Neachtain.

The case has become more urgent since the Israeli pledge to pull out by July, which could end the UNIFIL mission in Lebanon.

Pledge

The Army suspect Joyce was injured during the gun battle but later died from his wounds and secretly buried by his captors.

Minister Smith repeated his appeal for help on Lebanese TV and radio during the coverage of the St Patrick's Day celebrations in Camp Shamrock.

260

As. O Reilly / more 3/4/00
Ne Sbn.
Mrs. Cotter.
Ret. 3/4/00

Mr. O'Donoghue / *Mrs. Bassett*

(32)

Please see the attached letter from the Ambassador of Israel regarding the late Private Kevin Joyce.

The Minister wishes the matter to be pursued with the Palestinian Authorities via Dept. of Foreign Affairs.

Please have detailed note prepared regarding the circumstances surrounding Pte Joyce's disappearance with appropriate covering letter to Sec. Gen., Dept. of Foreign Affairs for my signature.

31 March, 2000.

30 June, 2000

Mr. Padraic Mc Kernan,
Secretary General,
Department of Foreign Affairs.

Dear Paddy,

The matter of the disappearance of Private Kevin Joyce while on service with UNIFIL on 27 April, 1981 was raised by the Minister during a meeting with the Israeli Ambassador on 1 February, 2000. ██████████████████████████████████████ A copy of the Ambassador's letter is appended hereto.

████████████████████████████ The background to the disappearance of Private Joyce is set out in the attached Information Note. I would greatly appreciate your assistance in this matter.

I might add that the Minister, during visits to UNIFIL, raised the issue of the disappearance of Private Joyce both in conversation with local representatives (Muktars) and with the Lebanese media and appealed for any information which might bring this sad chapter to a close.

Yours sincerely,

David J. O' Callaghan
Secretary General

262

Military Police Company,
McDermott Barracks, Defence Forces Training Centre,
Curragh Camp, Co. Kildare.

Tel: (045) 445290 (Officer Commanding & APM)
       (045) 445291 (Admin Officer)
       (045) 445292 (Orderly Room)
       (045) 445293 (Investigation Section)
       (045) 445383 (Crime Reader/Collator)

(045) 445294 (RSM)
(045) 445295 (Duty Room)
(045) 445296 (RQMS)
(045) 445299 (Pl Comd & Pass NCO)

MP DFTC/CS7/3

03 AUG 00

Lt Gen D. STAPLETON
Chief Of Staff

Sir

841576 PTE KEVIN JOYCE 48 INF BN UNIFIL - MIA 27 APR 81

References: A.   Conversation re above 10 JUL 00

            B.   PM/C/02/81 dated 30 JAN 87 - Investigation Report Capt F.E.
                DWAN

1.   In SEP 98, during a visit to 83 Inf Bn UNIFIL, you indicated that further
enquiries should be made to try to ascertain the whereabouts of the remains of Pte
K. JOYCE.

2.   Before departing for LEBANON with 83 Inf Bn I obtained a copy of Ref B and
studied it carefully. I was, and am, inclined to agree with the premise that Pte
JOYCE was killed within a very short time of being abducted. Based on the report I
developed what I considered to be a reasonable theory of the death of Pte JOYCE;
this also identifies a particular area where Pte JOYCE may have been killed.

      a.   Ref B, para 3.d outlines information that Pte JOYCE was killed shortly
            after, and within a few kms of where, he was taken.

      b.   Ref B, Annex D, is a letter dated 02 JUL 86, from Capt DWAN to Mr
            Nabih BERRI, then Minister of the South in the LEBANESE
            Government. Para 2.a refers to a statement that Pte JOYCE was
            killed approx two (2) hours after being taken and within a few miles of
            DAYR NTAR, and buried in that area. It also refers to an 'eye witness'
            - a local.

      c.   Para 2.c of the letter refers to ▓▓▓▓▓▓▓▓▓▓▓▓▓▓
            ▓▓▓▓▓▓ as a person who may have information on the matter.

3.   a.   The persons believed to have killed Pte DOHERTY and abducted Pte
            JOYCE may have come from ▓▓▓▓▓▓▓▓▓▓▓▓

b. The area of the village of MAZRA'AT AL MUSHRIF is the possible, perhaps probable, location where Pte JOYCE was killed and subsequently buried.

c. The geography of the principle locations is as follows:

(1) MAZRA'AT AL MUSHRIF lies approx 4 kms SW of DAYR NTAR, and approx 3 kms E of QANA.

(2) AYTIT is approx 4 kms NW of MAZRA'AT AL MUSHRIF.

(3) A likely line of march for persons moving from DYAR NTAR to the camp at AYTIT is through the wadis SW towards MAZRA'AT AL MUSHRIF, and then turning NW towards AYTIT.

(4) The time lapse alleged between the abduction and killing of Pte JOYCE makes MAZRA'AT AL MUSHRIF a very probable location.

(5) See also para 2.c above.

4. In SEP 98, after your visit to 83 Inf Bn UNIFIL, I discussed this matter with Lt Col B. GOULDING, SLO at HQ UNIFIL (presently SSO Pers Staff, 1 S Bde). I explained the above theory to Lt Col GOULDING. Lt Col GOULDING drafted a letter to the Senior Officer LEBANESE Army G2 at QANA. I can NOT now recall the exact content but I do recall that the emphasis was on the recovery of the remains of Pte JOYCE and that other matters were of little or NO importance. I do NOT know what response was received from LEBANESE Army G2. Lt Col GOULDING did inform me that he saw little possibility of getting into the area of MAZRA'AT AL MUSHRIF as at that time, SEP 98, it was an area where the resistance movements, principally HIZBOLLAH, had heavy weaponry stored/hidden.

5. Shortly after this, possibly late SEP or early OCT 98, OC 83 Inf Bn, Lt Col M. O'DWYER, instructed me to prepare a briefing note for the local (TIBNIN) LEBANESE Army G2 officer, Capt SIRHAN. I did this, cleared the content with Lt Col GOULDING, and passed the note to MIO 83 Inf Bn to pass to Capt SIRHAN. I heard nothing more.

6. I should state that another reason for selecting MAZRA'AT AL MUSHRIF is it appears a reasonable size of area to conduct a search and enquiries; I believe at this remove that a focused search would be more practicable than trying to cover a vast amount of the area of SOUTH LEBANON.

7. I believe the political climate in LEBANON is more conducive now, than at any time in the past, to resolving the whereabouts of the remains of Pte JOYCE. I also believe that there is nothing to be gained, and indeed much to be lost, by trying to establish the identities of the persons responsible for the abduction of Pte JOYCE and his killing and that of his comrade, Pte DOHERTY. The focus must be on the

covery of his remains and their return to his family for burial in his native land. I also believe that best results would be achieved through the LEBANESE Army and the military wings of the resistance organisations in SOUTH LEBANON – soldiers would understand!

8. A final point is that if remains were recovered there must be proper identification; there should also be NO publicity or premature release of information lest the family of Pte JOYCE be further distressed.

9. I hope the above is useful. I would be happy to discuss this matter further if required.

10. As requested.

R.M. STEWART
Comdt
Officer Commanding

CONFIDENTIAL

PDFORRA

**Permanent Defence Force
Other Ranks Representative
Association**

136 Capel Street
Dublin 1

Tel: (01) 872 3388
Fax: (01) 872 3506
Email: hq@pdforra.ie
Freephone: 1 800 200250

21st September 2000

Michael Smith,
Minister for Defence,
Defence Force Headquarters,
Parkgate,
Dublin 8.

Dear Minister,

You will remember that I wrote to you in July last concerning my belief that additional efforts should be made to attempt to recover the body of Pte Kevin Joyce.

I have the full approval of the National Executive of PDFORRA to further explore this crucially important and sensitive issue.

In the past days I have met with Kevin Joyce's sister and she has now given the blessing of the family to myself and PDFORRA to do whatever possible to attempt to locate her brother's body. You may be aware of a situation, which developed some years ago when the Joyce family did not wish to have any further interaction with the Defence Forces on this matter.

I request a meeting with you at year earliest convenience so that I can discuss this important matter with you. I will be asking you to raise this matter as a matter of urgency with the Department of Foreign Affairs so that they can pursue it with the new Palestinian Government and the governments of Lebanon and Syria.

Yours sincerely,

EAMONN LAFFERTY
PRESIDENT
PDFORRA

Copy to Cancl.

No 22/9/

266

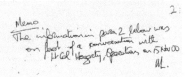

Memo
The information in para 2 below was
on foot of a conversation with
Lt Col Hegarty, Operations on 15 Nov 00
ML

2:

FAX TRANSMISSION

Overseas/Internal Security Unit, Department of Defence,
Parkgate, Infirmary Road, Dublin 7, Ireland.

To: Mr. Conleth Brady
      Department of Foreign Affairs
      Fax no: 4785949   Date:15 November, 2000.
              5946   Pages: 4 including cover sheet.

From: Margaret O'Leary at Fax no: 8042022

Re: Disappearance of Pte. Kevin Joyce in Lebanon on 27 April, 1981

Conleth,

I refer to our telephone conversation this afternoon and recent correspondence (copies
attached) regarding the above.

The military authorities have reported that Dr. Beverley Edwards, Queens University, Belfast,
who is an expert in Middle East affairs and who acts as Special Adviser to the EU Special
Representative to the Middle East, Mr. Moratinos, has been in contact with the 88th Irish
Battalion which has just completed its tour of duty with UNIFIL. Dr. Edwards has paid
several visits to the Irish Battalion while in the Middle East and the OC IRISHBATT had
asked her to use her good offices to assist in this case. She has now suggested to the military
authorities that the Minister for Foreign Affairs might raise the matter with the EU Special
Representative to the Middle East in the margins of tomorrow's meeting of the Euro
Mediterranean Partnership Council in Marseilles with a view to his Office assisting in
ascertaining any information on the whereabouts of the remains of Private Joyce.

It would be appreciated if consideration could be given to this suggestion by your Department.
I understand that Dr.Edwards has discussed the case of Pte. Joyce's disappearance with Mr.
Moratinos.

Regards,

P.S.
Sorry for late notice of this which
was unavoidable. I've spoken
to Mr T. Mannix since I spoke to you.
ML

_____
MARGARET O'LEARY

c.c. Director of Operations (Attn: Lt Col G. Hegarty)

molé23b.aam

Mrs Barrett advised of above.
1 Ml

Office of the Director of Operations,
Defence Forces Headquarters,
Parkgate, Dublin 8.

24 Nov '00

Ms Margaret O Leary
Overseas / Internal Security Unit

Miss Reilly
Pl prepare reply for ~~DDOPS~~ signature by
PSM.7
4/5/12

- 5 ...

Dear Margaret,

841576 PTE KEVIN JOYCE (I INFANTRY BATTALION)
48 INFANTRY BATTALION UNIFIL (MISSING IN ACTION)

1. Ref : PDFORRA letter to Minister dated 21 Sept 2000 and your query of 16 Oct 2000.

2. Pte Kevin Joyce was abducted on the 27 Apr 81 from an OP (6-22A) near Dayr Ntar.
    Efforts to obtain information on his whereabouts have continued with each successive
    battalion since 1981. The present battalion has also been tasked to pursue the matter.
    In addition, the EU Special Representative to the Middle East has recently been
    advised on the case, and it is hoped that he will persue it through his own channels.

3. PDFORRA should be informed of the continuing efforts being made to ascertain what
    happened to Pte Joyce; that we are acutely aware of the anguish of the Joyce family
    and that we will continue to do everything within our power to resolve this matter.

G. HEGARTY

LIEUTENANT COLONEL

OIC OVERSEAS SUBSECTION

J:\OS\EOPS\MISSIONS\UN\UNIFIL\UNIFIL\JOYCE.SAM

Ref: 0486/2000

January, 2000.

Mr. Eamonn Lafferty,
President,
PDFORRA,
136 Capel Street,
Dublin 1.

Dear Eamonn,

I have been asked by the Minister for Defence, Mr. Michael Smith, T.D., to refer to your letter of 21 September, 2000, concerning efforts to locate the body of Private Kevin Joyce, who was abducted on 27 April, 1981, from Irish UNIFIL post 6-22A near Dayr Ntar, Lebanon.

The Minister would like to assure you that efforts to obtain information on Private Joyce's whereabouts have been ongoing since his disappearance. In this regard, the Minister himself has raised the matter of the disappearance of Private Joyce with the Israeli Ambassador and, at his instigation, the matter has also been pursued by the Department of Foreign Affairs with the Palestinian authorities. During a meeting in the Department of Foreign Affairs last August, the Palestinian Representative to Ireland, Dr. Youssef Allan undertook to pursue the matter with his authorities. The Department of Foreign Affairs has also asked their Representative in Ramallah, Israel, to make enquiries with the Palestinian authorities there. It is also understood that the EU Special Representative to the Middle East has recently been advised on the case.

The Minister has taken every opportunity during his visits to UNIFIL to raise the issue both with local representatives and with the Lebanese media. In addition, each successive Irish Battalion since 1981, including the present battalion, has been tasked with pursuing the matter.

I trust that this outlines that position in this case to date.

Yours sincerely,

MICHAEL O'SULLIVAN
PRIVATE SECRETARY
MINISTER FOR DEFENCE

Setback in hunt for soldier

The Star

31st January

Setback in hunt for soldier

EXCLUSIVE by MICHAEL O'TOOLE

A PALESTINIAN diplomat who died in Dublin this month had been playing a crucial role in the search for the remains of the only Irish soldier missing in action.

The soldiers' union, PDFORRA, said yesterday that the death of Dr Yusef Allan was a setback in its efforts to have Private Kevin Joyce's body returned to Ireland.

But sources told the Star they were determined to bring the soldier's body home.

Meeting

Ironically, senior PDFORRA officials had scheduled a meeting with Dr Allan in Dublin, due to take place days after he died two weeks ago.

Private Joyce (21) has not been seen since an attack on his south Lebanon UN post in which comrade Hugh Doherty was killed in April 1981.

To this day, no group has claimed responsibility for the attack on Pte Joyce's outpost at As Sultaniyah, but it is widely accepted that the PLO was behind the brutal killings.

It is believed Pte Joyce was abducted after Pte Doherty was killed by a gang of PLO raiders - and then executed away from the bunker.

The Irish Army mounted a massive search for Pte Joyce after his disappearance, covering hundreds of square kilometres in vain.

Dr Allan was the PLO's representative in Ireland and had been part of secret negotiations reviewed by The Star last month -to recover the soldier's body.

A source said: "This is definitely a set back." "But we will just have to keep going and use other avenues and we are still hopeful

Dr Allan was found at the bottom of the stairs in his house on Hi Haddington Road. Ballsbridge. It is thought Dr Allm died of a heartattack.

Previous   Headlines   Next

Information Note on Private Kevin Joyce (Caomhán Seoighe) for Minister of State at the Department of Foreign Affairs, Liz O'Donnell T.D.

On 27 April 1981, an observation post at Dayr Ntar near As Sultaniyah manned by Private Hugh Doherty and Private Kevin Joyce came under attack. Private Doherty was later found dead from gunshot wounds and Private Joyce was missing. Some equipment was also missing. The attackers are unknown.

The UNIFIL investigation into the whereabouts of Private Joyce has continued but there have been no indications of his possible whereabouts or to suggest that he is still alive. It would appear that Private Joyce was killed a short time after his abduction.

The situation in UNIFIL is that the case remains open. Efforts are made from time to time in Lebanon to establish his whereabouts. Ongoing enquiries into the location of Private Joyce's remains continue and, if located, efforts will be made to repatriate his remains.

The Minister for Defence, Mr. Michael Smith, T.D., accompanied by the Secretary General of the Department of Defence and the Chief of Staff met the local religious leader, the Muchtar of Tibnin, during their visit to the Lebanon in September, 1998 and requested that the militia suspected of being involved return the remains of Private Joyce. At that time, Lebanese television had been showing a picture of Private Joyce in a bid to jog the memories of locals who may know something about the abduction.

The Minister also raised the matter of the disappearance of Private Kevin Joyce when the Ambassador of Israel to Ireland, H.E. Mark Sofer paid a courtesy call to him in February 2000

During a meeting in the Department of Foreign Affairs in August 2000, the Palestinian Representative to Ireland, the late Dr. Youssef Allan undertook to pursue the matter with his authorities. The Department of Foreign Affairs also asked their Representative in Ramallah, Israel, to make enquiries with the Palestinian authorities there. It is also understood that the EU Special Representative to the Middle East has been advised on the case.

The Minister has taken every opportunity during his visits to UNIFIL to raise the issue both with local representatives and with the Lebanese media. In addition, each successive Irish Battalion since 1981, including the present battalion, has been tasked with pursuing the matter.

█████████████████████████████████ Private Joyce joined the Defence Forces ██████████████ and was stationed with the Western Command's first battalion at Renmore Barracks, Galway. He is still Ireland's only 'Missing in Action' soldier and is remembered by his unit at Renmore each year during a ceremony for deceased members.

██████ The Military Star Medal (An Realt Mileata) was presented to the family of Private Joyce at a special awards ceremony in Collins Barracks, Dublin on Sunday 8 November, 1998.

272

DEFENCE (AMENDMENT) (NO. 2) ACT, 1960

Record of the death of a member, or the wife of A member, or a relative or dependant of a member ordinarily residing with the member, of the Permanent Defence Force occurring outside the State while the member is serving outside the State with an International United Nations Force.

No. (1)	Date and place of death (2)	Name and Surname (3).	Sex (4)	Marital condition (5)	Age last birthday (6)	Number, rank and unit, or occupation (7)	(a) Cause of death (b) State if Certified (c) Duration of illness (8)	Signature, number, rank and unit of officer compiling this record and date of signature (9)	Signature of Adjutant-General and date of signature (10)
	Thirty Seventh Day of April 1981. Dair Ntar Lebanon.	Kevin Joyce	Male	Bachelor	20 yrs.	841576 Private 48 Inf Bn.	Missing In Action Presumed Dead Wef 27 April 1981. (See Attached Correspondence)		

CONFIDENTIAL

[handwritten annotations]
Min. Bennett action & please
for early issue
M.O. Pl. ann - &
appropriate to DFA,
approach this matter
Do 9/4/01.

Office of the Chief of Staff,
Defence Forces Headquarters,
Parkgate,
Dublin 8.
Phone: 01-8042600
Fax: 01-6703823
Email: cosoffice@eircom.net

6 April 2001

Mr Michael Smith T.D.,
Minister for Defence.

SEARCH FOR PRIVATE CAOMHAN SEOIGHE (KEVIN JOYCE) IN LEBANON

MISSING IN ACTION - 27 APRIL 1981

Minister,

1. As you are aware from the detailed briefings you received at Camp Shamrock, UNIFIL, on 14 March 2001, Lieutenant Colonel D. Ashe and the staff of 88 Infantry Battalion, are making every effort to locate and retrieve the remains of Private Caomhan Seoighe.

2. In the latest report to this office, Lieutenant Colonel Ashe has offered a number of "suggested official approaches" in order to advance the investigation, namely,

    a. <u>Syrian Government</u> be asked to:-

        (1) Assist by getting the PFLP and the PFLP-GC to appoint a Liaison Officer (LO), in Lebanon, to Irishbatt.

        (2) Have the Syrian Security Services in Lebanon;

            (a) Specifically tasked with liaison and co-operation with Irishbatt.

            (b) Seek any information that would lead to a discovery of the remains of Private Seoighe from the Damascus based PFLP and PFLP-GC.

        (3) Assist by getting Saiqa and the Iraqi Baath Party to appoint Liaison Officers (LOs) to Irishbatt.

<u>CONFIDENTIAL</u>

274

b.   Please note that on my visit to Damascus on 17 March 2001 I requested Lieutenant General Tourkmani, the Syrian Forces Deputy Chief of Staff, for assistance in this matter. He replied that it would be a matter solely for the Lebanese authorities. Consequently I feel that it will take a Government to Government request for the desired action to be taken.

c.   **Palestinian Authority**   Request that the Palestinian Authority be asked to instruct the following personnel to give their full commitment to Irishbatt;

    (1)   **Sultan Abu al Aynain**   -   Political Chief in Lebanon for Yasser Arafat and his official spokesman in Lebanon.

    (2)   **Munir al Maqdah**   -   Military Leader of Fatah in Lebanon.

3.   May I request that the assistance of the Department of Foreign Affairs be obtained in the matters as outlined in Para 2 above.

C.E. MANGAN

LIEUTENANT GENERAL

CHIEF OF STAFF

486/2000

27, April, 2001.

<u>For attention of Mr. Tony Mannix</u>

The Secretary General,
Department of Foreign Affairs.

<u>Re: Disappearance of Private Caomhan Seoige (Kevin Joyce)
on 27 April, 1981.</u>

I refer to previous correspondence concerning the above.

The Minister during his visit to Lebanon on 14 March last was briefed on efforts being made by the Irish Battalion (IRISHBATT) to locate and retrieve the remains of Private Joyce.

The Chief of Staff has now reported to the Minister that the Irish Battalion has offered a number of "suggested official approaches" in order to advance the investigation, namely,

a.   **<u>Syrian Government</u>** be asked to:-

    (1)   Assist by getting the Popular Front for the liberation of Palestine (PFLP) and the Popular Front for the liberation of Palestine-General Command (PFLP-GC) to appoint a Liaison Officer (LO), in Lebanon, to IRISHBATT;

    (2)   Have the Syrian Security Services in Lebanon;

        (a)   Specifically tasked with liaison and co-operation with IRISHBATT;

        (b)   Seek any information from Damascus based PFLP and PFLP-GC that would lead to the discovery of the remains of Private Seoighe.

    (3)   Assist by getting Saiqa and the Iraqi Baath Party to appoint Liaison Officers (LOs) to IRISHBATT.

276

[**Note:** On his visit to Damascus on 17 March, 2001, the Chief of Staff, Lt. Gen. C. Mangan, requested Lt. Gen. Tourkmani, the Syrian Forces Deputy Chief of Staff, for assistance in this matter. He replied that it would be a matter solely for the Lebanese authorities. Consequently the military authorities consider that it will take a request through the normal diplomatic channels for the desired action to be taken.]

b.   **Palestinian Authority** Request that the Palestinian Authority be asked to instruct the following personnel to give their full commitment to IRISHBATT:

    (1)   **Sultan Abu al Aynain**   -   Political Chief in Lebanon for Yasser Arafat and his official spokesman in Lebanon.

    (2)   **Munir al Maqdah**   -   Military Leader of Fatah in Lebanon.

The Minister, accordingly, wishes that your Department would pursue the matter, as appropriate, with the Syrian Government and the Palestinian Authority as suggested by the military authorities. Your assistance in this matter is greatly appreciated. In view of the fact that the Battalion about to depart will be the last Irish Battalion to be deployed to UNIFIL the Minister is most anxious to explore all avenues which might bring this sad chapter to a close.

MARGARET BARRETT
PRINCIPAL
EXECUTIVE BRANCH

. J years on the thin blue line-1

The Sunday World

13rd May

23 years on the thin blue line-1

Report by DECLAN POWER

THE LAST batch of Irish troops to serve with UNIFIL will leave Lebanon next November, having completed their final mission of peace.

Since the Irish deployed with UNIFIL, 45 Irish soldiers have been killed helping Lebanon on her turbulent path to peace.

Now, after 23 years which saw two full-scale Israeli invasions and 47 battalions of Irish UN soldiers holding the blue line, Southern Lebanon is finally at peace.

As the Irish troops departed for South Lebanon for the last time earlier this month, Defence Minister Michael Smith talked exclusively to the Sunday World about his vision for future Irish peacekeeping involvement.

Legacy

This minister also spoke about his hopes for a lasting Irish legacy to help South Lebanon get back on its feet.

He said that the ending of Irish service with the United Nations Interim Force In Lebanon (UNIFIL) would be "a very historic moment, tinged with a certain sadness".

"We said when we started we would finish the job, and we did," Minister Smith told the Sunday World.

The UN forces came to Lebanon in 1978 to effect a separation of the invading Israeli army from Palestinian Liberation Organisation (PLO) fighters.

However, even though the PLO eventually left Lebanon, conflict continued between the Israelis and the Lebanese version of the IRA, the Hizbollah or "Party of God", a radical Islamic guerrilla army.

The Hizbollah regularly staged rocket attacks and sent suicide bombers into northern Israel. The Israelis often retaliated with merciless air and artillery bombardments of Southern Lebanon.

The Irish no longer have to run a gauntlet of attacks from either Hizbollah gun men or the Israeli-backed backed militias to patrol their area. Irish soldiers now patrol right up to the border with ıel.

Minister Smith believes the greatest legacy the Irish can leave is the fact that communities there can begin to grow again.

To help this along, the Minister told the Sunday World he plans to set up a third-level institute for education for the local South Lebanese population.

"When I think how Ireland has developed, I think 'what were the pillars that underpinned this?' The first thing was education the opening of the minds the breaking of new territories," he said.

"Now I hope we can enable the Lebanese to reach the same heights the Irish have done," added a clearly enthusiastic Minister Smith.

Sacrifices

Talking of the Irish who died in Lebanon, the Minister said it was the Taoiseach's express wish to have the memorial that exists out there brought and home and consecrated as a lasting memorial "to remind people that peacekeepinginvolves sacrifices".

The Minister stressed that he and his department are not forgetting the deaths of Privates Smallhorne and Barrett, the two soldiers who were murdered by militia gunmen after the Battle of At Tiri in 1980.

He said he had "great sympathy for the families of the two soldiers", and indeed for their comrade, Kerryman John O'Mahony who, though wounded, survived the incident.

Mohammed Bazi, a former militia gunman and alleged murderer of Smallhorne and Barrett, now lives in Detroit in the USA.

The Minister said he was happy to give the families access to the records of how their men died and was surprised it hadn't been done earlier.

He also said discussions are ongoing with the Attorney General and both the Lebanese and US authorities to "pursue all legal avenues open to seeing justice done".

However, perhaps the most fitting legacy to the men of At Tiri is the fact that it still exists today as a thriving rural community.

In 1980 it was set to be obliterated by Israeli militia, but Irish troops held the line and fought running battles to protect the village.

This is in stark contrast to the village of Srebrenicia in Bosnia. When Dutch peacekeepers pulled out, Serb soldiers massacred the village's male population.

Lashing out at the those who claim Ireland's participation in European- or UN- mandated peace enforcement operations erodes neutrality, the minister had this to say:, "Ireland is not neutral when it comes to fundamental wrongs. I would hate to think Irish people would turn their backs on societies emerging from conflict in different parts of the world."

The minister confirmed Ireland is preparing to play its role in more UN-mandated missions when the Lebanon mission ends.

Neglected

He said there would be a deepening of our peacekeeping involvement in the former Yugoslavia. Speaking about other forthcoming missions, he added: "Parts of Africa have been very neglected and we will be looking at the possibility of taking part in peacekeeping and humanitarian missions there."

In a direct response to organisations like AfrI and the Peace and Neutrality Alliance, Mr Smith said he would hate to think he represents a community that stands idly by while wrongs are being perpetrated on innocents.

Stressing Ireland's desire to participate in "spreading the line of peace", the Minister said: "We will stay involved and will think about each mission case by case.

"We have no colonial baggage, we did not oppress we were oppressed- and everywhere we have gone we have been accepted."

Tragedy of the soldier who never came home

THE IRISH Army has one final heartbreaking task to complete before finally withdrawing from the Lebanon in November.

It is to try and discover precisely what happened to Private Kevin Joyce who was kidnapped while serving there 20 years ago.

The brave soldier left his family home in Castlevillage on Inisheer in the Arran Islands for the last time in October 1980 to serve with the 47th Irish battalion in Lebanon.

He disappeared six months later when the observation post he was manning in the village of Dyar Ntar came under attack from a Palestinian militia.

Private Hugh Doherty, a colleague from Donegal who was serving alongside him, died at the post after befog shot three times in the back

Negotiate

The Irish Army launched a major and massive search of the area for 20-year-old Private Joyce after learning of the attack, but failed to discover where he was being held or what had happened to him.

A special team of unarmed United Nations officers, known as Observer Group Lebanon, weredrafted in to negotiate with senior Palestinian figures over the abduction, but also failed to get any results.

The Palestinians were either unaware of the missing soldier's whereabouts or were keeping quiet.

Investigators believe that the aim of the guerrillas had been to kidnap both soldiers.

The Palestinians would then have used them as a powerful bargaining chip to have the post at Dyar Ntar closed down.

280

hile the remains of Private Doherty were flown home for burial, the search for his missing colleague continued.

It is thought that Private Joyce was kept alive for about a month by his captors before being killed.

Although the horror murders happened 20 years ago, senior Irish Army officials are still hopeful that they may yet be told where his remains are and they can be returned to hisnative inisheer for burial.

Previous   Headlines   Next

Minister,

Re:- Disappearance of Private Kevin Joyce on 27 April, 1981.

A number approaches suggested by the Chief of Staff in his minute to you dated 6 April, 2001 in relation to the above were conveyed to the Department of Foreign Affairs with a request that they be pursued, as appropriate, with the Syrian Government and the Palestinian Authority.

In response, the Department of Foreign Affairs have informed

Accordingly, the attached draft letter to Defence Minister Mustafa Tlass, whom you have met on a couple of occasions is submitted for your approval, please.

Regarding the other approaches suggested by the COS, the Palestinian Authority has been formally approached through the Representative Office of Ireland to the Palestinian Authority and a response is awaited. Meanwhile the matter is being pursued assiduously by the present battalion in Lebanon and, in this regard, there has been contact between military personnel there and Ambassador Gunning.

DAVID J. O'CALLAGHAN
SECRETARY GENERAL

May, 2001.

Chief of Staff,

Re: Disappearance of Private Kevin Joyce on 27 April, 1981

Further to your minute to the Minister dated 6 April, 2001, the Department requested the Department of Foreign Affairs on 27 April, 2001, to pursue, as appropriate, with the Syrian Government and the Palestinian Authority, the approaches suggested by you.

On 11 May, 2001, that Department forwarded letters which it had received from Ambassador Gunning in Cairo in the matter. Arising from the advice of the Ambassador ▮▮▮▮▮▮
▮▮

Copies of the relevant correspondence in this matter are enclosed. You might advise of the reasons why, following Irishbatt contacts with the Palestinians, it is now considered that an approach to Syria, as suggested earlier, is not appropriate - in other words, the nature of the Palestinian advice. I would like to keep the Minister advised of any further developments as they occur.

DAVID J. O'CALLAGHAN
SECRETARY GENERAL

June, 2001.

CONFIDENTIAL

**Headquarters
89 Inf Bn
UNIFIL**

IRISHBATT

Chief of Staff
Through
D COS (Ops)
Through
D OPS

28 May 2001

Sir,

SEARCH FOR PTE JOYCE

1. The above case was taken over by Comdt J. J. O' Reilly, Adjt 89 Inf Bn, from Comdt G. Aherne, MIO 88 Inf Bn on 14 May.

2. On 22 May the Irish Ambassador to Egypt, Syria and Lebanon, Mr Peter Gunning, visited 89 Inf Bn HQ, at his own request, for a briefing on the Joyce case. ▇▇ He took the opportunity to visit Irishbatt while in Beirut on official business, which included attending a reception on board the L.E. Aoife.

3. The Ambassador was given a detailed briefing on the case, most of which was new to him, since the briefing from DFA was incomplete in many respects. He was also taken to former post 6-22D in Dyar Ntar and the surrounding area, where the incident occurred in 1981. Following the briefing, the ground orientation and our discussions, he fully appreciated the difficulty of the task, the sensitivities involved and the discretion required.

4. I discussed with the Ambassador the possible benefits of using diplomatic pressure, but impressed upon him the need for discretion in so doing. The Ambassador agreed and reiterated his view, expressed in his reply to the DFA, ▇▇▇▇▇▇▇▇▇▇▇▇ ▇▇▇▇▇▇▇ He did, however take a great interest and offered to help in any way which would be appropriate and of value.

5   The optimism expressed by FATAH in Apr, when it was indicated that the discovery of Pte Joyce's body was imminent has now faded and the prospects of a resolution have receded somewhat. However, in his initial meeting with the FATAH contacts on 26 May, Comdt O' Reilly was informed by them that they are continuing their efforts and they are hopeful of a conclusion before Irishbatt withdraws from Lebanon.

CONFIDENTIAL

During the meeting Comdt O' Reilly twice asked if there was anything Irishbatt could do to help them advance matters, to which they replied in the negative. Accordingly, I suspect that any attempts to influence events from Syria, *at this point*, could be resented by these men and prove detrimental to relations on the ground. I am satisfied that Ambassador Gunning shares this view.

6. If any diplomatic pressure is to be exerted at this stage, it should be on the Palestinian Authority. I have been informed by Ambassador Gunning that the Palestinian Minister for Planning and International Co-Operation, Dr Nabil Sha'ath met the Minister for Foreign Affairs in Dublin in recent days and the subject of Pte Joyce was discussed in a general way. It would be of help if this meeting could be built upon and further official contact be made with President Arafat, thanking him for his help to date and impressing on him our desire to advance the investigation given the limited amount of time left to the Irish contingent in Lebanon.

7. I have also spoken with the Lebanese army LO appointed to the case, Col Kanafir, at a reception in the house of the Irish Consul in Lebanon, on 24 May and stressed the need for restraint and discretion on the part of the Lebanese authorities if, and when the body of Pte Joyce is located. He readily agreed, while pointing out the difficulties faced in attempting to find mortal remains in Lebanon after such a long time lapse.

8. Having fully aquainted myself with all aspects of this case, through the comprehensive documentation left by the 88 Inf Bn, through briefings, orientation on the ground and meetings with people associated with the investigation, I would caution against excessive optimism and unrealistic hopes at this stage. Nevertheless, every effort will be made to continue to build on the excellent work done by our predecessors and this Bn will spare no effort in trying to bring this case to a resolution in the time we have left in this mission.

G HEGARTY
LT COL
OC 89 INF BN

In search of the unknown grave of missing soldier

Ireland on Sunday

19th August

In search of the unknown grave of missing soldier

INTENSE EFFORTS involving top level negotiations with key PLO representatives are underway in a last ditch attempt to locate and repatriate the remains of missing Irish soldier Lt Kevin Joyce.

The 20 year old soldier from Inisheer in the Aran Islands disappeared on April 27, 1981 - his family visited Camp Shamrock in Tibnin for the 20th anniversary of his death earlier this year - while manning an observation post in Dyarntar with Lt Hugh Doherty from Donegal who was a found dead at the scene.

The alarm was raised when the two men failed to report back from duty after their shift finished at 6pm.

Officers attending the scene discovered Lt Doherty's body with three shots in his back. However, there was no trace of Lt Joyce also known as Caomhin Seoige who was due to go home within a week.

The men's equipment - rifles, binoculars and a radio - was missing.

At first it was almost impossible to discover what had happened at the time was one of intense shelling by the Israelis and none of the factions was prepared to admit to killing a UN soldier.

However, in the intervening years intelligence from locals, on the ground has indicated that the men were targeted by the PLO.

In recent months PDFORRA offered to finance efforts to discover where Lt Joyce's remains are, so that they could be recovered before the Irish troops return home.

'There were several times during the past year when we thought we were on the verge of bringing him home,' said a senior army source.

Information

"But all of our information is third hand. It's a bit like the search for Jean McConville of the IRA Disappeared. Even after you have a search area located it is still next to impossible to actually pinpoint the area you need to search. Negotiations are extremely sensitive and in involved trips by senior army personnel to Damascus to meet PLO representatives. "There are no strings attached to our discussions. We do not want revenge. We have no agenda. We don't care who did this and we don't want justice. We just want to bring him home," the source said.

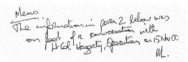

Memo
The information in para 2 below was on foot of a conversation with Lt Col Hegarty, Operations on 15 Nov 00.
ML.

FAX TRANSMISSION

Overseas/Internal Security Unit, Department of Defence,
Parkgate, Infirmary Road, Dublin 7, Ireland.

To: Mr. Conleth Brady
      Department of Foreign Affairs   Date: 15 November, 2000.
      Fax no: 4785949   Pages: 4, including cover sheet.
              5946

From: Margaret O'Leary at Fax no: 8042022

Re: Disappearance of Pte. Kevin Joyce in Lebanon on 27 April, 1981

Conleth,

I refer to our telephone conversation this afternoon and recent correspondence (copies attached) regarding the above.

The military authorities have reported that Dr. Beverley Edwards, Queens University, Belfast, who is an expert in Middle East affairs and who acts as Special Adviser to the EU Special Representative to the Middle East, Mr. Moratinos, has been in contact with the 88th Irish Battalion which has just completed its tour of duty with UNIFIL. Dr. Edwards has paid several visits to the Irish Battalion while in the Middle East and the OC IRISHBATT had asked her to use her good offices to assist in this case. She has now suggested to the military authorities that the Minister for Foreign Affairs might raise the matter with the EU Special Representative to the Middle East in the margins of tomorrow's meeting of the Euro Mediterranean Partnership Council in Marseilles with a view to his Office assisting in ascertaining any information on the whereabouts of the remains of Private Joyce.

It would be appreciated if consideration could be given to this suggestion by your Department. I understand that Dr. Edwards has discussed the case of Pte. Joyce's disappearance with Mr. Moratinos.

Regards,

P.S.
Sorry for late notice of this which was unavoidable. I've spoken to Mr T. Marvix since I spoke to you
ML.

MARGARET O'LEARY

C.C. Director of Operations (Attn: Lt Col G. Hegarty)

287

return on Tuesday 21 March, 2000.

The main purpose of my visit was to observe at first hand the work of Irish military

personnel serving in the region and to assure them, on behalf of the Government and the

people of Ireland, how proud we are of the outstanding manner in which they have

consistently performed their duties on United Nations service. I also wanted to express my

sympathy and that of the Government following the recent tragic deaths of Privates

Lawlor, Fitzpatrick, Murphy and Deere in a traffic accident on 14 February, 2000.

During the course of my visit to Lebanon, I met with the Lebanese Prime Minister Dr.

Selim Hoss, the Lebanese Chief of Staff and Commander in Chief of the Lebanese Army,

General Michel Suleyman, the UNIFIL Force Commander Major General Obeng and

Deputy Force Commander Brigadier General James Sreenan (from the Defence Forces) as

well as other local representatives and dignitaries. During the course of these meetings I

reiterated my concern for the safety of Irish troops in the event of a unilateral withdrawal

of Israeli Forces from the Israeli occupied area in South Lebanon. It will be recalled that

the level of their casualties in Lebanon led the Israeli Government to declare its intention to

withdraw unilaterally from Lebanon by July, 2000. A disorderly Israeli withdrawal

without the agreement of the Lebanese and Syrian Governments could create difficulties

for the UNIFIL contingent in Lebanon. This scenario could call for a revision of the role of

UNIFIL in a post withdrawal situation.

I also indicated that while Ireland would wish to maintain a commitment to UNIFIL until

such time as its mandate was discharged, I nevertheless, stressed the fact that the safety of

Irish troops was of paramount concern to me and to the Government. It is my view that, should the situation prevail where the safety of Defence Force personnel was seriously compromised there may be no option but to withdraw them. The emerging situation is being followed closely by the United Nations. Ireland and other UNIFIL troop contributing states are considering, in consultation with the Department of Peacekeeping Operations of the UN in New York, the implications of the various scenarios attendant on Israeli withdrawal. I will continue to keep the matter under close review in consultation with the military authorities and the Department of Foreign Affairs with particular regard to likely developments in the post-July, 2000 situation. While I was in Lebanon, it was reported that Prime Minister Barak favoured a full withdrawal south of the international border between Israel and Lebanon, thus complying with UN Resolution 425 of March, 1978 . I was heartened to hear of this development.

While in Lebanon, I again raised the issue of the disappearance of Pte. Joyce in 1981 both in conversation with local representatives (Muktars), and with the Lebanese media, and I appealed for any information which might bring this sad chapter to a close.

In all of the discussions that I had, there was consistent praise for Irish troops and a desire that they should continue in service in South Lebanon. I was greatly impressed, as always, by the commitment of all our troops in the Middle East to the important work they are undertaking in the cause of international peace.

I also visited Damascus, Syria, where I met with the Syrian Defence Minister, Lieutenant

General Mustafa Tlass who briefed me on recent developments on the Israeli/Syrian track of the Middle East Peace Process. While there, I met with Irish personnel serving with the United Nations Truce Supervision Organisation (UNTSO). There are currently ten personnel serving with UNTSO in the Middle East.

MICHAEL SMITH, T.D.,
MINISTER FOR DEFENCE

Question No. 77

To ask the Minister for Defence the position regarding the search for the remains of a person (details supplied) who has been missing in the Lebanon since 1980; and if he will make a statement on the matter.

DEPUTY SEAN RYAN

FOR ORAL ANSWER ON TUESDAY, 15TH MAY, 2001.

REPLY

On 27 April 1981, an observation post in South Lebanon manned by Private Hugh Doherty and Private Kevin Joyce of IRISHBATT came under attack. Private Doherty was later found dead from gunshot wounds and Private Joyce was missing. *All* Some equipment was also missing. The attackers are unknown.

I wish to assure the House that efforts to obtain information on the whereabouts of Private Joyce have been ongoing since his disappearance. I have raised the matter with the Israeli Ambassador and, the matter has also been pursued by the Department of Foreign Affairs with the Palestinian authorities. During a meeting in the Department of Foreign Affairs in August last year, the then Palestinian Representative to Ireland, the late Dr. Youssef Allan undertook to pursue the matter with his authorities. The Department of Foreign Affairs has also asked the Representative Office of Ireland to the Palestinian Authority, Ramallah, to make inquiries with the Palestinian authorities there. The EU Special Representative to the Middle East Peace Process, Ambassador Moratinos has also been advised on the case by the Department of Foreign Affairs and asked for any assistance he may be able to provide.

During my visits to UNIFIL I have taken every opportunity to raise the issue both with Government and local representatives and with the Lebanese media. In addition, each successive Irish Battalion since 1981, including the present battalion, has been tasked with pursuing the matter.

With the imminent withdrawal of the Irish Contingent from Lebanon later this year, my Department and the Department of Foreign Affairs are giving high priority to the ongoing efforts to locate the whereabouts of Private Joyce and bring this tragic incident to a conclusion. In April 2001 Private Joyce's brother and sister visited the scene of the incident in South Lebanon.

MICHAEL SMITH T.D.,
MINISTER FOR DEFENCE.

Supplementary Questions

Q. **Will the Minister give details of the circumstances surrounding the abduction of Pte. Joyce?**

A. On 10 April 1981, IRISHBATT opened a daylight observation post near Dayr Natr village. This post was manned by two personnel. On 27 April 1981, a patrol was sent to the post when the two soldiers on duty there failed to rendezvous with scheduled transport. At 1855 hours the patrol reached the post and found Pte. Hugh Doherty dead from gunshot wounds. The other soldier Pte. Joyce was missing and remains missing since that time Detailed searches and inquiries have been carried out since 1981 with no positive results. High level contacts through military and diplomatic channels have failed to locate Pte. Joyce. With the imminent withdrawal of the Irish Contingent from Lebanon in November 2001, the Department of Defence in conjunction with the Department of Foreign Affairs is redoubling efforts to locate Pte. Joyce and bring this tragic incident to a conclusion.

Q. **What recent efforts are being made by your Department in relation to this matter?**

A. As late as 27 April, 2001 my Department requested the Department of Foreign Affairs to pursue a number of specific avenues of inquiry, suggested by the Chief of Staff, through diplomatic channels. The Department of Foreign Affairs has confirmed that tit is actively pursuing the matter through its representatives in the region.

Q. **Would the Minister indicate what those inquiries entail?**

A. In view of the sensitive nature of this matter I am sure that the House will appreciate that I do not wish to go into any great detail at this stage.

Appendix G—Unifil 6 Clippings

'C' COY 49TH IRISHBATT

'C' Coy moved from As Sultaniyah on 4 July and took over operational control of the Brashit area from 'B' Coy. Unlike As Sultaniyah where we had men to spare, Brashit stretches the Coy resources to the limit with only a handful of men remaining at HQ. However, having spent over a month at our new location, most will agree that the non-stop atmosphere here is more preferable.

'Charlie' Coy, like most other Coys, has its fair share of sporting talent, entertainers and general characters. Among those worthy of note is Sgt. Tom Jinks of the weapons platoon. Apart from being an all-rounder sportwise, he has won premier awards in shooting competitions in Ireland and is the Coy's No. 1 sniper. Entertainers in the Coy come in all shapes and sizes as was borne out in our recent talent competition. Who will forget the "Dun Ui Mhaolaoise" players with Cpl Martin Scanlon to the fore? TPR Kevin McBride played the leading role in "the court case" and is now open to offers from all dramatic societies, or bands of strolling players. So good was the talent unearthed that the Coy is confident of taking most of the prizes at the Battalion concert.

Due to the heavy operational commitment, time available for sporting activities is naturally limited. However, we have

Personnel of 'C' Coy at Brashit. From (L-R) are Lt. E. Caulfield, Cpl F. Lambe, Pte S. McNamee, Pte J. O'Donnell and Pte J. Folan. (L-R kneeling): Pte P. Faherty, Pre M. Conroy, Pte J. McDonagh.

teams taking part in all battalion competitions. Our soccer team is worthy of note and our volleyballers are quietly confident that they might cause a shock or two.

Coy Sgt Michael Chapman has served overseas on five different occasions in the Congo, Cyprus and Lebanon, and says, "While

O the r Personnel of 'C' Coy at Branshit

former missions may have been pleasant, service with UNIFIL taxes a man to the full and makes him a better soldier". Pte Paul Browne is on his first trip overseas' and says, "The duties are rough but because of that the time passes quickly". He also mentions the transport, saying, "If we had a few more serviceable trucks in the Coy, it would make life an awful lot easier". He says he would return but being a married man, he would naturally have to consult the better-half.

The most memorable post in this area is 6-19 Charlie situated on Hill 839 overlooking the Enclave. It consists of a shelter with a "glass house" tower perched atop. At present, engineer work is taking place at this area and what enormous difference will there be on completion!

Re – supply of "Charlie" takes place along a track that is barely negotiable by landrover. Other posts are located at Bayt Yahun, the "Black Hole", the "Green Rooms", and in Brashit village,

while the Coy HQ is in Brashit Camp Post 6-16.

There is no shortage of overseas service in 'C' Coy and apart from extensive service in other UN missions, sixteen members of the Coy are on their second tour of duty in Lebanon. The record for service in Lebanon is held jointly by three NCOs, Sgt William Thompson, Cpl Tony Doyle and Cpl Peter Ruance, who are on their third tour.

'C' Coy Officers and men are proud of their UN service record and of their contribution to the UNIFIL mission.

By Lt. A. Bracken

IRELAND

IRISHBATT 49TH 'A' COY

A Coy 49th Irishbatt under the Command of Comdt. Mick Lucey took over operational control of the Haddathah Coy area on 4th May '81. Among the other villages in the area are, At Tiri, Ar Ruaysah and Rshaf. The Coy consists of 2 Rifle Platoons, a weapons Platoon and Coy HQ.

'A' Coy comprises mainly soldiers from the Irish Army's Eastern Command, which has responsibility for a large sector of the border with Northern Ireland and the men of 'A' Coy have much experience of manning Checkpoints and Observation Posts and mounting patrols, as a result.

No 1 Platoon is almost entirely drawn from the 2nd Infantry Battalion based in Dublin City and is commanded by Lt. Jim McCarthy. Among the many notables in the platoon are Sgt Andrew «Darts» Bardon and Cpl Mick «Moggy» Kelly. The platoon provides personnel for Haddathah Check Point and the remainder of the platoon are based in Ar Ruaysah, opposite the «Cuckoo's

FORCE COMMANDER inspects 'A' Coy Post Guard at HADDATHAH.

Pte TOM HICKEY 'B' Coy on Sentry Duty at Post 6-16 Bra Shit Camp.

Nest» a nearby DFF position.
No. 2
Platoon is made up of men mainly drawn from two of the Army's Border Battalions, the 27th and 29th Battalions. It is Commanded by Lt. Ger Davis who was stationed in Dublin, and the platoon Sgt is Sgt Brian Branagan. The Platoon is based in Haddathah village and among its tasks are the provision of Coy HQ Guard as well as mounting Patrols, listening posts and escorts in the area.

The main strength of the Weapons Platoon comes from the 5th Battalion, based in Dublin, along the banks of Dublin's famous waterway the river Liffey. The platoon commander is Capt. Matt Murray from the 29th Battalion and another «blow in» is Sgt John De Lacy a well known Weapons Instructor from the Eastern Command Training Depot. All the members of the platoon are experts in the use of mortars and anti ¦rank weapons. The Recce section which forms part of the Weapons Platoon is commanded by Lt. Peter Marron from the 1st Cavalry Squadran based in County Cork and he is now on his second tour of duty in the Lebanon. This section provides mobility and firepower with Panhard APCs and AML 90.

The Coy HQ is based in Haddathah village in a house called after the Gresham Hotel, one of Dublin's most famous Hostelries. The kingpins here are the 2 i/c Capt Ger Aherne, Coy Sgt Michael Smith and CQMS Derek Gaffney, who look after all administrative and logistic problems, ably assisted by Cpl William Lingwood on his «trusty» typewriter.

As already stated 'A' Coy personnel have wide experience gained on border duty with Northern Ireland and twenty per cent of the Coy have previous UN service. This experience together with a tough 8 weeks training period in Ireland's Wicklow mountains, which are somewhat similar to the terrain in South Lebanon have ensured that 'A' Coy 49th Irishbatt are very much on top of the situation in their new environment and are well geared for the task of helping to bring peace and stability to South Lebanon.

By Comdt G. BO,Y LE
PRO IRISHBATT

Pte William O'Neill 'B' on Sentry at Bra Shit.

TRANSPORT GROUP – 49th IRISHBATT

One of the most vital elements of any Unit is it's Transport section and with the 49th Irish Battalion, the Transport Group of HQ Coy is no exception. The group is Commanded by Comdt. Tony Egar and the senior NCO is Coy/Sgt Harry Mulhearn.

Daily throughout the Irish AO, they can be seen performing their varied tasks of patrolling, drawing water and rations etc. It requires a superhuman effort on everybody's behalf to keep our transport in a roadworthy condition as the majority of our vehicles are well past middle age. This unenviable task falls to the lot of Sgt Jim Burns of whom it was heard said that he was born with a pair of metric spanners instead of hands. He is ably assisted by Pte Paul Mulreany and Pte Martin Cummins.

The daily grind of repair and overhaul and servicing of vehicles is carried out 'neath the Southern slope of Tibnin at Total garage. Here,under the hot Lebanese sun, the members of the Transport group carry out first line repairs and such major jobs as the fitting of new engines, clutches and gear boxes. These tasks are usually carried out away from the glare of the spotlight, but the transport group are mindful of their great contribution to helping the 49th Bn fulfil it s mission.

One of the most noticeable and, indeed, vital tasks of the Transport group is the drawing and the distribution of water supplies throughout the Bn area. In summertime this becomes an even more important function and here the group is lucky to have the services of the likes of Cpl Paul Walsh who drives his water truck from dawn to dusk at this labour of love. The vehicles in use for water supply vary from purpose-built water trucks to ordinary trucks fitted with plastic tanks and these vehicles more than any others require constant maintenance to keep them in a roadworthy condition. To this end CQMS Con Dennehy is kept at full stretch supplying spare parts.

The tasks of the Transport group are indeed onerous, however, their willing spirit and dedication to their job are obvious and we take this opplortunity of expressing our gratitude.

By Gombt G. Boyle
PRO IRISHBATT

UNIFIL'S OPERATIONAL HISTORY : A summary

Tyre, Sud Liban, 27 Avril 1978. Trois officers Sénégalais entrain, d'étudier une carte.

A view of part of Fijibatt HQ at Qana in the early days. Left top is an Observation post. Office and living acco. odations were all in tents.

on Jabal Kabir. On 15 and 31 October Fijian positions were attacked. On 31 October and 1 November Dutch patrols were ambushed by a Palestinian group near Mazraat al Musrif. In December, a serious confrontation developed at Wadi Jilu between Fatah/LNM and Fibatt. Also attributed to AE's were firings five times at UNIFIL helicopters, mostly while on medical evacuation flights.

In the summer, NorMedCoy was replaced by SwedMedCoy.

1981

On 14 February 1981, Maj-Gen. William Callaghan (Ireland) took over as Force Commander om Maj-Gen. E.A. Erskine Ghana) who was appointed as CHIEF-OF-Staff, UNTSO and the secretary General's representative on operations in the Middle ast.

Chief of -Staff, UNTSO.

In the first half of 1981, especially in February and March there were heavy and frequent exchanges of fire between IDF/DFF in the enclave and armed elements positioned in the Tyre pocket and north of the Litani River. On 2 March, following an Israeli air raid, AE's fired into northern Israel. Until 9 April, shellings continued daily. On 9 April, Israeli gunboats fired into Tyre area. On 10 April, AE's fired rockets into Israel. Israel retaliated with an air strike. During 20 April exchange, many rockets were fired into northern Israel. Meanwhile Norwegian, Dutch, Fijian and Ghanaian (north) positions were endangered by rounds falling near their positions.

27 April was a day of typically intense hostilities. Firing in the north-eastern sector was

initiated by IDF/DFF and continued almost 24 hours. Close to 800 artillery, mortar and tank rounds were fired by this side. AE's fired approximately 340 artillery/mortar rounds and rockets in this sector, with some impacts inside Israel. In the western sector 41 rockets were fired from Rashidiyeh area, most of them falling into western Galilee, while IDF shelled Rashidiyeh. Same day, Israeli jets conducted a series of attacks against the Tyre pocket and other targets north of the Litani. Exchanges continued through May but tapered off towards the end. June was comparatively calm.

One of the most serious incidents of the first half of 1981 was on 16 March when DFF, apparently opposing further deployment of Lebanese army troops with UNIFIL, fired about 60 mortar rounds into the village of Al-Qantara, killing one Nigerian officer and two soldiers and wounding 20 Nigerian soldiers. Four Lebanese soldiers and 10 civilians were also wounded.

During the second-half of 1981, the activities of armed elements, the DFF and IDF in and near the UNIFIL area of operation continued. Mid-July witnessed a serious outbreak of hostilities affecting areas outside UNIFIL control, which led to an influx of people into the UNIFIL area from other parts of Lebanon seeking safety.

On 18 June, soldiers of the Fijian battalion who were laying

a telephone line at Wadi Jilu, came under rocket-propelled grenade, heavy machine-gun and rifle fire from armed elements of the LNM. One Fijian soldier was wounded.

On 19 June, a militant of a Lebanese National Movement faction was denied entry at a Fijian check-point for being in uniform and carrying a weapon. A short time later, armed elements of various Lebanese and Palestinian factions surrounded the check-point and opened fire. One Fijian soldier was injured. During the ensuing exchange of fire, three Fijian soldiers were captured and taken away. A local cease-fire was arranged. While negotiations were in progress with a PLO liaison officer, two of the captured soldiers were murdered. The third, an officer, was able to escape after having been tortured. ⟶

Nothing like a good wash after a hard days work. This was one of the early days Fijian wash point.

A single-deck Observation Post being rebuilt to a double deck post.

DEATH AT DEIR NTAR

When Private Hugh Doherty of the 49 Irish Battalion bade his widowed mother, Elisabeth Doherty that pleasant goodbye in Dublin shortly before he emplaned the 'Austria Air's Boeing 747 to Tel-Aviv to begin a six months tour of duty with UNIFIL, little did it occur to both mother and son that, that agreeable farewell wish was indeed the very last.

For exactly five days after setting foot in south Lebanon on (22 April, Pte Doherty, 21, was a dead man. He was killed by an unidentified armed elements whilst on duty with another Irish soldier, Private Kevin Joyce, at Check point 6-22 Delta, on 27 April.

His body was found at an outpost near the village of Deir Ntar, a location approximately four kilometers north west of Tibnine and three kilometers southwest of Jwayya. Initial medical examination revealed that the time of death was at about 1630 hrs. Pte Doherty's death brought to 62 the number of UNIFIL soldiers who had lost their lives whilst on this operation and the eleventh of the Irish Battalion since the operation began some three years ago. Hugh's greatest ambition was to serve with UNIFIL. His mortal remains was sent to Ireland on 1 May.

Meanwhile the search for his missing partner, Pte, Joyce, continues. Pte Joyce was due to return home with the 48 Irish Battalion in May this year. 1981.

BY Osabu-Quaye

Friday, May 25, 2012

Minister rules out inquiry into death

BY C.J.MCGINLEY

A FORMER army colleague of a Letterkenny soldier killed in the Lebanon 31-years ago has accused the authorities of a 'cover up'.

Speaking to the Donegal News yesterday (Thursday) Michael Walker said he would continue to campaign on behalf of the family of Private Hugh Doherty from Ballymacool, Letterkenny for a full independent inquiry into the circumstances surrounding his death.

Private Hugh Doherty (20) of Ballymacool Terrace was shot dead while on UN peacekeeping duties on April 27, 1981. The body of his partner, Private Caomhan Seoighe (20) from Innisheer, Galway has never been recovered.

Both men were on observation duty near the Moslem village of Dayr Ntar when they were killed. A Palestinian rebel group claim they know where the body of Private Caomhan Seoighe (Kevin Joyce) lies buried and had admitted it was also responsible for the killing of Private Doherty, a single man, at the South Lebanon lookout post.

The killing of Private Doherty was the subject of a UN Board of Inquiry in No-vember 1981 and by the then Director of Operations for the Defence Forces, Col Salvino in 1982. However, Mr Walker, who was on duty with the two men claims there was never a proper inquiry as key personnel hadn't been interviewed and the army wasn't coming clean about the threat assessment at the time.

He claims the two men were sent out away from their post without an NCO. However, in a letter last week the Department of Defence said while the Salvino report identified inadequacies in the conduct and in the location of the outpost there was no increased threat at the time to Irish or UN personnel.

"As such, the Minister considers that there is no reasonable basis to accede to your request for an independent inquiry into the circumstances of this incident at this time," the Department stated.

While it is over three decades ago since the tragic death of Hugh Doherty it is still remembered to this day in Letterkenny where he had a full military funeral. He has a brother Eunan who resides in McNeely Villas and two sisters, May (Dr McGinley Road) and Phylis Tuohy (Clara, Co Offaly).